Passion and Cunning

Passion and Cunning

and other Essays

CONOR CRUISE O'BRIEN

Weidenfeld and Nicolson

London

First published in Great Britain by
George Weidenfeld & Nicolson Limited
91 Clapham High Street, London SW4 7TA

ISBN 0 297 79280 6

Photoset by
Deltatype Ltd, Ellesmere Port, S. Wirral
Printed and bound by
Butler & Tanner Ltd
Frome and London

For Patrick and Margaret

Contents

Introduction

WITH ONE EXCEPTION, all these essays and reviews appeared within the last four or five years. The exception is the Yeats essay which first appeared in the collection *In Excited Reverie* edited by A. N. Jeffares and K. G. Cross and published in 1965 for the centenary of Yeats's birth. Possibly partly because it was initially published during a year of 'tributes' to the poet the essay gave a certain amount of offence to Yeats scholars and others at the time and it has continued to be a subject of controversy.

Some of those who entered the controversy – particularly in its earlier phases – became so angry at what they thought I was saying that they had difficulty taking in what I actually said. Terence de Vere White, reviewing the Jeffares-Cross collection in the *Irish Times*, accused me of practising double standards by referring to the death of Francis Sheehy-Skeffington as murder while avoiding applying the term murder to the death of Kevin O'Higgins. (In the Irish context, this particular kind of selectivity of expression would have implied an anti-British and pro-IRA bias; something of which the reviewer, unlike some of my later critics, assumed me to be in the grip.) When I pointed out that I had in fact used the word murder, not only in referring to the murder of Francis Sheehy-Skeffington, but also to the murder of Kevin O'Higgins, Mr de Vere White, being a fair- minded and courteous man, handsomely acknowledged his mistake. He added that the essay had made him so angry that 'the print swam before my eyes'. And somehow it has managed to go on swimming, before other eyes.

Not long before his lamented and untimely death, the late Leland Lyons – who was working on the Yeats biography at the time – referred to my essay, in the *Yeats Annual* (number 2). He called my essay 'brilliant'. That was ominous for starters; I knew Leland Lyons well enough to know that that particular adjective did not occupy an elevated place in the hierarchy of his terms of commendation. He went on to describe a statement which he attributed to me as 'probably the most offensive remark in the entire canon of Yeats criticism'. The remark which he attributed to me was that 'if Ireland had been occupied by the Nazis one would have expected to see [Yeats] at least a cautious participant, or ornament, in a collaborationist regime'.

But that is not what I said, and not what I meant. The essay is reprinted here exactly in its original form and the reader will see – p. 50 – that the situation I was contemplating was one in which *England*, not Ireland, was occupied by the Nazis. If Ireland had been occupied by the Nazis, Yeats, if alive and well, would have been in exile and writing against the German occupiers. He was, as he said himself, throughout his life an Irish nationalist; sometimes manically, sometimes depressively so. The situation I was in fact contemplating was one in which the Germans had won the war and the European ex-neutrals would have been collaborating with the victors (they wouldn't have had much choice in the matter). Yeats' explicitly anti-British writings on the eve of the war, some of them with apparently pro-German overtones, would – when taken in conjunction with his great international cultural eminence – have made his participation or at least support desirable to an Irish government in that situation. That is the hypothetical situation I was considering. I realize that many people – especially among Yeats's British admirers – will still find the remark offensive. But I don't think the author of 'The Ghost of Roger Casement' would have found it in the least offensive.

I came across Leland Lyons' comment only after his death, and very shortly after. I read it with a pang, because I would have loved to go and talk to him about it. Not least because, for the first time in my life – and we had worked together in the same field, on the life and times of Charles Stewart Parnell – I had caught that meticulous scholar out in a mistake of fact. But I know how it had happened; the print had swum.

Yet I acknowledge now, as I think about the matter further, that the passage as it stands *is* unjust to Yeats. It is unjust because of where it stops. He might indeed have accepted participation in the kind of government I have hypothesized; he could well have been persuaded that it was his duty to do so. But I cannot imagine him as *remaining* in such a government, or continuing to support it, while it complied with the actual demands of the new masters of Europe. The Nazis had drawn up lists of the 4,000 or so Jews in Ireland and their first demand would have been one for the handing over of those Jews. I don't believe that Yeats could ever have gone along with that, and I should not have left my hypothesis in a state that suggested that he might. I am glad that republication gives me a chance of clearing that one up.

The controversy about Yeats's politics goes on and has continued to revolve, to some extent, around that essay of mine. The main challenge to the view expressed in that essay has been Elizabeth Cullingford's book *Yeats, Ireland and Fascism* (1981). I attended the Yeats International Summer School at Sligo in the summer of 1985 – as Elizabeth Cullingford also did – and found that the discussions on this particular subject were lively, but not unpleasantly heated, as they might have been some years back. If I am not mistaken, the general impression among those Yeats scholars who are interested in his politics is that I may have overstated my case a bit but that is better than sweeping the subject under the rug, as had been the general practice in Yeatsian studies in the period before publication of the essay in question.

As regards the other essays, I think the ones that call for comment are those on Nicaragua and South Africa, in view of developments in the situations there in the period since the essays were originally published.

As far as Nicaragua is concerned, things have got a bit worse than they were at the time I wrote. The pressures have increased and the people are suffering more, especially from the results of an enormous increase in inflation. The Contras have got more money and more modern weapons. Apart from that, there have been no great changes. It is not yet clear what the effect of the enormous publicity around Irangate may be. The great drop in Ronald Reagan's popularity and the revelations of corruption, illegality and duplicity surrounding the support for the Contras offer reasons for hoping that the next American administration may drop the Contras. But to anyone who, like myself, cherishes such hopes the popular enthusiasm engendered by the televised appearance of Lieutenant-Colonel Oliver North was profoundly disquieting. Polls continue to show the majority of Americans disapprove of supporting the Contras. But the trouble seems to be that many of those who disapprove are really not much interested in the subject, whereas many of those who approve are passionately committed. But I still hope that the repercussions of Irangate may prove to be such as to be discouraging to adventurism of the Contra type.

There have been some significant developments in Central America, and especially Nicaragua, in the second half of 1987 (time of going to press). The Sandinista Government took some quite far-reaching measures of internal liberalization, recommended by its Central American neighbours, on the initiative of Costa Rica. The Nicaraguan censorship was relaxed. *La Presna* – closed by Government order shortly after my visit – was allowed to reopen. Overtures were made to the internal opposition. A Commission of National Reconciliation was set up, headed by Cardinal Miguel Obando y Bravo, of all people. The Cardinal's acceptance of this nomination may be no less significant than the Sandinista acceptance of the Cardinal, in the role of reconciler, (*see* pp 85–87 and pp 106–107). All the Sandinista moves in the direction of liberalization were instantly dismissed by the Reagan administration as entirely cosmetic. The administration apparently cannot be influenced by any internal change, as long as the Sandinistas remain in power. The position of the United States continues to be that it refuses to negotiate with the Sandinistas but insists that the Sandinistas must negotiate with its own servants, the contra leadership. The Sandinistas continue to refuse that demand, but offer 'cease-fire talks' with individual contra groups in the field. No early end to the struggle appears in sight, and so the liberalization moves may well be fragile.

Since the publication of 'What Can Become of South Africa?', the apartheid regime has secured what can best be described as a remission. Such international sanctions as have been applied have been less effective than had been feared. The actual application of sanctions has tended to bring the business community and the regime together – for the purpose of sanction-busting – whereas the *threat* of sanctions tended to separate businessmen from politicians. The imposition of stringent media controls – and particularly controls on television – under the state of national emergency have been effective in reducing the volume of adverse international publicity and apparently the level of public interest. The elections on 6 May 1987 showed the white electorate swinging to the right. The Progressive Federal Party lost ground and the Conservatives under Andries Treurnicht became the main opposition party. P. W. Botha's National Party remained securely in office, its losses to the Conservatives being compensated by support from English speakers, moving away from the Progressives. In the light of Afrikaner history the new situation looks rather ominous for P. W. Botha. His position has now become rather closely analogous to that of Jan Smuts fifty years ago. At that time Smuts's power-base consisted of a coalition of Afrikaners and English speakers. He was challenged by the predecessors of today's National Party, the 'purified' Nationalists, under D. F. Malan. 'Purified' meant that they were a purely Afrikaner party, free from any taint of Britishness.

By 1938 the challenge mounted by the 'pure' Afrikaners to the mixed Afrikaners was such that Smuts was not able to show his face during the great Afrikaner celebration of the 100th anniversary of the Voortrekkers, the Covenant and the Battle of Blood River.

This year brings the 150th anniversary of those same events. Treurnicht, at the head of his 'pure' Afrikaners, can reasonably hope to upstage Botha much as Malan upstaged Smuts. (He is unlikely however to achieve the same

4

degree of success, as English speakers are now very much hangers-on in an Afrikaner-led movement, and also Botha controls much more patronage than Smuts ever did.)

In July 1987, the visit of about sixty white South Africans to Dakar, Senegal to meet the ANC excited a good deal of international media interest. Some of the comment developed the 'Afrikanerdom crumbling' theme. This matter is discussed in my essay (p. 122) and I see no reason to revise my comments there. A minority of Afrikaners – mainly intellectuals and clergy – have moved to the left but there are no signs that Afrikanerdom as a whole is beginning to follow them. Quite the other way; in the elections Afrikaners in large numbers deserted the Nationalists but they went to the more hardline Conservatives, not to the Progressives. And the very gifted Afrikaner leader of the Progressives Frederick van Zyl Slabbert had resigned from the leadership of the Progressives before the elections. In doing so, I believe, he implicitly recognized that there was no hope of the development on which PFP hopes had rested: that of beginning to attract Afrikaner votes in sizeable numbers.

I spoke earlier of a 'remission' secured by the regime. I think the remission has happened, and ought to be clearly recognized, but that it cannot be more than a remission. The basic problems still remain. It is a continuing crisis of demography and of legitimacy. The growth of the black population continues to outrun the white; black unemployment and black desperation continue to increase; the regime, in whatever efforts it may make to deal with these problems, has no legitimacy in the eyes of a great and growing majority of its subjects. There may be a lull now, but there are greater troubles coming. On the whole I believe the analysis presented in 'What Can Become of South Africa?' remains sound.

There was one very interesting new development in July 1987, which on the whole I take as tending to confirm the general validity of my analysis. In that month, the main black trade union organization, COSATU, called for 'mandatory and general economic sanctions' against South Africa. I think that if such sanctions were to come into being, they would have to be ordered by the Security Council of the U.N., with consequently the support of the superpowers, and that the sanctions could not become effective without the application of a blockade, supported by the superpowers, as envisaged in 'What Can Become of South Africa'?

Pending the application of the 'mandatory and general sanctions' called for COSATU saw no merit in the kind of piecemeal and limited sanctions applied by a number of Western countries. These, in COSATU's opinion, cannot damage the regime but can cause widespread black unemployment.

Although the positions here adopted by the principal black trade union movement in South Africa would appear startling in their implications, they seem to have aroused very little comment in the West.

There have also been some developments in relation to the matters considered in 'South Africa and the Academic Boycott'. A three-man commission appointed by the University of Cape Town considered the matter of the forcible breakup of my lectures by mobs of militant students and others. The commission decided to put much of the blame for these disorders on me personally. It seemed that my 'mercurial and volatile temperament' so provoked the poor students that they could not be held fully accountable. This line may have been convenient for the University administration – which feared more trouble if it had to discipline the rioters – but it did not win the approval of the faculty. Professor David Welsh, chairman of the Department of Political Science at the University – and who had invited me to lecture there – resigned from that chairmanship on learning of the comments made in the commission's report. David Welsh's position was strongly supported by a number of other members of the University and at the end of April 1987 the Senate of the University of Cape Town, by a large majority, formally repudiated the comments made about me by the commission. I should like here to express my warm thanks to the faculty of the University of Cape Town, and to my friends David Welsh and Peter Collins in particular.

In general, the idea of the 'academic boycott' seems now to be questioned, even in some quarters from which it earlier received support. Oliver Tambo, on behalf of the ANC, is reported as having said the academic boycott should not be applied to people who oppose apartheid. I would not be particularly happy with that formula myself, but it does seem to indicate a degree of movement in the right direction, and an implicit acknowledgement that there have been excesses. I think there is also some recognition that the kind of rampaging militancy which zeal for the academic boycott brought to the University of Cape Town in October 1986 endangers the very institutions on which the future of higher education for blacks depends. The people who whipped up those riots seem to believe that the future of higher education didn't matter because the revolution was around the corner and would take care of everything. But in the present mood of relative disillusion, people can see that the revolution is not exactly around the corner and that in what looks like a longish 'meantime' people either get educated or don't.

The on-campus violence, legitimized by the international 'academic boycott' and increased during 1987, finally supplied the Pretoria regime with

6

a credible pretext for introducing – for the first time – legislation which will place campus discipline under State control. Normally such legislation – placing as it does English-speaking universities under Afrikaner control – would have been fiercely resented by the English-speaking community. But the English-speaking community is now more alarmed about the present chaos in the universities than the Afrikaners are. So what 'the academic boycott' has accomplished is an extension of the power of Pretoria, over the universities.

In an article on the South African University troubles published in the *Guardian* on 28 October 1987, David Beresford wrote: 'Recently a student at Cape Town confessed (and the government confirmed) that he was a police spy. He had encouraged students to stone police vehicles and had helped disrupt the O'Brien visit'. Strange bedfellows of the 'academic boycott'.

Most of the other essays don't seem to me to need updating or other comment here. However, I should like to conclude with a word about the Pope, by way of a kind of footnote to the essay 'The Liberal Pole'.

Some friends have suggested to me that my comments on Pope John Paul II were unduly harsh. This worried me a bit for a while but I stopped worrying in July 1987 when I read a certain news item. The news item concerned a meeting between Dr Kurt Waldheim, President of Austria, and Pope John Paul II.

I had known Kurt Waldheim at the United Nations – since before he became Secretary-General – and had worked quite closely with him at one point on a resolution about the South Tyrol. Like most people, I didn't know then that Kurt Waldheim, during the war, had served on the staff of a general later hanged for war crimes, and that he had served in the theatre and at the time where these crimes were committed. The Pope, however, when he received Dr Waldheim did presumably know these things which were by then in the public domain. This however did not prevent the Pope from praising Dr Waldheim's 'life-long services to peace.' 'Life-long' in the circumstances might seem a trifle fulsome, but that didn't worry Dr Waldheim a bit. Like the competent diplomatist he is, he returned the compliment in such a way as to turn it to his own advantage. 'The Pope is the conscience of the world', said Kurt Waldheim.

With admirers like that, John Paul II doesn't have to worry about critics like me.

Passion and Cunning
An Essay on the Politics of W. B. Yeats*

THE DAY THE NEWS OF YEATS'S DEATH reached Dublin I was lunching with my mother's sister, Hanna Sheehy-Skeffington. Hanna was the widow of Frank Skeffington, pacifist and socialist, who had been murdered on the orders of a British officer, Bowen-Colthurst, in Easter Week 1916. She was not consistently a pacifist, but an Irish revolutionary; Madame MacBride and Countess Markievicz were among her close political friends, Countess Markievicz being, however, politically the closer. Physically, she looked a little like Queen Victoria and – a comparison that would have pleased her better – a little like Krupskaya. Mentally she was extremely and variously alert. Her conversation, when politics were not the theme, was relaxed, humorous and widely tolerant of human eccentricity; when politics were the theme she always spoke very quietly and economically, with a lethal wit and a cutting contempt for 'moderates' and compromisers. Hers was the kind of Irish mind which Yeats could call – when he felt it to be on his side – 'cold', 'detonating', 'Swiftian', or when, as in this case, it was not on his side, 'bitter', 'abstract', 'fanatical'.

On this day I tried to tell her something of my generation's sense of loss by Yeats's death. I was genuinely moved, a little pompous, discussing a great literary event with my aunt, a well-read woman who loved poetry.

Her large, blue eyes became increasingly blank almost to the polar expression they took on in controversy. Then she relaxed a little: I was young and meant no harm. She almost audibly did not say several things that occurred to her. She wished, I know, to say something kind; she could not say anything she did not believe to be true. After a pause she spoke:

'Yes,' she said, 'he was a Link with the Past.'

I had been speaking of the poet; she was thinking of the politician.

At the time I thought this attitude exasperating and even ludicrous. Who

*Contribution to the Yeats Centenary Volume *In Excited Reverie* (edited by A. N. Jeffares and K. M. Cross, 1965).

cared about Yeats the politician? What mattered was the poetry; the fact that Yeats had been at sea in politics – as I then thought – was irrelevant, Yeats the poet was all-in-all.

This opinion was characteristic of my generation – which is partly why I cite it – and, as that generation is now middle-aged, it is now perhaps the dominant one. On rereading Yeats's poetry, and some of his prose – and reading some of the prose for the first time – I no longer think this opinion quite adequate. I no longer believe Yeats's political activities to have been foolish or fundamentally inconsistent or his political attitude to be detach-able from the rest of his personality, disconnected from action, or irrelevant to his poetry. His politics were, it now seems to me, marked by a considerable degree of inner consistency between thought and action, by a powerful emotional drive, cautious experimentalism in action, and, in expression, extravagances and disengagements which succeeded one another not without calculation and not without reference to the given political conjuncture of the moment.

It is true that warrant – rather too much warrant – can be found in his poetry for the conventional picture of the impractical poet drawn to politics by romantic love and generous emotion, and recoiling ruefully from each political failure to poetry, his proper sphere:

> All things can tempt me from this craft of verse
> One time it was a woman's face or worse –
> The seeming needs of my fool-driven land (1909)

And again:

> I think it better that in times like these
> A poet's mouth be silent, for in truth
> We have no gift to set a statesman right (1916)

And again:

> Dear shadows, now you know it all
> All the folly of a fight
> With a common wrong or right (1927)

And finally:

> I never bade you go
> To Moscow or to Rome
> Renounce that drudgery
> Call the Muses home (1938)

Such apolitical or anti-political pronouncements, scattered over thirty years of Yeats's writing, represent 'the true Yeats' for three large classes of Yeats's admirers: those who are bored by Irish politics, those who are bored by all politics, and those who are frightened by Yeats's politics. 'We have no gift to set a statesman right' is particularly popular because it sets a neat and memorable dividing line between literature and politics. Yet the poet who wrote it was exercising a political choice: he was refusing to write a war poem – probably solicited for the cause of the Allies in the First World War, a cause which did not move Yeats. He politely and elegantly refused to be drawn. That the aphorism produced in the process was not, for him, a guiding maxim, he was to prove a few months later when he wrote a series of noble war poems in a cause which did move him, that of Ireland. He who had no gift to set a statesman right was no longer troubled by this disability when he wrote after the executions of the leaders of the 1916 Rebellion:

> You say that we should still the land
> Till Germany's overcome;
> But who is there to argue that
> Now Pearse is deaf and dumb?
> And is their logic to outweigh
> MacDonagh's bony thumb?

When the Muses came home, they came full of politics; there is a far higher proportion of poems with political themes in the last book than in any other, and the last four poems of all, when there was no longer time for politeness or pretence, carry a burden of politics. Throughout his life as a writer Yeats had abiding, and intensifying, political interests and passions. It is misleading to make him essentially non-political, on the strength of certain disclaimers, refusals and ironies. The fact that General Ludendorff carried out a number of tactical withdrawals did not necessarily make him a pacifist.

This essay is concerned, not primarily with Yeats's 'political philosophy', but with the forms of his actual involvement, at certain critical times, in the political life of his own day.[1] Yeats's biographers have recounted some of his political activities, and in some of what follows I am indebted in particular to J. M. Hone's *W. B. Yeats*, Dr Richard Ellmann's *Yeats: The Man and the Masks* and Dr A. N. Jeffares' *W. B. Yeats, Man and Poet*. But a biographer may feel that he cannot – without toppling his book over – give the detail necessary to situate a given action, or inaction, in the political context of its time. In biographies, as in literary histories, we necessarily find, instead of the complexities of actual political conjunctures, a generalized 'political background', lacking the texture and the weight of real politics. It is often assumed, I think, that this does not matter much in the case of a writer like Yeats because his politics, if they existed, were probably rather vague and generalized themselves. In what follows I shall present some reasons for believing that Yeats's politics were less vague than is commonly supposed.

At the bottom of it all was the Anglo-Irish predicament. The Irish Protestant stock from which Yeats came was no longer a ruling class but still a superior caste, and thought of itself in this way.[2] When he wrote towards the end of his life of 'the caste system that has saved the intellect of India',[3] he was almost certainly thinking not so much of India, as Ireland. His people were in the habit of looking down on their Catholic neighbours – the majority of those among whom they lived – and this habit Yeats never entirely lost. But when he went to school in England Yeats was to find, as Parnell and others had found, that this distinction had lost much of its validity. Unsophisticated Englishmen – including all the young – made no more distinction between 'Protestant-Irish' and 'Catholic-Irish' than they did between Brahmin and untouchable. The Irish were known by their brogue – which in Yeats's case must have been quite marked at this stage – and they were all comic, inferior and 'mad';[4] among the sophisticated classes these same categories found gentler nuances: witty, impractical, imaginative. The Irish Protestant thus acquired two basic bits of information: the important thing about him, in relation to Ireland, was that he was a Protestant; in relation to England, that he was an Irishman.

For proud and sensitive natures, exposed at this period to the English view of the Irish, a political reaction was predictable, starting from the premises: 'I, an Irishman, am as good as any Englishman. Ireland is therefore as good as England. Yet England governs herself; Ireland is governed by England. Can this be right?'

Parnell thought not; Yeats's father thought not; Yeats thought not.

It used to be widely assumed in Ireland that Yeats became entangled in politics by Maud Gonne. This is of course wrong; Yeats had been drawn into politics before he ever heard of Maud Gonne, and the most active phases of his political life were to come after he had quarrelled with Maud Gonne. Yeats entered politics under the influence of John O'Leary, the Fenian convict and exile, who returned to Ireland in 1884. Yeats now became what he was to remain all his life – as he was to repeat towards the end – 'a nationalist of the school of John O'Leary'.

What was the school of John O'Leary? Its central doctrines were those of classical, uncompromising Irish Republicanism: 'the tone', as O'Leary himself said, 'of Wolfe Tone' – but scarcely less important were certain limitations placed, by O'Leary himself, on the practical application of the doctrine. 'There are certain things,' he used to say, 'that a man ought not to do to save his country.' It was a phrase that Yeats was often to repeat. The 'certain things' included – along with some pleasant personal taboos such as 'a man ought not to cry in public for his country' – some of practical political

11

importance. The school of John O'Leary withheld its endorsement from parliamentary action, frowned on agrarian agitation, and vehemently condemned acts of individual terrorism.

Now in the 1880s these, and no others, were the methods effectively used to weaken the foundations of English rule. The successful application of agrarian ostracism had just given a new word – boycott – to the language of the world, and the dynamite of the Clan-na-Gael had reinforced the arguments of Parnell's disciplined parliamentary party so that Englishmen were beginning, for the first time in their lives, to feel that self-government for Ireland was a question within the bounds of practical politics. 'Violence', as William O'Brien so rightly said, 'is the only way of ensuring a hearing for moderation.' O'Leary had little use for O'Brien's kind of moderation and no use for the kinds of violence O'Brien had in mind. The Dublin Fenians whom O'Leary led – and whom Yeats was to join – spent their time not in causing but in preventing acts of terrorism. Their task, it seems, was to keep an organization in being for the day when a general rising would become a practical possibility. The distant future was to show that their work was not in vain, but in the 1880s insurrection seemed – and was – a very remote contingency. In the 1880s the people who were hanged were political and agrarian terrorists; the people who were beaten by the police and put in jail were the 'moderate' agrarian nationalists of the Plan of Campaign. O'Leary's group, shunning alike agrarian action, terrorism and moderation, was left alone by the police.[5]

The school of John O'Leary, then, was in the 1880s and 1890s extreme but not dangerous. This combination has a natural appeal to two of Yeats's most enduring characteristics: his pride and his prudence. With the power he knew to be in him he had much to be both proud and prudent about. The prudent Yeats, the sound calculator of chances, is as it seems the manager of the poet. A poet, if he is to survive long enough to be recognized as a great poet, has need of such a manager. The poet Yeats is drawn to nationalism by a deep sense of injured dignity and by a hatred proportionate to his power: hatred is always strong in him, and by far the strongest of his political emotions. 'There are moments', he wrote, 'when hatred [of England, in the context] poisons my life and I accuse myself of effeminacy because I have not given it adequate expression.'[6] Yeats the manager was always there to see that he gave it just the right degree of expression for any given time. One can imagine him saying to the poet trembling on the verge of national politics: 'Oh well, if you must you must, but for God's sake don't do anything – like getting jailed or killed – that would stop your poetry. I'll tell you what – I'll arrange an introduction to John O'Leary.'

Yet there were some things no manager could have arranged. How could it come about that the extremist politician most likely to attract the manager, should also have the magnificence – in moral stature, in style of speech and in personal appearance – which could hold the poet:

> Beautiful lofty things, O'Leary's noble head.

Or what manager could have arranged that the young woman, ablaze with politics,[7] who called on him with an introduction from the O'Learys on that fateful winter day in 1889 should be the most beautiful woman of her time:

> Pallas Athene in that straight back and arrogant head
> All the Olympians – a thing never known again.

One has to remind oneself that O'Leary and Maud Gonne were historical figures and not simply invented by Yeats, like Michael Robartes and Owen Aherne:

> As if some ballad-singer had sung it all

Yeats's long and splendidly unhappy relation to Maud Gonne had, of course, profound effects on his life and work but I do not find that it had any proportionate effect, at least directly, on his political alignment. It is true that it was after he met her – and probably at her urging – that he actually joined the Fenian brotherhood, but they were O'Leary Fenians, he was already closely associated with them, and joining them committed him, as we have seen, to little of practical consequence. There was also a sound practical argument for going with the Fenians. 'In this country', O'Leary had told him, 'a man must have upon his side the Church or the Fenians, and you will never have the Church.'[8] His letters, just after he first met Maud Gonne, do show some trace of her specific influence. He wrote to Katherine Tynan, about the murder in America of a supposed informer by members of the Clan-na-Gael: 'He seems to have been a great rascal. It was really a very becoming thing to remove him . . . a Spy has no rights.'[9] These ferocious sentiments are definitely not 'school of John O'Leary'; they are character- istic of Maud Gonne, whom Yeats had met six months before. The difference was that Maud Gonne perhaps meant them, and might conceivably have acted on them;[10] Yeats probably did not mean them and certainly would not have acted on them. His letter went on: 'There! You will be angry with me for all these dreadful sentiments. I may think the other way tomorrow.'

In practice, where Maud Gonne differed from O'Leary – as she did in favouring agrarian agitation – Yeats does not seem to have followed her, although he did intercede for her with O'Leary.[11] Maud Gonne did not affect Yeats's political course at this time so profoundly as is usually assumed. What did affect it were events which took place two to three years later – the fall and death of Parnell.

'The modern literature of Ireland,' Yeats told the Swedish Academy in 1925, 'and indeed all that stir of thought which prepared for the Anglo-Irish war, began when Parnell fell from power in 1891. A disillusioned and embittered Ireland turned from parliamentary politics; an event was conceived and the race began, as I think, to be troubled by that event's long gestation.'[12] Elsewhere he speaks of Four Bells, 'four deep tragic notes' in Irish history, the first being the war that ended with the Flight of the Earls (1603), the fourth being the death of Parnell in 1891.

'I heard the first note of the Fourth Bell forty years ago on a stormy October morning. I had gone to Kingston [sic] Pier to meet the Mail Boat that arrived about 6 a.m. I was expecting a friend, but met what I thought much less of at the time, the body of Parnell.'[13]

The friend was, of course, Maud Gonne, who came over on the boat that brought Parnell's body back to Ireland.

Few historians, I think, would challenge Yeats's estimate, in his Swedish address, of the impact of Parnell's fall and death, or his summary account of a process in which he himself played an important part. His historical sense was keen, as his political sense also was. For he not only saw in retrospect the crucial importance of the fall and death of Parnell. He saw it *at the time*, immediately, and he saw in it his opportunity and took that opportunity. He had not been a follower of Parnell's before his fall – the 'school of John O'Leary' forbade it – and does not seem to have become intensely interested in Parnell until the moment of his fall. Since, in later life, he made Parnell a symbol, almost a god indeed, in whose name he as priest excommunicated prominent public figures of the day, it is interesting that in his letters of the time there is no note of grief at his fall or even at his death. The first note is one of rather gleeful excitement at an event and an opportunity; the creation of a vacuum. 'This Parnell business', he wrote to O'Leary after the divorce case, 'is most exciting. Hope he will hold on. As it is he has driven up into dust and vacuum no end of insincerities. The whole matter of Irish politics will be better of it.'[14] In a later letter to O'Leary Yeats expresses an optimism, which sounds a little artificial, about Parnell's chances and gives some not altogether random reasons for being on Parnell's side: the priests and 'the Sullivan gang' were on the other side. Then Parnell died. Yeats wrote a poem about him on that day for publication that evening. The poem was called, 'Mourn and then Onward'.[15] It concluded:

> Mourn – and then onward, there is no returning
> He guides ye from the tomb
> His memory now is a tall pillar burning
> Before us in the gloom.

There is not much gloom in the covering letter with which the poet sent this dirge to his sister:

> I send you a copy of *United Ireland* with a poem of mine on Parnell written on the day he died to be in time for the press that evening. It has been a success.
> The Funeral [which Yeats did not attend] is just over. The people are breathing fire and slaughter. The wreaths have such inscriptions as 'Murdered by the Priests' and a number of Wexford men were heard by a man I know promising to remove a Bishop and seven priests before next Sunday. Tomorrow will bring them cooler heads I doubt not.[16]

Yeats, according to Dr Ellmann, 'had grasped instinctively that the time had come for him to act'. The word 'instinctively' may be misleading. Yeats in later life, when he had no more use, for the moment, for nationalist political activity, used to write as if his political activity at this time had been a sad mistake, committed mainly because of his passion for Maud Gonne. Critics and biographers have tended to follow him in exaggerating, as I believe, the importance of the Gonne factor in his politics. This influences presentation: thus Dr Ellmann reserves the entrance of Maud Gonne into his narrative for the moment of Parnell's death, although the natural moment to have brought her in would, one would have thought, have been the time at which Yeats first met her and fell in love with her, almost three years before. Keeping her back intensifies the drama but blurs the politics. It helps to perpetuate Yeats's myth of himself as 'a foolish passionate man', whereas the weight of the evidence suggests that he was something much more interesting: a cunning passionate man.[17] In this case the cunning was more in evidence than the passion.

Yeats was still almost unknown. He had been glad to get space, through O'Leary's influence, in a paper like *The Gael* – the organ of the Gaelic Athletic Association – and was sometimes in danger of being squeezed out by a big football match. Now he had an opportunity of reaching, with powerful impact, at a time of maximum national emotion, the widest possible Irish audience. *United Ireland* was Parnell's last paper and Irish people everywhere must have fought for copies of its issue of 10 October, to see what it had to say about the death of the Chief. And they found there the poem and the name of W. B. Yeats. There can have been few – and hardly any on the Parnellite side – who were not more moved by 'Mourn and then Onward' than Yeats was. A name almost unknown the day before became known to most of Ireland overnight.

I can see no reason to suppose that, in writing this poem and above all in getting it to the press with the necessary celerity, Yeats was just reacting instinctively or trying to please Maud Gonne. He had an eye for an opportunity – a politician's eye, and a politician's sense of timing.[18]

Some will perhaps find offensive the suggestion that Yeats used Parnell's coffin for a platform. Parnell, who made his own name out of the Manchester Martyrs, would have approved Yeats. Parnell knew, as Pearse knew, by Rossa's grave, that in Ireland there is no better platform than a hero's coffin.

Yeats had seen Parnell, after consolidating his Irish fief, impose himself on the politics of the United Kingdom. 'Mourn and then Onward' was not exactly a bid for the mantle of Parnell – a garment which was just then, as Yeats well knew, being thoroughly torn to pieces – but may reasonably be interpreted as an attempt, by bringing poetry into the political vacuum left by Parnell's death, to become as a poet something of what Parnell had been in politics: a virtual dictator in Ireland: a power, and sometimes an arbiter, in England. If so, it was not a wild aim, and Yeats in large measure made it good. Not that power, in itself, was the object, as it is for the man who is primarily a politician, but that the power already in him needed living-space. The poet Yeats wanted elbow-room and an audience, and the politician Yeats saw to it that he got them.

Ireland was now, as he said, 'like wax' and he set about shaping it. In later years – after the fighting had begun – the phrase 'the litherary side of the Movement' came to be used derisively, but in the 1890s and in the early years of the new century 'the litherary side of the Movement' was the only side that was moving, and its leader was Yeats. In founding the Irish Literary Society in London and the National Literary Society in Dublin, and the theatre which later became the Abbey Theatre, the politician Yeats was about the poet's business, using for the ends of poetry the political energy diverted by the fall of Parnell. Later, he liked to talk as if he had been duped, and wrote bitterly of evenings spent with 'some small organizer' pouring his third glass of whiskey into the spittoon.[19]

One may feel that, if anyone was duped, it was more likely to be the unfortunate 'small organizer' than Yeats, the big organizer. But there is no need to speak of dupes at all; both Yeats and the 'small organizer' were serving, in their different ways, the dignity of the nation to which they both belonged. For the small organizer the end was a political one, and poetry a means; for Yeats the end was a poetic one and the means political. They had to part in the end, but there is no need now to regret, or to quarrel over, the road they travelled together.

They parted, of course, in 1903, with the marriage of Maud Gonne to Major John MacBride. Nature, deferential to the poet, made this 'the year of the big wind', in which trees blew down all over Ireland, including in Lady Gregory's park at Coole. It was the great turning-point in Yeats's life, in politics as well as in other ways. The fact that he broke – for a time and in a way – with Irish politics after Maud Gonne's marriage has naturally contributed to the romantic belief, encouraged by himself, that his politics were 'just Maud Gonne'. The evidence does not warrant this conclusion. As we have seen he had made his political choice before he met Maud Gonne, and his entry into effective politics dates, not from his meeting with Maud Gonne, but from the political opportunity created by the fall of Parnell. The most that can be said of Maud Gonne – politically – is that she deepened his political involvement, and probably kept him politically involved for some time after he would otherwise have quit. For her he had written *Cathleen Ni Houlihan*, and she played the part, so that a member of the audience could write this:

> The effect of *Cathleen Ni Houlihan* on me was that I went home asking myself if such plays should be produced unless one was prepared for people to go out to shoot and be shot . . . Miss Gonne's impersonation had stirred the audience as I have never seen another audience stirred.[20]

After the curtain fell on *Cathleen Ni Houlihan* (1902) it could fairly be said that Yeats's work for the Irish revolution had been accomplished. It seems, in retrospect, considerate of Maud Gonne to have married in the following year.

The poet – having acquired in his political years a name, an audience and the dramatic society that was about to become the Abbey Theatre – now turned aside from Irish politics. He did not cease – he never ceased – to be an Irish nationalist, but his nationalism now became aristocratic and archaizing, instead of being popular and active. Aristocratic nationalism was not, in Ireland, practical politics, because the aristocracy was almost entirely Unionist, that is to say anti-nationalist. This did not matter to Yeats, who had had enough, for the moment, of practical politics. In his new aristocratism he was releasing a part of his personality he had been forced to try to suppress during the years of political activity. In those years this Irish

Protestant had necessarily emphasized his Irishness, minimizing or denying the separate and distinct tradition which the word Protestant implies. The Protestant now re-emerged with an audible sigh of relief. It had been stuffy in there, and getting stuffier. For, in the first years of Yeats's involvement in active politics there had been special circumstances making political life among Irish nationalists tolerable for a Protestant: by 1900 these special circumstances had disappeared.

The fall of Parnell had produced, as well as a 'clerical' party, led by Dillon, an anti-clerical Parnellite party led by John Redmond. Parnellite circles – to which Yeats had directed his first appeal, and which probably made up the larger part of his audiences – were distinguished by a scarcity of priests and a minimum of priestly authority. The glee with which Yeats in his letters chronicles threats against priests is significant. It was not that he necessarily hated priests himself – though he certainly did not like them – but that an atmosphere of priestly authority, in which for example priests tended to be arbiters of taste, was inimical to Protestant and poet. This atmosphere was temporarily dissipated in a considerable part of Ireland, including Dublin, in 1891, and Yeats must have found the going relatively easy then. By 1900, however, with the reunification of the Irish party and the burying of the Parnellite hatchet – which was an anti-clerical hatchet – the clergy had recovered most of their former authority, and life among nationalists must have become proportionately depressing for Protestants.[21] It was already depressing enough, for reasons of class. Yeats has left us a collective picture of his political associates of the 1890s: 'Men who had risen above the traditions of the countryman, without learning those of cultivated life, or even educating themselves and who because of their poverty, their ignorance, their superstitious piety, are much subject to all kinds of fear.'[22]

This is a classical statement of the Irish Protestant view of the rising Catholic middle class. From this class Yeats was now recoiling and the violence of his recoil did much to determine the political direction of his later years.

'One thing that Marxist criticism has not succeeded in doing,' as George Orwell points out, 'is to trace the connection between "tendency" and "literary style".'[23] Orwell goes on, in the essay on Yeats, to reveal, unconsciously, some of the reasons for that failure. He seeks, in Yeats's work, 'some kind of connection between his wayward, even tortured, style of writing and his rather sinister vision of life'. He finds this connection, as far as he finds it at all, in Yeats's archaisms, affectations and 'quaintness'. This does not fit very well, for the 'quaintness' was at its height in the 1890s, when Yeats's vision of life was, from either an Orwellian or a Marxist point of view, at its least sinister: when he was identified with the popular cause in his own country and when, in England, he sat at the feet of William Morris and looked on Socialism with a friendly eye. Unfortunately for Orwell's thesis, it was precisely at the moment – after the turning-point of 1903 – when Yeats's vision of life began to turn 'sinister' – aristocratic and proto-Fascist – that he began to purge his style of quaintness, and his greatest poetry was written near the end of his life when his ideas were at their most sinister.

A Marxist critique which starts from the assumption that bad politics make for bad style will continue 'not to succeed'. The opposite assumption, though not entirely true, would be nearer to the truth. The politics of the left – any left, even a popular 'National movement' – impose, by their emphasis on collective effort and on sacrifice, a constraint on the artist, a constraint which may show itself in artificialities of style, vagueness or simple carelessness. Right wing politics, with their emphasis on the freedoms of the elite, impose less constraint, require less pretence, allow style to become more personal and direct.

It is not necessary to claim that these generalizations are universally valid; they were, I think, valid for Yeats and for many of his generation and that immediately following. Snobbery – 'abhorring the multitude' – was then a more acceptable, and therefore comfortable, attitude than it now would be. A hero of François Mauriac's, after a day spent among workers in some Christian Socialist movement, used to change into black silk pyjamas in the evening and read Laforgue, *pour se désencanailler*. Yeats after 1903 *se désencanaillait* in the company of Lady Gregory and her circle. Now that he had withdrawn for the time from active politics, politics became explicit in his poetry. His bitterness about Maud Gonne's marriage took a political form:

> Why should I blame her that she filled my days
> With misery or that she would of late
> Have taught to ignorant men most violent ways
> Or hurled the little streets upon the great
> Had they but courage equal to desire?

If the snobbery endemic in his class and generation takes in his writing from now on an almost hysterical intensity, it is, I think, that he felt himself to have undergone, in his political years, a kind of contamination, a loss of caste, through 'the contagion of the throng' and that in the end, he had suffered a deep injury to his pride. 'One must accept', he had written to Lady Gregory near the end of his political involvement, 'the baptism of the gutter.'[24] 'The foul ditch' and 'the abounding gutter' became recurring symbols of disgust in his later poetry. In the same letter in which he accepted the baptism of the gutter, he spoke of trying to get someone to resign from something 'in favour of MacBride of the Irish Brigade' – the man whom Maud Gonne was to marry three years later:

> My love is angry that of late
> I cry all base blood down
> As though she had not taught me hate
> By kisses to a clown.

There were moments when he felt ashamed of this hate,[25] but it proved enduring. Hatred of England had been with him early; hatred of 'the base' in Ireland now joined it. The two hates represented an abnormal intensification of the normal dualism of the Irish Protestant. They formed an unstable and potentially explosive combination: a volcanic substance which would from time to time erupt through the often placid surface of Yeats's public life.

Although Yeats withdrew in a sense from Irish politics about 1903, this did not mean that Irish politics withdrew from him. His theatre, because of *Cathleen Ni Houlihan*, had just become a kind of Holy Place of Irish nationalism and his new frame of mind – fortunately for the theatre – was far from that of a custodian of such a Holy Place. Militant nationalists, of whom the most vocal Dublin leader at this time was Arthur Griffith, the founder of Sinn Fein, naturally wanted the theatre to serve the cause actively, as it had done with *Cathleen Ni Houlihan*. They also – and with them a wider public – insisted that it must not 'play into the enemy's hands' by presenting a 'degrading' image of Irish life. Here nationalist pressures and Catholic pressures – which often worked against each other, as Parnell and the Fenians knew – converged in turbulent menace. Plays that showed Irishmen as sinful – or, even, for example, coarse in speech – were hurtful to many militant nationalists as denigrating the inherently virtuous and refined character of 'the Irish race' (a phrase much in use at the time); to many militant Catholics such plays were both inherently immoral and scandalous, and also offensive by the suggestion that the Catholic education of the Irishman left something to be desired. 'An insult to Ireland', cried the first set of voices, and the second set responded: 'an insult to Catholic Ireland'.[26] 'Audience', telegraphed Lady Gregory on the first night of *The Playboy of the Western World*, 'broke up in disorder at the word *shift* [chemise].'[27]

It seems in retrospect surprising – and it is a tribute to the courage, tenacity and skill of Yeats and Lady Gregory – that the theatre should have been able to survive at all under the combined pressure – only fitfully applied it is true – of the two most powerful forces in Irish life. Yeats had many battles to fight and fought them with gusto. 'Into the dozen or so fairly important quarrels in the theatre movement from 1903 till 1911 he threw himself with something like abandon. The issue was in almost every case national art versus nationalist propaganda.'[28]

The art that he defended in his theatre was that which belonged to 'life' as against – his words – 'the desire which every political party has to substitute for life a bunch of reliable principles and assertions'.[29] He never, as we say in Dublin, said a truer word. He was here taking his stand as an artist, in defence of the life of art in his country. For him then – and for us now – the politics of the matter come on a much lower level. But it is with that lower level – in which he took an ever-renewed interest – that we are concerned here. On that level the defence of 'national art' against 'nationalist propaganda' represented a political shift; for Yeats, in *Cathleen Ni Houlihan*, had produced one of the most powerful pieces of nationalist propaganda ever written. Yeats could be an excellent propagandist when he wanted to, and he often did want to. 'You have been liable at times, only at times,' his father wrote to him anxiously, 'to a touch of the propaganda fiend.'[30] And he himself affirmed more sweepingly: 'I have been a propagandist all my life.'

Those who looked to him and his theatre for nationalist propaganda, and did not get it, had therefore some reason to feel confusion and disappointment. The fact was that their cause – the nationalist cause – did not sufficiently stir Yeats at this particular time (between 1903 and 1916) to make him write (or encourage others to write) in a way which would have had the effect they desired – as he had written before and as he was to write again. The nationalist in him was dormant, and the aristocrat wide awake, dominating the mob from the stage.[31] For those in whose bloodstream *Cathleen Ni Houlihan* was still working this was an unfortunate conjuncture; for those who detested all that that play stood for, it was an auspicious one. The young men from Trinity came to the Abbey to defend artistic freedom by singing 'God Save the King'.[32]

There is one important apparent break in the otherwise consistently aristocratic line of thought and action which he pursued in these years and – with the partial exception of certain nationalist flare-ups – throughout his life from about 1903 to the end. This apparent break is constituted by the stand he took on the great Dublin Lock-out, when the Dublin employers led by William Martin Murphy tried to starve the Dublin workers into submission[33] in order to break Jim Larkin's Irish Transport and General Workers' Union. Few who had read Yeats's writings, or considered his attitude to public questions in the preceding ten years, could have expected him to come out on the side of Larkin's men. William Martin Murphy – if he had had time for Yeats or for his poetry – might plausibly have claimed that if ever there was a man who:

> . . . taught to ignorant men most violent ways

that man was Big Jim Larkin. He could also have contended – and proved his case, certainly to the satisfaction of a Dublin court of the time – that it was actually Larkin's policy to:

> . . . hurl the little streets upon the great.

For this Larkin himself, if not all his followers, had 'courage equal to desire'. 'My advice to you', Larkin had told his men, 'is to be round the doors and corners, and if one of our class should fall, then two of the others should fall for that one. We will demonstrate in O'Connell Street [Dublin's principal thoroughfare]. It is our street as well as William Martin Murphy's. We are fighting for bread and butter. We will hold our meeting in the streets, and if any one of our men fall, there must be justice. By the living God if they want war they can have it.'

A conservative admirer of Yeats could reasonably have expected to find him, in such a war, on the side of public order, the rights of property and the rule of the educated. What Yeats did, however, was to come out explicitly and vehemently against the activities of the employers' principal allies – police, press and clergy. His protest – in the form of a letter to Larkin's *Irish Worker* – is important enough, in the context of the present discussion, to be quoted in full:

> I do not complain of Dublin's capacity for fanaticism whether in priest or layman, for you cannot have strong feeling without that capacity, but neither those who directed the police nor the editors of our newspapers can plead fanaticism. They are supposed to watch over our civil liberties, and I charge the Dublin Nationalist newspapers with deliberately arousing religious passion to break up the organization of the workingman, with appealing to mob law day after day, with publishing the names of workingmen and their wives for purposes of intimidation.
>
> And I charge the Unionist Press of Dublin and those who directed the police with conniving at this conspiracy. I want to know why the 'Daily Express', which is directly and indirectly inciting Ulster to rebellion in defence of what it calls 'the liberty of the subject' is so indifferent to that liberty here in Dublin

that it has not made one editorial comment, and I ask the 'Irish Times' why a few sentences at the end of an article, too late in the week to be of any service, has been the measure of its love for civil liberty?

I want to know why there were only (according to the press reports) two policemen at Kingsbridge on Saturday when Mr. Sheehy Skeffington was assaulted and a man prevented from buying a ticket for his own child? There had been tumults every night at every Dublin railway station, and I can only assume that the police authorities wished those tumults to continue.

I want to know why the mob at North Wall and elsewhere were permitted to drag children from their parents' arms, and by what right one woman was compelled to open her box and show a marriage certificate; I want to know by what right the police have refused to accept charges against rioters; I want to know who has ordered the abrogation of the most elementary rights of the citizens, and why authorities who are bound to protect every man in doing that which he has a legal right to do – even though they have to call upon all the forces of the Crown – have permitted the Ancient Order of Hibernians to besiege Dublin, taking possession of the railway stations like a foreign army.

Prime Ministers have fallen, and Ministers of State have been impeached for less than this. I demand that the coming Police Inquiry shall be so widened that we may get to the bottom of a conspiracy, whose like has not been seen in any English-speaking town during living memory. Intriguers have met together somewhere behind the scenes that they might turn the religion of Him who thought it hard for a rich man to enter into the Kingdom of Heaven into an oppression of the poor.

'It may be surmised', wrote the late J. M. Hone about this letter, 'that Yeats was not actuated solely by humanitarian zeal.'[34] It may indeed – as we shall see – but Hone's comment needs itself to be treated with some reserve. Hone was a friend of Yeats, and in tune with his political views, but his conservatism was of a colder and more intellectual stamp than Yeats's. It is clear from Hone's references to the Lock-out – he pays tribute to Murphy's services to Dublin – that the employers, rather than the workers, commanded such store of sympathy as he possessed.[35] The very use of the words 'humanitarian zeal' conveys as much. Granted his premises this was a logical position. But Yeats was not logical in this chilly way. He was an enthusiast, in the old sense of the word; he was not only capable of generous indignation – he positively revelled in it, as he was to show again and again. We may – and I do – accept the view that Yeats on this occasion was not activated *solely* by humanitarian zeal, but we need more stress on the 'solely' than Hone, in the context, seems to imply. The events of the Dublin Lock-out – including the events which Yeats described – aroused strong emotions and there can be no doubt that Yeats's indignation was genuine, and that it sprang, in part, from those human feelings which, when we find them inconvenient, we call 'humanitarian zeal'.

Yet, as Hone suggests, feelings of this kind would hardly by themselves explain the phenomenon of the letter. There is no reason to suppose that Yeats was either peculiarly accessible, or peculiarly resistant, to such feelings. He could, like most other politically-minded people, modulate the expression of such feelings – and perhaps even, to some extent, the feelings themselves – in accordance with his judgement of the social and political context in which the 'crimes' or 'regrettable incidents', as the case might be, occurred. Thus, in later years, Yeats did not, as we shall see, allow his humane feelings to overpower his political judgement in connection either with the repressive measures of the first Free State government, or with the penal achievements of the Fascist governments. Nor, in these later contexts, did he show the marked specific concern for civil liberties which he shows here. It is true that he became more conservative – and more than conservative – as he grew older, but a conservative aristocratic pattern had already, by 1913, become quite distinct. The concern about the 'oppression of the poor' in this letter does not fit more easily into this pattern than the apparent Christian piety of the last sentence fits into the pattern of Yeats's religious ideas.

The explanation of the letter which Hone suggests is, as far as it goes, helpful. This is that Yeats was already violently incensed against Murphy on an artistic issue: Murphy's opposition, in his powerful paper *The Irish Independent*, to the housing by Dublin Corporation of the Lane collection of paintings, in the manner prescribed by Lane. When Murphy attacked Lane, Larkin praised Lane. Yeats, it is hinted – no more than a hint is given – came to the support of Larkin for similar reasons to those that made Larkin come to the support of Lane. The poet was naturally no more predisposed in favour of the labour leader, than the labour leader was in favour of the art connoisseur, but all three had a common enemy in the person of the arch-philistine and arch-bourgeois, William Martin Murphy. This is illuminating, and the reminder that Murphy had been a prominent anti-Parnellite is also highly relevant. If this were all, however, the letter would be little more than an incident in something like a personal feud, with little relevance to the wider pattern of Yeats's politics. I believe, however, that this is not all, and that the letter is both more relevant to that pattern, and more consistent with it, than appears at first sight.

'Yeats', according to Hone, 'chose to regard Martin Murphy as a representative type and leader of the middle class which had begun to rise to power under the shadow of the Land League. . . .'[36] Both Yeats and Hone

24

are rather vague about this middle class; it is possible to be a little more specific. The Land League (1879–81), with its successor movements, had profoundly weakened the influence, formerly overpowering, of the old Protestant Ascendancy, with which Yeats liked to identify himself; it threatened also the privileged social position – and sometimes directly hit the incomes – of the Protestant middle class to which Yeats did, in fact, belong.

The boycott, in which the people had received and absorbed effective instruction from the Land League times on, was certainly not intended by its organizers as a lever to help in bringing about the emergence of a Catholic middle class, but it is probable that that is one of the ways in which it actually worked. People who sold goods to, or had dealings with, boycotted farmers, land agents, etc., were themselves boycotted; those who attempted to break the boycott in this way had a high propensity to be, in politics Unionists, and in religion Protestant. It may be imagined that a 'Nationalist' shopkeeper would not be backward in urging the boycott of a 'Unionist' competitor; in this way a socio-political movement could shade over into a communal-religious one.

This process is still a reality of life, within the experience of the present writer, in parts of Northern Ireland. I remember being gently chided, by a group of nationalist friends in a northern city, for not staying at the 'nationalist hotel'; in fact, they not only chided me, but with two telephone calls, neatly transferred my hotel-political allegiance.[37] These friends were quite conscious about their intent: to shift as much economic power as possible from 'their' hands into 'ours'. They had not the air of having invented the idea and I believe that it was an important, though seldom mentioned, feature of Irish life for many years. Conditions between the invention of the boycott and the first war – that is during the first phases of Yeats's active life – must have been particularly propitious to it. Yeats, in associating as he did – rather strangely at first sight – the 'new middle class' with the agrarian agitation, had this set of phenomena in mind. For the class from which Yeats had come – the Protestant merchants and professional people – 'the shadow of the Land League' meant the boycott, in its wide variety of forms, as an instrument for the transfer of economic power out of their hands into those of the more astute, energetic and rapacious of the conquered caste, now beginning to form a 'new middle class'.[38]

Yeats was not wrong in seeing in 'the Sullivan gang' – that clan from Bantry, Co. Cork, of which the economic head was William Martin Murphy and the political head Tim Healy – representative leaders of this new class. The qualities of acumen and energy all Ireland, friend and foe, conceded to them; the quality of unscrupulous rapacity was persistently attributed to them by their numerous enemies. They had not been particularly closely associated with the Land League, but they were associated with the varieties of religious-communal economic and social activity which I have been describing as arising from the successful operation of the boycott. The Land League itself had not been clerically inspired or dominated – far from it – but, in its successor body, the National League, the clergy began to play a direct and recognized political part.[39]

After the Parnell divorce case 'the Sullivan gang', led by Healy and backed by Murphy's money, emerged as the spearhead of the clerical attack on Parnell. Other, more important leaders who went against Parnell – John Dillon and William O'Brien – carefully eschewed 'the moral issue' and tried to spare Parnell. It was left to Healy and his clan, with the active support of the clergy, to hammer away at this issue, often in scurrilous language, and to Parnell's undoing. To the young Yeats – whose dislike of 'the Sullivan gang' antedated these proceedings – the spectacle of the plebeian Healy taunting the falling aristocrat was a powerful symbol. Paradoxically, the Parnell split closed – for a time – the schism in his political soul between the 'Protestant/aristocrat' and the 'Irish/nationalist'. The unified nationalist movement of 1880–90 – a movement in which 'the Sullivan gang' had followed Parnell – had been putting pressure on England, and there Yeats approved them, but they were also putting pressure on the superior caste in Ireland, and that he very much disliked. When Parnell and 'the Sullivan gang' flew apart, this tension in Yeats was relaxed. Parnell was fighting England and – no longer the Ascendancy, which began to discern merits in him for the first time – but the Catholic middle class, encouraged by the clergy and led by 'the Sullivan gang'.

We know with what intensity this struggle revived in Yeats's mind in 1913 when, in the poem 'To a Shade' he apostrophized the ghost of Parnell. The line:

> Your enemy an old foul mouth

refers to a collective Sullivan orifice – the tongue of Healy and the teeth of Murphy. The immediate occasion for the attack – the art-gallery controversy – was aesthetic, but the roots of the controversy, and its emotional charge, were social and political and – in the communal sense – religious. It is true that the poet attacked 'the Sullivan gang' for its philistinism – and Murphy's *Irish Independent* was indeed, and long remained, a philistine bastion – but he had hated them long before any artistic controversy arose; in any case the Sullivan clan were certainly, intellectually, well above the general level of

26

the Irish middle and upper class as a whole (both Protestant and Catholic) and, aesthetically, did not lag conspicuously behind these.[40] It was not primarily as art critics but as representatives of a class – the new middle class – and exponents of a method – clerical pressure – that they were obnoxious.

Yeats's intervention in the 1913 industrial conflict came just at the moment when the leader of the obnoxious class brought the obnoxious method to bear. Murphy, supported in this by Archbishop Walsh, had enlisted clerical aid to prevent children of the Dublin workers from being sent to the homes of English sympathizers. From the Archbishop's point of view the children's departure involved a danger to their faith; from Murphy's point of view it represented a danger to his economic blockade. If the children were not on hand, to go hungry – and be seen and heard to go hungry – then the men might be able to hold out, and Larkin would win. So the cry 'the faith in danger' was used to starve the children.

Yeats's attack is directed first and foremost at Murphy's use of 'religion'. This first charge is against 'the Dublin nationalist newspapers' – which were led by Murphy's *Irish Independent* – for 'deliberately arousing religious passion to break up the organization of the workingman'. The other charges are all ancillary to this – charges of connivance in Murphy's methods of defending the faith, and some details of these methods.

One can discern, then, in this letter, honest disgust at an odious piece of cruel hypocrisy, a human desire for a crack at Murphy, and the wish to illuminate a particularly unlovely example of the social influence of the Catholic clergy. Concern for the workers is also present, but it must be noted that this, in itself, had not been sufficient to arouse Yeats to intervene. The Lock-out (of some workers) and strike (of others) and the police brutalities had begun in August, and protests began soon after. Yeats did not, however, protest until after the publication on 21 October of the letter from the Catholic Archbishop of Dublin, in which he told the workers' wives that, if they allowed their hungry children to go to England to be fed they would 'no longer be held worthy of the name of Catholic mothers'.

Yeats's indignation at the 'saving of the children' was spontaneous, comprehensible and creditable. It does not constitute – appearances to the contrary – an isolated pro-working class outbreak, unique in his career.[41] The anti-clerical feelings in themselves were habitual in the class from which he himself sprang. Other members of that class could, however, muffle the expression of these feelings when, as now, it suited their economic interest to do so – that is the meaning of the charge of 'connivance' which Yeats directed against the (Protestant) *Irish Times* and *Daily Express*. Yeats himself could do some muffling at times, but when the provocation was great

27

– as now – he had to give vent to his feelings, against the formidable alliance of savings and prayers.

> What need you, being come to sense
> But fumble in a greasy till
> And add the halfpence to the pence
> And prayer to shivering prayer until
> You have dried the marrow from the bone;
> For men were born to pray and save
> Romantic Ireland's dead and gone
> It's with O'Leary in the grave.
>
> (September 1913)[42]

Most of the leaders who planned the rising which proved – three years later – that romantic Ireland was not yet dead and gone, belonged to the general class which Yeats distrusted; not to the climbing 'Sullivan gang' section of it, but to the 'clerks and shopkeepers' whom he thought of as 'the base'; they included the basest of the base – from Yeats's point of view – Major MacBride himself. They had all been engaged for years in the kind of politics on which he had turned his back. But in 1916 they were shot by the English:

> All changed, changed utterly
> A terrible beauty is born

The poems 'Easter 1916', 'Sixteen Dead Men', 'The Rose Tree' and 'On a Political Prisoner' drew strength from the complexity as well as from the intensity of the emotions involved; the sense – which became explicit years after – of his own share in the 'gestation' of the event,[43] and the presence in the event of the strongest love and the strongest personal hatred of his life. They showed an old hate, and even a kind of disgust, for much of what the insurrection meant,

> Blind and leader of the blind
> Drinking the foul ditch where they lie

an even older and deeper hate for those who crushed the insurrection; and finally a prophetic sense of the still more bitter struggle yet to come:

> But who can talk of give and take
> What should be and what not
> While those dead men are loitering there
> To stir the boiling pot?

By the time when 'Easter 1916' and 'The Rose Tree' were published, in the autumn of 1920, the pot had boiled over. The Black-and-Tan terror was now at its height throughout Ireland. To publish these poems in this context was a political act, and a bold one: probably the boldest of Yeats's career. Yeats could be fearless on issues where artistic integrity was involved – as he showed for example in facing the riots over *The Playboy of the Western World* in 1907 – and also when clerical meddling aroused his anger. But in national politics, even where he felt passionately, he usually acted prudently. And even at this point, although he acted with unusual boldness, he did not allow himself to be carried away. What he published in 1920 concerned a historical event of four years earlier; even on that event he did not publish, in England, the poem 'Sixteen Dead Men' which, with its 'boiling pot', had the most explicit bearing on contemporary politics. He did not publish, at all, the poem 'Reprisals' written against the Black-and-Tans and addressed to the ghost of Lady Gregory's son, killed in the Great War:

> Flit to Kiltartan Cross and stay
> Till certain second thoughts have come
> Upon the cause you served that we
> Imagined such a fine affair:
> Half-drunk or whole-mad soldiery
> Are murdering your tenants there.
> Men that revere your father yet
> Are shot at on the open plain
> Where may new-married women sit
> And suckle children now? Armed men
> May murder them in passing by
> Nor law nor parliament take heed
> Then close your ears with dust and lie
> Among the other cheated dead.[44]

Yeats's indignation was spontaneous: his method of giving public expression to that indignation seems calculated.[45] By publishing the 1916 poems in 1920 he placed himself openly 'on Ireland's side' in the fight with England, but he closed no doors in terms of contemporary politics. For it was known, in 1920, that Ireland was going to get some form of self-government. If the rebels were beaten, it would be the Home Rule (with partition) of the British Act of 1920. If the rebels won, it would be the Republic proclaimed in 1916. The two poems that Yeats chose to publish covered, as it happened, both eventualities neatly. The spirit of the Proclamation of the Republic was in them:

> 'But where can we draw water'
> Said Pearse to Connolly
> 'When all the wells are parched away

> As plain as plain can be
> There's nothing but our own red blood
> Can make a right Rose Tree'

But there were also in them the doubts and reservations which most Irishmen had felt about the Proclamation of 1916: the doubts and reservations of those for whom Home Rule and the Act of 1920 represented an acceptable settlement:

> Was it needless death after all?
> For England may keep faith
> For all that is done and said.
> We know their dream; enough
> To know they dreamed and are dead;
> And what if excess of love
> Bewildered them till they died?

In the event the Anglo-Irish Treaty brought to Ireland the realities of the Act of 1920 with some of the trappings of 1916. This treaty set up, not the Republic proclaimed in 1916, but a Free State within the Empire and without the six counties of the north-east. Many – probably more than half – of those who had been fighting the Black-and-Tans while Yeats had been publishing his 1916 poems, felt that this was a betrayal, as Yeats's Pearse and Connolly might have felt:

> Maybe a breath of politic words
> Has withered our Rose Tree

Those who felt in this way tried to reject the treaty and carry on the struggle. The majority of the people, tired of war, had voted, in effect, for the acceptance of the treaty. The Free State Government, with the aid of British artillery and armoured cars, now set about liquidating the Republican forces. Whether it had behind it, in this effort, all of those who had given it its majority may be doubted. It certainly had behind it all the wealthier elements in the country, including the Anglo-Irish, and it had W. B. Yeats, nominated by President Cosgrave to the Senate of the Irish Free State in December 1922. The Civil War had now been raging for six months.

The Free State forces, in destroying the Republican forces, were obliged to use some of the same methods as the Black-and-Tans (flogging, shooting of hostages), but applied these with greater efficiency, based on far better intelligence, and with proportionately less accompanying publicity.[46] It was a pattern that was to be repeated – perhaps copied – after the mid-century, in many ex-colonies, and came to be assailed as neo-colonialism. Many of those who had denounced the excesses of the Black-and-Tans were plunged in deeper horror by what happened during the Civil War and in its aftermath. These included Lady Gregory, whose journals tell a story:[47]

[During the Civil War] Jan 23 [1923] These floggings in my mind. I wrote to Yeats in protest. The young men taken away were flogged as well as those left 'with a thonged whip'. I was not surprised to hear Hogan's house at Kilchreest has been destroyed. Hatred must grow – 'death answering to death through the generations like clerks answering one another at the Mass'.

[After the Civil War] Aug 23 W. B. Yeats here yesterday. I say the fault of the Government is this hatred of the Republicans they show in their speeches. He says it is justified or at least excused by the information they have had from America that it is to be said, in case 'of a Republican defeat', that the elections were not carried out fairly and assassinations are threatened. But with the Republicans saying the prisoners are flogged or tortured they probably have the same hatred. . . .

Nov 10 . . . There has been some talk about the hunger strike, Esmonde saying the Government would not yield. And this is Yeats' view. I had some talk with him after we came home, the first time I had seen him close and again this morning. He says the Government cannot give in. That if they had let Miss MacSwiney die when she began it this new hunger strike would not have begun, but they had a sentimental feeling for her for her brother's sake.[48]

We talked a long time this morning. I had had a bad night and thought it over a long time, and had come to a determination of writing to the papers about it, asking that the crime or accusation against these four hundred remaining on [hunger] strike might be told out, that we might know if consenting to their suicide is in accordance with the conscience of Christian nations and the law of God. I mean to go and consult 'A.E.'[49] about them. But Yeats is violently against any protest, says it is necessary to the stability of Government to hold out, says they cannot publish the accusations because many are on suspicion, or as they think certainty, but they have not evidence that can be shown. . . .

I ask if that might not come under an amnesty at the conclusion of the war, for the Government themselves signed death sentences during it. But he says no, and he says the Government cannot publish the real reason for the detention of this thousand, they themselves are in danger of being assassinated by some among them.

I asked if they could not, on their side, try to get rid of the Oath [of Allegiance to the Crown]; that would do away with the real cause of trouble, the keeping of Republicans out of the Dail. He said they cannot in the present state of English feeling, it would be useless to ask for it, and besides we may probably want English help in getting the Loan. And the Senate can make no move in the matter. . . .

Nov 11 . . . Went on to Jack Yeats [the painter, the poet's brother] . . .

Lennox Robinson . . . said: 'Can we not do anything about the hunger strikers? Write a letter perhaps.' Strange, because I had not spoken of my own restless night or my talk with Yeats. So we walked and planned and at last went into the Arts Club and wrote a letter. We thought Stephens [James][50] and Jack Yeats might join in signing it. He called in Cruise O'Brien[51] from another room to ask if the *Independent* [pro-Government paper] would put it in. He thought so, made one or two slight alterations, thinking it showed a slight prepossession against the Government; then I came back to Merrion Square [to Yeats's house].

Later Lennox Robinson telephoned that Jack Yeats had refused to sign, 'he is much too red to do so', and asked if we should still send it on with our own names and Stephens', who has agreed. I said 'Yes'. It may perhaps bring letters or suggestions from others and possibly save some lives. Then I told Yeats (W.B.) what I had done and proposed leaving his house for the hotel, as he might not approve. He would not allow that and after talking for a while thought perhaps we had done right. Of course one won't have any gratitude from either side. But I slept better.

Nov 16. On Monday night 'A.E.' and Lieutenant 'X' were with Yeats. I looked in but didn't stay. Yeats said they had talked of the prisoners. 'X' said they were not on hunger-strike, were being fed. And that the stories of ill-treatment are not true – gave instances, thinks it 'likely only half a dozen men will die'. Dreadful, I think, even if that half-dozen were not of the bravest.[52]

Yeats was now an established public figure. Having become a senator in December 1922, he received an honorary doctorate from Trinity College in 1923 and the Nobel Prize for Literature in the same year. The Yeatses had now a house in Merrion Square, 'the Berkeley Square of Ireland', as he said. He was soberly pleased about his political position and prospects. 'We', he wrote of himself and his fellow senators, 'are a fairly distinguished body and should get much government into our hands.'[53] His political ideas were now explicitly reactionary: 'Out of all this murder and rapine', he wrote in 1922, 'will come not a demagogic but an authoritarian government.'[54] And again: 'Everywhere one notices a drift towards Conservatism, perhaps towards Autocracy.'[55] His ideas for Ireland were explicitly linked with the rise of Fascism in Europe:

We are preparing here, behind our screen of bombs and smoke, a return to conservative politics as elsewhere in Europe or at least to a substitution of the historical sense of logic. The return will be painful and perhaps violent but many educated men talk of it and must soon work for it and perhaps riot for it.

A curious sign is that 'A.E.' who was the most popular of men is now suffering some slight eclipse because of old democratic speeches – things of years ago. I on the other hand get hearers where I did not get them because I have been of the opposite party. . . . The Ireland that reacts from the present disorder is turning its eyes towards individualist [i.e. Fascist] Italy.[56]

This letter was written just before Yeats's nomination to the Senate of the Free State and just after Mussolini's March on Rome (22 October 1922).

Many of Yeats's contemporaries, younger admirers and subsequent writers about him refused to take all this very seriously.[57] The Dublin to which Yeats belonged – in so far as he belonged to Dublin at all – the Dublin of the Arts Club, liked to treat Yeats's politics as a joke, and this tradition went a long way back. More than twenty years before, when Yeats and Maud Gonne were stirring up opinion against Queen Victoria's visit to Ireland, Percy French had made the Queen protest:

> And there must be a slate, sez she
> Off that Willie Yeats, sez she
> He'd be betther at home, sez she
> Frinch-polishin' a pome, sez she
> Than writin' letthers, sez she
> About his betthers, sez she
> Paradin' me crimes, sez she
> In the Irish Times, sez she.

This mood of affectionate raillery persisted, and perhaps did something to protect Yeats from possible adverse consequences of his political involvement. My father, at the Arts Club, used to poke gentle fun at Yeats's 'Fascism', parodying him as referring in a speech to 'that very great man, Missolonghi' and then, when corrected, saying majestically: 'I am told the name is not Missolonghi but Mussolini – but, does it . . . really . . . matter?'

Yeats enjoyed, and even encouraged, this kind of joke about himself and others:

> And thought before I had done
> Of a mocking tale or a gibe
> To please a companion
> Around the fire at the club
> Being certain that they and I
> But lived where motley is worn

For those who admired Yeats, but were made uneasy by his politics, the idea that his politics were vague, ill-informed and funny, offered a way out; a way out, left open by Yeats himself. Yet his politics had this much serious about them: that practice and theory tended to concur. The poet admired Mussolini from afar:[58] the senator admired, and worked with, Ireland's strong man, Kevin O'Higgins.[59] O'Higgins, in Irish politics – he was

Minister of Justice in the Free State Government – was thought to stand for what was most ruthless and implacable in the party of property: seventy-seven executions and the famous words, 'if necessary seven hundred and seventy-seven'. This was not repugnant to Yeats; the 'right of the State to take life in its own defence' became dear to him. O'Higgins was 'their sole statesman'; Yeats did him the honour of including him, along with Grattan, Parnell and Berkeley, in a list of great Irishmen – a list in which the sole Gaelic and Catholic name is that of O'Higgins. His portrait is among 'my friends' in 'The Municipal Gallery Revisited':

> Kevin O'Higgins' countenance that wears
> A gentle questioning look that cannot hide
> A soul incapable of remorse or rest.

Those who – like Yeats – admired in O'Higgins a potential autocrat, would not have taken it for granted that he, as his colleagues were to do in 1932, would have tamely allowed the party defeated in the Civil War to come to power through impeccably conducted free elections. But by then O'Higgins was no longer there; he had been assassinated in 1927:

> A great man in his pride
> Confronting murderous men

'Nobody', he had said in a phrase which impressed Yeats, 'can expect to live who has done what I have.'[60] How deeply hated he was not only by his political opponents, but by some of 'his own side' including his own police, I can remember myself. I was ten years old and returning from a drive in the country – my first drive in a motor-car – with my aunt Mrs Skeffington and a friend of hers. We were stopped at a road-block and the sergeant, recognizing my aunt, smiled broadly and said: 'Ye'll be delighted to hear, Ma'am – Kevin's been shot!'

Countess Markievicz – 'Madame' as she was known among the poor of Dublin who loved her – died after O'Higgins was murdered. She had a great following among the street-traders of Moore Street; famed hecklers and the bane of every Free State politician, they were known at this time as 'Madame's wans'. About O'Higgins's death, one of them said: 'poor Madame's last wish'.

It was of her that Yeats had written:

> Did she in touching that lone wing
> Recall the years before her mind
> Become a bitter, an abstract thing,
> Her thought some popular enmity:

> Blind and leader of the blind
> Drinking the foul ditch where they lie.

All Ireland was divided by the end of that week between those who mourned Countess Markievicz and those who mourned O'Higgins. The latter were probably fewer but more 'respectable'. From a window in Parnell Square I watched O'Higgins's funeral go by. I had not imagined there were so many top hats in the world; I was never to see so many again.[61] They were there to honour a man who had defended what they stood for at the cost of many lives including his own. Senator Yeats must have been under one of the top hats. The poet had stayed away from Parnell's funeral; the senator would not, I think, have stayed away from that of Kevin O'Higgins.[62]

In 1928, the year after O'Higgins's death, Yeats lost his Senate seat; his term had expired and the government made no move to renew his nomination. For some time past the going had been increasingly difficult, for similar reasons to those which had applied at the turn of the century. That is to say that the specific influence of the Catholic Church in politics was growing more palpable again. It is true that the regime to which Yeats belonged had always been supported by the Church, but in the beginning it had also needed Protestant support. When it was struggling for its life, and needed money and guns from England, it had to reassure English opinion by giving places of prominence to the Protestant middle class, most of whom, though not Yeats, were classified as 'Southern loyalists'. When the emergency was over, and 'the Loan' negotiated, the need to placate English opinion, by showing deference to Protestants, subsided. The government no longer needed British artillery; it still needed to have its position fully covered by the Canons of the Church. The vital principle for the party now in power was one later reduced by a member of that party to a lapidary formula – never to risk 'a clout of a crogier'.

The fact was that 'the Sullivan gang' – Yeats's old bugbears from 1890 to 1913 – were an important component in the regime which had made Yeats a senator. Healy was Governor-General and Yeats had called on him in that capacity; the Murphy press – which had called vociferously for the execution of the 1916 leaders – was a pillar of the Cosgrave regime; Kevin O'Higgins himself was a member of the clan, a nephew of Healy's. Granted that Yeats's hostility to this clan – and the 'clerical bourgeoisie' for which it stood – was sincere, as it surely was, how did he become so easily reconciled to them in 1922? The answer is, I think, a double one. First, the Civil War had changed many things. The Protestant middle and upper classes, which had so long regarded the social and political influence of the clergy as either a baneful or contemptible phenomenon, had now seen its advantages as a barrier against 'anarchy'; the propertied classes had been made more conscious of a common danger and common interests, less insistent on differences and group competition. Yeats – who worked in the Senate generally in concert with the representatives of the Protestant propertied classes – could also move with them in suppressing his repugnance for what 'the Bantry band' represented. Second, the reconciliation was only partial and temporary:

A patched-up affair if you ask my opinion

As long as the 'clerical bourgeoisie' showed consideration for the suscepti-bilities of Protestants, it was possible to work with them. When the bishops began to dictate, the strain, for Yeats, became too great. The Irish bishops, crogier-happy, now extorted the legislation they wanted, forbidding divorce and the sale of contraceptives and later setting up a censorship of publications. The government party, which Yeats had supported on all major issues, carried out the wishes of the bishops on all these matters.

Irish Protestants generally did not care for the new trend, but most of them now made their political choices, not as Protestants but as bourgeoisie. The Government was obnoxiously Papist but it was sound on the essential: the rights of property. Nor did Protestants wish to say anything to confirm their fellow countrymen in an opinion to which they were already too prone: that the distinguishing characteristic of Protestantism is a devotion to divorce, contraceptives and dirty books. The new legislation was, in practice, not much more than a minor irritant; Belfast is not far away.

Most Irish Protestants therefore took a guarded line in the matter. But not Yeats.[63] Yeats's aristocratic feelings, and his pride as a senator, were hurt; the sage oligarchy to which he had felt himself to belong, the 'fairly distinguished body' which 'should get much government into its hands', was now taking its orders from a bunch of peasants in mitres.[64] The 'base' were dictating to their betters. The peroration of his speech on divorce was not a liberal one; it was the statement of the spokesman of a superior caste, denying the right of inferior castes to make laws for it:

> We against whom you have done this thing are no petty people. We are one of the great stocks of Europe. We are the people of Burke: we are the people of Grattan; we are the people of Swift, the people of Emmet, the people of Parnell. We have created the most of the modern literature of this country. We have created the best of its political intelligence.[65]

Some have felt that Yeats's own political intelligence was not at its best on this occasion. Certainly he seemed to be committing political – or at the very least parliamentary – suicide. Yet he could not do otherwise; to remain in politics he would have had to swallow his pride, and pride was essential to his political life. His dilemma – the dilemma which, happily for his work, pushed him away from the centre and towards the margins of politics – was that he had become an anti-clerical conservative in a country where the clergy were an indispensable element of any practical conservative politics. Because of his conservative option in the Civil War he had cut himself off from all the forces in the country which were, in any notable degree, resistant to clerical pressure (or, for that matter, to the temptation of manipulating religious signs for their own ends). His political friends now showed themselves to be a clerical party, the direct heirs to the anti-Parnellites of the 1890s. What was still living in the Parnellite tradition had gone on the Republican side in the Civil War and regarded Yeats with aversion and a sense of betrayal. He now, by openly defying the Church, cut himself off, for a time at least, from the modern 'anti-Parnellites'. Politically, he had become for the moment completely isolated.

The year 1932 was a turning-point in Irish political history. In that year the party, led by Mr Cosgrave, which had won the Civil War and ruled the country since the foundation of the State, fell from power. The party, led by de Valera, which represented the losers in the Civil War, now won a general election and took over the Government. The respect for democratic process shown by Mr Cosgrave's government was, in the circumstances, rather remarkable. It was, indeed, too remarkable to please many of the members of the fallen party, and some of these now set about organizing a paramilitary movement, on the Fascist model, for the intimidation of their opponents and the recovery of power. 'They have the Blackshirts in Italy,' said one of the politicians concerned, 'they have the Brownshirts in Germany, and now in Ireland we have the Blueshirts.'

Yeats took part in the launching of this movement and wrote songs for it:

> What is equality? Muck in the yard.

It was necessary, he explained, to break 'the reign of the mob' and:

> If any Government or Party undertook this work it will need force, marching men (the logic of fanaticism whether in a woman or a mob is drawn from a premise, protected by ignorance and therefore irrefutable); it will promise not this or that measure but a discipline, a way of life; that sacred drama must to all native eyes and ears become the greatest of the parables. There is no such government or party today; should either appear, I offer it these trivial songs and what remains to me of life. (April 1934)

Several months later he added this postscript:

> P.S. Because a friend belonging to a political party wherewith I had once had some loose association told me that it had, or was about to have or might be persuaded to have, some such aim as mine, I wrote these songs. Finding that it neither would nor could, I increased their fantasy, their extravagance, their obscurity, that no party might sing them. (August 1934)

The picture presented in the postscript is that of a dreamy, unpractical poet hardly even on the fringes of politics, and innocent with regard to them, moved by an impulse, and misled by a friend, into a political gesture which he later regretted. On the whole this picture has been accepted. Yet the evidence of the letters suggests that his involvement was considerably deeper, and more conscious than he found it convenient, in retrospect, to say.

'At the moment,' he wrote in April 1933 to Olivia Shakespear, 'I am trying in association with [an] ex-cabinet minister, an eminent lawyer and a philosopher to work out a social theory which can be used against Communism in Ireland. This country is exciting. I am told that de Valera has said in private that within three years he will be torn to pieces.'[67] A few months later to the same correspondent:

> Politics are growing heroic. De Valera has forced political thought to face the most fundamental issues.[68] A Fascist opposition is forming behind the scenes to be ready should some tragic situation develop. I find myself constantly urging the despotic rule of the educated classes. . . . I know half a dozen men any one of whom may be Caesar – or Catiline. It is amusing to live in a country where men will aways act. Where nobody is satisfied with thought. There is so little in our stocking that we are ready at any moment to turn it inside out and how can we not feel emulous when we see Hitler juggling with his sausage of stocking. Our chosen colour is blue, and blue shirts are marching about all over the country and their organizer tells me that it was my suggestion – a suggestion I have entirely forgotten – that made them select for their flag a red St Patrick's cross on a blue ground – all I can remember is that I have always denounced green and commended blue (the colour of my early book covers). The chance of being shot is raising everybody's spirits enormously. There is some politics for you of which your newspapers know nothing.[69]

To the same, 23 July 1933:

> The great secret is out – a convention of blue-shirts – National Guards – have received their new leader with the Fascist salute and the new leader announces reform of Parliament as his business.
>
> When I wrote to you, the Fascist organizer of the blue-shirts had told me

that he was about to bring to see me the man he had selected for leader that I might talk my anti-democratic philosophy. I was ready, for I had just rewritten for the seventh time the part of *A Vision* that deals with the future. The leader turned out to be a Gen[eral] O'Duffy, head of the Irish Police for twelve years and a famous organizer . . . Italy, Poland, Germany, then perhaps Ireland. Doubtless I shall hate it (though not so much as I hate Irish democracy) but it is September and we must not behave like the gay young sparks of May or June. The *Observer*, *The Sunday Times*, the only English newspapers I see, have noticed nothing though Cosgrave's ablest ministers are with O'Duffy. O'Duffy himself is autocratic, directing the movement from above down as though it were an army. I did not think him a great man though a pleasant one, but one never knows, his face and mind may harden or clarify.[70]

To the same, 17 August 1933:

The papers will have told you of the blue-shirt excitement here. The government is in a panic and has surrounded itself with armoured cars. The shirts themselves are made in batches of 600 and cannot be made fast enough. The organization is for an independent Ireland within the commonwealth. Whether it succeeds or not in abolishing parliamentary government as we know it today it will certainly bring into discussion all the things I care for. Three months ago there seemed not a trace of such a movement and when it did come into existence it had little apparent importance until that romantic dreamer I have described to you pitched on O'Duffy for a leader. About him the newspapers have probably told you enough. He seemed to me a plastic man but I could not judge whether he would prove plastic to the opinions of others, obvious political current or his own will ('unity of being').

To the same, 20 September 1933:

I wonder if the English newspapers have given you any idea of our political comedy. Act I. Capt. Macmanus, the ex-British officer I spoke of, his head full of vague Fascism, got probably from me, decided that Gen[eral] O'Duffy should be made leader of a body of young men formed to keep meetings from being broken up. He put into O'Duffy's head – he describes him as 'a simple peasant' – Fascist ideas and started him off to organize that body of young men. Act II. Some journalist announced that 30,000 of these young men were going to march through Dublin on a certain day (the correct number was 3,000). Government panic. Would not O'Duffy, who had once been head of the army, and more recently head of the police, march on the Government with 30,000 plus army and police? Result, martial law – in its Irish form – armoured cars in the streets, and new police force drawn from the I.R.A. to guard the Government, and O'Duffy's organization proclaimed. Act III. O'Duffy is made thereby so important that Cosgrave surrenders the leadership of his party to O'Duffy and all the opposition united under him. Two months ago he was unknown politically.

That was the climax; from then on the references to O'Duffy in Yeats's letters become much sparser and increasingly disparaging, and Yeats soon adopts an attitude of political disengagement, which becomes explicit in the poem 'Church and State' (November 1934):

> Here is fresh matter, poet,
> Matter for old age meet;
> Might of the Church and the State
> Their mobs put under their feet.
> O but heart's wine shall run pure
> Mind's bread grow sweet
>
> That were a cowardly song
> Wander in dreams no more
> What if the Church and the State
> Are the mob that howls at the door?
> Wine shall run thick to the end,
> Bread taste sour.

It is customary to say that, at this point, Yeats had become 'disillusioned with Fascism'. One may accept this judgment, but must also remark that the principal illusion which had been dissipated was the illusion that Fascism in Ireland stood a good chance of winning. In the spring and summer of 1933, the Fascism of the Irish Blueshirts looked to many people like a possible winner and in this phase Yeats was with the Blueshirts. By the autumn and winter of 1933–34, the Government's energetic measures – described by Yeats as 'panic measures' – made it clear that de Valera was no von Papen. O'Duffy, failing to devise anything effective in reply, revealed that he was no Hitler. The blue began to fade, and Yeats's interest in it faded proportionately.[71]

Commenting on a mildly anti-Blueshirt anecdote in a letter of Yeats's, Professor Jeffares says: 'This ironic attitude to the Blueshirts reveals the true Yeats, detached and merely playing with his thoughts, except for the intervals when he wanted to achieve complete directness and accuracy.'

The date of the anecdote in question is February 1934, by which date the Blueshirts were beginning to look a little silly. The thoughts Yeats had 'played with' in the days when they had looked possibly formidable were less 'detached'. I cannot see on what grounds we are to regard the Yeats who began to sneer at the Blueshirts when they proved a flop, as being more 'real' than the Yeats who was excited about them when he thought they might win.

It was the same Yeats, strongly drawn to Fascism, but no lover of hopeless causes.

In April 1934 – as we have seen (p. 37) – he was still advocating 'force, marching men' to 'break the reign of the mob', but professing somewhat disingenuously that 'no such party' as would undertake this work had yet appeared. By August 1934 – when the party for which he had in fact written the songs was on the verge of public disintegration – he had found that that party 'neither could nor would' do what he proposed for it. This, it will be noted, does not amount to a disavowal of the programme of 'force, marching men' to 'break the reign of the mob'. The irony and detachment of the poem 'The Church and the State' belong to the period after the final break-up of the Blueshirt movement.

Comment on the question of Yeats's attitude to Fascism has been bedevilled by the assumption that a great poet must be, even in politics, 'a nice guy'. If this be assumed then it follows that, as Yeats obviously was a great poet he cannot really have favoured Fascism, which is obviously not a nice cause. Thus the critic or biographer is led to postulate a 'true Yeats', so that Yeats's recorded words and actions of Fascist character must have been perpetrated by some bogus person with the same name and outward appearance.[72]

If one drops the assumption about poets having always to be nice in politics, then the puzzle disappears, and we see, I believe, that Yeats the man was as near to being a Fascist as the conditions of his own country permitted. His unstinted admiration had gone to Kevin O'Higgins, the most ruthless 'strong man' of his time in Ireland, and he linked his admiration explicitly to his rejoicing at the rise of Fascism in Europe – and this at the very beginning, within a few weeks of the March on Rome. Ten years later, after Hitler had moved to the centre of the political stage in Europe, Yeats was trying to create a movement in Ireland which would be overtly Fascist in language, costume, behaviour and intent. He turned his back on this movement when it began to fail, not before. Would the irony and detachment of this phase of disillusion have lasted if a more effective Fascist leader and movement had later emerged? One may doubt it. Many in Germany who were 'disillusioned' by the failure of the Kapp putsch and the beer-cellar putsch were speedily 'reillusioned' when Hitler succeeded – and 'disillusioned' again when he lost the war (see Introduction p. 2).

Post-war writers, touching with embarrassment on Yeats's pro-Fascist opinions, have tended to treat these as a curious aberration of an idealistic but ill-informed poet. In fact such opinions were quite usual in the Irish Protestant middle class to which Yeats belonged (as well as in other middle classes) in the 1920s and 30s. The *Irish Times*, spokesman of that class, aroused no protest from its readers when it hailed Hitler (4 March 1933) as 'Europe's standard-bearer against Muscovite terrorism' and its references to Mussolini were as consistently admiring as those to Soviet Russia were consistently damning. But the limiting factor on the pro-Fascist tendencies of the *Irish Times* and of the Irish Protestant middle class generally was the pull of loyalty to Britain – a factor which did not apply, or applied only with great ambivalence – in the case of Yeats. Mr T. R. Henn is quite right when he says that Yeats was 'not alone in believing at that moment of history, that the discipline of Fascist theory might impose order upon a disintegrating world'. I cannot follow Mr Henn, however, to his conclusion that 'nothing could be further from Yeats's mind than [Fascism's] violent and suppressive practice'.[73] 'Force, marching men' and 'the victory [in civil war] of the skilful, riding their machines as did the feudal knights their armoured horses', surely belong to the domain of violent and suppressive practice.

Just as one school is led to claim that the pro-Fascist Yeats was not the 'true' Yeats, so another tries to believe that the Fascism to which Yeats was drawn was not a 'true' Fascism.

Several critics have assured us that he was drawn not really to Fascism, but to some idealized aristocracy of eighteenth-century stamp. 'In all fairness,' writes Dr Vivian Mercier, 'we should allow that his views were closer to Hamilton's or even to Jefferson's than they were to Mussolini's'.[74] As far as political theory is concerned this is probably correct – though the name of Swift would seem more relevant than those of Hamilton or Jefferson. But it ignores one important reality: that Yeats was interested in *contemporary* politics and that he was a contemporary, not of Swift's or Jefferson's, but of Mussolini's.[75] He would have certainly preferred something more strictly aristocratic than Fascism, but since he was living in the twentieth century, he was attracted to Fascism as the best available form of anti-democratic theory and practice. Mr Frank O'Connor, who knew him well in his last years and – politics apart – greatly admired and liked him, has told us plainly that, 'He was a Fascist and authoritarian, seeing in world crises only the break-up of the "damned liberalism" he hated.'[76]

George Orwell, though critical, and up to a point percipient, about Yeats's tendencies, thought that Yeats misunderstood what an authoritarian society would be like. Such a society, Orwell pointed out 'will not be ruled by noblemen with Van Dyck faces, but by anonymous millionaires, shiny-bottomed bureaucrats and murderous gangsters'. This implies a degree of innocence in Yeats which cannot reasonably be postulated. O'Higgins and O'Duffy were not 'noblemen with Van Dyck faces', and Yeats had considerable experience of practical politics, both in the 1890s and in the early 1920s. 'In the last forty years,' wrote J. M. Hone in the year of Yeats's death, 'there was never a period in which his countrymen did not regard him as a public figure.'[77] When he thought of rule by an elite, it was a possible elite, resembling in many ways the nominated members of the Senate in which he had sat.[78] Its membership – bankers, organizers, ex-officers – would correspond roughly to what Orwell, in more emotive language, describes. Nor should it be assumed – as Orwell with his 'murderous gangsters' seems to imply – that the sensitive nature of the poet would necessarily be revolted by the methods of rule of an authoritarian state. Yeats – unlike, say, his brother, or Lady Gregory – was not, in politics, a very squeamish person. Seventy-seven executions did not repel him; on the contrary, they made him admire O'Higgins all the more. At least one of his associates of the early 1930s – 'the gunman I have told you of'[79] – might have been described as a 'murderous gangster'. And when, in 1936, Ethel Mannin appealed to him for a gesture which would have helped the German writer, Ossietski, then in a Nazi concentration camp, Yeats refused. 'Do not', he said, 'try to make a politician out of me. . . .'[80]

It is true that neither Yeats nor anyone else during Yeats's lifetime knew what horrors Fascism would be capable of. But the many who, like Yeats, were drawn to Fascism at this time knew, and seemed to have little difficulty in accepting, or at least making allowances for, much of what had already been done. 'The Prussian police', wrote the *Irish Times* in an editorial of February 1933, 'have been authorized by Herr Hitler's Minister to shoot Communists – a term which in Germany has a wide political connotation – on sight.' The same editorial which contained this information ended with the words: 'Naturally the earlier phases of this renascence are crude, but Germany is finding her feet after a long period of political ineptitude.'[81]

Yeats read the newspapers; he also read, as Hone records, several books on Fascist Italy and Nazi Germany. If, then, he was attracted to the dominant movements of these countries, and if he supported a movement in his own country whose resemblances to those continental movements he liked to stress, it cannot be contended that he did so in ignorance of such 'crude' practices as the *Irish Times* described.

Some writers – notably Professor D. T. Torchiana – in his well-documented study, *W. B. Yeats, Jonathan Swift and Liberty*[82] – have insisted that in spite of Yeats's authoritarian and Fascist leanings he was essentially a friend of liberty. 'Both Swift and Yeats', Torchiana concludes, 'served human liberty.' The senses in which this is true for Yeats are important but clearly limited. He defended the liberty of the artist, consistently. In politics, true to his duality, he defended the liberty of Ireland against English domination, and the liberty of his own caste – and sometimes by extension, of others – against clerical domination. Often these liberties overlapped, and the cause of artist and aristocrat became the same; often his resistance to 'clerical' authoritarianism (his position on the Lock-out, on divorce, on censorship) makes him appear a liberal. But his objection to clerical authoritarianism is not the liberal's objection to *all* authoritarianism. On the contrary he favours 'a despotism of the educated classes', and, in the search for this, is drawn towards Fascism. It is true that Fascism was not in reality a despotism of the educated classes, but it was a form of despotism which the educated classes in the 1920s and 30s showed a disposition to settle for – a despotism proportionate to the apparent threat, in their country, of Communism or 'anarchy'. In assessing Yeats's pro-Fascist opinions, there is no need to regard these as so extraordinary that he must either not have been himself, or not have known what he was about.

Yet, in challenging the assumption that Yeats's pro-Fascism was either not 'truly Yeats' or not 'truly pro-Fascist', one must not overlook the intermittent character of his pro-Fascism and of all his political activity. If his pro-Fascism was real, his irony and caution were real too, and his phases of detachment not less real than his phase of political commitment. The long phase of nationalist commitment (1887–1903) was followed by a long phase (1903–16) of detachment from almost all practical politics (except those to which the theatre exposed him) by a critique of Irish nationalist politics, and by the formation of an aristocratic attitude which did not find practical political expression until after 1916, when – after a new flare-up of nationalist feeling – he re-entered Irish politics on the right, in the Free State Senate. After clerical pressures had made the Senate uncongenial to him and had extruded him from it, he withdrew again from active politics (1928–33), only returning when a situation propitious to Fascism seemed to present itself. When O'Duffy's Irish Fascists failed ignominiously, he turned away from politics again. And always, in the long phases of withdrawal, he tended to write of all politics with a kind of contempt, a plague-on-both-your-houses air.[83]

In that same letter in which he refused to try to help Ossietski he wrote: '. . . if I did what you want I would seem to hold one form of government more responsible than any other and that would betray my convictions. Communist, Fascist, nationalist, clerical, anti-clerical, are all responsible according to the number of their victims.'[84] This was 'the true Yeats' – the true Yeats of a period of political inactivity when he watched, bitterly or sardonically, a game he had no chance of playing. But when he had a chance, when he saw political opportunities, as in 1891 or 1920, or thought he saw them, as in 1933, he wrote differently, and with excitement. These 'manic' phases of political activity were no less real or important than the 'depressive' phases which followed them. And the options of the 'manic' phases were not haphazard or middle-of-the-road. They were either anti-English or – in Irish politics – aristocratic and, from the time Fascism had appeared, distinctly and exultantly pro-Fascist.

It was Yeats's misfortune as a politician, and his good fortune as a poet, that his political opportunities or temptations were few and far between. Irish politics in their normal run have not, since the introduction of universal suffrage, been receptive to poets, aristocrats or Protestants – there have been distinguished exceptions, but that has been the general rule for many years. It is only in rare conjunctures, times of great national stress and division, that an Irish party is likely to find room for such exotics for, in such times, men welcome an ally with a name and a voice. Such moments of excitement and emotion, which offered opportunities, were also the moments which most stirred the poet. Such times were the Parnell split of 1891 and the Sinn Fein split of 1920–22. The abortive Fascist movement of 1933 seemed to be, but was not, the opening of another profound fissure in Irish political life. In the first two cases, the world of Irish politics proved, when 'normalcy' had returned, no place for the poet. In the third case the poet retired from a political movement which had lost momentum. It is fairly safe to say that, if it had succeeded, it would have dropped him or forced him out; not through any great aversion on his part from thugs in coloured shirts, but because an Irish Fascism, to have any chance of staying in power, would necessarily have to become an intensely clerical Fascism. In fact the successor movement to the Blueshirts – the Christian Front – was a noisily Catholic clerical-Fascist movement. This was a kind of Fascism – perhaps the only kind – which Yeats could not accept or tolerate, since his authoritarian view of life derived ultimately from his concept of the caste to which he belonged, and the distinguishing mark of that caste was its Protestantism.

In the political writings of his last years the two elements in his politics – the 'Irish' and the 'Protestant' elements – entered into a new set of relations. The 'Irish' element became more vocal than it had been since 1916 and the 'Protestant' element was obliged to break finally with the traditional right wing in Irish politics. Anti-English feeling, long dormant in Yeats, became increasingly pronounced in the period 1937–39. A series of poems, 'Roger Casement', 'The Ghost of Roger Casement', 'The O'Rahilly', 'Come

Gather Round Me Parnellites', both expressed and did much to rekindle, the old pride in Irish nationalism which the cynicism that followed the Civil War had dulled. The Casement poems especially had a powerful anti-English charge:

> O what has made that sudden noise
> What on the threshold stands?
> It never crossed the sea because
> John Bull and the sea are friends;
> But this is not the old sea
> Nor this the old sea shore
> What gave that roar of mockery
> That roar in the sea's roar?
> The ghost of Roger Casement
> Is beating on the door.

No Irishman, reading these lines on the eve of the Second World War, had forgotten that Casement had been hanged, as well as 'morally assassinated' for trying, in 1916, to bring help to Ireland from Germany. And some Irishmen, at least, must have reflected that if the sea was no longer the old sea, which had been friends with John Bull, the reason for this might be that the nation from which Casement had tried to bring help now possessed a powerful air force.

Potentially, 'The Ghost of Roger Casement' was as explosive as *Cathleen Ni Houlihan*.

Just at this time Yeats was writing to Ethel Mannin that, while he liked neither side in Spain, and did not want to see his old leader O'Duffy – now fighting for Franco – return to Ireland with enhanced prestige to 'the Catholic front',[85] he was attracted by the thought that a Fascist victory would weaken England.

> I am an old Fenian and I think the old Fenian in me would rejoice if a Fascist nation or government controlled Spain because that would weaken the British Empire, force England to be civil to India and loosen the hand of English finance in the far East of which I hear occasionally. But this is mere instinct. A thing I would never act on. Then I have a horror of modern politics – I see nothing but the manipulation of popular enthusiasm by false news – a horror that has been deepened in these last weeks by the Casement business. My ballad on that subject has had success. . . .[86]

The success of the ballad was mainly among those who had been Yeats's political enemies and against whom he had conspired: de Valera's party. It was in de Valera's paper, the *Irish Press*, that the ballad appeared. Yeats wrote:

On Feb 2 my wife went to Dublin shopping and was surprised at the deference everybody showed her in buses and shops. Then she found what it was – the Casement poem was in the morning paper. Next day I was publicly thanked by the Vice-President of the Executive Council (Mr de Valera's deputy in the Government) by de Valera's political secretary, by our chief antiquarian and an old revolutionist, Count Plunkett who called my poem 'a ballad the people much needed'. De Valera's newspaper gave me a long leader, saying that for generations to come my poem will pour scorn on the forgers and their backers.[87]

There were adequate reasons for a degree of reconciliation between Yeats and his former foes. First, from Yeats's point of view, the events of the early 1930s had shown that, if there was a 'strong man' in Irish politics it was not O'Duffy but de Valera.[88] Second, five years of de Valera's government had dissipated the theory – once cherished by Yeats's former political friends – that de Valera meant Communism. Third, de Valera was the main barrier[89] against what Yeats then saw – with considerable justice – as a rising tide of clericalist power, a tide which threatened all that Yeats had built in Ireland:

> I am convinced that if the Spanish war goes on or if [it] ceases and O'Duffy's volunteers return heroes, my 'pagan' institutions, the Theatre, the Academy will be fighting for their lives against combined Gaelic and Catholic bigotry. A friar or monk has already threatened us with mob violence.[90]

In the same letter, Yeats noted how de Valera had carried in Parliament, against a pro-Franco opposition, a measure to stop Irish volunteers from going to Spain.

The fourth reason for a *rapprochement* with de Valera's party is more complex. Just as Yeats's own mind was hopelessly divided about the Spanish war – the authoritarian and Anglophobe in him desiring a Franco victory, the Irish anticlerical dreading the results – so the party of his former friends was also in confusion. But their confusion was almost the mirror-image, the inversion, of his. They wanted, or said they wanted, a Franco victory, on Catholic grounds. But also, as the party of the Anglo-Irish Treaty, the 'Commonwealth Party', they contained the most pro-British elements in Irish life: the people who, in the event of Britain's going to war, would try to see to it that Ireland came in on Britain's side.

De Valera at this time was engaged, with the Chamberlain Government, in negotiations which led to the return of the Irish ports, which the treaty had retained under British control. Without the return of these ports Ireland's neutrality in the coming war, which it was de Valera's policy to ensure, would scarcely have been practical politics. Yeats – who, as Frank O'Connor has told us,[91] in his last years, admired and defended de Valera –

put his name and influence explicitly behind the recovery of the ports; implicitly but clearly behind a policy of neutrality.

> Armament comes next education. The country must take over the entire defence of its shores. The formation of military families should be encouraged. I know enough of my countrymen to know that, once democratic plausibility has gone, their small army will be efficient and self reliant, highly trained though not highly disciplined. Armed with modern weapons, officered by men from such schools as I have described, it could throw back from our shores the disciplined, uneducated masses of the commercial nations.[92]

From the point of view of de Valera's party, Yeats's tentative overtures – for such, I believe, they were – would have presented some advantages. The patriotic poems undoubtedly struck a genuinely responsive note among most Irish people: their appearance in de Valera's newspaper was helpful, especially at this time, in Ireland; the prestige – by now great – of Yeats's name in England would be helpful there in relation to the ports and to neutrality. Yet, while there were reasons on both sides for some degree of *rapprochement*, it may be doubted whether this would ever have become close or warm. Irish political life between the wars had been too bitter for that. De Valera's memory had not the reputation of being short or inaccurate. Yeats's activities in 1922–23 and in 1933 would have been quite fresh in de Valera's mind. It is believed also that he had read, with distaste and distress, the lines:

> Had de Valera eaten Parnell's heart
> No loose-lipped demagogue had won the day
> No civil rancour torn the land apart.

Real reconciliation had to wait for the next generation. After the war Yeats's son, Michael, joined de Valera's party and became a senator.

The two main currents in Yeats's active politics – his Anglophobe Irish nationalism and his authoritarianism – necessarily converged in the years immediately before the war, thrusting him in the direction of desiring the victory of the Fascist powers. The doctrine of John O'Leary, to whose school Yeats always claimed to belong, was Tone's doctrine: that 'England's difficulty is Ireland's opportunity'. The caution and scepticism, which were also permanent features of his personality, worked, together with his repulsion from Irish clerical Fascism, to prevent him from being carried too far by Tone and O'Leary. But an underlying wish found voice, at this time, when the prestige and authority of England were lower than they had been for centuries, in an increasingly anti-English tone, in verse and prose and in his conversation. This did not happen without a violent inner struggle. 'The "Irishry" ', he wrote in *A General Introduction for my Work* (1937),

> . . . have preserved their ancient 'deposit' through wars which, during the sixteenth and seventeenth centuries, became wars of extermination; no people, Lecky said at the opening of his *Ireland in the Eighteenth Century*, have undergone greater persecution, nor did that persecution altogether cease up to our own day. No people hate as we do in whom that past is always alive, there are moments when hatred poisons my life and I accuse myself of effeminacy because I have not given it adequate expression. It is not enough to have put it into the mouth of a rambling peasant poet. Then I remind myself that though mine is the first English marriage I know of in the direct line, all my family are English and that I owe my soul to Shakespeare, to Spenser and to Blake, perhaps to William Morris, and to the English language in which I think, speak and write, that everything I love has come to me through English; my hatred tortures me with love, my love with hate. I am like the Tibetan monk who dreams at his initiation that he is eaten by a wild beast and learns on waking that he himself is eater and eaten. This is Irish hatred and solitude, the hatred of human life that made Swift write *Gulliver* and the epitaph upon his tomb, that can still make us wag between extremes and doubt our sanity.

In *On the Boiler*, written the following year, the writer assumes – without however being altogether explicit about it – that the Fascist powers are winning and England is in contemptible decline. 'The Fascist countries', he writes in the section 'Tomorrow's Revolution', 'know that civilization has reached a crisis, and found their eloquence upon that knowledge.' The only fault he has to find with them is that 'perhaps from dread of attack' they encourage large families. He assumes in 'Ireland after the Revolution' that 'some tragic crisis shall so alter Europe and all opinion that the Irish government will teach the great majority of its school-children nothing but' . . . a list of manual and menial occupations follows.[93]

At the time when this was written the 'tragic crisis' many expected was that which was to lead Pétain's France to adopt somewhat similar educational policies. It is hard to resist the conclusion that Yeats when writing this, expected, and hoped, that Ireland 'after the revolution' would be a sort of satellite of a Fascist-dominated Europe. As regards England, his contempt, in this year of Munich, is unqualified and savage. After saying some hard things about King George v, he concludes 'Ireland after the Revolution' with the words: 'The Irish mind has still, in country rapscallion or in Bernard Shaw, an ancient cold, explosive detonating impartiality. The English mind, excited by its newspaper proprietors and its school-masters, has turned into a bed-hot harlot.'

Dorothy Wellesley, who was troubled by his increasingly anti-British attitude in the last years of his life, made a shrewd comment: 'Why then, in the twentieth century and when the Irish are freed from their oppressors the English, does he despise and dislike us increasingly? Because he dislikes the stuffed lion and admires the ranting, roaring oppressors.'[94]

During Yeats's life, the English Government gave him a Civil List pension, and the Athenaeum Club gave him the signal honour of a special election. Since his death, the British Council has presented him to the world as one of England's glories. There is therefore some irony in the thought that there was something in him that would have taken considerable pleasure – though not without a respectful backward glance at Shakespeare – in seeing England occupied by the Nazis, the Royal Family exiled, and the Mother of Parliaments torn down. Meanwhile in Ireland one would have expected to see him at least a cautious participant, or ornament, in a collaborationist regime, (but see Introduction p. 4).

It is probably fortunate for his future reputation, and especially his standing with the British Council, that he died in January 1939, before the political momentum of his last years could carry him any farther than *On the Boiler*.

Yeats was, as he said, 'a propagandist all my life'; deeply immersed in political interests, politically active whenever opportunity presented itself. His best poetry – that of his maturity and old age – had often a political theme, sometimes a political intent. The argument of this essay has been that his politics deserve to be taken more seriously than they have been, were not fundamentally inconsistent, vague or irrelevant to his 'real self' and were, in his maturity and old age, generally pro-Fascist in tendency and Fascist in practice on the single occasion when opportunity arose.

How can those of us who loathe such politics continue, not merely to admire but to love the poetry, and perhaps most of all the poems with a political bearing?

An important part of the answer is supplied by the poet himself in a note on 'Leda and the Swan':

> I wrote 'Leda and the Swan' because the editor of a political review asked me for a poem. I thought, 'After the individualist, demagogic movement founded by Hobbes [*sic*] and popularized by the Encyclopaedists and the French Revolution, we have a soil so exhausted that it cannot grow that crop again for centuries.' Then I thought, 'Nothing is now possible but some movement from above preceded by some violent annunciation.' My fancy began to play with Leda and the Swan for metaphor, and I began this poem;

but as I wrote, bird and lady took such possession of the scene that all politics went out of it, and my friend tells me that his 'conservative readers would misunderstand the poem'.[95]

They would have been puzzled certainly:

> A sudden blow: the great wings beating still
> Above the staggering girl, her thighs caressed
> By the dark webs, her nape caught in his bill,
> He holds her helpless breast upon his breast.
>
> How can those terrified vague fingers push
> The feathered glory from her loosening thighs?
> And how can body, laid in that white rush,
> But feel the strange heart beating where it lies?
>
> A shudder in the loins engenders there
> The broken wall, the burning roof and tower
> And Agamemnon dead.
>
>   Being so caught up,
> So mastered by the brute blood of the air,
> Did she put on his knowledge with his power
> Before the indifferent beak could let her drop?

Very little seems to be known – and perhaps little can be known – of how this process of transformation works. How can that patter of Mussolini prose 'produce' such a poem? How can that political ugly duckling be turned into this glorious Swan? It is in a sense like the transmutation, in 'Easter 1916', of those whom Yeats had thought of as commonplace people:

> All changed, changed utterly
> A terrible beauty is born

Is the connection then between the politics and the poetry only trivial and superficial? There is, I think, a deeper connection: if the political prose and the poetry are thought of, not as 'substance' and 'metaphor', or 'content' and 'style' but as cognate expressions of a fundamental force, anterior to both politics and poetry.

That force was, I suggest, Yeats's profound and tragic intuitive – and intelligent – awareness, in his maturity and old age, of what the First World War had set loose, of what was already moving towards Hitler and the Second World War. That he is conscious of the danger a letter shows as early as 1923: 'Unless Europe takes to war again and starts new telepathic streams of violence and cruelty.'[96] But the poetry is already responding to the telepathic streams as early as 1920, when he wrote 'The Second Coming':

> Things fall apart: the centre cannot hold
> Mere anarchy is loosed upon the world
> The blood-dimmed tide is loosed. . . .
>
> . . . .
>
> And what rough beast his hour come round again
> Slouches towards Bethlehem to be born?

Years afterwards, just before the Spanish Civil War, he drew Ethel Mannin's attention to this poem: 'If you have my poems by you look up a poem called "The Second Coming". It was written more than sixteen or seventeen years ago and foretold what is happening. I have written of the same thing again and again since.'[97]

The words 'violence', 'hatred', and 'fanaticism' became keywords in Yeats's poetry. He often uses them in condemnation of the left in Irish politics – the politics of Constance Markievicz and of Maud Gonne:

> I thought my love must her own soul destroy
> So did fanaticism and hate enslave it

But he is also increasingly conscious of these same forces in himself:

> Out of Ireland have we come
> Great hatred, little room,
> Maimed us from the start
> I carry from my mother's womb
> A fanatic heart.

The 'fanatic heart', an unusual capacity for hatred and an unusual experience of it, probably made him more sensitive and more responsive to the 'telepathic waves' coming from Europe than other writers in English seem to have been. The forces in him that responded to the hatred, cruelty and violence welling up in Europe produced the prophetic images of 'The Second Coming' and the last part of 'Nineteen Hundred and Nineteen':

> Violence upon the roads: violence of horses;
> Some few have handsome riders, are garlanded
> On delicate sensitive ear or tossing mane,
> But wearied running round and round in their courses
> All break and vanish, and evil gathers head:
> Herodias' daughters have returned again.
> A sudden blast of dusty wind and after
> Thunder of feet, tumult of images,
> Their purposes in the labyrinth of the wind;

It may be objected that 'Nineteen Hundred and Nineteen' and 'The Second

Coming' were written not about the coming of Fascism but about the Anglo-Irish War and the Black-and-Tans. The distinction is less than absolute: the Black-and-Tans were in fact an early manifestation of an outlook and methods which the Nazis were later to perfect. The *Freikorps* on the Polish-German border were at this time trying to do exactly what the Black-and-Tans were doing in Ireland and the *Freikorps* were the direct and proudly acknowledged predecessors of Hitler's Nazis. There is even a direct link between the Black-and-Tans and the Nazis in the person of 'Lord Haw-Haw' – William Joyce – who fought for the British Government in the first movement and was hanged by it for his work in the second.

Bruno Brehm, one of Hitler's novelists, made the assassination by Irish revolutionaries of Sir Henry Wilson – the principal exponent of intensified Black-and-Tan measures in Ireland – symbolic of the tragic confrontation of hero and submen. Wilson was seen in the same relation to the Irish as Hitler to Jews and Bolsheviks.

In *A General Introduction to my Work* (1937) Yeats made specific the connection between his own hatred and what was happening in Europe:

When I stand upon O'Connell Bridge in the half-light and notice that discordant architecture, all those electric signs, where modern heterogeneity has taken physical form, a vague hatred comes up out of my own dark and I am certain that wherever in Europe there are minds strong enough to lead others the same vague hatred arises; in four or five or in less generations this hatred will have issued in violence and imposed some kind of rule of kindred. I cannot know the nature of that rule, for its opposite fills the light; all I can do to bring it nearer is to intensify my hatred. I am no Nationalist, except in Ireland for passing reasons; State and Nation are the work of intellect, and when you consider what comes before and after them they are, as Victor Hugo said, of something or other, not worth the blade of grass God gives for the nest of the linnet.

By the time the *General Introduction* was written, Fascist power and 'rule of kindred' were already in full swing: the length of time – 'four or five generations' – is odd and perhaps calculated: it brings to mind the retrospective 'commentaries' on the songs for O'Duffy. The paragraph itself may be taken as a kind of retrospective commentary on 'The Second Coming'.

In 'The Second Coming' the poet, perhaps from the foretaste of the Black-and-Tans, augured the still more terrible things that were to come. The sort of 'premonitory' intuition present in 'The Second Coming' and in other poems necessarily affected Yeats in his ordinary life as well as in his poetry. Yeats the manager, the senator, the politician, stands in a diplomatic relation to these intimations of power. His references to Fascism, though sometimes mildly critical, are never hostile, almost always respectful, often admiring, and this especially in years of Fascist victories: 1922, 1933 and 1938. Some reasons for this have already been suggested; it might be added that for Yeats a bandwagon had the same high degree of attraction that it has for other political mortals:

> Processions that lack high stilts have nothing that catches the eye

If a Marxist, believing that history is going in a given direction, thinks it right to give it a good shove in the way it is going, it is natural enough that one who, like Yeats, feels that it is going in the opposite direction, should accompany it that way with, if not a shove, at least a cautious tilt.

In the poetry, however, the raw intimations of what is impending – the 'telephathic waves of violence and fear' – make themselves known, not in the form of calculated practical deductions, but in the attempt to reveal, through metaphoric insight, what is actually happening. The poet, like the lady, is

> . . . so caught up
> So mastered by the brute blood of the air

that he does indeed take on the knowledge of what is happening with the power to make it known. The political man had his cautious understanding with Fascism, the diplomatic relation to a great force; the poet conveyed the nature of the force, the dimension of the tragedy. The impurities of his long and extraordinary life went into its devious and sometimes sinister political theories and activities. The purity and integrity – including the truth about politics as Yeats apprehended it – are in the poetry concentrated in metaphors of such power that they thrust aside all calculated intent: bird and lady take possession of the scene.

Notes

1 On that aspect see J. M. Hone, 'Yeats as a Political Philosopher' (*London Mercury*, April 1939); Grattan Freyer, 'The Politics of W. B. Yeats' (*Politics and Letters*, Summer 1947); D. M. Torchiana, 'W. B. Yeats, Jonathan Swift and Liberty' (*Modern Philosophy*, August 1963). The last two also discuss his political activities, but the stress is more on theory and less on practical choices – in an Irish context – than is the case with the present essay. The two lines of approach give significantly different results.

2 Yeats belonged, not to the 'Ascendancy' in the strict sense of the word, but to

the Protestant middle class of merchants and professional people: '*une famille de bonne bourgeoisie protestante*', in the words of Paul-Dubois. But, like many members of this class, he preferred, particularly in his later years, to think of himself as belonging to an aristocracy.

3 *On the Boiler.*

4 See *Reveries over Childhood and Youth.*

5 I now find this paragraph somewhat regrettable. (1987).

6 *A General Introduction for my Work* (1937). The important passage from which this is taken is quoted at greater length on p. 49.

7 'It was you was it not,' Yeats wrote to O'Leary, 'who converted Miss Gonne to her Irish opinions. She herself will make many converts.' (1 February 1889, *Letters*, edited by Alan Wade, (London, 1954). P. 108).

8 *Autobiographies*, p. 209. I tried going against O'Leary's Law and have experienced its force.

9 To Katherine Tynan, 25 July 1898. *Letters*, p. 151.

10 In practice, when an occasion offered, she did not.

11 Maud Gonne, *A Servant of the Queen*, pp. 206–7; Stephen Gwynn (ed.); *Scattering Branches: Tributes to the Memory of W. B. Yeats* (London, 1940), p. 49.

12 Lecture on accepting the Nobel Prize. Text in *Autobiographies*, p. 559.

13 Commentary on the poem 'Parnell's Funeral'. Text in Allt and Alspach, p. 834.

14 Letter dated 'c. 4 December 1890' in Volume I of Collected Letters of W. B. Yeats: edited by John Kelly, (Oxford, 1986). Footnote of 1987.

15 Full text in Ellmann, p. 103. The poem was never republished by Yeats.

16 *Letters*, edited by John Kelly, Volume 1, p. 265. Letter dated 11 October 1891.

17 That I may seem though I die old
    A foolish passionate man
    The use here of the word 'seem' seems to have been overlooked by some critics.

18 Those who doubt the existence of an element of calculation in Yeats's behaviour at this time should consider a sentence in a letter of his advising a young Irishwoman to write about 'Irish legends and places': 'It helps originality and makes one's verses sincere, and gives one less numerous competitors.' (31 January 1889, *Letters*, edited by Alan Wade, p. 104.)

19 *Autobiographies*, p. 355.

20 Stephen Gwynn, quoted in A. N. Jeffares', *W. B. Yeats*, p. 138. This is not at all an isolated judgement: P. S. O'Hegarty stated that to him and his revolutionary contemporaries *Cathleen Ni Houlihan* was 'a sort of sacrament' ('W. B. Yeats and the Revolutionary Ireland of his Time', *Dublin Magazine*, July–September 1939). For Constance Markievicz, a person under sentence of death after the 1916 Rising: 'That play of W.B.'s was a sort of gospel to me.'

21 How little the trend to reconciliation between the factions was to Yeats's taste may be gathered from the following: 'John Dillon [leader of the anti-Parnellite faction] is making the first speech he has made before a popular Dublin audience

since the death of Parnell. . . . [He] is very nervous. . . . I am almost overpowered by an instinct of cruelty: I long to cry out, "Had Zimri peace that slew his master?" ' (*Autobiographies*, p. 366.) Yeats has been represented as himself seeking to make peace between Parnellite and anti-Parnellite. This is true only in the sense that he and Maud Gonne, in helping, for example, to organize the centenary commemoration of the 1798 Rebellion (a commemoration in which parliamentarians of both factions took part), hoped that they were beginning to build a unified national movement of Fenian inspiration, in which all nationalist Irishmen, whatever their past political differences, could join. The support of former anti-Parnellites – being the majority of the Irish people – was essential to the success of any Irish movement. But the quotation from *Autobiographies* (above) shows how Yeats continued to feel about the anti-Parnellite parliamentarians – of whom Dillon was not only the most eminent, but also the most moderate.

22 'The Cutting of an Agate' (1907) in *Essays and Introductions*, p. 260.

23 'W. B. Yeats' (1943) in *Critical Essays*.

24 10 April 1900. *Letters*, p. 338. In later years he liked to tell the story of the speaker at the Socialist picnic: 'I was brought up a gentleman and now as you can see associate with all sorts.'

25 Cf *The People* (1916).

26 Those who find it hard to understand such hypersensitivity should look through the back files of *Punch*. It was natural – though silly – that some Irish people, depressed by being seen as Caliban, should insist on getting 'from our own theatre' a much more flattering reflection.

27 To be fair to the much maligned Abbey audiences, the survival was also due to recognition, by small – but qualitatively significant – sections of Catholics and nationalists, that the *Playboy* rioters had made fools of themselves.

28 Ellmann, p. 179.

29 Quoted in Hone, p. 194.

30 J. B. Yeats, *Letters* (11 December 1913).

31 This always latent hostility to 'the crowd', including his own audiences, was generously stimulated when, on a night in 1905, some members of an Abbey audience hissed Maud Gonne on her appearance after her separation from Major MacBride. 'He felt that never again could he touch popular politics.' (Hone, p. 210.)

32 Not at all to Yeats's pleasure.

33 This is not just a rhetorical flourish. 'You will recollect when dealing with a company of this kind,' said Murphy in an address to his tramway workers on 19 July 1913, 'that every one of the shareholders, to the number of five, six or seven thousands, will have three meals a day whether the men succeed or not. I don't know if the men who go out can count on this.' Quoted in *1913: Jim Larkin and the Dublin Lock-out* (Workers' Union of Ireland).

34 *W. B. Yeats*, p. 268. Hone's reference to the letter is brief and he does not quote it.

35 Typically, he refers to events which followed the lock-out, decided on by the Dublin employers, of members of the Transport and General Workers' Union, as 'the great strike led by Larkin which paralyzed the life of Dublin'.

36 'This,' adds Hone rather cryptically, 'Murphy certainly was not.'

37 The 'nationalist hotel' was not a political centre but the only hotel owned by a Catholic. The owner gave no signs of objecting to the political status quo and even, for business reasons, kept 'Protestant Bibles' in the hotel rooms.

38 The Land League was primarily an agrarian body, but its successor bodies extended their operations to urban areas. Michael Davitt boasted that a 'run' organized by the League broke the Munster Bank in Cork: the Plan of Campaign certainly brought economic life to standstill in the town of Tipperary.

39 This was by the decision of Parnell himself at a time when he wanted to break the revolutionary landowners and the movement. See the present writer's *Parnell and his Party*, Clarendon Press, 1957.

40 It is true that, as in comparable situations elsewhere, the new middle class as a whole was inferior to the old in education as in money. In the novels of Somerville and Ross we get glimpses of this new class, as they appear to two pairs of brightly observant Ascendancy eyes.

41 It was no way inconsistent with his 'Protestant/aristocratic' position to attack the leaders of the rising Catholic middle class, and their clerical allies, or to defend their enemies. The leaders of that alliance had always inspired in him distrust and repugnance – feelings which 1913 fanned into flame.

42 John O'Leary died in 1907.

43   Did words of mine send out
        Certain men the English shot?

44 Full text in Allt and Alspach, p. 791. It has been stated that he intended to publish this, 'but cancelled the publication on hearing that it would distress Robert's widow'. (Hone, p. 338.)

45 He could hardly, of course, have published any of them in the United Kingdom in wartime, but could have published at least 'Easter 1916' in America; it was written in September 1916 and the United States did not enter the war until the following April. 'Easter 1916' was printed at the time in an edition of twenty-five copies for distribution among friends, but the series was withheld from the sight of the general public until 1920. (Hone, p. 301.)

46 A friend who read this in draft objected to this comparison and pointed out that the Free State forces, unlike the Black-and-Tans, did not use indiscriminate terror against the civilian population. This is a valid point, though even the Black-and-Tan terror was not *altogether* indiscriminate.

47 *Lady Gregory's Journals, 1916–1930*, edited by Lennox Robinson, (London, 1946).

48 Mary MacSwiney was the sister of Terence MacSwiney, the famous Lord Mayor of Cork, who had died on hunger strike as a prisoner of the British. The Government may or may not have had 'a sentimental feeling for her'; some of its

members probably had: all of them knew that to let her die as her brother had died would discredit them in the eyes of most of their countrymen.

49   Pseudonym for George Russell, Irish poet and mystic.

50   Irish poet and novelist.

51   Father of the present writer, at the time a leader-writer on *The Irish Independent*.

52   While refusing to protest publicly about the Government's policy on hunger-striking, Yeats may have interceded privately. Patrick McCartan informed Mr Terence de Vere White, many years later, that, 'I got Mrs Green, W. B. Yeats and others to intercede for them, but it was futile.' (White, *Kevin O'Higgins*, p. 179.)

53   To Edmund Dulac, 1 December 1922, *Letters*, p. 694.

54   To Olivia Shakespear, May 1922, *Letters*, edited by Alan Wade, p. 682.

55   To the same, October 1922, *Letters*, p. 690.

56   To H. J. C. Grierson, 6 November 1922. Dr Ellmann quotes (pp.248–9) a public speech in the same vein nearly two years later (2 August 1924).

57   Thus Mr Arland Ussher has said that, 'Yeats, in spite of his desire to be a public figure, was more apolitical than any fully responsible person alive.' (*Three Great Irishmen*, p. 91.) Another critic has said that even his 'superficially political poems' are 'not really so'. (M. L. Rosenthal, in *The Nation*, 23 June 1956.) It is hard to see how these judgements can be reconciled with the known facts of Yeats's life and work.

58   'Students of contemporary Italy where Vico's thought is current through its influence upon Croce and Gentile think it created, or in part created, the present government of one man surrounded by just such able assistants as Vico foresaw.' (Introduction to 'The Words upon the Window-pane' (1931); *Explorations*, London, 1962, p. 355.)

59   O'Higgins's biographer, Mr Terence de Vere White, while noting that it became the fashion to call him 'the Irish Mussolini', maintains that he was in fact 'an intense believer in democracy'. This may well be so; as far as the subject of this essay is concerned, the important point is that it was as 'an Irish Mussolini' that Yeats rightly or wrongly saw him, and that he admired him for that.

60   To Olivia Shakespear, April 1933, *Letters*, p. 809.

61   I was not alone in being impressed by the top hats. 'Rarely', noted the Dublin *Evening Mail*, 'has there been such a display of silk hats and frock coats.' The same paper recorded that, 'The Fascisti in Dublin were present with their flag and black shirts and they were given a place in the procession by the police.' (13 July 1927.)

62   The Senate attended the funeral as a body: the press did not report the names of individual senators present. Senate records show that Yeats was present on the previous day at the meeting which unanimously decided that the Senate would attend the funeral as a body.

63   The *Irish Times*, representative of Irish Protestant opinion, editorially regretted the manner of Senator Yeats's intervention on this subject (12 June 1925).

64 Yeats's resentment of the Irish bishops found vent, as early as 1924, in a criticism of the style of the Pastorals: 'a style rancid, coarse and vague like that of the daily papers'. (Leading article in *Tomorrow*, quoted in Ellman, pp. 250–51.) Yeats prudently did not sign this article, but got two other people to sign it.

65 11 June 1925.

66 'Commentary on the Three Songs', December 1934, in Allt and Alspach, pp. 836–7.

67 *Letters*, p. 808.

68 Earlier he had written as if he thought de Valera a Fascist. 'You are right', he wrote to Olivia Shakespear in February 1933, 'in comparing de Valera to Mussolini or Hitler. All three have exactly the same aim so far as I can judge.' (*Letters*, p. 806.) It is hard to reconcile this ambiguous and untrue statement with the organization of a Fascist opposition to de Valera.

69 13 July 1933. *Letters*, pp. 811–12.

70 *Letters*, pp. 812–13.

71 The sequence of events described by Yeats in his September letter involved, in reality, a climbdown by O'Duffy, who had announced a mass parade of the Blueshirts (National Guard) for 13 August, the anniversary of Collins's death. When the National Guard was proclaimed illegal, the parade was called off and a 'quiet ceremony at the Cenotaph' was held instead. O'Duffy immediately became, as Yeats noted, leader of the Opposition United Party, but, as a historian sympathetic to the opposition has observed: 'From the very outset the new arrangement was thoroughly unsatisfactory; it quickly became apparent that O'Duffy did not possess the special qualities that equip a man for leadership in public life.' (D. O'Sullivan, *The Irish Free State and the Senate*, p. 406.) O'Duffy resigned his chairmanship of the United Party in September 1934.

72 (There is a sense of course in which the poet, actually engaged in writing his poetry, is 'the true Yeats', but that is another matter.)

73 *The Lonely Tower*, p. 467.

74 'To pierce the dark mind', *The Nation*, 10 December 1960.

75 He had, in any case, the assurance of his friend Ezra Pound (*Jefferson and/or Mussolini*) that the Duce was translating Jeffersonian ideas into twentieth century terms.

76 'The Old Age of a Poet', *The Bell*, February 1941. He also records an Abbey dispute over an attempt by Yeats to stage *Coriolanus* for purposes of 'Fascist propaganda'. Mr Sean O'Falain, a more cautious observer, who also knew Yeats at this time, speaks of his 'Fascist tendencies'. (*Yeats and the Younger Generation*, Horizon, January 1942.)

77 'Yeats as a Political Philosopher', *London Mercury*, April 1939.

78 'In its early days,' Yeats wrote of the Senate, 'some old banker or lawyer would dominate the House, leaning upon the back of the chair in front, always speaking with undisturbed self-possession as at some table in a board-room. My imagination sets up against him some typical elected man, emotional as a

youthful chimpanzee, hot and vague, always disturbed, always hating something or other.' (*On the Boiler*)

In another mood, however, he wrote about 'these oligarchs' in a more
disparaging vein. (*A Packet for Ezra Pound*)

79 *Letters*, p. 880. The late Louis MacNeice in *The Poetry of W. B. Yeats* seems to
have been the first to lay much stress on Yeats's relation to Fascism, but could
not quite make up his mind what that relation was. He refers to Yeats at one
point as 'the man who nearly became a Fascist' (p. 174), having spoken of him
earlier as having arrived at 'his own elegant brand of Fascism' (p. 41).

80 To Ethel Mannin, April 1936. In fairness to Yeats it must be noted, however, that
in order to help Ossietski, he would have had to recommend him to the Nobel
Committee for consideration for the Nobel Prize – something which, on artistic
grounds, he may well have been unwilling to do. His degree of 'toughness' on
political matters, minimized as it has been by some of his admirers, should not be
exaggerated either. In the Senate he supported an amendment to the Government's Public Safety Bill intended to secure independent inspection of prisons
(Senate Debates I, Cols 1440–41; 1638–9). He also sent 'warm blankets' to Maud
Gonne when his government put her in jail (*Letters*, p. 696). But in all essentials he
supported the Government's policy of firmness. 'Even the gentle Yeats', wrote
Sean O'Casey, 'voted for the Flogging Bill.'

81 It is true that the Blueshirts did not even try to go to anything like the lengths of
their continental models. It is also true that, unlike in the case of their models,
the Communists whom the Blueshirts were fighting were, in Ireland, largely
imaginary.

82 *Modern Philosophy*, 1963.

83 'Contempt for politics' is of course a characteristic conservative stance.

84 *Letters*, 8 April 1936. In a similar, but significantly different mood he wrote to
the same correspondent six months later: 'Some day you will understand what I
see in the Irish national movement and why I can be no other sort of
revolutionist – as a young man I belonged to the I.R.B. and was in many things
O'Leary's pupil. Besides why should I trouble about communism, fascism,
liberalism, radicalism, when all, though some bow first and some stern first but
all at the same pace, all are going down stream with the artificial unity which
ends every civilization.' (30 November 1938, *Letters*, p. 896.)

But in his letters to Ethel Mannin, who was herself of the left, Yeats tended to
understate the specifically right-wing elements of his thought; he more than
once used John O'Leary to fend her off. (cf. *Letters*, p.291); his letters to Olivia
Shakespear are in some ways more revealing.

85 His worries on this ground were needless.

86 1 March 1937. The occasion of the ballad was the publication of Dr W. F.
Maloney's *The Forged Casement Diaries*, which claimed that British officials
had forged documents in order to impute homosexuality to Casement.
Controversy on this question still continues.

87 To Dorothy Wellesley, 8 February 1937, *Letters*, p. 880.

88 Even before his Blueshirt phase, Yeats had been impressed by de Valera at his first meeting with him: '. . . I was impressed by his simplicity and honesty though we differed throughout.' (To Olivia Shakespear, 9 March 1933, *Letters*, p. 806.)

89 At least he could plausibly be seen as something like that at the time (1977 footnote).

90 To Ethel Mannin, 1 March 1937, *Letters*, p. 885.

91 'The Old Age of a Poet'.

92 *On the Boiler*. In what is probably his last letter to Maud Gonne, Yeats writes of *On the Boiler*: 'For the first time I am saying what I believe about Irish and European politics.' (16 June 1938, *Letters*, pp. 909–10.)

93 '. . . ploughing, harrowing, sowing, curry-combing, bicycle-cleaning, drill-driving, parcel-making, bale-pushing, tin-can-soldering, door-knob-polishing, threshold whitening, coat-cleaning, trouser-patching, and playing upon the Squiffer . . .'

94 'Comments and Conversations', p. 195, July 1938. In Introduction to *Letters on Poetry to Dorothy Wellesley*, Oxford, 1940.

95 June 1924; Allt and Alspach, p. 828.

96 Letter to Olivia Shakespear, 28 June 1923, *Letters*, p. 699.

97 8 April 1936, *Letters*, p. 850–51. This was the same letter in which he refused to help Ossietzki.

Virtue and Terror
Rousseau and Robespierre*

NOTHING, I THINK, IS KNOWN WITH CERTAINTY about the Robespierre-Rousseau relationship, except that the great revolutionary always expressed love and admiration for the philosopher.

And that in itself doesn't tell us very much, because virtually everybody in France, who could read, in the last quarter of the eighteenth century, seems to have loved and admired Rousseau. Marie Antoinette, whom Robespierre guillotined, loved and admired Rousseau. The Thermidorians, who guillotined Robespierre, loved and admired Rousseau.

A common love of Rousseau doesn't seem to have been a very reliable bond, when the heat was on.

Part of the problem was, and is, that there are several Rousseaus; he is a writer of curiously copious contradictions, which overlap, in disconcerting ways. One pair of contradictions is particularly important in the present context. There is a tender, hypersensitive Rousseau, much given to tears. And there is also a stern, Spartan Rousseau, with a thirst for justice and blood. In short a 'nice cop' Rousseau and a 'tough cop' Rousseau.

The nice cop is the author of the epistolary novel, *La Nouvelle Héloïse*, of the *Rêveries d'un Promeneur Solitaire*, of *Emile*, and especially, *La Profession de Foi du Vicaire Savoyard*. The tough cop wrote most, though not all, of *Du Contrat Social*.

The nice cop was in high favour at Court in the years before the Revolution, especially in the circle of Marie Antoinette, in the days of the Petit Trianon, the simple life, and playing at milkmaids. The tough cop comes in with the Revolution. *Du Contrat Social* seems to have been the *least* read of Rousseau's works before the Revolution. But it was published thirteen times between 1792 and 1795 – the years of Robespierre's ascendancy and of the Terror. One edition was published in pocket Bible size for the use of the soldiers defending *la patrie*.

* Valedictory Public Lecture as Montgomery Fellow at Dartmouth College, 29 May 1985.

Robespierre's own style was deliberately austere, stern, Spartan. But it would be a mistake to think of him as exclusively devoted to the tough cop. If *Du Contrat Social* was claimed as his political inspiration, his favourite reading – his 'Bible' according to Aulard – was *La Nouvelle Héloïse*, and his guide in matters of religion was *La Profession de Foi du Vicaire Savoyard*. In time of war and revolution, the Spartan Rousseau was required; the triumph of the Revolution would (it was hoped) bring back the tender Rousseau. Robespierre felt that indulgence, the failure to crush the internal enemies of the Revolution, would be a cruel betrayal of future generations. The Terror – which Robespierre generally preferred to call simply 'Justice' – was a way of keeping faith with those generations. The guillotine was kind, teleologically speaking.

The cult of Rousseau accompanied the Terror. But the cult of Rousseau also accompanied the formal repudiation of the Terror. Indeed it was the Thermidorian period which saw Rousseau's apotheosis. In the days of Robespierre, at the height of the Terror, there had been grandiose plans for giving Rousseau special honours, and setting him, at least implicitly, above the other great Enlightenment figures, as *the* philosopher of the Revolution. On the fifth Floreal of the Revolutionary calendar – that is, 24 April 1794 – the great Committee of Public Safety, Robespierre's committee, called on all the artists of the Republic to compete in designs for a large statue of Jean-Jacques Rousseau, to be erected on the Champs Elysees.

That was Robespierre's plan, but Robespierre did not live to have it carried out. Two and a half months later, on 9 Thermidor, 1794, Robespierre fell and then was killed. Robespierre's overthrowers, the Thermidorians – most of them terrified ex-terrorists – had their own reasons for being eager to do honour to Jean-Jacques. Although the Thermidorians were not particularly nice people – and several of them had shown themselves to be more bloody-minded than Robespierre – it was the 'nice cop' aspect of Rousseau that they wished to honour. Their idea was that Robespierre – whom they presented as entirely to blame for the Terror, which he was not – had been a sanguinary hypocrite, who had really been jealous of Rousseau, and had failed to do him proper honours. The Thermidorians would now prove their own virtue and sincerity, and loyalty to the basic principles of the Revolution, by solemnly doing honour to Jean-Jacques. So on 14 September 1794, the Thermidorian-dominated Convention ordered that Rousseau's remains be brought from his original burial place at the Isle of Poplars, Ermenonville, and placed in the Panthéon in Paris with appropriate ceremony. Gordon McNeil tells that story:

The preparations for the ceremony, which included decorations, illumin-ations, sculptures, a replica of the Isle of Poplars, and hymns commissioned for the occasion, were elaborate and detailed. A cortège composed of officials, musicians and various delegations accompanied the remains from Ermenon-ville, and there were appropriate celebrations at each of the stops *en route*. On its arrival in Paris, the coffin was placed on the replica of the Isle of Poplars which had been erected in the Tuileries gardens.

The ceremony of Panthéonization took place on October 11. There was a special service in the Convention, and then a procession to the Panthéon. In the line of march were mounted police, a band playing Rousseau's com-positions, and various groups, each with an appropriately inscribed standard: botanists, artists and artisans, mothers and children, war orphans, and Genevans. The *Contrat Social*, the 'beacon of legislators', was carried on a velvet cushion, and a statue of its author in a cart pulled by twelve horses. At the Panthéon, a civic hymn was sung, the president of the Convention delivered a eulogy, and ended the ceremony by placing flowers on the coffin. That evening there was dancing on the Place du Panthéon, and the theatres presented the favorite Rousseau plays, and a new one, *La fête de J.-J. Rousseau*, written especially for the occasion.[1]

As you can see, it would be hard to identify a specific influence of Rousseau's thought on the course of the French Revolution. *Du Contrat Social* may have been the 'beacon of legislators', but it was quite a shifty beacon. Yet Rousseau was obviously important, to all concerned. Robespierre had made certain uses of Rousseau to legitimize his own rule, and his version of Justice. The Thermidorians used their Panthéonization ceremony to legitimize their own authority, and de-legitimize their predecessor.

Yet, even if it is primarily a matter of legitimization, presumably influence comes in, in *some* way. If a writer is to be seen as legitimizing the activity of a politician, presumably that activity must be seen to resemble, at least in some respects, what the writer seems to be saying. And – again presumably – that need to resemble should inflect the actual conduct of the politician, at least in some degree. Yet the case of Rousseau and the Thermidorians, enthusiastic and mutually hostile disciples of Rousseau, suggests that the degree of inflection of conduct may be more limited than might be expected. And of course the history of religions is rich in examples of this kind.

While brooding a bit over this question of influence and legitimation, I came across a relevant sentence in Ralph Korngold's *Robespierre and the Fourth Estate* (New York, 1941). The sentence runs:

> Rousseau's relation to the French Revolution is not unlike that of Marx to the Russian Revolution, and Marx's influence upon Lenin may be compared with Rousseau's upon Robespierre.

Well, 'may be compared' is always safe of course, since anything may be compared with anything else. The question is what happens when you do the comparing. In this case, the writer issues, as it were, a license for comparing, without actually doing the comparing. So let us have a slightly closer look.

In so far as 'Rousseau–Robespierre' resembles 'Marx–Lenin' it is, I think, again primarily a matter of legitimation rather than of inherited doctrine. The legitimacy on which Robespierre – and also his Thermidorian enemies – drew was double, intellectual as well as moral. Intellectually, *Du Contrat Social* came to be seen as the culmination, in terms of political wisdom, of the Enlightenment, the *siècle des lumières*. As became clear, during the course of the Revolution, commitment to the book could be interpreted in widely different ways. But the capacious ambiguities of *Du Contrat Social* did nothing to impair its legitimizing authority. Indeed the book's ambiguities seem to have been the condition of the scope of its authority.

The moral authority of Rousseau, which I think was considerably more important than his intellectual authority, derives from the apparently almost universal perception of Rousseau himself as the archetype of the virtuous person, peculiarly in harmony with nature. I shall come back to that, in relation to Rousseau himself, a little later. But there are some points to be made at this stage, about archetypal virtue as a revolutionary force, and as a source of political legitimation.

The mainstream of the French Enlightenment – around Voltaire and Diderot – had largely completed, by about 1770, the work begun by Spinoza a hundred years before, in discrediting the intellectual authority of revealed religion, and specifically, in France, of the Catholic Church. This left a huge emotional and moral vacuum. The secret of Rousseau's appeal is that he, for many people, was able to fill that gap. In *Emile*, with *La Profession de Foi du Vicaire Savoyard*, Rousseau brought God back, as a blend of virtue and nature: a form of God to which many, in the post-Enlightenment world, were most grateful to be able to turn. More than that, Rousseau's eloquence – and especially his pervasive, seductive and contagious self-pity – made him personally into a kind of saint and protomartyr of his own vague but intoxicating religion.

Now the revolutionary potential of all that may not be immediately apparent, but it is strongly there. The mainstream Enlightenment had made its *intellectual* superiority to the *ancien régime* crushingly clear, first in relation to the Church, through Voltaire and Diderot, and then in relation to the nobility, as in Beaumarchais's *Marriage of Figaro*. But now, in Rousseau and Rousseauism, many could see the emergence of *spiritual and moral* forces markedly superior to the *ancien régime*, whether in its secular or ecclesiastical manifestations. Rousseau is holier than St Peter; and a song to that effect was sung during the Revolution. French society was divided into *les purs* – the followers of Rousseau – and *les corrompus*, who were affluent, arrogant, materialistic, and beneficiaries of the *ancien régime* (and later the traitors to the Revolution). Many of the nobility and clergy (as well as the bourgeoisie, especially the lower bourgeoisie) came to see things in the same way, and to bow before the moral superiority of Rousseau, as many of the same people had bowed before the intellectual superiority of Voltaire. Thus the abdication of the ruling classes was already quite far advanced, well before 1789.

The basic *political* achievement of Maximilien Robespierre was that he felt himself to be, and convinced others that he was, the moral and spiritual successor of Jean-Jacques Rousseau. He was, and was repeatedly hailed as, 'the Incorruptible', the indicated leader of *les purs* in the decisive battle against *les corrompus*.

I shall come back to that. But first let us take a look at the Marx and Lenin comparison. When Lenin went back to Russia in 1917 to implement Marx's teaching, what did that implementation have in common with Robespierre's implementation of Rousseau? I think it did have some basic things in common. There was, in both cases, both an intellectual and moral inheritance. And in both cases, in my opinion, the moral inheritance was of more fundamental importance than the intellectual.

The main intellectual inheritance in Lenin's case was of course *Das Kapital*. And I think *Das Kapital*, in this context, is quite closely comparable to *Du Contrat Social*, as inherited by Robespierre. It was a 'beacon of legislators', an impressive intellectual property, that was supposed to clarify everything. *Das Kapital* was, in one way, however, superior to *Du Contrat Social*. *Das Kapital* was predictive, as well as analytical. It was supposed to prove scientifically that the victory of the proletarian revolution was inevitable. And even if the book did not in fact prove anything of the kind, the belief that it did prove it was helpful to the morale of the revolutionaries. And the morale was more important than the alleged science. Lenin was Marx's spiritual heir, as Robespierre was Rousseau's. Lenin had Marx's indomitable fighting spirit; his thirst for revolution; his polemical skills; his hard, malicious scorn and capacity to frighten. These qualities had much more to do with Lenin's revolutionary success than whatever science may be contained in *Das Kapital*.

Edmund Wilson suggests in *To the Finland Station* that, when Lenin arrived at that Petrograd terminus, 'for the first time a philosophical key fitted a historical lock'. But in fact it was Lenin's Bolshevik colleagues who were fiddling around at the time with that philosophical key; and not getting anywhere because the key was intended for a quite different lock: the lock of the advanced countries, not a Russian lock. Lenin's achievement was to throw away the useless key – or rather, put it quietly in his pocket – and follow his own pragmatic hunch: that since Russia was going out of the war anyway, the faction that was most determined to help Russia out of the war would be the one that would win.

The Rousseau–Robespierre connection is unlike that Marx–Lenin one in many ways, but the two connections are alike in this: that it is the spiritual inheritance, the likeness of mind, that is of fundamental importance, while the letter of the inherited doctrine does little more than legitimize the spiritual inheritance, by proclaiming it.

The dominant, though by no means the sole, tradition of French historiography about the Revolution has been the Thermidorian one, or – as Ernest Hamel puts it, more comprehensively, the Thermido-girondin one.[2] In terms of that tradition, the cruel tyrant, Robespierre, was a hypocrite, who put on a blood-stained travesty of the life and teachings of the gentle Jean-Jacques.

It wasn't really much like that. Jean-Jacques wasn't all that gentle, and Robespierre was less cruel than some of the revolutionary leaders who talked loudest about their own devotion to Rousseau, and how unworthy Robespierre was to use that name.

J. L. Talmon saw Rousseau as among the founding fathers of what Talmon calls 'totalitarian democracy'. Certainly, the spirit of Rousseau's main political writings is profoundly, though delphically, authoritarian. True, the source of all authority, the sovereign, the General Will, consists of all the citizens, associated in one moral and collective group. This sovereign, according to Rousseau, is incapable of doing wrong: 'The sovereign in virtue of the mere fact that it exists, is always what it ought to be.' The very style there is ominous: peremptory, swaggeringly paradoxical, absolute, and unassailable, because consisting entirely of gratuitous assertion. It is the style of the Supreme Court of a despotism – though in a good period, stylistically speaking. One is hardly surprised to read on the following page – at the end of Chapter VII of the First Book, the following: 'So that the social pact may not be an empty formula, it tacitly implies the engagement, which alone can supply the force of the rest, that whoever will refuse to obey the general will be constrained to obey, by the whole social body: which means nothing else than that he will be forced to be free.' Again the style fits the matter to perfection. The high and insolent paradox – 'forced to be free' – suggests the pleasures of authoritarian jurisprudence and law enforcement.

There are many contradictions in *Du Contrat Social*, as in the rest of Rousseau, and some commentators manage to see the work, balancing one thing against another, as on the whole basically liberal and democratic. Phasing out startling and meaningful statements through the soporific invocation of 'the perspective of the whole work' is a technique greatly favoured by certain schools of academic commentators. Apparently the idea is to defend the respectability of prominent writers within one's field of specialization by putting liberal interpretations on work which is in fact not liberal. The process has been defined as gentling or 'gentlification'. For obvious reasons, the gentlifiers have been kept busiest in the area of German studies. There are gentle Fichteans, gentle Hegelians, gentle Wagnerites and, most assiduous of all, gentle Nietzscheans. But there are also, for example, gentle Yeatsians and gentle Rousseauists. I cannot, within the limits of this lecture, engage in the detailed and voluminous argument with these last which their well-chosen ground of controversy would require. I can only indicate my disagreement with them, as gently as possible. And there is a specific objection to the 'gentle Rousseau' case which requires mention, because it is not a question of theoretical analysis, but of practice, in a concrete case. Rousseau had become such an accepted sage in his own day that he was asked to draft constitutions for two countries – Corsica and Poland – then struggling to be free. In the case of Corsica (for which he produced only a fragment of a constitution), he sets out how the social pact is actually to be arrived at. The leader – it was to be the famous General Paoli – lands on the island and addresses his people in the following words, provided for him by Rousseau:

> 'Corsicans be silent: I am going to speak in the name of all. . . . Let those who will not consent, *depart*, and let those who consent raise their hand.'

There follow the words of the oath of the social pact.

According to the teaching of *Du Contrat Social* itself, those who departed, on that occasion, would not be citizens of the land they lived in, but strangers in it. And apparently that was to be the case whether those who departed were in a minority, or actually in a majority. The social contract, as designed by Rousseau for the population of Corsica under Paoli, consisted in:

(a) shutting up;

(b) being those in whose name the General spoke;

(c) raising your hand, on request.

La volonté générale, c'est la volonté du Général.[3] Or you could adapt Louis xv and say: *La volonté générale, c'est moi*. That formula is pretty much how Robespierre understood the matter. And I can't see that he was anything but a most faithful disciple, in that, of his master, the author of *Du Contrat Social*.

The spirit of *Du Contrat Social* is not compatible, in my belief, with the spirit or practice of a democratic and liberal State. But it is quite compatible with the spirit and practice of the Fatherland in danger, *la patrie en danger*: the conditions of revolutionary France, under threat from external and internal enemies. Those were the conditions which prevailed in France in the years 1792–94, the years which saw the emergence of Robespierre as the leading revolutionary figure, and the emergence also of the Terror as an institution of the State.

This is not to say that Robespierre was dictator, or even Head of State or of the Government. He was not even a minister, though he was more than a minister. Only in his last year did he accept even a share in any form of collective executive authority, as one of the nine members of the great Committee of Public Safety.

Robespierre controlled no government department, no funds, no police, no troops. His was essentially a moral authority. But it was an extraordinary moral authority; perhaps a greater moral authority, extending over the political domain, than has been exercised by any other elected politician, without administrative functions or governmental role. And it was an authority in part derived from the Rousseau myth, in part conferred by Robespierre's own character, and in part apparently suggested by certain formulations in *Du Contrat Social*.

That last aspect is not necessarily the most important of the three, but it is curious, and I don't know that it has attracted as much attention as it deserves. In *Du Contrat Social*, the connection between the theoretical sovereign, 'the general will', and any practicable scheme of governance here on earth is generally far from clear. But there are two categories of people who do provide a kind of link. There is the 'guide' or 'legislator' who makes his appearance in Chapters VI and VII of the Second Book. The guide is necessary because of the mysterious incapacities of the theoretically infallible sovereign, the General Will. As Rousseau puts it: 'The General Will is always right (*droite*) but the judgement which guides it is not always enlightened.' So there is a need for this special personage, the guide or legislator, whose job it is to *show* the General Will, in Rousseau's words, how 'to see objects as they are, sometimes as they ought to appear to it'.

To help the General Will, which is always right, 'to see objects as they are' . . . The General Will is infallible, but not particularly well-informed. Rather like the Pope.

And again, more startlingly, it is sometimes the duty of the guide to show the General Will *not* the objects as they actually are, but as they 'ought to appear' to the 'not always enlightened' General Will. (*Il faut lui faire voir les objets tels qu'ils sont, quelquefois tels qu'ils doivent lui paraître.*) So it seems that the guide or legislator has sometimes the duty, apparently at his own discretion, to make a monkey out of this metaphysically exalted creature, the General Will. Varying the zoological metaphor, the guide or legislator who has charge of the perceptions of the General Will is really the keeper of a sort of sacred crocodile: a formidable-looking beast, and greatly to be venerated, but dumb, dim-witted, purblind and not to be let out on its own.

Clearly this guide, legislator, monkey-maker and crocodile-keeper is a redoubtable functionary. And no one can read Robespierre's revolutionary speeches without feeling that he considers himself to be a guide in this sense. Especially in his most continuous role throughout his short political career – his role as resident pundit of the *Société des Amis de la Constitution*, alias the Jacobin Club – he appears in the capacity, and with the vocabulary, of Grand Interpreter, articulating the demands of the General Will, and correcting its defects of vision. In his 'Address to the French of the eighty-three Departments' in the summer of 1792, Robespierre came forward confidently as spokesman for the General Will:

> *Pour nous, nous ne sommes d'aucun parti, nous ne servons*
> *aucune faction; vous le savez, frères et amis, notre*
> *volonté, c'est la volonté générale.*[3]

It is clear that many supporters of the French Revolution accepted this identification.

But there is another functionary, besides the guide or legislator, within the system of *Du Contrat Social*, whose role was filled by Robespierre, with no less impressive an authority, and to more directly terrifying effect. This functionary is Rousseau's 'Censor'. The Censor's functions are carefully set out in Chapter VII of the Fourth Book, *De la Censure*, 'Concerning Censorship'. Rousseau's Censor, like the old Roman one, is a censor of morals, and an interpreter of public opinion. Rousseau takes an example, as he likes to do, from ancient Spartan practice. In Sparta, the ephors were the magistrates who acted as censors of morals (as well as in other capacities). As Rousseau tells the story: 'A man of bad morals once offered a piece of good advice in the Council of Sparta. The ephors, without taking any overt notice of his remark, had the same advice proposed by a virtuous citizen.'

This role of censor was one for which Robespierre had a marked predilection, and an awesome credibility. And in the Paris of the Revolution, this became a more central role, with more tragic implications, than had ever been the case in ancient Rome or Sparta. Revolutionary Paris was a Manichean world in which there were only the virtuous and the vicious, *les purs* and *les corrompus*. To be a prominent man, identified as *corrompu*, was, by late 1793, to be well on the way to the guillotine. And Robespierre, the Incorruptible, was generally accepted as the authority on who was *pur* and who was *corrompu*. So life or death could hang on a Robespierre speech.

It is worth noting that Robespierre *combined* the roles of 'guide' and 'censor' which appear as separate in Rousseau. And Robespierre's entire revolutionary activity is defined by that combination of roles.

Virtue was the governing principle of the whole system, as Montesquieu (endorsed by Rousseau) had said it should be in a Republic. Virtue, during the Revolution, hinged on the defence of Revolutionary France, against its external and internal enemies. In an article published in the summer of 1792, Robespierre defined *la vertu* as consisting of '*l'amour du bien, de la patrie et de la liberté*'.[4] And Robespierre spoke as confidently on behalf of virtue, in his role as censor, as he did on behalf of the General Will, in his role as guide. And virtue alone could legitimize Terror (alias Justice). In the autumn of 1793, the great Committee of Public Safety, under Robespierre's inspiration, in a circular to local revolutionary authorities, gave the instruction: '*Méritez par la vertu le droit de punir le crime.*'[5] Robespierre was regarded as the archetype of those whose virtue had earned them that right.

The virtuous Maximilien was seen as the heir and interpreter of the virtuous Jean-Jacques, guide and censor, worthy of trust, and guarantor of the gains of the Revolution and the integrity of the nation. And he *was* worthy of trust, in his loyalty to the Revolution, and freedom from corruption, whereas many of his rivals were crooks, and scoundrels of various other descriptions.[6]

Toward the end of his life, Robespierre was trying to bring the Terror – which was never entirely or even largely under his control – to an end. And that is why he had to be killed. The pacemakers of the Terror in the provinces – Fouché, Tallien, Carrier – saw that they were about to be cast in the role of the last victims, unless they could cast Robespierre in that role, and emerge themselves in the role of *modérés*. They brought it off, I think, mainly because most of the French people, being a little bit *corrompus* themselves, like other people, got tired of hearing so much about *les purs*, once the royalist danger was over and the national territory and the revolutionary gains by the bourgeois and peasants were no longer in danger. Like the English people, the French preferred cakes and ale (or wine) to the rule of the saints, though the saints had had their uses in their day.

As Maximilien himself put it: 'Virtue is always in a minority on earth.' *La vertu est toujours en minorité sur la terre*. Amen, says the majority.

Notes

1 Gordon H. McNeil, 'The Cult of Rousseau and the French Revolution', *Journal of the History of Ideas*, vol. 6 (1945), pp. 197–212. There is something phoney about Rousseau's Thermidorian apotheosis. As Albert Meynier puts it neatly: '*C'est au moment ou l'on va commencer à s'éloigner de lui qu'on le glorifie.*' (*Jean-Jacques Rousseau, Révolutionnaire*, Paris, 1921[?], p. 220.)

2 (Louis-) Ernest Hamel, *Histoire de Robespierre* (three volumes, Paris, 1865–6). This is still the most useful biography of Robespierre, because it quotes his speeches at length, putting them in context. Hamel was passionately pro-Robespierre and conducted a running (and most entertaining) feud with his contemporary, Michelet. Recommended reading as a supplement (and in part a corrective) to Michelet.

3 'The General Will against the will of the General', was one of the slogans of the Paris student rebels of May 1968, against de Gaulle.

4 Quoted in Hamel II, p. 336; for another quotation, of similar purport, see p. 699 of the same volume.

5 Hamel II, p. 277.

6 Hamel III, p. 171.

7 Robespierre's virtue, in private life, is best attested by the fact that his Thermidorian enemies were extremely anxious to find dirt about his private life and never found any. As in the case of Spinoza, nobody who knew Robespierre in his private life could be induced to say a word against him. In fact, Robespierre's reputation for virtue is much less assailable than that of his master, Rousseau, who handed over his five children (by his common-law wife, Thérèse Levasseur) to the foundling asylum, immediately after birth. Edmund Burke, for one, felt that Rousseau's pattern of paternal conduct fell well below the general level of mammalian morality. 'The bear', said Burke, 'loves, licks and forms her young; but bears are not philosophers.' (*Letter to a Member of the National Assembly*, 1791.)

The Liberal Pole
Pope John Paul II*

I N 1870, THE FIRST VATICAN COUNCIL publicly proclaimed as dogma
something which many, though not all, Catholics had long believed: that
the Pope was infallible in matters of faith and morals. In the early 1960s
the Second Vatican Council summoned by Pope John XXIII sought to remove
the emphasis from the personal authority of the Pope, to put more emphasis
on the collegiate authority of bishops and in general to begin the process of
liberalization and modernization – *aggiornamento* – of the Catholic Church.
Karol Wojtila, as auxiliary Archbishop and then Archbishop of Krakow,
played an important part in the Second Vatican Council whose general
impetus he then seemed to favour. In the aftermath of the Council,
however, he helped John XXIII's conservative successor Paul VI in his
cautious reassertion of papal authority. And from the time he became Pope
in 1978, Wojtila, as John Paul II, has firmly put the clock back.

I propose to examine Wojtila's emergence as a powerful figure in the
Church, and the principal features of his Pontificate. At the Second Vatican
Council, which Wojtila attended, participants in the Council were impressed by his liberal language and by his apparent accord with the general
trend of the Council. He was 'the liberal Pole'. At the Second Vatican
Council there was a Church commission – set up by Pope John XXIII and
opened by Pope Paul VI – to look into contraception. The fifth session of the
commission, in April 1966, produced a majority report which did not uphold
the Church's traditional absolute ban on contraception, and a minority
report which did. The Commission's report fell to be reviewed, in June 1966,
by the sixteen cardinals and bishops who were members of the commission.
A majority approved the removal of the absolute ban on contraception. And
how did Archbishop Wojtila vote, on this momentous occasion? He didn't
vote at all. He just wasn't there. Why? If he had attended, he would have

*This is the full text of a television programme transmitted on Channel 4 on 24 August
1985.

had to vote with the minority, led by Cardinal Ottaviani, widely regarded as the leader of the party of reaction within the Church. Wojtila would have forfeited his reputation as 'the liberal Pole'.

In 1968 the conservative Pope Paul VI issued the famous, or notorious, encyclical, *Humanae Vitae*, reaffirming the traditional absolute ban on contraception and setting aside the majority report of the commission, and the majority vote of the commission's bishops and cardinals. The Synod of the following year was expected to provide confrontation between Pope and bishops, but didn't. Cardinal Wojtila seems to have played a leading part among those, in the Synod of 1969, who successfully counselled against rocking the boat, and who chose instead to spread oil on troubled waters. It was Wojtila who delivered at the Vatican the Synod's final declaration on 27 October 1969. 'There is nothing more important', Wojtila declared, 'than the testimony of union and the spreading of peace. The union in the Church, which is desired so ardently by the Christian people, depends very largely on the collaboration between the Supreme Pontiff and the bishops' conference.' In the context, 'collaboration' is an exquisite euphemism, characteristic of the style which Wojtila, as Pope John Paul II, was to make familiar. Language which suggested a sustained momentum of Vatican II was used with connotations designed to restore the authoritarian principle.

Wojtila was then, and Pope John Paul II still is, a man of profound convictions, and of high personal courage, proved in the frightful conditions of wartime Poland. But he is also a man of great astuteness, even deviousness, in tactical matters. And the tactical skills served then, and still serve, to conceal the full depths of his traditional Tridentine Catholicity and of an authoritarianism gentle and unassuming in style, but implacable in substance.

At the Conclave to elect a successor to Pope John Paul I, in October 1978, the Italian cardinals were bitterly divided among themselves. Once serious consideration had to be given to non-Italians, the choice soon fell on Cardinal Wojtila, 'the liberal Pole'. Nobody thought he was *very* liberal; in the expression, 'liberal Pole', the noun qualifies the adjective. What Wojtila seems to have been expected to do was to work in the spirit of Vatican II, and maintain some of its momentum without going too far. No well-informed cardinal would have expected Wojtila personally to favour the reversal or dilution of *Humanae Vitae*, but he was expected to be a staunch upholder of the Vatican II principle of collegiality or consensus and therefore not to let his personal views close the door to reinterpretation of *Humanae Vitae* or anything else.

Wojtila at this time was perceived as essentially standing for 'Collegiality', possibly through a misunderstanding of his role in the Synod of 1969. Yet John Paul II's first statement as Pope seemed to confirm the trust which moderate liberals had placed in him. In his discourse of the morning after his election he used the word 'collegiality' five times, and seemed to commit himself strongly to Vatican II. He said:

> We consider our primary duty to be that of promoting, with prudent but encouraging action, the most exact fulfilment of the norms of the [Second Vatican] Council. Above all, we favour the development of conciliar attitudes. First we must be in harmony with the Council. One must put into effect what was in its documents; and what was implicit should be made explicit in the light of the experiments that followed, and in the light of new emerging circumstances.

A sensitive nose might perhaps have picked up, from the last phrase, a whiff of the impending counter-revolution. But the blessed word 'collegiality' seems to have reassured the liberally-minded, at this stage. It was after all, going to be the Synod of Bishops which would make 'explicit' those things which were said to be 'implicit' in the documents of Vatican II. Only it wasn't going to be the Synod of Bishops. It was going to be the new Pope. Henceforward the language of Vatican II would mean whatever John Paul II said it meant, which would be the reverse of what liberally-minded Catholics had understood it to mean.

Let us look at some examples of this. Consider 'collegiality' (or consensus), 'dialogue' and 'ecumenism' – key concepts of Vatican II – in their new Wojtila Humpty Dumpty meanings.

'Collegiality' or consensus first. One of the major documents – indeed *the* major document – of the Wojtila Pontificate, is *Familiaris Consortio* (1981) dealing with the Christian Family in the Modern World. This is the document which (among other things) reaffirmed *Humanae Vitae* and the traditional absolute ban on contraception. According to a statement made by the Pope in August of 1984, the words of this document 'reflect the consensus of the 1980 World Synod of Bishops in the Modern World'. And they certainly do reflect that consensus – as defined and interpreted by the Pope, and by the Pope alone.

The Synod in question lasted a month. Many bishops called for a new look at the traditional teaching. The Pope listened and took notes. He then reaffirmed the traditional teaching. That was the consensus, and the new meaning of consensus is sufficiently apparent from the title of the document which is supposed to reflect consensus. The full title, in the official English version, runs: 'Apostolic Exhortation. *Familiaris Consortio* of his Holiness

Pope John Paul II. To the Episcopate, to the Clergy and to the Faithful regarding the role of the Christian Family in the Modern World'. In short, consensus, as defined and interpreted by the Pope, is an attribute of those Pontifical utterances which are delivered at the end of meetings of bishops.

Then take 'dialogue'. It would not be right – not quite right – to say that dialogue now means monologue. The Pope is generally quite prepared to listen, or at any rate to allow himself to be addressed. But what is said to him, if it differs from his own inner convictions, seems incapable of impinging. In extreme cases, where the words addressed to him are extremely distasteful, it seems that the Pope can become physically deaf.

There was a poignant case of such a dialogue during the Pope's visit to America. At a service in Washington, Sister Mary Theresa Kane made a speech of welcome to the Pope, on behalf of 700 nuns. She urged the Pope

to listen with compassion and to hear the call of women who comprise half of mankind. As women, we have heard the powerful messages of our Church addressing the need of dignity and reverence of all persons. As women, we have pondered upon those words. Our contemplation leads us to state that the Church in its call for reverence and dignity must respond by providing the possibility of women as persons being included in all ministries in our Church.

The Pope then addressed the nuns. He made no reference to Sister Mary Theresa's appeal. 'It was said afterwards', according to his biographer, 'that he had not been able to hear what she said.' The Pope reminded the nuns, many of whom were wearing suits, of the desirability of wearing 'a simple and suitable religious garb'. The Pope has conducted dialogues on similar lines in other places – in Bavaria, for example, and with the recalcitrant Catholics of Holland.

The fate of 'ecumenism' has been much the same as that of dialogue, and consistently so. John Paul II is in favour of ecumenism, as strictly defined by himself. For him, ecumenism is a form of Catholic missionary work. In the Encyclical *Redemptor Hominis*, in the first year of his Pontificate, John Paul II said: 'We approach them' – in the context, non-Catholics – 'with the esteem, respect and discernment that since the time of the Apostles has marked the *missionary* attitude, the attitude of the *missionary* [the Pope's italics].' Much more recently – in January 1985 – the Pope spelled out what Christian unity means; 'as it is told to us through the great ecclesiastical Tradition, as it is professed in the one faith, in the celebration of the same sacraments, in the communion of all bishops constituted to shepherd the People of God – and united among themselves around the Successor of Peter'. And all this – the present successor of Peter happily went on – 'with respect for the values and the riches of each particular tradition and each culture, according to the teaching of the Second Vatican Council in the decree on ecumenism the twentieth century anniversary of whose promulgation we are observing'.

I can't help feeling a little sorry for those Anglican divines who have been attempting ecumenical dialogue with the missionaries of the current successor of Peter.

And what a pity George Orwell did not live to see the Pontificate which has included the year 1984! With what unholy joy the author of *Nineteen Eighty-Four* would have exploited the current bonanza of Papal Newspeak. Orwell, who detested Roman Catholicism, and obsessively equated it with Stalinism, did not live to see even Vatican II, let alone John Paul II's neo-Tridentine annexation and transmogrification of Vatican II. Orwell's assumption would have been upset by Vatican II, but reaffirmed by John Paul II, and above all by John Paul's imperious reversals of the ordinary meaning of the words and concepts. Orwell would have recognized in John Paul – with a characteristically bitter satisfaction – a corruptor of human language, and an enemy of the human intellect. The Rome Orwell knew, and did not love, is back with us.

Without accepting that Orwellian equation, we may trace a certain connection between John Paul II's kind of authoritarianism and the Marxist dispensation under which he lived for so long. In the face of an authoritarian and dogmatic secular power, backed by overwhelming physical force, it must have seemed right and proper to affirm a symmetrical spiritual alternative, and so to reaffirm infallible authority, and unity under the authority. Also Wojtila's diplomatic astuteness, and marked propensity to double-talk, may be seen as qualities exercised and enhanced by his position as spokesman for a captive people: wily shepherd of a threatened flock. Those who voted for 'the Cardinal from behind the Iron Curtain' may not have realized that, in that sense, he would have to bring a piece of the Curtain with him, to the Vatican.

All this may seem a far cry from the Pope the world knows best: the sunnily perambulating, baby-kissing figure, supremely at his ease among the crowds and before the cameras. But in reality, there is no conflict. 'John Paul Superstar', as *Time* magazine called him, and the author of *Familiaris Consortio*, are the same father-figure in different contexts. Bonhomie on festive occasions is entirely compatible with sternness, when thought appropriate, in the bosom of the family, and in relation to the family. And it is above all within the family of the Church, and in relation to the sexual life of the Catholic family, that this particular Pope most feels the need to be stern.

On general subjects, the Pope can often sound like a modern liberal. His general utterances about the Third World, for example, sound very like the Brandt Report. But even in relation to the Third World, whenever specific Catholic issues come in, the swish of discipline can be heard in the Pope's utterances. He has been cold towards the religious who have devoted their lives to work among the poor of the Third World; these religious appear to be seen by him mainly in the role of potential victims of alien ideas, in the guise of 'Liberation Theology'. And the Pope has set his face against the notion that contraception can be of any legitimate use in relation to the frightful demographic problems of Africa, Asia and Latin America. At Santo Domingo, in October last year, John Paul II called on the Church in Latin America to: 'Resist the agents of neo-Malthusianism who want to impose a new colonialism on the Latin American peoples, weakening their life force with contraceptive practices, sterilization, liberalization of abortion and disintegrating the unity, stability and the fertility of the family.'

It is on subjects connected with sexuality that this Pope is at his most emotional and most negatively authoritarian: no contraception, no abortion, no release from vows of celibacy, no women priests, no legitimation of any homosexual activity.

At the centre of the Wojtila pattern of feelings and ideas about these matters appears a vision of the Virgin Mary at the foot of the Cross on which her Son is crucified. This is of course a traditional and poignant Catholic image, but it dominates the mind and imagination of the present Pope with a peculiar intensity. This appears most notably in his pronouncements on the family, sexual morality, celibacy and gender discrimination in relation to the priesthood. These matters have had a central place in this Pontificate, and John Paul's teaching in relation to them is animated, permeated and dominated by his intense personal devotion to the Virgin Mother at the foot of her Son's Cross. The culminating passage of *Familiaris Consortio* runs as follows:

> May the Virgin Mary, who is the Mother of the Church also be the Mother, in 'the Church of the home'. Thanks to her motherly aid, may each Christian family really become a 'little Church' in which the mystery of the Church of Christ is mirrored and given new life. May she, the Handmaid of the Lord, be an example of humble and generous acceptance of the Will of God. May she, the Sorrowful Mother at the foot of the Cross, comfort the sufferings and dry the tears of those in distress because of the difficulties of the families.

Obviously, this teaching exalts women, in a way. But the way is a way defined and interpreted by male celibates, the closed caste from which the elite of the Church is drawn. The Pope stresses again and again the 'dignity' of women – another Vatican II term, now applied in a special sense. This 'dignity', in practice, seems to consist entirely in submission to rules laid down by male celibates; in avoidance of contraception and abortion, in all circumstances; in unquestioning acceptance of women's exclusion from the priesthood; and especially in a sustained effort to emulate the Virgin Mother, however difficult that may be, especially for married women. And if it proves too difficult, there is always the Cross to contemplate. 'Spouses', according to John Paul II's *Familiaris Consortio*, are 'the permanent reminder to the Church of what happened on the Cross.'

In his play, *Le Soulier de Satin*, Paul Claudel has the Moon put the following queries to his heroine: 'Is it not your marriage night to-night? And where did you think you were going to spend your marriage night, except upon the Cross?' Commenting on this passage, I once wrote that Claudel's Moon sounded like a demented Reverend Mother. That was circa 1960. But in 1985, it is painfully clear that this is precisely the kind of Reverend Mother who would find favour in the sight of the present Holy Father.

In its spirit, the Pontificate of John Paul II is a tremendous archaism, a splendid example of Polish Baroque. But in its outward appearance, this Pontificate seems hearteningly modern, open in style, no longer reclusive. Most lay Catholics probably pay much more attention to the Pope's attractive appearances than to his sombre teaching. 'The Pope is a very nice man, and a credit to us all, even if he does have this hang-up about contraception,' probably sums up the attitude most general among urban lay Catholics. But for the many earnest and troubled religious whose hearts had lifted at the promise of *aggiornamento*, this Pontificate is a period of captivity. Perhaps the next Synod, summoned by the Pope for the coming autumn, will bring them deliverance. But I doubt it.[1]

Personally, as I studied the writings of John Paul II, I found my faith revive: my faith, that is, in the eighteenth-century Enlightenment; in Voltaire and Diderot, as liberators of the human mind from an oppressive and obfuscating dogmatism. Faith in the Enlightenment is hardly the faith this Pope wants to revive, but never mind. If God can move in a mysterious way, I suppose Enlightenment can too.

Note

1 I find it didn't.

God and Man in Nicaragua*

G OD IS CENTRAL to the current public debate in Nicaragua, and both sides constantly invoke His name. On all the main roads, near the larger centres of population, there are huge printed posters reading simply:

> PARA NOSOTROS NO HAY
> MAS QUE UN SOLO DIOS
>
> 1 Corinthians, 8,6.

'For us there is not more than one single God.' But, someone has been going round adding to each poster, in large manuscript, after 'Dios', the words:

> . . . EL DIOS DE LOS POBRES!!

The 'one single God', without further qualification, is the God of the Nicaraguan Catholic Hierarchy, led by Cardinal Miguel Obando y Bravo, Archbishop of Managua. And this is also the God of Nicaragua's middle class opposition, all of which – including Protestant oppositionists – looks to the Cardinal as its political leader. The posters are assumed to be funded by the Cardinal's North American friends.

'The God of the poor' is the God of the governing *Frente Nacional Sandinista*, of the three (formerly four) Catholic priests who are members of the Government – in defiance of the hierarchy and of the Pope – and of the many Catholic (and some Protestant) clergy and lay men and women, Nicaraguan and non-Nicaraguan, who have worked among the Nicaraguan poor, and who see the Sandinista Government as generally promoting the interests of the poor.

Both sides are deeply in earnest, with passions that approximate to those of civil war. Indeed they are very closely related to the civil war now being waged, with outside support, in many parts of Nicaragua.

The Cardinal's public position on the war has been identical, in essentials,

*From *The Atlantic Monthly*, August 1986.

to that of President Reagan. Like the President, the Cardinal calls for immediate negotiations between the Sandinista Government and the American-backed *contras*. In adopting this position, the Cardinal sees himself as doing his duty as a Christian leader, seeking peace, *la paz*. The Sandinistas, on the other hand, believe that they are the ones who are seeking peace, through negotiations between the two sovereign Governments concerned, the United States and Nicaragua. The Sandinistas see *la paz* as withheld by the United States' refusal of direct negotiations, and by its humiliating insistence that, instead, the Nicaraguan Government must negotiate with the *contras*, the paid paramilitary agents of the United States.

It follows that the Sandinistas regard the Cardinal as promoting war, not peace, and helping the cause of Nicaragua's enemies.

The Cardinal genuinely does not see the issue in this light, but the light he does see it in does not tend to make relations with the Government look any better. The Cardinal has consistently refused to condemn *contra* atrocities. Asked why, he adopts an agnostic position. He has read allegations about such things, in the Government press, he says, but as he knows a lot of things the Government press says are not true, he can't comment. (*Newsweek* int?rview with Joseph Contrera: 18 November 1985.) This hardly holds water. The Catholic clergy, anywhere in a Catholic country, are in a position to provide their bishops with a very good national news service; they don't have to be dependent on a Government-controlled press. And the *contra* campaign of terror against peasants in northern Nicaragua is notorious; so much so indeed that President Reagan, at one point, was driven to claim that the Sandinistas were in the habit of dressing up as *contras*, in order to commit atrocities, in order to discredit the *contras*.

The Cardinal's claim not to know did not go down well with some, even, of his senior clergy, in the exposed areas. 'Tell him to come to my parish', said one of these, 'and help me bury the dead.'

It is not, however, just a question of not wishing to know what the *contras* may have done. It is a question of signalling support for the *contras*. After receiving his Cardinal's hat from the Pope in May 1985, and before returning to Nicaragua, the new Cardinal said Mass in Miami: a Mass attended by the *contra* leadership and by the photographers. *Contra* leaders Adolfo Portocarrero and Eden Pastora were prominent in the audience at the Mass. 'I do not object to being identified with the people who have taken up arms,' the Cardinal commented after the ceremony.

At Miami, with a confidence enhanced by the new and signal mark of the Pope's approval, the new Cardinal went a step further than he had ever gone, while he was no more than an archbishop. But it was a step in the direction in which he – and following him the Nicaraguan Hierarchy – had been moving for more than five years; initially hesitantly, but openly and with conviction from 1983 on. The Pope's visit to Nicaragua came on 4 March of that year. I shall come back to that event, momentous in the history, not merely of Nicaragua and Central America, but of Latin America as a whole and of the Catholic Church. It is enough for the present to say that, in its immediate impact, the visit was a disaster for the Sandinistas, and that it fortified the position of Archbishop Obando and his supporters; at least for a time.

Later in that year, the Sandinista Government, under growing pressure from the Reagan Administration's efforts to destabilize it, introduced compulsory military service: *Servicio Militar Patriotico (S.M.P.)*. The response of the Nicaraguan Episcopal Conference, in a document called 'General Considerations on Military Service', was to call in question the legitimacy of the Nicaraguan State itself, in its existing form, and to legitimize rejection of its authority, specifically in the form of refusal of military service. (Implicit legitimation of an opposing form of military service was left until later, at Miami.)

La Prensa, on 1 September 1983, published the bishops' explosive challenge under the appropriate title: 'Nobody can be obliged to take up arms for a party'. The bishops said, among other things:

> The absolute dictatorship of a political party, which is constituted by force as the only arbiter and owner of the state, its institutions and every type of social activity, poses the problem of its legitimacy as well as the legitimacy of its institutions, including the army. . . . It is not correct to mix, confuse or identify the concepts of fatherland, state, revolution, and *Sandinismo*. . . . The attitude towards this Bill, for all those who do not share the Sandinista Party ideology, has to be that of 'conscientious objection' and no one should be punished, persecuted, or discriminated against for adopting this position.

The document ends with the words, 'May the Virgin Mary, Queen of Peace, help us to live according to charity so that this Holy Year of Reconciliation may produce in each of us and our society sincere fruits of justice, love and peace.'

The document embodying the general considerations on military service of the Nicaraguan Episcopal Conference is something of a curiosity in the history of the post-Reformation Church. Medieval popes, and counter-Reformation popes de-legitimized princes, and then sought to depose them, with considerable abandon. But in more recent times – and especially in the twentieth century – the instruction to 'Render unto Caesar the things that are Caesar's' has not generally been interpreted as including an obligation to verify the credentials of each particular Caesar. In Latin America, in particular, the Church has generally felt no need to challenge 'absolute dictatorships' of the right, or to insist on that blood-fraught revolutionary (or counter-revolutionary) distinction between 'the regime' and 'the State'. But in little Nicaragua, as out of one of its volcanoes, the old Hildebrandine fires erupted, with the assertion of the right and duty of the Church to pronounce on the legitimacy of princes, and to prepare their deposition. As in other parts of the world, in the closing years of the twentieth century, the notion of Holy War is showing that it has not yet lost all its power to intoxicate and to inflame.

It is fair to note at this point that, in the last five years of the Somoza dictatorship (1974–79), Archbishop Obando and the rest of the Nicaraguan hierarchy were increasingly critical of the regime, and strongly so in the dictator's last year. After the fall of the dictator, the *Frente Sandinista* – in words which it was later to regret – acknowledged the significant role which the Bishops, 'especially Monsignor Obando y Bravo', had played in the revolution, in that they had 'valiantly denounced the crimes and abuses of the dictatorship'. But until 1978–79 – when Somoza was visibly collapsing and bereft of American support – the Archbishop never seems to have attacked him in the fundamental way in which he has attacked the Sandinista regime, or with the same accents of Holy War. To denounce abuses of power is not as radical as to deny the legitimacy of power.

But it is not *really* Holy War, most of the Cardinal's opponents claim. The 'General Considerations' are only formally a doctrinal document; they are in reality a political document, dictated by the social conservatism of the Cardinal and some of his colleagues, and by their desire to help bring about the restoration of the old order (minus Somoza) under the benign hegemony of the United States. There is certainly some truth in that view of the matter, but it can be exaggerated, and sometimes is. Thus the Sandinista newspaper, *Barricada*, likes to depict the Cardinal as a puppet, manipulated by Ronald Reagan. This is not credible. You cannot watch the Cardinal, or listen to him for a hour or so, without being aware that, whatever else may be said about the man, he does not belong to the order of puppets.

On the first Sunday of our stay in Nicaragua, my wife and I went to the little Church of San Domingo de las Sierritas, near Managua, to hear the Cardinal say Mass, and preach. San Domingo is a pretty little church, high and cool. It lies in a relatively affluent area, and the congregation was a middle-class one. There were also several television crews: the Cardinal is always news. We followed the crews into the sacristy, where the Cardinal was christening a baby, and being filmed. I thought an elderly nun, beside the Cardinal, looked a bit tight-lipped about the publicity – distracting from the sacrament – but the Cardinal had clearly given permission. International publicity, after all, is part of his armour in his struggle against the Sandinistas and their allies.

After the christening, we all went back into the church. By mistake, my wife and I took the places intended for the parents of the christened baby, beside the grandparents. Nobody even murmured. Nicaraguans are an unusually gentle people, in most contexts. The Cardinal is something of an exception. Even when saying Mass, he seemed that morning to be spoiling for a fight. As he put on his vestments, I thought he looked like a boxer getting ready for the ring. He is a small, powerfully built man, now running to fat; markedly Indian features – more so than most of his congregation; bullet head, thick neck, heavy jaw. His most marked expressive character-istic – perhaps especially marked that day – is that the corners of his lips turn sharply down. As he sat at the altar, while lessons were being read, the tips of his short fingers, joined in prayer, crossed the line of his mouth. My notes carry the hieroglyph: ⌁

That the Cardinal was cross was obvious; that he was cross with the Sandinistas and their allies was also obvious. I think now that he had other, stronger reasons for being cross, though I did not guess at them at the time.

The Cardinal read out, in a firm, strong, clear voice a letter of the Nicaraguan Episcopate on 'The Eucharist, Source of Unity of Inspiration', dated 6 April 1986. It was a well written statement, in a high Castilian style, with classical overtones: 'They blame the Church for silence, while they silence it. . . .' It contained a long passage – which the Cardinal read out with especial resonance – attacking what the Cardinal and his followers call 'the popular Church' (*iglesia popular*) meaning those who regard themselves as followers of *el Dios de los pobres* (who retort with the phrase '*iglesia institucional*', applied to people like the Cardinal and his supporters). The attack on the *iglesia popular* began with the words:

'A belligerent group of priests, religious, nuns and lay people, insisting that they belong to the Catholic Church, in reality, by their acts, works actively in undermining the unity of the same Church, collaborating in the destruction of the foundations on which rests unity in the Faith and in the Body of Christ.'

These words – and much more to the same tune – were spoken with passionate conviction. But there was another passage, read with no special emphasis, which may be of more significance, as regards the evolution in 1986 of the struggle between Church and State in Nicaragua (and the related struggles within the Latin American Church). This passage was part of a section headed: 'The Church, Waging Peace'. The key sentence in the passage read: 'We judge that any form of aid, whatever its source, which may lead to destruction, pain and death for our families or to hatred and division between our peoples is to be condemned.'

At the time I thought that passage was pretty anodyne. I thought that because I was not then aware of how far the Cardinal – especially in 1985 at Miami – had committed himself to the *contra* side. Against that background, the sentence looks a lot more interesting. And it has aroused interest, especially among that 'belligerent group' which the belligerent Cardinal so detests. Government press censorship did not allow that Episcopal Letter (or several others before it) to appear in the newspapers. But it was readily available from diocesan press offices in Nicaragua, and became the subject of delighted comment in the April issue of *Envío*. *Envío*, a monthly review published by the *Instituto Historico Centroamericano* in Managua, reflects the views of an influential group of Catholic intellectuals (priests and lay people) who are, as they say in Managua, 'with the process'. The process in question is the revolutionary process, especially in its social aspects; being 'with the process' implies broad support for the Sandinistas, without necessarily being committed to support all their policies and actions. At the end of an article entitled '*La Iglesia de los Pobres en Nicaragua*', *Envío* singles out that passage from the Nicaraguan Hierarchy's statement, underlining parts of it, calling it a historic step, *paso historico*, and claiming that it means 'the condemnation of the military aid of Ronald Reagan's administration to the counter-revolution'.

Certainly, it comes a lot nearer to meaning just that than anything the Nicaraguan bishops had ever said before; and it even seems an implicit condemnation of the Cardinal's own position at Miami, less than a year before.

It doesn't seem an unreasonable inference that a section – perhaps a majority – of the Nicaraguan Hierarchy is becoming refractory against the Cardinal's leadership, in relation to civil war. As regards the *iglesia popular*, he still calls the tune, but no longer on the *contras*, it would seem. Some of the bishops, especially from the northern and eastern dioceses, where they know most about *contras* at first hand, are believed to have had misgivings about the Cardinal's lead on this matter for some time, on moral and humanitarian grounds. Others, more politically minded, may well feel that the Cardinal's line simply doesn't make sense today, in terms of the Church's interests. The *contras* have never looked as if they could overthrow the Sandinistas, and they look even less like it now than they did in 1983–84 (which was their peak). To call, as the Cardinal has regularly done, on the

Sandinistas to negotiate with the *contras* is to call for what is not going to happen. Nobody who knows anything about the Sandinistas believes that they would negotiate with the *contras* even if Managua were about to fall, which it is not, or not to the *contras*. If it does fall, it will be to the invading armed forces of the United States.

To support the weaker side in a civil war, in the hope that it may be about to be rescued by foreign invasion, is an extraordinarily high-risk policy, which prudent churchmen – whatever their personal political inclinations – would always wish to avoid. It rather looks as if prudent churchmen may currently be a rising force in the Nicaraguan Episcopate, and that they may be beginning to rein in their impetuous Primate, the 'Cardinal of Central America'.

If all that is so – as I believe – it is not surprising if the Cardinal looked a bit grim, at Mass that April morning, in San Domingo de la Sierritas.

The Cardinal is still a force – a force of nature indeed – but he and what he represents may no longer be quite the force they were, in what looks in retrospect like their heyday: the period that began with the Pope's visit to Nicaragua in March 1983, and ended in May 1985 with the Cardinal's visit to Miami, in all the hubris of the new red hat.

The Pope's visit to Nicaragua is perhaps the most important, and certainly the most dramatic, episode in the great struggle between the institutional *un solo Dios* and *el Dios de los pobres* in Latin America in the late twentieth century. Both sides in Nicaragua had looked to the Pope for a blessing, legitimizing their particular interpretation of the Church's teaching. The Archbishop, of course, knew the Pope. The champions of *el Dios de los pobres*, for their part, seem to have been counting on John Paul II's social teaching, which seems strongly on the side of the Third World, and hostile to capitalist values and the consumer society. And the Pope had presided, very early in his Pontificate, over the second Conference of Latin American Bishops at Puebla de los Angeles, in Mexico, which had committed the Church to 'the preferential option for the poor' seen by some as the furthest the institutional Church has gone – since its adoption by the Emperor Constantine – in recognizing *el Dios de los pobres*.

In Managua last May, I asked a young Jesuit, an ardent and active liberation theologian very much 'with the process' in Nicaragua, where he thought the Pope stood on liberation theology. 'The Pope', said the Jesuit, '*is himself* a liberation theologian!' His eyes flashed as he said that, and then he laughed painfully, as at some unbearable paradox.

My own guess is that the Pope sees himself as not merely *a* liberation theologian but as *the* liberation theologian. It is for *him* to say how far liberation theology can legitimately go, and where it is to stop. It is for him to determine in what sense God is in very truth *el Dios de los pobres*; and also for him to repudiate false, and potentially heretical or schismatic, interpretations of those words.

Many other Catholics, in arguing about this or that formula of the Second Vatican Council, tend to ignore the *First* Vatican Council, which in 1870 declared 'the Roman Pontiff' – subject to certain conditions – to be 'endowed with that infallibility which, according to the will of the Redeemer, is vouchsafed to the Church when she desires to fix a doctrine of faith or morality'. Liberal and progressive Catholics tend to assume that the resolutions of Vatican I have somehow been superseded, implicitly rescinded, or qualified out of existence, by Vatican II (1962–65). Pope John Paul II makes no such assumptions. In the Encyclical *Redemptor Hominis*, at the very beginning of his Pontificate, he took care to quote Vatican I, as well as Vatican II, when he touched, rather enigmatically, on the subject of 'infallibility'. Since then, John Paul II has conducted what is in essence a Vatican I Pontificate, while making copious and adroit use of the style and formulae of Vatican II. Thus John Paul II, like Vatican II, is all in favour of 'ecumenism'; but he also makes it clear that the Church unity which he favours is to be 'around the Successor of Peter: a Successor of Peter who is also the successor of Pius IX, never repudiating Vatican I. 'Consensus', too, the present Pope favours, and 'dialogue', just like Vatican II; except that now, when bishops meet, it is the Pope who registers the true meaning of their dialogue, and issues the document which embodies what he says is their consensus. It is all rather Orwellian, and it seems fitting that the Pontificate of John Paul II should have included the year 1984. But the Orwellisms are dictated by the necessities of the situation, which require the re-edification of one kind of Church, behind the façade of another. The central meaning of this Pontificate is to restore papal authority seen as badly damaged by the effects of the Second Vatican Council. That restoration is no easy task; especially as it must perforce be conducted in terms of the very principles which did the damage.

The Pope's concept of his own authority is simply not compatible with the versions of liberation theology, and of *el Dios de los pobres*, which are fervently embraced by those Catholics who, in Nicaragua, are 'with the process' of the Revolution. On the other hand, it was natural for a pope, bent on restoring authority within the Church, to come to the support of an Archbishop whose own more limited authority was being challenged and subverted in Nicaragua. What was being challenged and subverted was not just the authority of Miguel Obando y Bravo, but the very concept of hierarchy, the whole structure of which the Pope himself is the apex.

And the challenge was – and is – not a petty, parochial or peripheral one. It is true that Nicaragua is a small and poor country. But the very fact that it is small and poor is a source of strength for it in the great debate within the Catholic Church. Tiny Nicaragua, standing up to the greatest power on earth, David against Goliath, evokes the admiration of millions of people throughout Latin America; and Latin America is where nearly half the world's Catholics live now, and where more than half the world's Catholics will be living by the end of the century. (And end of the millennium; not irrelevant, for the present Pope is very conscious of the approach of the Church's second millennial year, over which he personally hopes to preside.)

And as for poverty, many Latin Americans wonder why a Church committed to a preferential option for the poor should be severe on the Government of Nicaragua, simply because it contains priests who are committed to *el Dios de los pobres*, while almost all other Latin American countries are blatantly committed to *el Dios de los ricos*.

So – contrary to mundane appearances – this formidable Pope, in taking on Sandinista Nicaragua, was taking on an adversary no less formidable than himself: an adversary representing forces which may possibly defeat the entire purpose of his Pontificate and leave papal authority in ruins throughout Latin America – and so weakened throughout the rest of the world – before the end of the millennium, whether Karol Wojtila lives to see that ecclesial climacteric or not.

The mere existence of that tremendous latent challenge goes a long way to explain why the Pope himself engaged in a confrontation when he visited Nicaragua in March 1983. But it is also necessary to take account of certain preceding chronology:

October 1978: Karol Wojtila becomes Pope John Paul II.

January 1979: Second Conference of Latin American Bishops at Puebla de los Angeles in Mexico.

July 1979: Managua falls to the Nicaraguan Revolutionary forces. Inauguration of the Sandinista regime.

Puebla was the first major challenge in the new Pontificate. The previous Conference of Latin American Bishops at Medellin, in Columbia, had seen some notable victories for *el Dios de los pobres*. Some of its formulations have the marks of Latin American liberation theology. Medellin endorsed 'the clear perception that in man everything is mediated politically'. 'In our evaluation of popular religion,' declared the Medellin bishops, 'we may not take as our frame of reference the westernized cultural interpretation of the middle and upper classes; instead, we must judge its meaning in the context of the subcultures of the rural and marginal urban groups'.

For liberation theologians, Medellin marked a notable advance; some hailed it as 'the new Pentecost'. It followed that, for conservatives, Medellin was a disaster. As Paul Johnson writes, in his admiring *Pope John Paul ii and the Catholic Restoration*: 'The turning point, at which the ultra-radicals captured a section of the episcopate and first acquired a major voice in policy was . . . the Conference of Latin American Bishops held in Medellin in that fatal year 1968, the high tide of 1960s illusion.'

Pope Paul vi had been present at Medellin, without appearing to make much impact there. John Paul ii went to Puebla, where he showed a mixture of firmness and ambiguity, which has proved to be characteristic of his Pontificate. His aim was to reassert the *Magisterium*: the authority and discipline of the Universal Church, under the Successor of Peter. Medellin had seemed at times perilously close to launching a separate Latin American Church. But in reasserting papal authority, the new Pope had to take account of Medellin, as an accomplished fact, which the Latin American bishops were not about to reverse. So he handled Medellin, at Puebla, much as he has handled Vatican ii; he took over the style, while seeking to infuse into it a different spirit, tending towards more conservative interpretations. It is a subtle strategy, and works well in Rome; whether it can be made to work in Latin America is another matter. The partisans of *el Dios de los pobres* were not displeased with Puebla, which gave them that famous 'preferential option for the poor'. 'Medellin and Puebla' are commonly cited together, by radicals, with shared implied approval. The radicals also took favourable note of some of the Pope's Medellin-style language during his Mexican visit: his calls for 'bold transformations' and 'daring innovations to overcome the grave injustices of the past'.

On the whole, the Pope's Mexican visit of 1978 probably gave a lot more aid and comfort than he intended, to radical Catholics in Latin America. His biographer, Mary Craig, ends her chapter on that visit with the words: 'The Church in Latin America had received a shot in the arm and renewed hope was in the air.'

It certainly was. A little more than six months after Puebla, on 19 July 1979, Managua fell to the Sandinistas. 'Bold transformations' and 'daring innovations' were indeed under way. The Pope must later have wondered whether his own language in Mexico – his 'shot in the arm' – had helped 'the process' in Nicaragua.

Certainly, the radical currents in the Church, set in motion by Vatican ii, and swelled at Medellin, contributed to the Nicaraguan process. And the result of the process was something unique in history: a revolutionary government including four Catholic priests, having widespread Catholic support, and regarded by a significant section of the Catholic Church as an earthly manifestation of the will of the God of the poor. For these believers, the process is to culminate in *el Reino de Dios*: the Kingdom of God. For them, nothing less than that is what is at stake in Nicaragua.

In Sandinista Nicaragua – that is, among Sandinistas in Nicaragua – those words, 'the Kingdom of God', crop up, in speech and in print, with a frequency disquieting to the secular visitor; and to some religious visitors as well. What is most striking is the *casual* way in which the words are used. People refer to the coming Kingdom of God as if they were waiting for a bus.

I think it was that casualness that first brought home to me how serious these people are. You can actually feel around you, in Nicaragua, something going on that you know can't be switched off, either from Washington or from Rome: that most intractable thing, a new kind of Faith. And the Faith in question is not confined to those Sandinistas who are specifically identified as religious. The powerful *comandante* and Minister of the Interior, Tomas Borge – widely regarded as the most formidable Marxist in the Sandinista Directorate and in the Government – speaks of the Earthly Paradise and of Hell and Antichrist and of 'the integration of liberating Christianity with the Revolution'. Daniel Ortega, now President of Nicaragua, announcing to a large crowd in Managua his nomination of the Jesuit, Fernando Cardenal, as Minister for Education, gave that integrationist concept a simpler form in the slogan: '*Pueblo de Sandino! Pueblo de Cristo!*'

And the cult of the Revolutionary dead, which is such a conspicuous part of *Sandinismo*, is powerfully expressive of the same linkage. These dead are invariably referred to in countless official statements and inscriptions as *héroes y martires*: not merely national heroes but also martyrs, witnesses, through their death, to their faith in the God of the poor.

This 'synthesis of Christian vocation and revolutionary conscience' – as the F.S.L.N. has called it – has become a subject of deep concern to the Holy See. It seems to be widely supposed that what worries the Holy See about Nicaragua is the infiltration of Marxism into the Catholic Church. But I think that is Washington's worry rather than Rome's. The present Pope has had ample reason to take the measure of Marxism, and there can be little in his experience that could lead him to see Marxism in itself – as distinct from Soviet material power – as a particularly dangerous adversary. As it happened, the Pope was in Poland, for his triumphal visit, in that summer of 1979 in June, just as the Sandinistas in Nicaragua were sweeping towards their final victory.

The huge and loving crowds that came out for the Pope in Poland, welcomed him in the name of Faith and Fatherland. That potent combination had been able to set at defiance all the efforts of successive Polish governments, backed by Soviet power, to make Marxists out of the Polish people, or even any significant part of the Polish youth growing up under Marxist rule.

In Poland, Faith and Fatherland have been aligned for centuries, and still are. In Latin America, they have not been, up to now, but in *Sandinismo*, they are. That is the profound originality of *Sandinismo*, and the source of much of its power. (There is certainly also a Marxist component in *Sandinismo*, but it is in my opinion subordinate to the nationalist component, and to a great extent a vehicle for the expression of that. I shall come back to this.)

No one knows better than John Paul II the power that lies in the conjuncture of Faith and Fatherland. All the more reason therefore to view with alarm the form that the conjuncture has taken in Managua. For the Sandinistas, unlike the Poles, have not been content to take their faith on trust from Rome, but have been issuing their own definitions and interpretations, through their own trusted theologians, much as happened in the Reformation lands in the sixteenth century. And as Martin Luther found his princes, so the liberation theologians of Latin America have found *their* princes, in the nine *comandantes* of the *Frente Sandinista de Liberacion National*; with, no doubt, other princes to come, in other parts of Latin America.

Putting the thing another way, and invoking the memory of another Reformer, Managua is a potential Geneva for Latin America.

But the comparisons are only valid in so far as we remember that the original reformers were not setting out to form new churches, but to reform the Universal Church. Similarly, the liberation theologians and Christian Sandinistas are not at present setting out to found a new Church or churches in Latin America but to make over the Universal Church in the image of the God of the poor.

Whether the project is to lead to a breakaway Church or churches, or alternatively to a reform of the Universal Church, according to the prescriptions of Latin American liberation theologians, it must look about equally abhorrent from the point of view of a Pope bent on restoring and consolidating papal authority.

Nor can the Pope's forebodings have been in any way allayed by the flood of liberation theology that began to flow from the presses of Managua in the immediate aftermath of the Sandinista Revolution. I have one such publication before me as I write. It is called '*Cristianos Revolucionarios*'. It is one of a series of 'popular pamphlets', *folletos populares*, published by the *Instituto Historico Centroamericano* of Managua, who are also the publishers of the monthly review *Envío*, which I mentioned earlier.

'*Christianos Revolucionarios*' embodies the results of a seminar on 'Christian Faith and Sandinista Revolution' held at the *Universidad Centroamericana de Managua* in September 1979, when the Sandinista regime was just two months old. The cover shows a young man with a beret, wearing a crucifix around his neck, and carrying an automatic rifle in his left hand and Molotov cocktail in his right. But the cover seems likely to have been less disturbing, to Vatican circles, than some of the contents of the pamphlet (contents which incidentally are much more academic and subtle than the garish cover of the *folleto popular* seems to promise). One section of the pamphlet is boldly entitled: 'Jesus Christ is not enough for us'. *No nos basta Jesucristo*. The section argues that, as well as the Gospel, revolutionary practice is needed and also 'a theory' – which, while not explicitly named, is clearly some form of Marxism. The pamphlet goes on with some brilliance to explain the double position of the revolutionary Christians, within the revolution, and within the Church. They don't want to divide *either* the revolution *or* the Church, but to be an integral part of both. Far from seeking to create 'a parallel Church' (*una Iglesia paralela*) as their enemies claim, all the revolutionary Christians demand is 'a space' (*un espacio*). What do they want the space for? They want the space in order to 'confess [in it] explicitly how we belong [*nuestra pertinencia*] to the only Church of Christ [*la unica Iglesia de Cristo*]'. It is to be 'a space in which the popular classes would be able to appropriate [*apropiarse de*] the religious symbols, [and] in which this historical subject which was the people [*que era el pueblo*] will be able, as a people, to read the Bible and, reflecting on reality, to make theology (*hacer teologia*)'.

It is against a background of a spate of publications of that kind, that the reactions of the Nicaraguan Hierarchy, and of the Vatican, to the initial friendly overtures of the Sandinista Government have to be understood. In October of 1980, the National Directorate of the F.S.L.N. issued its communique on religion. This was certainly intended to be a conciliatory document; as I mentioned earlier, it praised Obando personally. The Sandinistas sincerely pride themselves on their magnanimous and positive approach to religion, and on having altogether abandoned that doctrinaire hostility to all religion, which had hitherto been common to all revolutions claiming any degree of Marxist inspiration. The key paragraph of the Sandinista communique ran:

We do not encourage nor [*sic*] provoke activities to divide the churches. Religion is the exclusive business of Christians and it does not concern political organizations. If there is division, the churches ought to look for the causes within themselves and not attribute responsibility to supposedly evil outside influences. Yes, we are frank in saying that we would look favourably upon a Church that, without prejudice, with maturity and responsibility, worked in the common effort to develop more and more avenues for dialogue and participation that our revolutionary process has opened.

What the Sandinistas had failed to realize was that their friendly overtures would be far more frightening to many bishops – including those of Managua and of Rome – than the normal degree of doctrinaire hostility to be expected from a purely Marxist government. With proper Marxists, churchmen knew where they stood: Marxists in one sphere, the Church in quite a different one: a tidy and tenable state of affairs. This new stuff was quite different. Not that liberation theology in itself was all that new; by 1979, liberation theology had been around for a little over a decade, since its beginnings in Germany in 1967. What was new in Nicaragua – and most alarmingly new – was that for the first time liberation theology had the *backing of a State*: a most undesirable precedent, for Latin America in particular.

The Vatican was, as usual, slow to react. But Archbishop Obando was prompt. His opposition to the Sandinista regime began as soon as those *folletos populares* started to promote liberation theology with official approval. That F.S.L.N. communique altogether failed to mollify him. As he must have seen it, those 'avenues of dialogue' which the F.S.L.N. was calling for could only lead into that ominous *espacio* demanded by the liberation theologians. As he saw the matter, not merely was the temporal sphere encroaching upon the spiritual, but a revolutionary state was making use of a Fifth Column within the Church in order to subvert the Hierarchy, and promote schism and heresy.

From these sources, and not from any nostalgia for the old social order, or need to do Washington's bidding, sprang the Archbishop's implacable hostility to 'the process'. But of course that hostility made the Archbishop a natural ally both of those who *were* nostalgic for the old social order, and of President Reagan, with whose inauguration the opening of the Archbishop's attacks on the Sandinista regime approximately coincided. And the Archbishop's complaints helped the President with the demonization of Sandinista Nicaragua. Thus the President, in claiming that the Church was persecuted in Nicaragua, could clinch that claim by quoting the Archbishop. To the general public, 'religious persecution' conjures up visions of churches being closed down by force, and of systematic physical ill treatment of priests and nuns. Nothing of the kind has been going on in Nicaragua. Obando, indeed, genuinely believes that the Church is being persecuted there. What he has in mind, when he talks about persecution, is primarily State encouragement to liberation theologians, and secondarily denial of access to the media, for himself and his colleagues, through government censorship, and thirdly a certain amount of rough barracking at times in the past by left-wing parishioners: the so-called *turbas divinas*. Those are the realities on which the charge is based. But the picture which the word 'persecution' brings to mind is different, and more frightening.

The battle between the Archbishop and the Sandinista Government was well and truly locked when Pope John Paul II came to Nicaragua, on 4 March 1983, to be welcomed by both sides.

In Managua last April, my wife and I watched the Pope's visit, on video, just as it had been broadcast at the time, for many hours, live on Nicaraguan television. We watched the video in the house of a woman whom I shall call Victoria. Victoria is a believing and practising Catholic and she is also 'with the process'. The Pope's visit had been a painful and distressing experience for her – and for many others like her – and she cannot have enjoyed the replay. On the other hand, she wanted us to see how it had been. Also, our presence there that evening was a distraction for her, at a time of suffering and anxiety. Her seventeen-year-old son, who had volunteered for his *Servicio Militar Patriotico*, had left the previous day for one of the 'war zones', penetrated by the *contras*. She told us how his ten-year-old brother had dressed up that day in his clown's outfit, in an effort to cheer them all up. As it happened, within a few days of our visit, Victoria had to call on another mother whose son, a class-mate of Victoria's son, had just been killed by *contras*. That boy's parents were *not* 'with the process', and the boy had not volunteered; he had been conscripted. In the circumstances, Victoria had wondered whether her condolences would be accepted. But they were.

Victoria is a member – in reality, a kind of leader – of one of the *comunidades de base* (basic Christian communities) in one of the poor *barrios* of Managua. The *comunidades* were set up under the impetus of Vatican II and Medellin, in an effort to remedy the shortage of parish clergy, chronic in Latin America. Most, though not all, of the *comunidades* appear by now to have become vehicles of liberation theology, and the *comunidades* generally are regarded with suspicion by conservatives in the Church. The *comunidades* were anxious to play their full part in the great event of the Pope's visit. And Victoria's *comunidad* had spent weeks preparing a big banner which they carried out to Sandino Airport, Managua, on the big day, 4 March 1983.

In any case there we were, in Victoria's living room, watching the Pope's visit, a little more than three years after the event.

There is the Pope's plane on the tarmac, and a long wait. My note reads: 'Plane pregnant with Pope'.

The Pope gets out and then, in accordance with established custom, kisses the ground of Nicaragua, which is hot. Rather neatly, the commentator says that the Pope is kissing the ground *de Nicaragua libre*. But that is the commentator, not the Pope.

The nine *comandantes de la revolución*, who make up the National Directorate of the *Frente Sandinista* are all there. Victoria's *comunidad*'s banner is there. It is a good big banner and it reads: BIENVENIDO JUAN PABLO EN LA TIERRA DE SANDINO.

There were other Sandinista slogans: 'Welcome to free Nicaragua, thanks to God and the Revolution'; 'Between Christianity and revolution, there is no contradiction'. And then there were what *Envío* was later to call 'more generic' slogans used by 'those Christians opposed to the process': 'I am happy the Pope is coming'; 'John Paul II, Nicaragua is waiting for you'.

The first to greet the Pope are the Papal Nuncio and a Foreign Office official. First sign that all is not well. Normally, the greeters should be the Archbishop of Managua (as head of the Nicaraguan Hierarchy), and the Foreign Minister, Miguel d'Escoto. Presumably the *Frente* objected to the Archbishop, because of his political role (as they see it). And the Pope must have objected to the Foreign Minister, since Miguel d'Escoto is a priest (of the Maryknoll Order), who has stayed on in the Government of Nicaragua, contrary to Church discipline. But both Obando and d'Escoto are around there, somewhere.

Now Daniel is welcoming the Pope on behalf of the three senior *comandantes* – Daniel Ortega, Co-ordinator of the National Directorate (and later elected President of Nicaragua). The press – except *La Prensa* – always calls him just Daniel, and so does everyone in Nicaragua who is 'with the process'. Daniel, with his spectacles and his mane of brown hair waving in the breeze, seems like a young, progressive headmaster anxious to make an impression on an extremely distinguished visitor. Too anxious, as it turns out.

I quote from my rough notes, made as I watched the Pope listen to Daniel:

'You are being received by a heroic people. . . . 50,000 dead – social and moral changes. . . .'

Pope looks as if he had toothache; holding jaw with left hand.

'American threat . . . worthy riposte to *intervención Norteamericana*.' *Barricada*-type speech goes on.

Pope's head bowed more and more on hand.
Daniel quotes from early (1912) letter of Nicaraguan Bishop to Yanks.
Pope folds arms on chest.
Long, long old letter. Daniel very boomy.
  'The soldiers killed . . .'

The reference here is to seventeen young soldiers killed by *contras* four days before the Pope's visit. The memory of these soldiers – all secondary school-boys – powerfully affected the ceremonies surrounding the Pope's visit. And that memory, and thoughts related to it, were also strongly present in Victoria's living room, while video made those scenes come alive again.

Daniel went on with his speech, getting a bit hoarse and wavery as if knowing that what he was saying wasn't going down too well. He spoke of the inalienable right to religious liberty, and then of Christians 'basing themselves on faith corresponding to the revolution'.

Pope back to holding jaw.

The Pope's response to Daniel's ill-judged discourse – even *Envío* says that it 'took longer than the time allotted' – seemed quite gracious, probably because most of it had been written beforehand. My notes read:

> 'Thanks God in land of lakes and volcanoes. . . . Noble people, rich in Christian traditions . . . sincere thanks to *junta*, [*sic*] and for its deference in coming to greet me. . . .'

This reference is significant, in that it seems to show that the Pope was indeed hoping – as the then Vatican Secretary of State, Cardinal Casaroli, is known to have hoped – that relations with the Sandinista regime might improve. The Pope, in thanking the *junta* – meaning the National Directorate of the nine *comandantes* – rather than the *Government* seems to have been making an important point. The Government included the four priests, who were *not* however members of the Directorate (or *junta*). The overture to the *junta*, ignoring the Government, seemed to imply that if the Sandinistas would drop the four priests – thus symbolizing a propensity to draw back from involvement in Church affairs – relations with the Vatican could be normalized. So the Pope seems to have been trying to mend some fences. But it didn't work out that way, not by any means.

In any case, even if he did mean to mend fences with the Sandinistas, he was not going to do so by publicly letting down the embattled Archbishop of Managua. He saluted his brother bishops, *hermanos obispos*, 'especially our beloved Miguel Obando'. Then a light, quick slap over the knuckles for Daniel, when, after sympathizing with 'those who suffer from the results of violence from whatever quarter it comes', the Pope condemned not only 'hatred' but also 'sterile accusations'.

Then the Government had to be greeted. This was the first really tricky bit, since the Government included those four priests. Still, governments are governments whatever they may contain, and the Pope has always greeted governments on his tours. Victoria told us that a way had been found round the difficulty, or so it was thought. The Pope was to pass along the line of Government members, acknowledging the Government's collective existence by some kind of comprehensive salutation, without having to greet each individual member. It was a sensible idea, but this was one of those days where everything that could go wrong, did. One member of the Government, apparently not having grasped the nature of the problem, stepped forward to greet the Pope. And then the fat was in the fire.

The next thing on that screen is the spectacle of the Minister for Culture, Father Ernesto Cardenal – a frail person with long white hair and a white beard – taking off his black beret and kneeling before the Pope, for a blessing. And the Pope, instead of blessing, wags a finger of admonition, saying sternly, 'You must regularize (*arreglar*) your situation with the Vatican.'

'Ernesto cried,' said Victoria, 'and everybody came over to comfort him.'

Ernesto Cardenal is something more important, in the eyes of many Nicaraguans, than either a minister or even a priest. He is a poet – one of the two most distinguished living Nicaraguan poets – in a land where poets are esteemed and appreciated, to an extent, I think, unknown in any other part of the modern world. It happens that the other leading Nicaraguan poet – Pablo Antonio Cuadra, director general of *La Prensa* – is one of the bitterest enemies of the Sandinista regime. He and Ernesto – who are cousins – were once also close friends, now separated by politics. 'He was like a son to me,' Cuadra told me. Clearly affection – though not the possibility of civil conversation – had managed to survive even the intense heat of antagonistic Nicaraguan politics.

When the Pope snubbed Ernesto, many Nicaraguans – all those who were 'with the process' and probably quite a few others as well – felt themselves snubbed, in the person of this admired and beloved Nicaraguan. Ernesto himself, though hurt, did not take the snub so heavily, or lose his sense of humour. He tells of how stricken his mother had been by the Pope's attitude. 'I thought he would treat you like a father,' she said. 'But he *did* treat me like a father,' said Ernesto. 'He just didn't treat me like a *mother*.'

Ernesto might feel no rancour, but others did, on his behalf. From the moment of the Pope's wagging finger, over Ernesto's uplifted face, the visit went sour, for many of those who – like Victoria – had worked hard to prepare a welcome for the Pope.

Victoria – like others we met – was puzzled, as well as distressed, by that rebuke. It seemed disproportionate, gratuitous, petty; a needless piece of humiliation, for the enforcement of some trifling and archaic ecclesiastical regulation. That is pretty much how I saw it myself, while I was watching that painful scene on video. But later, after I had looked more closely at what is at stake in Nicaragua for the Church – as the Pope conceives the Church – I felt rather differently about it. The Sandinista fusion of religion and politics – not only religion and Marxism, but also *religion and nationalism*, which is much more dangerous – puts at risk, throughout the whole vast spiritual battleground of Latin America, the Pope's mission to restore the *Magisterium*, the teaching authority of the papacy. Ernesto is a committed and enthusiastic agent of the Sandinista fusion. So when Ernesto knelt before the Pope, the Pope had to see, not just an estimable if misguided human being, but an insidious, incarnate threat to the Universal Church, and to the Pope's own mission. And not just a threat, but a trap as well. If the Pope gave Ernesto the blessing Ernesto was asking – guilelessly as it seemed, but perhaps with some guile in the background somewhere – would the Pope not be seen as blessing the Sandinista fusion itself? And if so, would he not – the Pope – be conniving at the sabotage of his own great mission, and of the Church entrusted to him?

Considering all that accumulated thunder in the air, I am surprised, in retrospect, at how lightly Ernesto got off. But that was certainly not the general impression at the time.

Thinking over that scene now, in terms of the forces represented by the protagonists, it is not Ernesto I am sorry for. It is the Pope. But I shall come back to that.

After that unpromising start, the Pope went on to León, a former capital of Nicaragua, for a purely religious ceremony, the Celebration of the Word. . . . There was a large crowd. 'Nobody did anything that day,' said Victoria glumly, looking at the scene. She also alluded to the cost of the visit. As soon as they realized that the visit was going to do them more harm than good, the Sandinistas, quite naturally, began to regret their investment in preparing to receive the Pope. Quite a large investment for impoverished Nicaragua: 'Approximately $3 million and two months supply of gasoline . . . used in bringing the people to Managua,' according to *Envío*.

Then the Pope went back to Managua and to the disastrous and chaotic last phase of his eleven-hour visit to Nicaragua. This was the Mass celebrated in Managua's main square, the 19th July Plaza. The crowd, which filled the plaza to overflowing, is said to have been the largest ever assembled in the history of Nicaragua: between 600,000 and 700,000 persons, or about one fourth of Nicaragua's total population. But not all of these, by this time, were well disposed to the Pope. The incident with Ernesto in the morning had set up a ferment.

The day had been terribly hot, even for tropical Nicaragua: 40°C (104°F). Tempers were frayed and distinct factions – Sandinistas and Obandists – made themselves heard – 'The Catholic chorus', according to *Envío* 'wanted only traditional religious songs to go out through the loudspeakers. But those controlling the audio, from the Sandinista system, were playing songs from the Nicaraguan Campesino Mass.'

This was already a bit rough, from the Pope's point of view. His very ears, during his own Pontifical Mass, were being assailed by the – to him – revolting strains of Sandinista fusionism and the dubious hymnal of liberation theology.

Then the Pope delivered his homily, and the whole thing came apart.

According to Victoria the text of the Pope's homily had been cleared with the Sandinista National Directorate. 'They thought it was all right when they read it,' she said, 'but when *he* read it aloud, it sounded quite different.'

I suppose that, on paper, the concepts of the homily – Church unity, the *Magisterium* and so on – may have looked abstract and abstruse, unlikely to arouse passion, or much interest. But when the Pope actually delivered this part of his homily, with barbed and fiery eloquence, it became apparent that he personally was very angry indeed, and that his anger was directed against the Sandinista process, in its relation to the Church:

> Church unity is put into question when the powerful factors which build and maintain it – the one faith, the revealed Word, the sacraments, obedience to the bishops and the Pope, the sense of vocation and joint responsibility in Christ's work in the world – are brought up against earthly considerations, unacceptable ideological commitments, temporal options, or concepts of the Church which are contrary to the true one.

'The word "true"', notes the *Envío* writer ruefully, 'was said in a tone of surprising firmness and with a sharp intonation.'

(The *Envío* writer also noted, sardonically, that the Pope, in the course of this homily, mentioned 'bishops' fourteen times and 'peace' only once.)

The Pope's tone – probably much more than what he said – sent up the temperature of the crowd. But it rose further – 'emotions boiled over', according to *Envío*, when the Pope called the *Iglesia popular* 'an absurd and dangerous project'. There were shouts of 'We want peace', '*Queremos la* paz!', 'People's power!', *Poder popular!*', 'They shall not pass!', '*No pasaran!*'. '*Silencio!*' shouted the Pope. '*He*'s not a Pope of the poor!' proclaimed a voice from the crowd. 'Look at his dress!' '*Silencio*', again. Then The Mothers took the stage, spreading further waves of emotion, which spilled over into the living room where we were watching the scene three years later. The Mothers are the members of Nicaragua's Association of Mothers of Heroes and Martyrs: that is, of sons who fell in the Revolution, at the hands of Somoza's National Guard, or in the current fighting at the hands of the *contras*. There are about fifty of these mothers – including some of the mothers of the recently killed seventeen – and these last were there, very near the altar and the Pope. 'The blood of our boys is crying out!' called one mother. 'We want a prayer for our Martyrs!' called another. The Pope, who was saying Mass, was unresponsive. Later another mother called out: 'We can offer you now only the sorrow. . . . The Reagan government. . . .' (her voice faded away). This particular interruption came at the actual moment of the Pope's Consecration of the Host, and was to give rise later to Vatican complaints about 'profanation of the Eucharist', during the Pope's visit to Nicaragua.

Victoria still, after three years, felt outraged by the Pope's refusal, as she saw it, to have the common decency to say a prayer for those dead boys, at the request of their recently bereaved mothers. I could understand and respect her feelings, but I also thought I could understand how the thing must have looked to the Pope. He must have felt, as in the case of Ernesto, that he was being set up. That association, heroes *and martyrs*, represented the very thing that was anathema to him in Nicaragua. The mere fact that he was asked for a prayer 'for our martyrs', made it impossible for him to say such a prayer, without tending to legitimize a cult which he regards as 'absurd and dangerous'. So he remained deaf to the entreaties of The Mothers, and there must be many, besides Victoria, who will never forgive him.

In any case, it was obviously a very angry – though controlled – Pope who took off from Sandino Airport that hot March evening. Whatever thoughts he may have entertained about mending some fences with the Sandinistas were banished, and would stay banished for years to come. Obando's harsh picture of what *Sandinismo* was like seemed abundantly vindicated. The Pope left to Obando the vestments he had worn during his Nicaraguan trip. And two years later the Pope made Obando a cardinal. All those feverish preparations the Sandinistas had made for the Pope's visit, and the money they had invested in it, had only helped (so it seemed) in the strengthening and promotion of their most implacable enemy.

That fourth of March, the day of the Pope's visit, is remembered in
Nicaragua as *el bochorno de Managua*. *Bochorno* is a beautifully appropriate word. The dictionary gives the English for it as: 'sultry weather. . . .
embarrassment'. The effects of the sultry embarrassment took a long time to
wear off: more than two years in fact. In this period, Miguel Obando was
riding high, and well into the political domain: legitimizing resistance to
military service, delegitimizing the regime, and then – as a new cardinal –
fraternizing with its enemies (as related earlier). He seemed to be daring the
Government to do something about him. The problem was that it didn't
seem possible to do anything about him, without appearing to persecute the
Church, and making the Pope into an open enemy. The minister responsible
for public order – Tomas Borge, senior *comandante* and Minister for the
Interior – publicly confessed that, though he could handle the other enemies
of the Revolution, he didn't know what to do about Obando's counter-
revolutionary activities: a most unusual confession for this powerful and
resourceful *comandante*, and exemplary Sandinista.

But there was one minister who thought he *did* know what to do about
Obando, and who acted on his thought. This was Miguel d'Escoto, Minister
for Foreign Affairs and Chancellor; and one of the three priests now in the
Government (the others being the brothers Ernesto and Fernando
Cardenal). Miguel d'Escoto was born in Hollywood, California, in 1933 and
educated in the United States, where he joined the Maryknoll Order. As
Foreign Minister, he has travelled enormously – seeming at times to be in
orbit – and much of the weight of Nicaragua's unique problems in foreign
affairs seems to be carried by the Vice President, the cool and politic Sergio
Ramirez (who is close to Daniel Ortega, and often consulted by him). It
would be easy, but wrong, to infer from that that Miguel d'Escoto is a bit of a
lightweight. Like each of his priestly colleagues, Miguel carries considerable
moral and intellectual, and even spiritual authority within the Sandinista
structures. *Comandantes* come and ask him questions about God; unlikely
as I know that will appear in Washington. Like Ernesto, Miguel has the gift
of inspiring affection as well as respect. When I asked a young Irishwoman,
in Managua, who knows Miguel well, what he was really like, she replied
simply: 'Miguel is a *dote*!' [a darling] But as well as being a dote, Miguel is
something of a prophet. Also he has a sense of theatre. He was not born in
Hollywood for nothing.

Through this combination of gifts, Miguel was able to find the way to lift
Sandinista spirits out of the uneasy leaden aftermath of *el bochorno*, and
also the way to wage spiritual war against Miguel Obando. The way was
through a form of sacred drama, which Miguel d'Escoto called *la*

insurrección evangélica. The 'evangelical insurrection' was carried out in two parts: the *ayuno*, or fast, and the *Viacrucis*, the Way of the Cross.

The *insurrección evangélica* began with the Foreign Minister's perception that – in his own words – 'The Government as a government cannot find an answer to a theological war.' It was the task of the Christian Sandinistas, specifically, to man that trench: 'We Christians have our own special arms which we must use: prayer, fasting, processions with hymns, vigils. . . .'

The first phase of the *insurrección* was the fast for peace, *el ayuno por la paz*. Here, of course, Miguel d'Escoto was consciously following in the footsteps of Gandhi and Martin Luther King. But he was following in his own way, and also breaking some new ground. His fast was unique in that it was carried out *by a member of a government*, with the support of his colleagues. The Government knew of his undertaking in advance, and it had their approval, informally. Daniel Ortega used to drop in to see him, during his fast. The idea of a government, through one of its ministers, using a fast as a religious-cum-political weapon is, I believe, wholly unprecedented.

The fast was also different from the Gandhi and King fasts, in that it was not a pacifist fast, although Miguel d'Escoto uses a lot of apparently pacifist language. His commitment to non-violence is personal and teleological, and does not exclude enthusiastic backing, in the present, for the Sandinista Army, the *Ejercito Sandinista*. In this respect, d'Escoto is less like Martin Luther King than he is like one of Cromwell's preachers; and indeed there seems to be something more Cromwellian than Catholic about *Sandinismo* generally (as I think John Paul II would agree). Teofilo Cabestrero, who has written a history of the d'Escoto fast (*Un Grito a Dios y al Mundo*, A Cry to God and the World) tells of a message from the fasting priest to the army, on the twelfth day of the fast. The message was conveyed to the army by Father César Jérez, S.J., head of the University at Managua, and d'Escoto's strongest supporter in the *insurrección evangélica*:

> At a solemn *acto de ascensos* [passing-out parade] of the *Ejercito Sandinista*, Father César Jérez read out to the soldiers a message from Father d'Escoto on which he praised their heroism and spoke to them of Christ and of [His] wish for [*voluntad de*] non-violent, prophetic methods, in order to bring about the coming of the Kingdom of God; he tells them that he is opening a new trench for peace with these means, fasting and prayer.

The idea of an encomium on non-violence being officially read out in the course of a military ceremony may seem odd to us, but it apparently doesn't seem odd to any of them: priests, soldiers or politicians. It is all part of *Sandinismo*. The *insurrección* itself did sometimes seem odd, even to Sandinistas, but it turned out to be oddly effective.

The *ayuno* began in the first week of July and d'Escoto kept it up for thirty days; others joined in for part of that time. D'Escoto was fasting, and keeping open house, and talking away, in a parish house in one of Managua's *barrios*. As Cabestrero describes it:

> Here come, on visits of solidarity to Father Miguel, young students, disabled people, villagers from Niguinohomo [Sandino's birthplace], peasants from Rio San Juan, Nicaraguan poets who give a night-time recital, combatants from nine Battalions of Irregular Warfare [*Batallones de Lucha Irregular*] who embrace Father d'Escoto, play the *Misa Campesina* and are applauded by the assembly.

And so on. It was an on-going show as well as a fast. And there were side-shows as well: a nocturnal panel on 'Prophetism' in Managua; a singing rosary at dawn in Esteli; processions and vigils all over Nicaragua, all part of the *insurrección evangélica*.

And d'Escoto himself continued to prophesy; the frontispiece to Cabestrero's book shows the fasting priest-Minister clutching a microphone in his right hand. This was early in the fast – and d'Escoto had been quite fat before he started – but his bearded face has already a set, hollow look and his sunken eyes are gleaming behind his horn-rimmed spectacles. He seems to be holding on to that mike as if it were some kind of lifeline; if he cannot eat, at least he can talk. He talks well, spontaneously, urgently, pungently; and – during the fast – a little feverishly. He talked to Cabestrero about the spiritual significance of Ronald Reagan's mendacity.

He had been listening to a speech of Reagan's, as he fasted, and it had hit him hard. The President has lied, he said 'with such a mastery, with such a great capacity for lying, for saying what is not so, and for saying it with such serenity and such conviction, that I, without becoming angry, felt an enormous sadness. And there came about a change in my vision of the problem that confronts us. . . . I thought, there is more in this than just a pathological obsession. . . . And one day, alone in my room, I thought that this incredible capacity for lying reveals something like a case of diabolical possession.'

But the primary target of the *insurrección* was not Reagan: it was Obando. Obando was generally not named, in this first phase of the *insurrección* – the *ayuno* – but the hierarchy was frequently either named or otherwise evoked. Right at the beginning, at the concelebrated Mass of twenty priests, which was the solemn opening of the *ayuno por la paz*, on 7 July 1985, one of the concelebrants, Monseñor Arias Caldera, said: 'May they depart from our sky, the crows who fly with the eagle of the North.' No one had to be told who the crows were, or the eagle. Later, d'Escoto, thinking aloud, was more specific:

> Then I saw the Church all bloody, guilty by omission and even more guilty than Reagan, because of the responsibility of its mission. . . . These are terribly sad things, like the conspiracy of the synagogue with the Empire and the forces of evil in order to condemn Jesus, things on which I have meditated much on retreat [en retiro].

Obando must have thought it was a funny kind of retreat.

The *ayuno* ended at the beginning of August 1985, after thirty days. D'Escoto had said he would keep it up until he was convinced that his spark – *chispa* – had got a fire going. By August, he thought – with reason – that there was a fire. The *ayuno* had caught the imagination of many Christians in many parts of the world, and especially in Latin America. Messages of 'prophetic solidarity' poured in from almost every country in Latin America and from many other countries. Thirty-five bishops (not all of them Catholic bishops) signified their support for the *ayuno*.

In Lent of 1986, Miguel d'Escoto, having recuperated his strength after his fast, started out on the second phase of the evangelical insurrection: *el Viacrucis por la paz*, the Way of the Cross. The *Viacrucis*, with its stations of the cross, is a traditional expression of Nicaraguan popular piety. D'Escoto intended his *Viacrucis* to be just that, but also to be an expression of support for the *Sandinista* position on peace, and so of insurrection against the position of the Nicaraguan hierarchy.

From a conservative point of view, of course, the d'Escoto *Viacrucis* represented an attempt to hijack a traditional devotion for political purposes. *La Prensa* – which of course is on the Cardinal's side – subjected d'Escoto's *Viacrucis*, throughout its progress, to a running fire of ridicule. I have sometimes wondered why the censors let that stuff through. *La Prensa* is subject to strict governmental pre-censorship. If people on *La Prensa* were able to mock that *Viacrucis*, it is because the censors decided to let them do so. This might be attributed to divided counsels within the Government, but I doubt whether that is the explanation. The Ministry of the Interior is responsible for censorship. The responsible Minister is *comandante* Tomas Borge. Borge is a subtle person, and if he let that mockery get by, it must be that he thought it would do the cause of the mockers more harm than good. And indeed mockery is not a particularly appropriate way to discredit a modern simulation of the *Viacrucis*, in the eyes of Christians. For Christians have to recall that mockery entered largely into the intentions of those who organized the *real Viacrucis*.

The traditional Nicaraguan *Viacrucis* is a local affair. D'Escoto's was larger and longer – '*un gran Viacrucis*' – setting out from Jalapa on the Honduran border on the first Friday in Lent, 14 February 1986, and reaching Managua, 300 kilometres away, on 28 February: two weeks of hot, dusty walking. Few of the pilgrims went all the way – perhaps no more than forty, including d'Escoto. Many more – from 5000 to 12,000, as reported – went along for a single stage of around 20 kilometres. Pilgrims stayed in peasant houses; peasants came out with plants and flowers as well as holy images. Not all that many peasants, but some peasants, for every stage. The pilgrims were accompanied by a car with a public address system which transmitted hymns and political speeches, alternately. Mothers, young men and children appeared, carrying crosses.

The parish clergy is sparse in rural Nicaragua, and it was divided on the *Viacrucis*. In several centres, the church doors were shut against the pilgrims, and in one the church door carried a placard reading: 'Don't make politics out of the *Viacrucis*!' But in other places, the parish priest welcomed the pilgrims, blessed them and walked with them.

The high point of the journey was in Esteli where, on 22 February, the Bishop, Monseñor Rubén López Ardón, personally ordered the Cathedral – which had previously been kept closed – to be opened to the pilgrims, embraced and blessed d'Escoto before about 20,000 people, himself asked for d'Escoto's blessing and said a prayer for peace. He recognized (according to the *Viacrucis Boletin*, No. 15) 'that the motives of this pilgrimage are of authentic Christian faith in the pursuit of peace and life'. The Bishop's statement was highly significant because it showed that the Nicaraguan hierarchy is no longer united behind the Cardinal, whose detestation of everything d'Escoto stands for is notorious. In fact the advent of d'Escoto's *Viacrucis* had obliged the Bishop of Esteli – whose northern diocese has suffered more than most from the depredations of the *contras* – to stand up and be counted. And he had – apparently after initial hesitation – chosen to be counted on the side of the pilgrims and not that of the Cardinal. It was the most notable victory to date of the *insurrección evangélica*.

Monseñor López Ardón also expressed the hope, at Esteli, that 'the procession towards Managua' should be 'orientated with maturity', meaning that he was asking d'Escoto to lay off the Cardinal. But there was no chance that the leader of the *Viacrucis* would do that. The whole enterprise was directed against the Cardinal's betrayal – as d'Escoto saw it – of both Faith and Fatherland. D'Escoto was now referring to Obando by name: 'It is intolerable,' said d'Escoto at Condega.

... that the medals of honour which the Government of the United States has offered to Cardinal Obando in order to make a political tool out of him [*para instrumentalizarlo politicamente*] should be accepted. If the attitudes of certain bishops don't change, we Christians will one day find ourselves in the painful position of asking ourselves: 'Can we celebrate the Eucharist in communion with those who use their religious influence against our people?

These words – with their strong hint of impending schism – were stuff to make even liberation theologians hold their breath. D'Escoto is their prophet, and they love him, but he frightens them. But then they also feel that that's what a prophet is *for*.

At Managua, in the Cardinal's own Archdiocese, on the last day of the *Viacrucis*, d'Escoto changed his tone, though not really his tune. Addressing a large crowd in front of the gaunt shell of Managua's Cathedral (ruined in the 1972 earthquake) Father d'Escoto held out his arms and entreated 'Brother Michael', *Hermano Miguel*, to come and join the *Viacrucis*. To no one's surprise, *Hermano Miguel* did not respond.

It is hard to gauge the impact of such a strange event as the *insurrección evangélica*. D'Escoto himself refuses to do so; he leaves all that to God, he says. Within Nicaragua, the *insurrección* never amounted to a mass movement. The maximum turn-out was that 20,000 at Esteli – a drop in the ocean compared with the 700,000 or so who came out to see the Pope in Managua. Yet the size of the turn-out – the 'gate' – is not necessarily what counts most. The intensity of the commitment behind the presence may count more. And d'Escoto's movement was one of high intensity. The psychic force of the storm it produced was enough to crack, at Esteli, the hitherto monolithic façade of the Nicaraguan hierarchy. And note had to be taken of that by all, both in Latin America and in Rome, who were concerned over the balance between the forces represented by the slogan '*un solo Dios*', and those represented by the slogan '*el Dios de los pobres*'. *El bochorno* had been the round of *un solo Dios*. The *insurrección* round went to *el Dios de los pobres*.

Whether by coincidence or not, the succeeding months have witnessed a certain relaxation of the ecclesiastical pressures against the Sandinistas, both from the Nicaraguan Hierarchy and from Rome. As mentioned earlier, the Nicaraguan Hierarchy, in its April Letter on the Eucharist, appeared to distance itself from the *contras*, whom Obando had previously appeared to back. A very senior Sandinista with whom I discussed this shift had a down-to-earth explanation of it, unconnected with the impact of the *insurrección*. (This particular Sandinista is of a cool, pragmatic temperament, and so not a natural d'Escoto fan.) 'The bishops', he said, 'were up for the *contras*, as long as they thought the *contras* might be going to win. But now that the *contras* don't look as if they could ever win, the Bishops draw aside a bit.'

I suspect that the two explanations – *insurrección* and *contra* failure – may not be incompatible or unconnected. The Sandinistas look a tougher nut to crack now than they did a few years back. And *one* of the things that makes them hard to destroy is the spiritual fire-power concentrated against the theological enemies of *Sandinismo*, by Miguel d'Escoto and his *compañeros*, out of 'the new trench for peace'.

During 1986, too, Rome greatly relaxed its pressure on 'liberation theology' – the culture from which *Sandinismo* derives so much of its vital force. The 'Instruction on Christian Freedom and Liberation' issued by the Vatican in April 1986 was welcomed by perhaps the most eminent liberation theologian, Gustavo Gutierrez of Peru, as 'the end of an era'. And it does indeed signal the end of the open season on liberation theology which the Vatican had been conducting, especially since the Pope's visit to Nicaragua: the attempt to stamp out 'deviations and risks of deviation' conducted on the Pope's behalf by Cardinal Joseph Ratzinger, prefect of the Congregation for the Doctrine of the Faith. Through Ratzinger, John Paul II was addressing a magisterial '*Silencio!*' to the worshippers of *el Dios de los pobres* in Latin America. But it simply did not work. Those concerned just carried on as before – or worse, from the Pope's point of view, as in the case of Nicaragua's *insurrectión*. What the April Instruction does – without of course acknowledging the fact – is to register the failure of an effort to exercise papal authority. Although John Paul II is generally regarded as a particularly strong Pope, that Instruction is one of the weakest documents ever to reach the world under the authority of a Roman Pontiff. Decoded, the message that went out *urbi et orbi* in April was: 'As you won't listen to what I've been trying to tell you, now I'm going to tell you something different, which I hope you'll like a bit better.'

What both the Pope and the Nicaraguan Hierarchy have been finding out and acknowledging in their way is that *el Dios de los pobres* is what Edmund Burke found 'the nature of things' to be: 'a sturdy adversary'. I mean *el Dios de los pobres*, not as He might be defined, contained and sanitized in Rome, but as He exists in the minds and hearts of those who call upon His name, throughout Latin America. His power was felt in Esteli in February, and in Managua and in Rome in April.

I said earlier that when I looked back on that scene in which the Pope admonishes Ernesto, the one I feel sorry for is the Pope. The reason for this is that Ernesto and his friends are engaged among living realities – the cause of the poor, the defence of Nicaragua – whereas the Pope has dedicated his life to the resuscitation of an extinct abstraction: the *Magisterium*, the teaching authority of the Church, of which the supreme exponent is the Pope. Some people think that the Pope is succeeding in bringing back this authority; that is the meaning of the phrase 'the Catholic restoration' used by Paul Johnson and others. It is true that this Pope is far more popular than any Pope has been before. But popularity is not to be confused with authority. Catholics love this Pope, but when he solemnly tells them that they must behave in some way that they don't find convenient, they just don't take a blind bit of notice of him.

The critical test, by which the *Magisterium* has been seen to fail, in our time, is that of contraception. If there is one matter in which the Church's teaching, in the second half of the twentieth century, has been clear and firm, that is the matter of contraception.

Pope Paul vi laid down the law on that, for Catholics, in the Encyclical *Humanae Vitae*; Pope John Paul ii, in *Familiaris Consortio*, has corroborated and fortified the law laid down in *Humanae Vitae*. The message of the *Magisterium* is crystal clear: Catholics are *not* to use contraceptives. And Catholics have gone right on using contraceptives: not only in North America, but in Catholic countries like Ireland and Poland, where Catholic education is strong, and Church attendance very high. If the very poor, in the poorest regions, still don't use contraceptives, this is not because they are mindful of the teaching of *Humanae Vitae* and *Familiaris Consortio*, but because they *are* very poor, and therefore ignorant, and therefore do not yet understand about contraception.

Then John Paul ii brought the weight of the *Magisterium* to bear against the liberation theologians, but again the thing didn't work. The spring seems to be broken.

John Paul ii is getting to look more and more like an international Canute, magisterially perambulating all the strands of the world, before huge and admiring audiences, without the slightest effect on the tides.

The contemporary failure of the *Magisterium* seems to have far-reaching implications for Latin America. The revolutionary Christians fought for their *espacio*; the traditionalist counter-attack has failed, and the revolutionaries now seem to be secure in control of that *espacio*, where they have 'appropriated' the symbols of the Catholic Church – such as the *Viacrucis* – with the emotional loyalties that go with these. Along with the revolutionary process, a new Reformation is in progress. Only the revolutionary reformers of *our* time don't need to break with Rome. They can keep the Roman symbols – and the Roman sacraments, which is more important – without Rome's retaining any vestige of real authority over them. Rome may discipline theologians for what they publish – though Rome seems by now to have realized that that too can be counter-productive. But what Rome can't possibly do is to supervise how Christianity is taught by thousands of ordinary priests, nuns, other religious, Delegates of the Word, and other lay people among the poor of Latin America. Many, probably most of those – the ones who are in regular contact with the poor, that is – have been radicalized by their experiences among the poor. Specifically, they have been radicalized by their experiences of what the rich, in most parts of Latin America, have been prepared to do to the poor and to those who try to help the poor. The church of *el Dios de los pobres* has its twentieth-century martyrs in Latin America, of whom the most venerated is the murdered Archbishop Romero of San Salvador. The teachers of the poor are teaching Christianity as a revolutionary doctrine, and there is nothing 'the Church' can any longer do about that. More than that, the Vatican, in calling off its crusade against 'deviations and risk of deviations' has itself 'deviated' into giving a kind of blessing to *los Cristianos Revolucionarios*. The most remarkable words in last April's Instruction are those which proclaim it 'perfectly legitimate that those who suffer oppression on the part of the wealthy or politically powerful should take action'. (A later passage makes clear that 'armed struggle' may be included under 'action'.)

Cardinal Obando may well wish to try to turn the words 'or politically powerful' into a kind of charter for the *contras*, but that is not how these words are likely to be read by most people in Latin America who know about them. Most people – whether of left or right – will read these words, in the context of the instruction that embodies them, as meaning that the Vatican can no longer be relied on as an ally for conservative forces in Latin America. If that interpretation is right, as I believe it to be, Miguel Obando y Bravo's life-line to Rome is endangered, within less than a year of his receiving that red hat for services to conservatism. Put not your trust in pontiffs.

Now all this has an important bearing on the prospects for *Sandinismo*, and also on the prospects for efforts to contain or extirpate *Sandinismo*. But before I try to explain the bearing and the prospects, as I see them, I had better try to explain what *Sandinismo* actually is; also, of course, as I see it.

Sandinismo is apparently regarded in Washington as an essentially alien ideology, cunningly decked out in some kind of Latin American fancy-dress. I don't know whether they really believe these things in Washington, or whether they only pretend to believe them, but if they do believe this one, they are in fundamental error, and headed for more unnecessary trouble. *Sandinismo* is a thoroughly Latin American ideology, with deep roots in

Latin American history, and specifically in the history of Nicaragua. Far from being an alien phenomenon in Nicaragua, *Sandinismo* is a native response to alien domination: the alien domination in question being that of the United States. Perhaps that is the basic reason why *Sandinismo*, viewed from Washington, looks so alien.

Augusto C. Sandino (1895–1934), the eponymous hero of this ideology, became a national hero to the Nicaraguans for the same basic reasons as those for which Joan of Arc became a national heroine to the French: he fought the foreigners who had invaded his country, and he was murdered by the servants of those same foreigners. (English historians – in the case of Joan – and American ones – in the case of Sandino – may define the issues differently, but I am talking about how the issues appear to *nationalists*, of France and Nicaragua, which is what matters in considering *Sandinismo*.)

The particular foreigners whom Sandino fought, at the head of a small but resolute band of guerrillas, were the U.S. Marines, who were in Nicaragua, at the invitation of Nicaragua's Conservative faction, from 1909–33. Sandino fought the Marines, with varying fortunes, from 1927–32. He was successful to the extent that the Americans were unable either to subdue him or buy him off – the latter being extremely unusual at the time in Central American politics, civil or military.

The last of the Marines left Nicaragua on 2 January 1933. They did not leave because they had been defeated by Sandino – as the simpler sorts of Sandinista rhetoric suggest – but because U.S. policy had changed, in favour of something subtler. But Sandino had probably quite a lot to do with the change in policy. The indomitable guerrilla leader had been news throughout the world and had caught the imagination of nationalists, not only in Latin America, but as far away as China. The publicity was judged to be bad for the United States. And it was possible to protect U.S. interests by other means. The means consisted of the Nicaraguan National Guard, selected and trained – and originally commanded – by U.S. Marines. The new commander of the National Guard, selected by the U.S. Ambassador, was Anastasio Somoza Debayle, the founder of the dynasty which was to rule Nicaragua until the Revolution of 1979. On 21 February 1934, Sandino and two of his generals, after dining in Managua with the then President of Nicaragua, Juan Bautista Sacasa – were abducted by members of the National Guard, driven out to Managua airfield and shot by firing squad. Two years later Somoza – who had been at a poetry-reading while Sandino and his comrades were being shot – ousted Sandino's host, Sacasa, and made himself President.

A marked feature of *Sandinismo*, as mentioned, is its cult of heroes and martyrs. Sandino himself is the supreme hero and protomartyr. '*Bienvenido a la Patria de Sandino!*' says a large sign at Sandino Airport, Managua, recalling the scene of the original martyrdom. There are portraits of him everywhere: a skinny, morose little man, invariably wearing a ten-gallon hat, and looking like a figure out of a 1920s cowboy movie. You see sketches of him in chalk on rocks along the Nicaraguan country roads; just lines, like a match-stick man, indentifiable only by the hat. And in at least one place, an economical artist has paid homage to Sandino by the simple hieroglyph: ⌒

Sandino's status as a martyr may appear a bit anomalous, since Sandino was not a Christian, although he did believe in God. Like many mavericks in the 1920s, he was a theosophist and a spiritualist. But Christian Sandinistas of today insist that whatever Sandino *thought* he was, he was indeed a true Christian martyr: one who fought and died for the God of the poor. He refused to call himself a Christian, because the most eminent Nicaraguan 'Christians' of his day – like that Bishop of Granada who blessed the U.S. Marines – were in the service of the enemy. These, however, were not really Christian at all, but worshippers of Mammon. Had Sandino lived to see the advent of liberation theology, he would have proclaimed himself a Christian Revolutionary. And on that last point, at least, I think the Christian *Sandinistas* are probably right.

To the U.S. media of his day, of course, Sandino was no kind of hero or martyr, Christian or other, but a bandit and a red. A bandit he certainly was not. The question of whether he was a red is more complex. In several ways, he *was* a red. In his Mexican years – 1922–26 – he associated with Communists and other revolutionary ideologues and picked up some of their outlook and vocabulary. He was not a Marxist – no one who was into theosophy and spiritualism could reasonably be described as a Marxist – and although he did often use the language of class war, I think it clear that, with him, the class struggle was secondary to the national struggle. This appears in the fact that Sandino stopped fighting once the Marines had been withdrawn. The *social* structure in Nicaragua was not changed by the departure of the Marines. The fact that Sandino spent his last evening on earth with the very 'moderate' President Sacasa seems to indicate that social conditions did not arouse in Sandino the same elemental passions that drove him on, over five years, to fight the foreign foe on Nicaraguan soil.

The primacy of nationalism also appears in the incident that led – according to his own account – to Sandino's departure from Mexico and return to Nicaragua. A Mexican revolutionary acquaintance of his, dismissing the possibility of revolution in Nicaragua ever, said that every Nicaraguan was a *vendepatria*. The mere thought of being taken for a *vendepatria* – a man prepared to sell his country – was so unbearable to Sandino that he determined to return to Nicaragua and raise an army to fight the U.S. Marines. And the expression *vendepatria* is even now the most deadly insult in the Sandinista lexicon. It is the word with which they brand people like Archbishop Obando.

In general, all Sandino's most passionate utterances, all those that are treasured by contemporary Sandinistas, are expressions of exalted nationalism. I could cite a number of examples, but there is just one that sums them all up. This consists of the four words of Sandino's that are the national motto of Sandinista Nicaragua: '*Patria Libre o Morir*!' 'Give me Liberty or give me Death'.

The second hero and martyr in the Sandinista pantheon is the poet Rigoberto López Pérez who in 1956 killed Anastasio Somoza Debayle, at a party in Léon, and was then shot down by Somoza's bodyguards. President Eisenhower called Lopez 'the murderer of a friend of the United States', but of course to Sandinistas he is not a murderer, but the executioner of Sandino's murderer. López's deed and fate were an inspiration to *Sandinismo*'s third hero and martyr, who was also its leader and principal ideologue, Carlos Fonseca Amadór, co-founder along with Silvio Mayorga and Tomas Borge, of the *Frente de Liberación Nacional Sandinista* in 1961. (Both Fonseca and Mayorga were later killed by the National Guard.)

In long 'Notes' which he wrote on López, Fonseca quotes Machiavelli's epithet on tyrannicides: '*rarisimos*'. Fonseca also quotes some of Lopez's own poetry, including the lines:

> Nicaragua is getting back to being
> (or may be for the first time)
> a free country
> without affronts and without stains:
> *una patria libre*
> *sin afrentas y sin manchas*

According to Fonseca the words 'or may be for the first time' have 'an extraordinary revolutionary transcendence' in their context. It is, I believe, this sense of national humiliation – Fonseca himself writes of '*la patria humillada*' – which supplies the basic drive of *Sandinismo*. Up to July 1979, the Sandinistas fought to wipe out what they regarded as the humiliation of their country. And since July 1979 – and especially since Ronald Reagan became President – they have been fighting to avert the re-imposition of national humiliation on their country. And to Sandinistas, national humiliation is precisely what Reagan insists on, when he refuses to negotiate with them, and tells them to negotiate with the *contras*. It is not in the nature of *Sandinistas* to negotiate with *contras*. *Not* negotiating with *contras* is what their tradition, their whole intellectual, moral and emotional formation are all about. *Patria Libre o Morir*.

As well as being inspired by Sandino, López and the Nicaraguan experience, Fonseca and his *compañeros* were immediately inspired by the Cuban Revolution, which had triumphed in Havana just before they established the *Frente* (in Honduras). Unlike Sandino, Fonseca and his *compañeros* were intellectuals, and committed Marxist-Leninists; and through them Marxism-Leninism became an element in *Sandinismo*. According to the thinking of President Reagan and his fellow-believers, this automatically makes Sandinistas into accomplices in the international Communist design, masterminded by Moscow. This kind of thinking is apparently impervious to the massive historical evidence which refutes it. In the 1950s, people like Reagan, by exactly this same reasoning, believed that the Chinese Communists, being Marxists, were *ipso facto* tools of Moscow. Those who, knowing China, argued that this was not the case, and that Chinese nationalism was still a major force in Chinese Communism, were dismissed as naïve – and in many cases also dismissed from their jobs. But the equation 'Marxist equals tool of Moscow', far from being called into question after it broke down in China, is still being applied, with exactly the same overbearing confidence, in Central America.

In fact, those Sandinistas who were, and are, Marxist-Leninists are no more apt to toe the Kremlin line than the Catholic Sandinistas are to toe the Vatican line. Carlos Fonseca despised the Moscow-line Marxist Nicaraguan Socialist Party, for being more faithful to the Moscow line than to Nicaragua. He called these Moscow-liners 'false Marxists'. Fonseca and his friends were 'the true Marxists'. That is a pretty solid refutation of the Reagan equation.

A good clue to the real nature of *Sandinismo* is contained in the Sandinista oath, as quoted by Fonseca, (who probably drafted it) which runs as follows:

> Before the image of Augusto César Sandino and Ernesto Che Guevara, before the memory of the heroes and martyrs of Latin America and all humanity, before history. I put my hand on the black and red banner which signifies '*Patria Libre o Morir*', and I swear to defend with arms in hand *el decoro nacional* [national decorum/decency/respect] and to fight for the redemption of the oppressed and exploited of Nicaragua and of the world. If I fulfil this oath, the liberation of Nicaragua and of all peoples will be a reward; if I betray this oath, a shameful death and ignominy will be my punishment.

You could take that oath, in good conscience, without being a Marxist.

But you could not sincerely take it, or repeat the Sandinista slogans, without being a nationalist. Within the Sandinista complex, nationalism and commitment to the cause of the exploited are as it were 'required' subjects. Marxism and Revolutionary Christianity are optional, at least as far as the rank and file are concerned. And even if all the nine *comandantes* are Marxists, as has been widely believed, their Marxism is still their own home-made version, not made in Moscow.

I believe that Marxism – even of the home-made variety – is now recessive within *Sandinismo*, and that the Christian Revolutionary element is becoming dominant. Education has been entrusted to Sandinista Jesuits. Fernando Cardenal is Minister of Education, and César Jérez – Miguel d'Escoto's friend – is head of the University. Perhap even more significant is what looks quite like a 'conversion' on the part of Tomas Borge. Borge – as the only survivor out of the three founders of the *Frente Sandinista* – is virtually the custodian of the Sandinista faith. And Borge – as noted earlier – has been increasingly using the language of *Christian* Messianism – 'the Kingdom of God' – rather than the Marxist variety. Granted Borge's immense authority, this can only make the Christian element less 'optional' and more central, within *Sandinismo*.

I think that, in the early days of the Revolution, revolutionaries like Borge were a bit wary about their Christian partners. Might not these *compañeros* defect, or at least wobble, when the theological heat was on? But that matter was put to the test, and the *compañeros* in question (with few exceptions) came out of it with flying colours. Paradoxically, it was the Pope's visit, *el bochorno de Managua*, that did most to increase the influence of the very people whose influence he (the Pope) wanted to diminish: the Christian Sandinistas. For there was the Successor of Peter in person, wagging a finger of reproach at these *compañeros*, and they had neither defected nor wobbled. On the contrary they had launched their counter-offensive, the *insurrección evangélica*. And finally, in the Vatican Instruction of April 1986, it was the Pope, not the Christian Sandinistas and liberation theologians, who was seen to give ground. The prestige of the revolutionary Christians had never been higher.

I think it would now be more accurate to speak of *Sandinismo* as a *faith* rather than an ideology. It is the most formidable kind of faith, the kind that is emotionally fused with national pride. And this kind of faith is now alight in every corner of Latin America. It is true that it is not the *only* kind of faith around. Latin America is now a melting pot, where faith is concerned. The traditional Catholic Church is collapsing, not just on one side but on two. On one side are the Christian Revolutionaries, enlarging that *espacio* of theirs, appropriating the symbols, and so on. On the other, lots of Catholics having been defecting to the Protestant fundamentalist sects. The Latin American bishops, in their reply to the Pope's Instruction, sought to ascribe the inroads of the fundamentalists to the activities of the C.I.A. I think the bishops overestimate the C.I.A. It looks as if there are a lot of people who are attracted neither to the old kind of Catholicism nor the new one, and who are looking for a different kind of faith; more individual, more quietist. But it is the new Catholicism that has the *political* dynamic, the capacity for revolutionary social transformation, and the capacity to fuse with national pride – as in earlier times millennialist Puritanism did, first in England and then in North America.

Is it necessary for the United States to take on the new Faith, by storming the new Geneva: Managua?

In which remains of this essay, I shall briefly consider three arguments by which it is alleged to be necessary to proceed in this way.

The first is that the new Faith is not really a faith at all, but a disguise under which Soviet power advances; the second, that even if the new Faith *is* native to Latin America, it is basically hostile to the U.S.; and the third that the new Faith is intrinsically oppressive and totalitarian.

As regards the first part, I have already discussed the native roots of *Sandinismo*, and shown – I hope – that one of its essential characteristics is the restoration of national pride. People who are as fiercely and proudly nationalist as the Sandinistas are, are not about to hand their country over to a new master, once they have got rid of the old one. Or rather, they are not about to do that *voluntarily*. They could be pushed into it. They could be pushed into it if they felt it was the only alternative to surrendering to the power of the United States. The Cuban precedent is there. The more 'successful' Reagan's pressure on Nicaragua is, the more Nicaragua is likely to be forced in that direction. If Soviet power does indeed come to extend into Central America, it will be courtesy of Ronald Reagan.

There is more substance in the second point. Latin American nationalism, including *Sandinismo*, *is* anti-American; or anti-*North*-American as they say, being Americans themselves. Sandino himself was fiercely and loudly anti-U.S.: as well he might be, seeing that the people he was fighting were the U.S. Marines, in his own country.

Latin American nationalism has always had to define itself *against* U.S. power. For Latin American nationalists, the national humiliations which they so deeply resented were consequences of the direct or indirect applications of U.S. power. The 'affronts' and 'stains' which Rigoberto

López Pérez felt he had to wipe out at the cost of his own life, were made in the U.S.A. For all these people, the eagle is, and long has been, a bird of ill omen.

At Sandinista rallies, the participants have a custom of breaking into ritual chants, at certain prescribed moments. Among these chants, there is one little number which runs:

> *Aquí, allá*
> *el Yanqui morirá!*
> Here, there
> the Yankee will die!

Being against *el Yanqui* is central to the Sandinista culture. But it is also important to see just what *el Yanqui* means in this context. *El Yanqui* is not just any old Yankee. Thousands of real, live Yankees come to Nicaragua every month, without needing a visa, and are welcomed warmly – as several of them told us – by Nicaraguans of all descriptions, both Sandinistas and others. *El Yanqui*, as in that ditty, is the North American who seeks to impose his will on Latin America. *That* is what must die.

Culturally, Nicaraguans (including Sandinistas) are closer to the United States, in some ways, than almost any other Latin American people. One morning at breakfast in the Hotel Intercontinental, Managua, I was reading *Barricada* – the official organ of the *Frente Sandinista* – when my eye was caught by a headline:

YANQUIS VENCIDOS: 'Yankees beaten'

Who, I wondered, had managed to inflict a defeat on the Colossus of the North – and if they had, why was *Barricada* running the story on page 14? Then I read the story and found that the people who had beaten the Yankees were the Cleveland Indians.

El beisbol is the national game in Nicaragua, and a national passion, for Sandinistas as well as others. You can see people playing it in every village, and kids practising on small patches of waste land, in any poor *barrio*. The only riots that took place during our stay in Nicaragua were between two lots of baseball fans. And all the papers – even *Barricada* – give lots of space, not only to Nicaraguan baseball, but also to *U.S.* baseball.

It is curious that the two Spanish-speaking countries where baseball is the national game – Cuba and Nicaragua – are also the two which have managed to shake off U.S. political hegemony. Baseball must be character-building.

The United States, it seems to me, possesses a tremendous *natural* attractive power over Latin America – a natural gravitational field – if successive U.S. administrations were not forever counteracting that pull by pushing the countries concerned around, in misguided and counter-productive efforts to make them more 'pro-American'. These are precisely the efforts that have in fact made them *anti*-American; to the extent that they are.

There is, I think, very little personal hatred in Nicaraguan anti-Americanism. Not even personal hatred for Ronald Reagan; Miguel d'Escoto did indeed fancy that the President might be a victim of diabolical possession, but even that was more in sorrow than in anger. There has been nothing in Nicaragua, about Reagan, that at all corresponds to, for example, the torrent of frantic and obscene iconography which Buenos Aires directed at Margaret Thatcher, at the time of the Falklands War. Sandinistas, indeed, understand Ronald Reagan rather better than most foreigners do. They understand and up to a point respect, his talk about 'standing tall', because 'standing tall' is what *Sandinismo*, too, is all about. They recognize in Reagan, *to that extent*, a partly kindred spirit. 'Ronald Reagan', one Sandinista told me, 'is the Che Guevara of imperialism.'

What Sandinistas cannot accept – and will resist, literally to their last breath – is the insistence that, for Americans to be seen to stand tall, Nicaraguans must cringe.

Neither the 'Communist' point nor the 'anti-American' point, as justify-ing intervention in Nicaragua, has any validity, in my view. There remains the third point: 'totalitarian oppressive. . . .'

I am concerned in this essay primarily with *faiths*: with the element of faith in *Sandinismo*, and with *Sandinismo as* faith. But it is necessary at this point to consider, more succinctly, the nature of the Sandinista polity.

The dominant characteristic of the Sandinista polity is government by a revolutionary elite: the *Frente Sandinista* itself, headed by the nine *comandantes de la revolución*, the National Directorate. This governing principle was already established in the formation of the *Frente* itself, twenty-five years ago, and maintained throughout the Revolution. The Revolution is not held to have been completed by the fall of Somoza but to be still continuing; the present phase being the defence of the Revolution against the counter-revolutionary forces in the pay of the United States.

In this phase, as in the earlier ones, the *Frente* sees itself as the Vanguard of the People, *la Vanguardia del Pueblo*. Those who make up the vanguard are, in Fonseca's words 'joined to the people and guiding it', *juntos al pueblo y guiandolo*. This concept may be Fonseca's – and so *Sandinismo*'s – principal debt to Lenin, but it is a lot older than Lenin and is probably inherent in every revolutionary 'process'; the Cromwellian Saints and

Robespierre's Jacobins saw matters in essentially the same light, subject to wide rhetorical variations.

The principle of rule by a revolutionary elite was overlaid, not super-seded, by the general elections held in November 1984. Not that the elections seem to have been rigged. There were many international observers around, including Western parliamentary delegations, and most of these agreed that, on the whole, the elections were fairly conducted – and a lot more fairly than most in Latin America. But of course the mere fact of being the incumbents gave the Sandinistas an enormous advantage, in conditions where voters had no previous experience of free elections. More fundamentally, it is extremely doubtful whether the opposition even if it had won an electoral majority, would thereby have attained real power. Throughout the whole thing, the army remained the *Ejercito Sandinista*, the police the *Policia Sandinista*. Elsewhere in Latin America, even the fairest elections generally lead to no change in the real structure of power, because the elected civilians never attain more than nominal control over the armed forces. And I don't believe the *Frente* would have allowed even a victorious opposition to desandinize the armed forces.

Indeed it seems clear that the *Frente* could not, *consistently with the Sandinista faith to which it is committed*, have accepted anything of the kind. At least as long as the Revolution is threatened by the Counter-revolution – and God knows how long that may be – no proper *Sandinista* can possibly consent to letting the *vendepatrias* take over again, either by elections or by force.

The idea of democratic process has no special sanctity in *Sandinista* eyes – or in many other Latin American eyes either. Elections may be tactically useful, in certain conditions, but no *Sandinista* could permit them to prevail against the truly sacred things: *la Revolución, la Patria, el Reino de Dios*. It is a question of faith, and articles of faith are not changed by counting heads. The same sacred things are also felt to be more important than freedom of expression. If censorship is useful for the defence of the Revolution, then let there be censorship, is the *Sandinista* position.

The *Sandinista* elite is unquestionably 'joined to the people', in that – unlike other Latin American *juntas* – it has worked to improve the conditions of the poor and to provide humane government. I would define the nature of this state as elitist and authoritarian, but not totalitarian, and not physically oppressive; although it can be held – and is held by the opposition – that rule by an elite, and press censorship, in themselves constitute oppression. That may be so, but if so, it is a milder form of oppression than the word generally conjures up or than prevails in most of

Latin America. The security forces are more restrained, and less apt to throw their weight around, than in other Latin American countries. The penal system is mild; this is no *gulag* State. And people – although not free to publish attacks on the regime in the media – feel absolutely free to attack it in private conversation, or from the pulpit. All that may, of course, change, under the pressures of the war, and other pressures. I am speaking of how things are now. The picture projected by the Reagan Adminstration of present-day Nicaragua as a sort of totalitarian inferno, is very far from the truth – as even American Embassy officials occasionally admit. In its early years, the regime made remarkable progress in the eradication of illiteracy and disease, and the replacement of sub-standard housing. But these achievements are now at risk – and there have been setbacks in all these fields – because of the economic pressures on Nicaragua and because of the disruption of production in the countryside – and flight of population – caused by *contra* attacks on villages and co-operatives. There are now shortages of virtually everything, even water. Even the privileged guests of the Hotel Intercontinental in Managua have to do without a water supply on Tuesdays and Fridays every week. In some of the *barrios* people count themselves lucky if they *get* water on two days a week. People are experiencing great hardship. One young mother – not an enemy of the regime – said to me with passion: 'Day after day, things are getting worse and worse.'

So in terms of making life miserable for most Nicaraguans, the Reagan pressures have been quite successful. But the success would only make some kind of sense – even of a nasty kind – if the misery were putting the skids under the Sandinistas. It is true that if elections were held now it is *possible* – though not in my opinion likely – that the public hardship might result in a majority against the *Frente*. But, as argued above – and as Washington must know – the Sandinistas have no intention of letting themselves be put out of power in this way. Nor are unarmed masses of people about to rise up and expel the Sandinistas. The pressures could only have effect if they tended to split the Sandinistas themselves, including the *Ejercito Sandinista*. But they don't work that way; quite the contrary. All this pressure, coming from Washington, tends to unite Sandinistas because it threatens the most cherished deity in their pantheon: *el decoro nacional*. Nicaraguans feeling a sense of national pride – almost always defined with negative reference to the United States – tend to rally behind the *Frente*, in answer to so blatant a challenge from the North. Some Nicaraguan nationalists did initially rally to the *contra* cause – around the theme of 'the revolution betrayed' – but several of these have now given up, the most prominent being Eden Pastora.

After these defections, the *contra* cause has been looking more and more like what the Sandinistas always said it was: a *vendepatria* enterprise.

It is true that there are sizeable numbers of Nicaraguans who care very little about *la patria* or *el decoro nacional*. For those in the Atlantic provinces for whom Spanish is not the first language, and whose religion is not Catholic – English-speakers of Jamaican origin and some Indians – neither the notion of *la patria* nor – consequently – *Sandinismo* can have much appeal. I was reliably informed in Bluefields that about four-fifths of local young males subject to call-up have left the country rather than undergo their *Servicio Militar Patriotico*. And it is also because of a lack of 'Nicaraguan' feeling in these provinces – and consequent resentment of *Sandinista* efforts to mobilize support – that the *contras* were initially able to make headway in this region; though they subsequently lost much support, because of the indiscriminately brutal behaviour of many of their number. Today the prevailing attitude in these provinces seems to be one of 'wait and see', with little enthusiasm either for the *Sandinistas* or for the *contras*.

But it is on the Spanish and Catholic Pacific side, where most of the population is, that *la patria* is, and has its devotees, the Sandinistas. The Sandinistas cannot, in my opinion, be driven from Managua except by the direct use of U.S. force. And if they are driven out of Managua they will still go on fighting, as guerrillas, and others will join them, and U.S. forces will have to stay there, in order to prevent a Sandinista come-back. And in that way, bogged down in Nicaragua, the United States will be taking on the forces of nationalism, not only in Nicaragua, but throughout Latin America. That did not work out well in Indo-China, and I don't think it would work well in Latin America either.

It is true that in the past the U.S. has been able to intervene in Latin America repeatedly and with impunity. But things are a bit different now; there is a new spirit around. In particular, the new alignment of *el Dios de los pobres* and *la patria* – Faith and Fatherland – is shifting the balance. Pope John Paul II took on that formidable alliance, without quite knowing what he was taking on, and then found that he had to back away. I hope that Ronald Reagan too may back away, before it is too late.

Conor Cruise O'Brien was given a Sidney Hillman Award for the above essay. He accepted the award on 19 May 1987 in the ballroom of the Sheraton Center in New York City, before a large audience consisting mainly of trade unionists. After the delivery of the acceptance speech the audience signified their approval by standing and observing a minute's silence.

I am honoured to accept the Sidney Hillman Award for my essay on Nicaragua.

The names of Sidney Hillman and of Nicaragua go well together today.

Throughout his active life, Sidney Hillman was assailed and smeared by the same forces in this country that in our time have created the *contras* and let them loose on the people of Nicaragua. Hillman in his day specifically condemned such interventionist policies. On 8 May 1922, addressing the Fifth Biennial Convention of his Amalgamated Clothing Workers at Carmen's Hall in Chicago, Sidney Hillman said:

> 'Our government should not assume . . . that it has the right to dictate conditions of life in another country . . . You do not commit murder only when you go out in the street and kill someone; you commit murder when you make it impossible for other people to live.'

Murder, yes. On 28 April last, a band of terrorists armed and paid by the Government of the United States murdered an American, Benjamin Linder, in cold blood. Linder was working on a rural electrification project in Nicaragua. It is for that reason, and no other reason, that he was murdered. That is what the *contras* are about.

Last week, David and Elizabeth Linder were in Washington to testify about their son's death. There they were basely insulted by a Congressman, who accused them of exploiting their son's death for political purposes.

Their son was a victim of political murder, and when they spoke out against that, they were accused of playing politics.

I think it is appropriate that we, who meet here in the name of Sidney Hillman, should take a stand on this matter on the side of David and Elizabeth Linder and against the murderers of their son.

In that spirit I ask you all to stand and observe a minute's silence, in memory of Benjamin Linder.

What Can Become of South Africa?*

'WHEN IS A BLACK PRESIDENT GOING TO RULE SOUTH AFRICA?' The question was put to State President P. W. Botha at a rally in Springs, Transvaal Province, in one of the critical by-election campaigns of late last year. The questioner appeared to be a supporter of one of the two parties to the right of Botha's National Party – parties then gaining ground at its expense – and the point was that the politics of Botha's government might open the way to the coming of black power.

President Botha's reply was: 'If we respect minority rights, we won't have black majority rule.'

'Minority rights', together with 'mutual respect', 'participation without dominion', 'co-operative coexistence', and 'joint responsibility', is Botha-speak for what used to be called apartheid. The official language, used in Botha's 1983 constitution, is 'the self-determination of population groups and peoples' (*selfbeskikking van bevolkingsgroepe en volke*). But it appears from all this lexical fumbling that the regime has not yet been able to find a new designation for apartheid which satisfies even itself.

The term *apartheid* ('separateness', often anglicized as 'separate development') is just fifty years old. It belongs by now in the embarrassing category of discredited euphemisms and is far more often heard from the lips of those who denounce it than of those who invented it. Some of the more 'enlightened', or *verligte*, Nationalists – basically those who are most concerned with trying to make a relatively favourable impact on international public opinion – have been saying for nearly ten years now that apartheid is dead, or dying. This is an acceptable official position. Dr Piet Koornhof, who told the National Press Club in Washington in 1979 that apartheid was dying, was minister of co-operation and development. 'Co-operation and development' is in fact another euphemism for apartheid, and Dr Koornhof was chief administrator of what he said was dying. President

* From *The Atlantic Monthly*, March 1986.

Botha, personally, doesn't go so far verbally as Koornhof has done; Botha has spoken of 'outgrowing apartheid in the discriminatory and negative sense'.

The term *apartheid* is out of favour, but the main structures – such as segregated residence – set up in the name of that concept are still in place. The concept is that of the separate development of the different peoples of South Africa, according to legal categories defined exclusively by whites, within political institutions established exclusively by whites, and within an overall system controlled exclusively by whites. There is no apparent disposition on the part of a majority of whites to change those realities of power. The argument that most interests most whites is over how best to protect those realities: whether by going down P. W. Botha's road of limited reform (that is, by removing irritations associated with apartheid but not those essential to its maintenance) or by digging in and telling the blacks and the outside world to go to hell.

The 'mini-general election' – five simultaneous by-elections at the end of October [1985] – showed the second school of thought as gaining, but not gaining very fast. The Nationalists have been losing Afrikaner votes to the parties on the right: the Conservative Party and the Herstigte Nasionale Party (which won a seat from the National Party in October). But these losses have been partly made good by a drift of English-speaking whites to the Nationalists, which enabled the Nationalists to hold four seats out of the five contested in the by-elections. Botha has had some success in projecting himself as not just the leader of the Afrikaner *volk* but the leader of 'South Africa', meaning all the whites, including those whom Afrikaners used to call *Neef Brit*, 'Cousin Brit'.

This need to attract Anglophones may have something to do with the disfavour into which the purely Afrikaans euphemism *apartheid* has fallen and the tendency to replace it with woozier formulas – like those quoted above – mostly drawn from the richer rhetorical resources of Anglo-Saxon hypocrisy.

Neef Brit has been welcomed and wooed at Nationalist election meetings for years past, although (or because) all these elections have resulted in a strengthening of the Afrikaner monopoly of power in Parliament, as well as in the civil service, the army and the police. Nationalist platform orators – almost invariably Afrikaner – are careful to alternate paragraphs of Afrikaans with paragraphs of English. Even the warm-up music for the National Party rallies includes not only old Afrikaans favourites but British tunes as well, slightly refracted through dim memories of Afrikaner schoolrooms. Thus the first three items on the musical program for Botha's election rally at Springs ran:

1 She'll be coming around the mountain when she comes
2 My Bonnie lies over the ocean
3 Daizy, Daizy, give me your anser do

Daizy (*sic*), Daizy (*sic*), give me your anser (*sic*) do. Nobody seemed to notice anomalies. There were obviously very few born English-speakers present, and any who were would be so fully committed to the politics of Afrikanerdom as to be past worrying about how to spell Daisy.

As you can sense, the atmosphere of a modern National Party rally is significantly different from what is presumably imagined by those who call the South African Nationalists Fascists and Nazis. At Nationalist rallies there is (so far) nothing reminiscent of the Fascist or Nazi *style*: no dramatic light-and-sound effects, no military precision or paramilitary presence, no apparatus for inducing hysteria, and no manifestations of hysteria. At Springs, I was reminded not of Nuremberg but of a meeting of the Parti Québécois at Rivière-du-Loup (except that the Québécois would never have sung 'Daizy'). These were middle-class (or upper-working-class) people from the same province, related to one another, speaking the same language, practising the same religion, familiar with the same history books, worried about the same things. They were stolid, undemonstrative people, a bit puzzled and a bit nostalgic. Most of them seemed to like P. W. Botha, without being wild about him. A few right-wingers in the audience didn't like him much but weren't wildly against him either. Any fanaticism that may have been present was not lying around on the surface.

Too much, of course, can be made of that impression of normality. This was an all-white meeting in an electoral district most of whose inhabitants are black and consequently disenfranchised for all elections on which power in South Africa depends. The only black person in sight was an American cameraman. If South African blacks had gained admission to that meeting, even without heckling, the stolidity level would have dropped dramatically. So also in Northern Ireland: Orange rallies are generally stolid, casual and good-humoured, but the detected presence of a Catholic, presumed hostile, can evoke some latent hysteria and violence; I speak from experience. (The Orange/Afrikaner comparison is quite a fertile one, provided it is not being used just for the stigmatization, or demonization, of one community or the other, or both.)

Similarly, if movie footage of South African police bashing black youths had been shown in that hall, it would have elicited sounds of approval, not disapproval. There is an organic connection between such orderly and peaceable gatherings as those election meetings and the episodes of violent repression required for the maintenance of apartheid (alias 'minority rights' and so forth).

The connection should be noted, but preferably without too simple an assumption of moral superiority over those respectable-seeming people who sustain all those brutal, *sjambok*-wielding, buckshot-firing policemen we have seen on television. For there is a scarcely less intimate connection between the international agitation against the apartheid state – the pressures for disinvestment and sanctions – and the internal violence applied against the servants and suspected servants of that state.

The greatest victory in the struggle against apartheid, so far, has been the replacement of white indirect rule in the black urban ghettos by the rule of those who are known as 'the children'. The children are those who attend school, when they choose to do so. Some of them are as old as twenty-four; most of them are teenagers; pre-teens, down to eight or so, play supportive enforcement roles. It is the children – in this context the militants among them – who have made life impossible, often literally, for the agents of white power in black townships. It is the children who enforce the boycotts, whether of schools or of white shops. It is the children who discipline those who are seen to step out of line (later the term 'comrades' replaced 'children').

The children see themselves as the peacemakers of the revolution, and, like other revolutionaries, they make use of terror. But the guillotine was merciful compared with the children's chosen methods of execution: burning alive, with a petrol-filled rubber tyre, 'the necklace', around one's neck. The children humorously refer to each such case as a 'Kentucky', after Kentucky Fried Chicken. A Kentucky and its necklace do not represent spontaneous outbreaks of popular rage. They are a standard ritualized penalty applied to black men and women designated as informers or collaborators.

On a university campus one bright afternoon in the South African spring I discussed the children and their works with an elderly black theologian, a clergyman resident in one of the townships – as the segregated urban locations for blacks are known. For obvious reasons, connected with the laws of South Africa, I don't identify this source; let us call him Ezra. I found Ezra in his study, reading a work by a mid-Victorian Methodist missionary. Ezra was chuckling, and read out the passage that tickled him. It was one of those 'mysterious Africa' bits, a purple patch about the almost infinite depths of the black man's inherent incapacity to comprehend anything whatever. 'He's talking about *my grandfather*!' Ezra cried with delight.

Ezra has been a member of the African National Congress since the early days – long before the ANC was banned, in 1960 – and is still a firm supporter, and therefore committed, at least in theory, to aiding the armed struggle, ordered by the ANC, against apartheid. He doesn't like the

Marxist tendencies of some of the present ANC leadership but doesn't take them seriously. 'I don't fear an African who, while he is fighting, utters voluminous words of Marxism,' he says.

I asked Ezra a question about the state of the Church in the townships today. Very satisfactory, Ezra thought. The churches were always full on Sundays. 'The ministers are with the people definitely. In a tremendous way. Ministers were among the first detained – especially Methodist ministers. The black side of the Church is tremendously radicalized.' Ezra went on to talk about the police, who cause most of the violence, he said, especially by their attacks on funeral crowds as they disperse. 'You get disgusted by such clumsy forcefulness.' The pulpits of the townships, it is clear, condemn all that.

I asked whether the parish clergy also condemned what I called 'examples of popular violence'. The wording was mealy-mouthed, because the question was fraught. Somehow it seems difficult to ask a Christian clergyman who is also a supporter of the ANC exactly what he has to say about the children and their necklace. The ANC's position on this matter is equivocal. According to a source generally sympathetic to the ANC, Roger Omond's recent *Apartheid Handbook*, '[The ANC's] leaders say that it attacks military and security targets, and tries to avoid civilian deaths, but that it is impossible for civilians to be completely unaffected by an armed struggle.' It is certainly impossible to be completely unaffected by being burned to death.

Ezra did not care for my question, put though it was with almost Proustian delicacy. At first he tried to brush it aside. 'There are generally not incidents on Sunday,' he informed me.

How about Saturday? I wanted to know. Suppose an 'incident of popular violence' happened in a certain parish on a Saturday night. Would the parish clergyman take that as a theme for his Sunday sermon?

'No,' Ezra said. 'He would fear for himself.' Similarly, if a clergyman were asked to allow his church to be used for a political meeting, he could not refuse, in such circumstances. 'They are really in sympathy. . . . It is a ministry to a very angry people.'

True, there was the case of Bishop Tutu. The Bishop had not only condemned violence – whether popular or police – but had actually successfully interposed his person, at a funeral, between some children and their intended victim. But this transaction, Ezra seemed to think, had done little to enhance the brave Bishop's popularity among the young in the townships. Ezra had watched the scene on television. There were some children in the audience and they 'jumped up and down with rage' at the

Bishop's intervention. Ezra himself clearly thought that the Bishop had made a mistake in antagonizing the children in this way. Yet Ezra seemed to have his own reservations, very mildly expressed, about the temper of the young. Older people were 'a bit more irenic than the young ones', as he put it. 'You sober down. The children don't know how change works. . . . They are very optimistic.' The thought of what all that childish optimism might entail seemed to depress his spirit, for he added: 'I can't visualize what is going to happen. . . . I don't see much that is good in the future.'

In another region of South Africa, more deeply stricken than Ezra's home territory by what white South Africa calls the unrest, I got a slightly different perspective on a world run by children. My informants were a middle-aged businessman, Bob, and a young clergyman, Mark. Both lived in the local township. Both were resolute supporters of the ANC and prominent members of the United Democratic Front (UDF), the umbrella group of organizations following the ANC's political line. Mark had recently been detained. These men were more political than Ezra, and also more closely involved with what was going on politically. Mark was highly articulate, obviously used to dealing with liberal sympathizers, and good at this kind of party work. I found Bob more illuminating, probably because his English was not quite good enough to conceal the complexities and contradictions of his actual thoughts and feelings.

Both were concerned about what was happening in their township and about the tendency for criminals to take over from the politicals. This would get worse, they both thought, as long as the Government continued to refuse freedom of political organization. Nelson Mandela and other prisoners and detainees would have to be released unconditionally, and the ANC exiles allowed to return, also unconditionally, before the growth of anarchy in the townships could be checked. The Progressive MP for the area, who had brought us together, thought that was reasonable, and so did I. Reasonable, and therefore probably remote.

Both Bob and Mark spoke like men who have a lot more to lose than their chains and who thought they might be on the way to losing it. They supported the call for the withdrawal of the troops and riot police from the townships. But for ordinary policing, such as was known in the townships before the Emergency (declared in July 1985), they seemed to feel a certain ambivalent nostalgia. Mark said, 'People did retain a fair amount of faith in the police. If my house is burgled, for example. But now there's a tendency to say, "Get rid of them all." But some say, "Let them stay and operate as police"' (that is, not politically).

'Rev. is right,' Bob said, but corrected him slightly: 'Everybody respected the police before the riot police. But now there's no difference.' Bob is a big, stout man with a lot on his mind. Suddenly, out of the blue, he said, 'That type, now, of that little youngster . . .' Instead of finishing the sentence, he related an incident:

'On Friday night' – we were meeting on Tuesday – 'six thugs armed with pangas attacked an Indian home, beat the husband, and repeatedly raped his wife, who later died.'

Then, after some thought, Bob added a political gloss. In this urban area the Indian housing estate is 'a buffer zone' between the black and the white areas. So one had to 'get rid of the buffer zone, to get at the whites', he said. 'These youngsters, just seeing the white face, they attack.'

Bob's remarks lacked logical connection, and were therefore convincing, in the context. The six were seen in the first place as 'thugs': criminals, not comrades. But they were also seen as agents of a political-racial purpose: breaking up a buffer zone and clearing the way for the revolutionary attack on the white area, the heartland of apartheid. The dividing line between criminality and politics may be clear in theory and rhetoric; in practice, and emotionally, it is liable to get blurred.

Rhetoric and reality also tend to drift apart where Indians are involved. According to ANC-UDF rhetoric – as engaged in certainly by Mark, and probably also by Bob in formal party contexts – Indians are fellow blacks. In practice, it would seem, this is not exactly so. The youngsters of whom it was said, 'seeing the white face, they attack' were in fact, on this occasion, seeing Indian faces and attacking Indian people.

The children, it is plain, have a grip on the imagination of their elders. And it is not just through fear that this grip is maintained; admiration enters into it too. The elders are a bit ashamed of their own past submissiveness to things like the pass laws and are proportionately proud of their children's bravery in defying apartheid. The system is loathed – and not just by the highly politicized – and no less so for being rebaptized 'minority rights' or 'self-determination'. The system's black agents have been correspondingly hated, and the children are admired for taking on those agents, even though the frightfulness of the children's favoured penalty may be quietly deprecated by some of the elders.

Yet the children with the necklace are only some of the children. 'These youngsters, seeing the white face, they attack' is not, or not yet, true of most of the youngsters. I was able to find that out for myself – not altogether voluntarily – one Sunday morning, on my way to hear Bishop Tutu conduct a religious service at St Matthew's Church, Embeni, Soweto.

I went to Soweto because it was an opportunity to see Bishop Tutu –

whom I know already in the white context – at work among his black parishioners. Entering Soweto in a taxi that morning, I felt a bit nervous, and not only because of Bob's dramatic generalization. There were other reasons, both political and personal. Politically, it looked like being a rough weekend. On the previous Friday the political activist Benjamin Moloise, convicted on a murder charge, had been hanged in Pretoria Central Prison after two years' imprisonment, despite a general expectation that his sentence would be commuted. A commemorative service was held in Johannesburg – not Soweto – later that morning. As the mourners left the service, having been addressed by Winnie Mandela and others, a resident in a neighbouring white apartment block dropped a flowerpot from an upper window into the middle of the mourning crowd. This precipitated a riot – the first black riot in downtown Johannesburg, legally a white area. There were riot pictures in the Johannesburg *Business Day* the following morning. These aroused a lot more attention among the paper's white readers than the usual riot pictures. The usual riot pictures were taken in Soweto (when they could still legally be taken there) and showed either 'white on black' (white policemen bashing black demonstrators, or at any rate blacks of some description) or 'black on black' (black militants lynching black collaborators, or at any rate blacks of some description). For most white people, who never go near places like Soweto, all that seems almost as remote as it does to people looking at these same Soweto pictures in New York or London. But the pictures that appeared in *Business Day* on the morning of Saturday 19 October were taken not in Soweto but in downtown Johannesburg, and they belonged to a hitherto quite rare category of picture – 'black on white'. They showed black demonstrators shoving white people around – not shoving them all that drastically, and nothing remotely comparable to some of the horrors of black on black, but they were still more startling and more ominous than anything shown before, since those shoved were whites, those shoving were blacks, and this was Johannesburg, 1985.

Business Day is a pretty dull newspaper, but it made compulsive reading that morning.

Black on white is still rare among politically motivated happenings, but it is not so rare in what you might call the private sector. On the afternoon of that same Saturday, I myself became a small statistic of black on white in the field of urban crime. It was a warm afternoon, and I was taking a walk in the neighbourhood of the Carlton Hotel, where I was staying. There were not many people around – shops and offices close at one o'clock on Saturday – and most of those who were around were black. Suddenly, quietly, and quite gently, one of these grasped my arms from behind. Another appeared in front of me, very close. From a distance he might have seemed to be asking for a light. In fact he had a knife with a four-inch blade pointed at my throat. A third man frisked me expertly and removed all my valuables, but left me my passport and notebook. Then they made off, without physically molesting me in any way. They were not children but middle-aged men, and from their age and relative restraint you might infer that they were non-political: 'ordinary decent criminals', as they say in Northern Ireland.

So what? the reader may reasonably ask. A person can be mugged in any modern city. I know this. In fact, the last time I had been mugged – almost exactly twenty years before – was in Manhattan, at Morningside Park. Although that event occurred during a break in a Socialist Scholars' Conference at Columbia, it had no political significance and did not portend the imminent eclipse of the United States Constitution or the collapse of the capitalist system. Nor would the corresponding happening in Johannesburg justify conclusions about the impending collapse of law and order in South Africa, although it does suggest that the forces of law and order may be stretched thin by the combined impact of escalating political unrest and escalating ordinary crime, both drawing on the same huge and expanding pool of black unemployed. (With an additional 350,000 seeking work each year, South Africa's director general of manpower, Dr Piet van der Merwe, expects unemployment to have more than doubled in ten years: from 10.6 per cent of the labour force in 1977 to 21.9 per cent in 1987.) I mention the mugging not because of any such wider implications but mainly because of the slight subjective jolt that such a happening imparts to the perspective from which the writer so affected views the phenomena about which he is writing. If you have recently had a knife held at your personal and non-metaphorical throat even for fifteen seconds, you are unlikely to be able to write about violence with the same degree of composure and fluent capacity for abstract generalization on the subject as you could attain had you not been obliged to concentrate, intensely if briefly, on the blade of that knife. The middle-aged men whose acquaintance I made that afternoon in von Brandis Street, Johannesburg, were altogether silent for the whole period of our life together, but if you listen carefully during the discussion of violence which inevitably pervades this essay, you may occasionally be able to detect the faint sound of their breathing.

No, reader, I have not forgotten that I was about to proceed to St Matthew's Church, Embeni, Soweto, there to witness Bishop Desmond Tutu conduct an Anglican service. The sequence of events, both macro and micro, runs as follows:

Friday morning. A black man is hanged in Pretoria, and mourned in

Johannesburg, mainly by blacks. A white hand drops a flowerpot, from a height, onto the mourners. The mourners riot.

Saturday. Black-on-white pictures in the paper. I get mugged (co-incidentally).

Sunday. To Embeni, Soweto, to witness Bishop Tutu, and so forth. But before I go on to Embeni, please allow me yet another digression. It is through such digressions, I think, that I can best share with you a personal experience of South Africa.

Brief digression on having been mugged as a topic of conversation in white liberal circles in today's South Africa.

First of all, it isn't a topic of conversation. 'I have been mugged' is a conversation-stopper, and a veritable bazooka among conversation-stoppers. I found that out at a party in Johannesburg's northern suburbs on the evening of my little mishap.

The presence of a mugging victim, I found, is a great begetter of pregnant silences, the pregnancies being strictly of the unwanted variety, to judge from the expressions of those so affected. That much is a matter of observation. Why it should be so can only be guessed. My own guess is based on placing myself in the shoes of those concerned. This I do without much difficulty, because I am a white liberal myself (subspecies *Homo Candidus Liberalis Pessimisticus*) and I have lived in Africa (Central and West, not South). So I hear their underground train of thought as rumbling along the following lines:

By blacks, of course, though of course he doesn't say so. He would say so if they were white. But whites have other ways of robbing people, with less risk. And what can a black do, if he's out of work and has no one to help him, *except* rob, whatever the risk? There's no social welfare, and millions of blacks are unemployed.

So how can you tell the muggee how frightfully sorry you feel about his trouble? The muggers are far more deserving of sympathy than he is. He can stop his credit cards and traveller's cheques and be very little the worse for his experience. They continue their desperate, hand-to-mouth existence until they get caught and go to jail.

Yet the muggee's hard-luck story is hard to take for some other and quite different reasons. We ourselves are potential muggees, and worse than muggees, and we shall remain here, at high risk, long after this character has gone back to whence he came. And we ourselves hardly deserve more sympathy, even from ourselves, than we could legitimately offer this hard-luck man – perhaps even less. We, too, are affluent, within a system we oppose and despise, so we are also – at least to some extent – legitimate targets, not only of the violence of the black unemployed but also of the revolutionary political enemies of apartheid. Ideologically, we have to be on the side of those who pose a threat to our lives and property; existentially, we are unable to be on that side. Also, we are unable to change the colour of our skins, a matter that ought not to be of the slightest importance but that the white community over many generations has made into the touchstone of everything, the be-all and the end-all: a be-all that looks more and more like an end-all.

We have had to contemplate that desolate range of subject matter for quite a long time, and we never much like being gratuitously reminded of it. So I'm afraid our accident-prone friend would do well to pass on, without undue delay, to some other topic of conversation.

The words are imagined, but the predicament reflected in them is real. Like other predicaments – the Irish one, for example – it is fraught with ironies. In noting the ironies, in attributing language, it is very much not my intention to satirize those who are caught in the predicament, which is probably the grimmest that any liberals have ever been caught in. These South Africans are coping with it, in many cases with admirable courage, resourcefulness and cheerfulness combined with intellectual rigor. I am thinking in particular of South African scholars and writers who over many years have combated apartheid by all the means appropriate to their functions.

It is a crowning irony that while the apartheid regime is punishing the journalists in their function, by elaborate and expanding censorship provisions, some of the dottier foreign enthusiasts of anti-apartheid are trying to inflict precisely symmetrical damage on South Africa's academic community. Thus a group of Irish lawyers – with Mr Sean MacBride, the Nobel and Lenin International Prize for Peace-winning former director of Amnesty International, as its most eminent member – recently urged an academic boycott of South Africa. The institutions that would be worst hit if this disgusting proposal were acted on are those – like the University of Cape Town – that are totally desegregated and are major sources of accurate information about the workings of apartheid and agents of exposure of attempts to camouflage apartheid. The zealots of apartheid will be absolutely delighted if this scheme of the zealots of anti-apartheid ever catches on. The fact is that both lots of know-nothings hate liberalism and associated manifestations of disinterested intellectual activity.

After writing the paragraphs above I learned that the South African scholars invited to the World Congress of Archaeology in Southampton next year have had their invitations withdrawn by the organizers.

End of digression and on to Embeni. When I ordered a taxi, giving that destination, on the Sunday morning, the hotel porter told me that I should get a police escort. But somehow I didn't feel I would be all that welcome in Bishop Tutu's congregation if I turned up supported by a Casspir armoured personnel carrier – full of South African police. In any case, such support would be likely to attract a lot more trouble along the way than it might avert. That was my hunch, and it turned out to be right. So no police.

My taxi driver rated as 'coloured' (mixed-race) in terms of the basic document of apartheid, the Population Registration Act of 1950, so he wasn't a resident of Soweto (by virtue of the Group Areas Act of the same year). He told me he knew the way to St Matthew's, Embeni, but actually he didn't; he just knew the way to Soweto, a sprawling city of small houses, encompassing more than a million and a half people. Once in Soweto, he had to ask the way, and this he did about twenty times. The first few times, I sweated a bit. I have driven with Protestants through Catholic South Armagh, and with Jews in the vicinity of Hebron, and felt a bit nervous each time, but I felt more nervous this time remembering Bob's dictum 'seeing the white face, they attack' (and a white face is a lot more conspicuous in Soweto than, say, a Protestant face in South Armagh). They all saw the white face, but there was no attack. Among the first people consulted by my driver was a group of young males: children. They showed no signs of colour prejudice but gave directions in a friendly way. The same was true of all the people we talked to in other areas of Soweto. It was rather different from what you might think Soweto is like, and different also from what Soweto actually *is* like under other conditions – for example, at a funeral and in the presence of the police. Considering the high proportion of politicized militants among the youth of Soweto, it is improbable that there were not some of these among the people consulted by my taxi driver. My guess is that any militant children who took note of my presence considered that the only kind of white person fool enough to ride around Soweto in a taxi looking for directions would be a foreign sympathizer with 'the cause of the people' – that is, the ANC.

In any case, violent hatred of all whites as such is not a general condition among the people of Soweto. That much I can claim to have established experimentally, with the aid of my consultative taxi driver. Black leaders claim that their people hate apartheid without hating whites. That claim may seem improbable, but my experience is certainly a small piece of evidence in its favour.

St Matthew's, Embeni, is an unfinished church, only half roofed over, but entirely usable on such a bright, warm, South African spring morning. The church was crowded, for the most part with smartly dressed men, women and children, including choristers in brightly coloured gowns and boys in blazers. All eyes, all the time, were on Bishop Tutu. My notes taken in the church read:

> Tutu baptizing: firm plunger of struggling lambs; [not babies but] big kids. Tutu preaching in Xhosa; simultaneously translated into Tswana. Great facial mobility and range of gestures. Clutching lectern with both hands, then reaching out and seeming to snatch things out of the air. Dead-pan, with wide-open eyes, for jokes. Laughter, applause. Then he relaxes, smiles. Affection, approval, amusement, confidence of congregation/audience. A 'good turn' and spiritual solace, all in one. Then a few words in English. Change of persona: no comic effects; grave, academic tone. Limited range of gesture now, using left hand. [He said:]
>
> 'God looks down on South Africa and weeps when He sees how some of His children are treating His other children. . . . Christ's religion [is] a religion of the poor, the marginalized, the ghetto people. . . . But the others, whom we disagree with, are not to be killed.'

After that, my concluding note reads simply, 'Dances high-life in full Episcopal regalia.'

There is a danger of that sounding funny. It wasn't funny at all; it was profoundly moving, and precisely appropriate. Only once before had I seen a sight that moved me in the same way. (There is a danger of this comparison sounding funny too, but I intend it in the most reverent appreciation.) Twenty years ago I watched a ground hornbill, in a clearing in the bush in northern Ghana, dancing all by himself a solemn and triumphant dance, as if celebrating the Creation.

Even so, in the half-roofed Church of St Matthew in Embeni, Soweto, did Desmond Tutu dance before his Lord.

In what I have written up to now, I have followed a train of personal experience, and one that was far from newsworthy. In so doing, I hoped to supplement the impressions of South Africa that you may get from the media, especially television. Daily life in South Africa at present is not so charged with hatred and violence as the selected images on the screen suggest. There is no deliberate distortion; it is in the nature of news coverage to reflect not daily life but what is startling, alarming, shocking. There are a lot of such things in South Africa, but not everything is like that. As that veteran enemy of apartheid Alan Paton said to me in Durban, '[The foreign media] seem to see nothing in South Africa but white wickedness and black suffering. Those things are there, but they're not everything.'

No. Those Afrikaners in Springs were not like Nazis; those blacks at Embeni were not exclusively preoccupied with suffering or hating. Correction is needed, but there is a danger of overdoing the correction. To convey a reassuring message would be much more misleading than the television coverage is.

Television cannot reflect the routine of daily life, but the violence shown episodically on the screen pervades daily life, mostly in latent form, and governs the contexts in which daily life is lived. Those stolid Afrikaners are behind their police, in every sense, and all the talk of police brutality leaves them at best unmoved. That relaxed and joyous congregation at St Matthew's may see the children as their champions, though the champions are also scary. Bishop Tutu's warnings against violence seem to be taken as appropriate, coming from him, more than as binding on those addressed. I was reminded of Pope John Paul II in Ireland condemning political violence. Everybody, including IRA supporters, thought the Pope was a lovely man, but support for the IRA and its armed struggle was not in any degree diminished.

Afrikaners, for their part, are cynical about the Bishop's condemnation of violence, as veiled collusion. Across the gulf that separates the ruling Afrikaners from the rebellious blacks, even such conciliatory sounds as are wafted to the other side bear sinister connotations. At a Supreme Court session in Pretoria, I heard a judge refer sardonically to a priest who was supposed to have told his congregation, 'I don't know how long you can be held back from burning vehicles.' Clearly, the judge heard that priest as actually inciting to violence, egging the congregation on, in coded language. Across such a chasm constructive dialogue appears unattainable.

If the televised images and printed reports convey to you that South Africa is already in a state of civil war, then that impression is exaggerated. But if they convey to you that South Africa is drifting, at an accelerating rate, toward civil war, then that impression is, in my belief, correct.

What can be the outcome of this incipient civil war? That remains a difficult question.

In my visits to various South African cities – Cape Town, Port Elizabeth, Grahamstown, East London, Durban, Johannesburg – I put to a number of well-informed people the following propositions:

The maintenance of the status quo is impossible.

Reforms acceptable both to the white electorate and to politicized blacks are impossible.

Revolution is impossible.

The first of those three propositions needs no discussion here, since nobody disputes it. To the second proposition most of my informants replied, in substance: 'Maybe not impossible. We must continue to hope that reform is not impossible. But it will be extremely difficult, certainly.'

As regards the third proposition, most informants, black and white, thought that if reforms acceptable to most politicized blacks continued to be denied by the white electorate, revolution would become inevitable, but in the fairly long term. Hardly anyone considers revolution possible in the here and now – within the next five years or ten years; even the ANC is said to put the remaining life of the apartheid regime at no less than ten years.

I should now like to consider the forces making for acceptance of major change, those working for resistance to change and how the resistance might be overcome.

The argument in favour of the feasibility of major reform, as I understand it, runs more or less as follows:

Already a sizeable portion of the white electorate is in favour of major reform. That support is likely to grow, as white South Africa begins to understand the magnitude of the external pressures on it, of which the fall in the value of the rand – from fifty-four cents in July of 1985 to thirty-six cents in October of 1985 – is the most telling symbol and most painful symptom for the white population generally. The business community is enthusiastically in favour of sweeping reforms.

It certainly is. If Marx were right and capitalists were the real controllers of the political systems of societies with capitalist economies, then Nelson Mandela would now be esconced in Pretoria as state president, with Oliver Tambo, the ANC leader, as his minister for defence.

I talked in Port Elizabeth, in the Eastern Cape Province, with the secretary of the local Chamber of Commerce. Port Elizabeth's commerce was brought very nearly to a standstill by the almost hundred per cent effective black boycott of white business in the city. The secretary, representing a business community on the verge of desperation, sounded rather like a spokesman for the ANC, although he had earlier supported the Nationalist Party. I was reminded of Herman Melville's story 'Benito Cereno', in which, as you will recall, the man who is apparently master of a slave ship is in reality the captive spokesman for the slaves, who have successfully rebelled.

The business leaders who went to talk with the ANC leadership in Lusaka in September are already in a sort of 'Benito Cereno' condition in relation to the future – prisoners by anticipation of a slave rebellion of whose inevitable success they have begun to be convinced.

Also, the case for radical change is now vigorously and skilfully presented in Parliament by the small but compact and effective Progressive Federal Party, led by F. van Zyl Slabbert. (I should say that I am using *Parliament* here to mean what everyone still thinks of as the *real* Parliament – the white one. But strictly speaking, since the enactment of P. W. Botha's 1983 constitution, Parliament consists of three houses – the House of Assembly [white], the House of Representatives [coloured], and the House of Delegates [Indian]. The institutions of revamped apartheid are confusing, like its vocabulary, and for the same reasons. Although the House of Representatives and the House of Delegates are generally considered as façades masking the continued white monopoly of real power, and although fewer than 20 per cent of the eligible coloured and Indian voters bothered [or dared] to vote in the elections for their respective houses, it was the provision of these concessions to the coloured and Indian communities, while failing to offer *even* a façade to the black majority, that enraged blacks generally and precipitated the present wave of unrest, beginning in late 1983.)

For years after the National Party came to power in 1948 – a power that it has maintained unbroken since then – the demoralized opposition, the United Party, offered no serious challenge to apartheid. That challenge came, indeed, and incisively, but from just one member of Parliament, Helen Suzman. Now the old United Party, rebaptized the New Republic Party, is in terminal decline, as was manifest in the mini-election of last October. Its parliamentary place has been taken by the Progressive Federal Party, 'the Progs'. Helen Suzman is still going strong, and is as astringently alert as ever, but she is now a member of a PFP group with twenty-seven seats in the House of Assembly. That is still a small minority – twenty-seven out of 178 – but it does represent a significant rise in the level of rejection of apartheid in a section of the white community.

The quality of this opposition is exceptionally high. Dr Slabbert is an attractive and inspiring leader, forty-five years old, energetic, highly intelligent, humorous and entirely unpompous. In style he is rather like Pierre Trudeau. He was an academic, and he is quite startlingly candid for a politician, but he seems well able to live down those handicaps.

I talked with Progs in different parts of the country. I was struck by the strength of the respect and affection that Dr Slabbert inspires in his following. I didn't hear a single sour note, and this is rare, in my experience, when one talks in private with party members anywhere about their leader.

I heard Dr Slabbert address a rally in Cape Town on the eve of the mini-election. It was a large and enthusiastic gathering, very different from the turn-out for State President Botha at Springs (although the difference was not reflected in the election results). The leader outlined the present demands of the PFP:

1 Dismantle apartheid completely.
2 Release political prisoners and all who are detained without trial.
3 End the state of emergency, and allow freedom of organization.
4 Call a national convention to determine the new non-racial, democratic constitution of South Africa.

These demands correspond fairly closely to the current demands of the ANC-UDF leadership, and Dr Slabbert, like the business leaders, has visited the ANC leadership in Lusaka.

The business leaders and the Progs are mostly drawn from the English-speaking community (although Dr Slabbert himself is an Afrikaner). The English-speaking community – about 40 per cent of the white population – has, however, been excluded from power since 1948 by the representatives of the Afrikaner community, the majority community within the all-white electorate for the House of Assembly. There can be no progress in the direction of radical change – by constitutional means – unless there is first a significant change in Afrikaner attitudes. What signs are there of such a change?

Well, there are *some* signs. Afrikanerdom is no longer such a monolith as it appeared, say, in the first decade after 1948.

It is not only representatives of English-speakers who have taken – or at any rate tried to take – the road to Lusaka. Students at Stellenbosch, the oldest and most distinguished Afrikaner university, announced their intention of travelling to Lusaka to talk with the ANC. The Botha Government withdrew the students' passports, a step that, interestingly enough, it did not take in the case of the business leaders; apparently such conduct may be grudgingly accepted on the part of *Neef Brit* but may not be tolerated where children of the *volk* are concerned. Nonetheless, opinion at Stellenbosch, both student and faculty, supported the students and their right to travel. I myself found that one can spend an agreeable day on that beautiful campus at Stellenbosch, and have many instructive conversations, without ever meeting anyone who appears to support the National Party. And it's not only Stellenbosch. What some people call the Afrikaner thaw has also reached the Dutch Reformed Church, the central spiritual institution of Afrikanerdom, whose blessings in the past legitimized and sustained apartheid. Dr Beyers Naudé, the most eminent pioneer of anti-apartheid within the DRC, was deprived of his ministry in 1963 and remains an outcast from Afrikanerdom (greatly to the benefit of his reputation in the outside world). Last October, Dr Nico Smith and other DRC clergymen followed the example of the business leaders, of Dr Slabbert and of the

Stellenbosch students by announcing their intention of travelling to Lusaka to meet the ANC leaders.

When this announcement came, it caused shock waves throughout South Africa. It seemed to some that a breach had appeared in the ideological citadel of Afrikanerdom.

There have also been signs of change within the medical and legal professions, change that could not have occurred without the consent of the (mainly) Afrikaner members. In October of 1985 the South African Medical Council struck off its rolls one of the police doctors implicated in the death in September 1977 of the Black Consciousness leader Steve Biko, from injuries received while in police custody. And in December, before the Supreme Court, the state was obliged to withdraw the charges of treason that it had brought against a number of prominent members of the UDF. There have been several other signs of professional unease at some of the practices and demands of the apartheid state.

Afrikaner writers and intellectuals have also turned against apartheid, rejecting it not in the Botha sense but really and fundamentally. Afrikaans writing – some of it now translated into English – is full of a sense of foreboding and evil. I talked in Cape Town with J. M. Coetzee, the author of a number of novels, including *Life and Times of Michael K*, which I had just read. *Michael K*, like several other impressive Afrikaner novels and stories, is set in a desolate, ruined South Africa, felt as the South Africa of the future if the country's rulers persevere on their present course. 'I used to wonder,' Coetzee told me, 'why it couldn't become Brazil.' He has stopped wondering about that, but by even wondering about it he had already broken, as others like him have done, with the traditions of his people and the governing ideology of the state. He is a thin, controlled, matter-of-fact man; you might take him for an accountant. But his view of the facts and figures tallies with his artistic vision: 'When things begin to break down, people should start starving pretty soon. Whites live in pockets. They can be cut off. One single highway leading into Cape Town. . . .'

(And, indeed, along that highway you already get a whiff of incipient siege. On my last day in Cape Town my friend and host, David Welsh, drove me out that way to the airport. David is a well-known political scientist and the co-author with Dr Slabbert of *South Africa's Options: Strategies for Sharing Power*. As we got into the car, David handed me a cushion. This was in case people threw stones at the car. Stoning cars, along this and some other highways, has become perhaps the most prevalent form of black-on-white activity – or more likely, this being the Cape, coloured-on-white. Coloured militants seem to be more hostile to whites as such than black militants are. A white University of Cape Town student told me, 'It's mainly the coloured people who call you whitey.' As it happened, there were no stones that morning. But the Casspirs of the South African police could be seen occasionally, strung out along that 'single highway'.)

Academics, churchmen, writers, doctors, lawyers. . . . It is clear that a significant number of Afrikaner intellectuals are at least beginning to desert apartheid. And this must cause some concern to the regime. An ideology needs intellectuals to impart it, by writing and teaching. And intellectuals who can do this properly need themselves to believe in the ideology they try to impart. True, intellectuals can always be hired to say and write the proper things. But intellectual mercenaries seldom carry conviction. So the ideology of apartheid is in trouble.

The modern tendency for intellectuals to desert apartheid is a little ironic, since apartheid is largely the creation of intellectuals. Intellectuals, mainly teachers and *predikants* (Calvinist clergymen), were the originators and disseminators of Afrikaner nationalism, the politico-cultural movement that eventually produced the doctrine and system of apartheid, and it was also intellectuals who shaped and refined that doctrine and system.

To understand the present predicament of Afrikanerdom, and the significance within that predicament of the (partial) defection of Afrikaner intellectuals, we must here consider briefly the history of Afrikaner nationalism within the general history of South Africa.

The Afrikaners are the oldest white community in South Africa. They are descended from Dutch people who settled in, and spread out from, the vicinity of the Cape of Good Hope, after a fort and a vegetable garden had been established there, for the Dutch East India Company, by Jan van Riebeeck, in 1652. For nearly a century and a half these Dutch-speaking people – absorbing a number of Huguenot émigrés from France – were the only white inhabitants of South Africa, which they came to regard as their country. Their language evolved away from the original Dutch – similar to the evolution of Canadian French away from metropolitan French – to what is now Afrikaans. Their attitudes toward the native peoples they encountered in South Africa were similar to those of English-speaking settlers in North America toward the natives of that continent, during the same period. Many Afrikaners also owned slaves.

As a result of the French revolutionary wars, the Netherlands lost control of South Africa. By the peace treaties that closed the Napoleonic wars, victorious Britain's rule over South Africa was internationally recognized. Emigration to South Africa from the British Isles was encouraged. Friction soon developed between the new rulers and their Afrikaans-speaking subjects. British policy toward the natives was influenced in the early nineteenth century by English-speaking missionaries, as well as by Whig Enlightenment philanthropy. Afrikaners resented these novel ideas and also resented the new British settlers. In 1834 the Parliament of the United Kingdom declared slavery abolished throughout the British Empire. And by 1838 the new anti-slavery laws came into force in South Africa (then consisting of what is now the Cape Province).

Many Afrikaner farmers decided to get away from the British and their meddlesome innovations, and the Great Trek began. Thousands of Afrikaners – or Boers, as they were then known – set out in their ox wagons with their families, their arms, and their black ('Hottentot') servants for the north, well beyond the then existing zone of white settlement. After many vicissitudes (and historic clashes with the Zulus, to be considered below) the Afrikaner emigrants established two internally autonomous Afrikaans-speaking republics of their own – the Transvaal and the Orange Free State – under British 'suzerainty'.

Suzerainty seems originally to have meant little more than a warning from Britain to foreign powers to keep out of the Boer republics. However, everything changed in the mid-1880s, with the discovery of gold in large quantities on the Witwatersrand, where Johannesburg now is ('The city with the heart of gold', as a 1985 poster has it). Foreign immigrants – '*Uitlanders*' – arrived, and British governments promptly took on an active role as protectors of the *Uitlanders*. By the 1890s, the heyday of jingo imperialism, concern for the *Uitlanders* had become merely a pretext for escalating British demands, whose eventual rejection would be the *casus* for a war of annexation of the Afrikaner republics and their wealth – a war that was expected to be brief. It wasn't. The resistance of the Afrikaners proved unexpectedly stiff, and the Anglo-Boer war went on for three years (1899–1902). The last phase of the war involved severe measures against Afrikaner civilians: Lord Kitchener established 'concentration camps' – almost the first official use of that term – in which about 26,000 Afrikaner women and children died.

In the aftermath of the Anglo-Boer war a new British government decided on a policy of reconciliation in South Africa, and members of the Afrikaner elite, led by Generals Barry Hertzog and Jan Smuts, met them half-way. This process led, in 1909–10, to the creation of a self-governing Dominion of the British Empire: the Union of South Africa. The Union (which became today's Republic of South Africa in 1961) was governed from its foundation until 1948 by a 'white coalition' of English-speakers and Afrikaners. In this period the earlier tendency of English-speakers to protect the blacks – a tendency that had already faded during the nineteenth century – was replaced by a rhetoric of 'racial reconcilation'. Racial reconciliation meant reconciliation between Afrikaner and British and joint supremacy of both over all blacks.

But against that ruling concept there was a rising tide of Afrikaner nationalism. Afrikaner nationalism aimed at – and eventually got, in 1948 – an Afrikaner monopoly of political power in South Africa. Afrikaner nationalism, as a conscious movement, began in the mid-1870s, but it gained greatly in emotional power as a result of the Anglo-Boer war and felt a need to cancel out that defeat.

'Afrikaner nationalism, as a conscious movement, began in the mid-1870s.' That statement of mine is firmly based on modern Afrikaner historical scholarship. But it is also – and symptomatically – a proposition passionately resented by modern Afrikaner nationalists, because the modern Afrikaner nationalist credo lays it down that the Great Trek itself, in the 1830s, was the birth of Afrikaner nationalism. Afrikaner historiography can be a dangerous business. For having challenged some aspects of the received nationalist version of Afrikaner history, a distinguished historian, Professor Floors van Jaarsveld, was tarred and feathered in front of a theological conference at the University of South Africa, Pretoria, on 28 March 1979. The subject on which Professor van Jaarsveld had proposed to address the conference was the historiographical reassessment of the Day of the Covenant.

The Day of the Covenant is Afrikanerdom's National Day, celebrated on 16 December. It commemorates the crowning event of the Great Trek: the victory of Andries Pretorius's Boer *commando*, on 16 December 1838, in the Battle of Blood River, over the *impis* (regiments) of the Zulu king Dingaan – that same Dingaan whose *impis* had the previous February massacred a party of more than 300 Boer trekkers, mostly children, under Piet Retief. The Battle of Blood River is commemorated on the spot by sixty-four life-size bronze ox wagons. That battle is also the central event commemorated in the great Voortrekker Monument at Pretoria, probably the most impressive shrine of sacral nationalism to be found anywhere on earth.

It is unlikely that there was much sacral nationalism, or nationalism of any kind, among the followers of Piet Retief or Andries Pretorius in 1838. What there was was the sense of being a chosen people in a promised land, something closely corresponding to the sense of the Puritans of New England in the seventeenth century – a good seedbed of nationalism, but not yet nationalism itself. Sacral nationalism made its appearance about forty years later, bringing with it the legend of the Covenant with God supposed to have been sworn and repeated by Sarel Cilliers – the *predikant* who accompanied Pretorius – that if the Zulus were defeated, the day would be observed every year as a day of thanksgiving.

This sacral nationalism, still the creed of South Africa's governing National Party, was born in South Africa in a period when European nationalisms were increasing in intensity. Afrikaner nationalism was a latecomer, but tardiness seems to intensify nationalism: German nationalism, too, was a latecomer. The men who gave Afrikaner sacral nationalism its first expression, in the 1870s, were teachers and *predikants*, meeting in Die Genootskap van Regtes Afrikaners (the Society of True Afrikaners), which had been founded in Paarl on 14 August 1875. It was a prolific and enthusiastic society. It produced, in 1876, its own newspaper, *Die Afrikaanse Patriot*, the first publication in Afrikaans, a medium that had hitherto been regarded, even by those who spoke it, as a mere patois of Dutch. And the same movement brought the basic text of the new Afrikaner sacral nationalism: *Die Geskiedenis van ons Land in die Taal van ons Volk* (*The History of Our Land in the Language of Our People*).

That title contains the three key words – *land, taal, volk* – of modern Afrikaner nationalism and of the rhetoric of the governing party of today's South Africa. The words *land* and *volk* have emotional associations corresponding to those of the same two words in German. They may also have a *potential* charge corresponding to what happened to the same two words in defeated Germany after the First World War, when *völkisch* nationalism turned from obsessive into manic, and Nazism was born. I shall come back to the question of that potentiality and what might release it.

At the time of the British victory in the Anglo-Boer war, in 1902, Afrikaner nationalists became divided into *bittereinders* and *hensoppers* ('hands-uppers'). The same sort of division continued inside Afrikaner politics throughout the first half of the twentieth century. One set of Afrikaners – considered by the others as little better than *hensoppers* – favoured 'unity', meaning the unity of white South Africans. From the coming of autonomy, with the foundation of the Union of South Africa in 1910, South Africa was ruled, essentially, by coalitions based on (and usually led by) Afrikaners of this type, together with the English-speaking community.

The other set of Afrikaners regarded themselves as the only *regte* Afrikaners, the only true nationalists. They saw the Afrikaner community – now 60 per cent of all whites – as the rightful rulers of South Africa, with *Neef Brit* in second place, and all South Africa's other inhabitants outside the political process. To that end they worked to establish the solidarity of the *volk* against the Afrikaner leaders – notably Generals Hertzog and Smuts – who preached and practised Caucasian ecumenism, the solidarity of whites in general.

After its founding, in 1918, that extraordinary institution the Afrikaner Broederbond set out to provide the leadership of the *regte* Afrikaners. The Broederbond was a secret society, but it was no ordinary secret society. By the late 1930s it had attained the leadership of resurgent Afrikaner nationalism, and within thirty years of its founding it had led the National Party to a monopoly of political power that has never since been interrupted.

Since the victory of the National Party, in 1948, the Broederbond has been the establishment of Afrikanerdom: every head of government has been a member, as P. W. Botha is now; almost all ministers have been members; and all *regte* Afrikaners of consequence are members. It is now – and this is a symbol of the malaise of the Afrikaner elite – a *divided* establishment, with members divided between the National Party and the smaller Afrikaner parties to the right of it. Though divided, the Broederbond remains an establishment.

But in its beginnings the membership was young and hungry. As with the earlier Genootskap, many of the members were teachers, *predikants*, intellectuals. And as with the Genootskap, much of its work consisted in nationalist indoctrination, through the churches, the schools and colleges, the press. The nationalism was sincere in its fervour; it was also connected with a deliberate effort of social promotion for Afrikaners generally, and in particular for members of the Broederbond, through mutual help. The Broederbond soon came to see the eventual winning of permanent political power in South Africa – political power as an Afrikaner monopoly – as the key to the fulfilment of both its nationalist and its social ambitions. By the 1930s – under political conditions very different from those of the previous century – the fanning of nationalist excitement had definite political objectives, the first of which was the casting out from the *volk* of men like Hertzog and Smuts, the allies of *Neef Brit*. And this objective was largely achieved by 16 December 1938, the centenary of the Day of the Covenant.

Carefully prepared and organized by the Broederbond, the celebration of the centenary was a culminating event in the liturgy of the sacral nationalism of the *volk*. During the preparatory months ox wagons traversed the land from Cape Town to Pretoria, stopping at all the holy places of nationalism. Nationalist excitement steadily mounted. Henning Klopper, the first chairman of the Broederbond and the chief organizer of these celebrations, wrote: 'The whole feeling of the trek was the working not of man, not of any living being. It was the will and the work of the Almighty God. It was a pilgrimage, a sacred happening.' It was. It was also a political happening. The temperature of Afrikaner nationalism had been raised so high as to make it impossible for either Smuts or Hertzog to be present at the ceremonies. The Broederbond had succeeded in the first of its major objectives. The second – the conquest of political power – was achieved just ten years later.

(It is worth noting at this point that the 150th anniversary of the Day of the Covenant falls in 1988.)

It was in the same period, the late 1930s, as the Broederbond was methodically preparing itself for the advent of Afrikaner power over all the other people of South Africa, that the framework for the doctrine and system of apartheid was created. The practice of white supremacy, in a rough-and-ready sort of way, had been around ever since the Dutch came to South Africa, and while Boers and English-speakers had their different ways of legitimizing the practice, they were generally agreed on the necessity for it, whatever the reasons for the necessity might be. What was new about apartheid was its doctrinal and systematic character: the fact of being an ideology. And the ideology, once its exponents came to power, made for a far more pervasive and insistent form of white supremacy than anything known before: more drastic, more pedantic, more innovative, imaginative, bureaucratic and meddlesome, and therefore far more tormenting to those subjected to its maddening attentions than the old, relatively easygoing routines of white rule had been.

The Broederbond was the creator of the apartheid ideology, through the writings of three of its academic members, high pundits of nationalism: Dr N. Diederichs, Dr P. J. Meyer and Dr G. Cronjé.

This was the late 1930s, and the early ideologues of apartheid were influenced to some degree by the language and concepts of contemporary European right-wing authoritarianism – usually in its milder forms. (Though many leading Afrikaner nationalists were 'pro-Nazi' during the war, the affinity seems to have been less ideological than a matter of 'the enemy of one's enemy', as with other subject peoples' nationalists in the same period; compare the 'pro-Nazism' of Flemish, Breton and Palestinian nationalists. Many Afrikaners, as well as English-speaking South Africans, fought on the side of the British in both world wars. But Afrikaner nationalists – those who regarded themselves as the only *regte* Afrikaners – were opposed to South African involvement on Britain's side in either war. Some were pro-German; some favoured neutrality.)

In the main, however, apartheid was an Afrikaner answer to an Afrikaner

145

problem. The problem was this: Afrikaner nationalists saw themselves as essentially freedom fighters. They had fought for their freedom, at the dawn of the century, against the greatest empire on earth, and had given a good account of themselves. And now, under the leadership of the Broederbond, they were headed for the recovery of their freedom, in their own home. But black people were a large majority in that home. Were the Afrikaners, once they had liberated themselves, going to liberate the blacks, by giving them real votes, and so power over whites, including Afrikaners? Obviously not, since such a conclusion would make nonsense of the whole epic struggle of the *volk* for freedom. Were they, then, going to deny to others the freedom they prized so much for themselves? The accurate answer was yes. But the accurate answer was unacceptable to people who were, like all fervent nationalists, self-righteous in the extreme. A sham answer was needed, and was believed, since it was needed. And so apartheid was born.

'The Boer nation', said the ideologue G. Cronjé, 'can fully understand the sufferings of the Bantu. It is that same imperialism and capitalism, having them believe that the foreign is better than what is their own, which seeks to destroy their tribal life.' So the liberation of the blacks by the Afrikaners would consist in the restoration of their tribal life.

The liberation of the Afrikaners, however, would entail a monopoly of state power. 'In the future Afrikaner national state [*volkstaat*],' P. J. Meyer wrote, 'the undivided power granted by God rests with the Afrikaner state authority.'

So the circle was squared; the two liberations were fully compatible. The apotheosis of Afrikaner sacral nationalism under God's ordination (*Godsbestemming*) would also liberate the blacks.

The invention of apartheid was a major achievement of liberation theology.

That is not so outrageous a paradox as it may sound to some ears. In the early part of the twentieth century the Afrikaner nationalists were not merely accepted internationally as a national-liberation movement. They were admired by fervent nationalists in all the countries of the British Empire, and the other colonial empires, as the archetypal example of a national-liberation movement, the most heroic and determined of fighters against imperialism. It was the Anglo-Boer war that set the pace for the worldwide process of decolonization in the twentieth century. The Irish nationalists were the next to strike a blow against imperialism, and they were consciously imitative of the Boers. Mr Sean MacBride is an advocate of extreme measures against the Afrikaners, but his father, Major John MacBride, fought with the Boers against the British. And I suspect that many Irish people today actually do not know that the brutal Afrikaners whom they occasionally see on their television screens are the same people as the valiant Boers of Irish nationalist tradition.

The fact that a genuine national-liberation movement should invent the ideology of apartheid, and erect its institutions, should not surprise us much. People fight for freedom, but what some of them win is power. And the use they make of their power may not look at all like the freedom their admirers saw them as fighting for. That generalization is relevant not only to the past Afrikaner struggle for freedom but to the *anti*-Afrikaner freedom struggle of today. Joseph Stalin and Pol Pot were once fighters for freedom, champions of the cause of the people. And it would hardly be an inconsistent development of present revolutionary activities if among the children with the necklace, who are currently burning people alive in the name of the cause of the people, were to be found a potential Joseph Stalin or a future Pol Pot.

To come back to the Afrikaners, and to the Afrikaner intellectuals in particular: those among them who talk to us in the 1980s about minority rights, self-determination and so on may be conscious hypocrites, and I suspect they mostly are. But those who created apartheid, its theoreticians and early practitioners, were not hypocrites at all. It might have been better if they had been, because then they would have left apartheid where it began: in the domain of words.

Like Pygmalion, the creators of apartheid were in love with their creation and brought it to life. As soon as the Nationalists came to power, in 1948, the building of the institutions of apartheid began, and it proceeded apace after the appointment of a dedicated apartheid intellectual, H. F. Verwoerd, in October of 1950, as minister for native affairs (he later became Prime Minister). The principal institutions were the 'Bantustans', later 'Homelands' (under apartheid, euphemisms atrophy quickly). The Homelands are supposed to be nation-states, in which the Bantu is free to live his own tribal life, even if he doesn't want to. Under Verwoerd the Nationalists set up Bantustans with the same confident *élan* with which the Jacobins of revolutionary France had set up their sister republics (*Républiques soeurs*): the Cisalpine Republic, the Parthenopean Republic and what have you. The sister republics of the Afrikaner state have names like Ciskei, Transkei, Bophuthatswana and Venda. (These are the four that are supposed to be fully independent. There are also six others.) There is a crazy poetry about it all, but the attempt to turn crazy poetry into reality, an attempt sustained with fanatical energy, has produced vast amounts of unnecessary human suffering: peremptory uprooting, colossal movements of populations, constant police investigation of passes, the separation of families, unusually long journeys to work – the catalogue of evils is well known. But it is different to see it. Travelling through a densely populated resettlement zone in a remote and desolate valley in the Ciskei, I noted the general impression in my diary: 'Mad child scattering packets of shacks over valley floor.'

Nor was apartheid applied with any real respect for its supposed guiding principle: tribal affiliation. The theory of the thing was that the identity of each tribal group was to be cherished – that each was a kind of *volk*, which, given its own land, might aspire someday to become like the Afrikaners, in a black sort of way. The architects of apartheid might have believed all that intellectually, but in practice they couldn't bring themselves to respect any black *volk*, and they chopped up the land to suit themselves – the Afrikaners, the real *volk*. Thus a certain group of people, having once been South African, suddenly found themselves citizens of Transkei. Then they were out of Transkei and back into South Africa, because the boss of Transkei, Kaiser Matanzima, didn't like them. Then they were out of South Africa again and found themselves citizens of the newly created and now 'independent' state of Ciskei. And so on. The term *Homelands* became a mockery.

Nationalist faith in apartheid continued strong for nearly thirty years. It survived the enormous demonstrations against the pass laws, in March of 1960, which led to large numbers of arrests and to the killing of sixty-nine blacks by the South African police, at Sharpeville. Sharpeville sent shock waves around the world, but Nationalists saw it as a flash in the pan. It was not until 16 June 1976, when school riots began in Soweto and spread across South Africa, that Nationalist complacency began to be shaken. The riots were precipitated by a desire to reject the enforced teaching of certain subjects in Afrikaans. But it soon became clear that far more was involved. Young people, who had never known any institutions other than those of apartheid, were in rebellion against those institutions. Apartheid had failed conspicuously in the one area indispensable to its success: the education of young blacks.

If Nationalist complacency was shaken by Soweto, it has to be shaken even more profoundly by the present unrest. Sixteen years had separated Sharpeville from Soweto; less than half that time span separated Soweto from the unrest that broke out in the autumn of 1983, almost simultaneously with the introduction of P. W. Botha's new constitution. And the unrest that began in 1983 has continued without a let-up ever since, with an extent and intensity never previously known, and it has been accompanied by an unprecedented measure of international displeasure, all leading to the collapse of the rand, and the South African moratorium on repayments.

The defection of a significant part of the intellectual elite of Afrikanerdom set in after Soweto. But an even more disturbing kind of intellectual defection seems to have set in among the Nationalists who remained, especially the leaders: a partial defection of their own minds.

Watching members of the Nationalist establishment in South Africa both in the flesh and on television, and reading or listening to their words, I formed the impression that these gentlemen had become incapable of thinking, at least on the subject about which they talked the most. It is understandable that this should have come about. The initial strain of attaining a belief in the fantasies of apartheid must have exacted a considerable mental toll. That was followed by the strain imposed by the divergence, combined with the denial of the divergence, between apartheid in theory and apartheid in practice. And that was followed in turn by the growing discredit of apartheid, leading to the combined necessities of assuring the international community that apartheid was to all intents and purposes dead while reassuring the Nationalist rank and file that apartheid in all essentials was very much alive. And on top of all that was the frantic quest for some euphemism adequate to describe the new reality that was to replace apartheid. This quest is doomed to failure, because the new reality – this is the minimum requirement of Nationalists – has to have at its core the prime substance of the *old* reality: white supremacy, and Afrikaner supremacy within white supremacy. And that is the reality that apartheid was created to disguise, not only from others but – and especially – from the creators of apartheid themselves.

All that is more than enough to boggle the mind, and the minds in question appear by now to be well and truly boggled.

While I was in Pretoria, I collected, from the State President's splendid offices in Union Building, a big bunch of P. W. Botha's speeches. I read all of these, and the experience went far toward boggling my own mind. Botha and his aides, it seems, have been so long in the business of churning out nonsense of the ideological sort that they can no longer discern and eliminate ordinary nonsense. Take the following gem, from a speech delivered by the State President on the occasion of the unveiling of a monument at the Burgher Memorial in Delareyville, on 10 October 1985. Botha was speaking in honour of Delareyville's eponymous Boer War hero General J. H. De la Rey, to whom he paid the following tribute:

> General De la Rey, after whom this town is called, laid down his life in the service of freedom and the principles of justice. Later, for the sake of these same principles, he revolted against the unfair attempts on South West Africa.

General De la Rey's posthumous exploit eclipses that of Hilaire Belloc's hero of the Napoleonic wars, who 'Lost a leg at Waterloo,/At Quatre-Bras and Ligny too!'

I have seen Botha in action in person twice – addressing the faithful at Springs and addressing a critical audience, the Foreign Correspondents' Association, in Johannesburg – and I have often watched him on South African television, which his picture dominates. On television his face in close-up doesn't look like much – it is puffy, the mouth a bit slobbery. But on the platform he is more impressive – a big, well-built man, with a demeanour that contradicts the flow of bland, conciliatory euphemisms that often pours from his mouth. When he is being abrasive – as he was with the foreign correspondents – he appears to mean what he says. But whether what he says is meant to please or to rasp, he looks the same: grim, unsmiling, determined – his little, rather porcine eyes darting from side to side as if searching for enemies, his gestures suggestive less of oratorical emphasis than of chopping something or somebody. His mind may be a bit gone, but his will appears intact.

I don't believe that Botha and his colleagues are anywhere near to agreeing to hand over a significant share in power to any blacks. They may eventually agree, in order to ease the international pressure, not only to gestures like the release of Nelson Mandela but to quite far-reaching reforms: to end influx control, to reform the pass laws, even to abolish the Group Areas Act (although most groups would have to remain in the areas in which they were put during the imperious heyday of apartheid). These reforms would make life a bit easier for ordinary blacks, but it is not likely that they would do anything to reduce the unrest. The unrest at this stage is a struggle for power, conducted on the black side by people who believe that the apartheid regime is beginning to collapse under the combined pressure of the unrest itself and the international pressure it generates. Quite rightly, these people see such reforms as have come and such as may be coming as fruits of the unrest, and so they will keep up the unrest, and pile on the pressure, by every means they can. And the elemental hatred of large numbers of blacks for the whole apartheid system will support them in keeping the pressure up as long as the regime refuses to begin handing over power to the revolutionary leaders.

So, because the National Party will refuse, the unrest will continue – no doubt with ups and downs in intensity – at least as long as the National Party remains in power. It will do so for a little under three years, until the next general election. But for how long after that?

Not all that long, runs one line of argument. There are those defections, that confusion at the top: premonitory signs. There is that queue to Lusaka, leaving the sinking ship. More generally, the Afrikaners of today are not the stern, embattled colonial farmers of Nationalist legend. They are urbanized, *embourgeoisés*, softened – part of the consumer society, part of the permissive society. They are no longer securely hooked to the culture represented by the Voortrekker Monument.

They spend less time, the argument goes on, in contemplating the exploits of the immortal General De la Rey, or the vexed question of what Sarel Cilliers may or may not have said to Andries Pretorius on the eve of the Battle of Blood River, than they do in contemplating the latest American situation comedy, courtesy of South African Television. They, whose ancestors so staunchly resisted anglicization, have shown far less resistance to Americanization. Even the hold of the Afrikaans language, the sacred *taal*, is weakening. It was weakening prior to television; as early as the 1950s the circulation of the English-language press was rising faster than that of the Afrikaans press. But televised entertainment is a far more effective agent of Anglophone acculturation than the printed word is. And televised entertainment is overwhelmingly American (and depicts an integrated society). Where *Neef Brit* failed, *Neef Yank* has won.

And – continues the argument – these Americanized bourgeois are not going to die in the last ditch, on some kind of spiritual ox wagon. Ox wagons are for the birds. Once these people realize that the game is really up, they are going to desert the National Party in droves. In such a situation the only Afrikaner tradition that can make sense to the Americanized Afrikaner is that of the *hensoppers*.

I can accept a large part of this argument – even the bit about the permissive society. In Pretorius Street, Pretoria – of all places – I saw a conspicuously placed poster supplying the telephone number of the Rentagirl Escort Service. I don't know what Sarel Cilliers may be saying, in heaven, to Andries Pretorius about *that*.

I agree with most of the descriptive part of the argument. White South Africans, English-speakers and Afrikaners together, respectfully attended by cheap black servants, may form, as has been said, 'the most spoiled society in the world'. What I find much less convincing, though, are the political inferences from all this. In particular I think that the argument greatly overstates the *political* (and politico-cultural) impact of television in deeply divided societies.

In Northern Ireland, Catholics and Protestants have been watching virtually the same television programmes, and very often the programmes that Afrikaners have been watching, for about a quarter of a century. But this common experience has in no way mitigated the ancient antagonism of the two communities. While the set is switched on, both communities are in the world of admass. But when the set is switched off, each is back in its separate world, Green or Orange. Similarly, I suspect that many an Afrikaner, switching off his set, returns to the *laager* as if he had never left it.

Basically, I think people distinguish between reality and make-believe more precisely than some commentators give them credit for. The stuff on the screen is make-believe. The alien community, on the ground and near you, is unfortunately part of the world of reality. You have to wake from the sweet dreams on the screen and keep your guard up.

If the 'softening up' argument proves to be correct, there should be a poor turnout for the commemorative ceremonies culminating on 16 December 1988 – the 150th anniversary of the Battle of Blood River.

My own guess is that there will be an impressive turnout. True, the mood will be far from the ebullient one in which the centenary was celebrated, in 1938. At that time Afrikanerdom was on the way up, and on the road to power. The ox wagon was also a bandwagon. Nothing of that now. The mood required in 1988 will be one of grim determination, because the *volk* is confronted with the greatest perceived threat to its existence since the Zulu king Dingaan treacherously murdered Piet Retief and his followers, in the *kraal* at Umgungundhlovo, on 6 February 1838. But the very fact of enhanced danger is likely to make the year 1988 – commemorating in February the disaster at Umgungundhlovo, as well as in December the deliverance at Blood River – a most appropriate time to display the determination of the threatened *volk*.

I think it probable that many of those who take part in the commemorative ceremonies of 1988 will be drawn from the ranks of the Afrikaners who are supposed to have become Americanized. And it may be that their determination will be registered a shade more grimly for a certain sense of guilt about having, in those long leisure hours before the TV screen, allowed their attention to wander far from the Vow that Sarel Cilliers swore, on behalf of all Afrikaners, in the terrible days between Umgungundhlovo and Blood River.

It is not, of course, all a matter of Afrikaner pride, legends, memories. There are also Afrikaner *interests*. Some of these are general interests, shared by all whites. But some are specific to Afrikaners, and the nature of these makes it particularly difficult for Afrikaners to contemplate a transit of power to blacks. The basic problem here is that the power that would be in transit is *political* power, which has been an Afrikaner monopoly since 1948. And the political power in question here is not a matter that affects just a few elected officials. The fruits of political power have become the mainstay of life for a very large number of Afrikaners.

This phenomenon, like much else in South Africa, dates from 1948 and the first electoral triumph of the National Party. Dr D. F. Malan, the first Nationalist Prime Minister, found an elegant and unchallengeable formula for turning the South African Civil Service into an Afrikaner monopoly. He simply decreed that future entrants into the civil service would have to be competent in both Afrikaans and English. And what could be fairer than that in (white) South Africa's bilingual society? In practice most Afrikaners knew at least some English – perforce, since English was the language of business. True, the English of many Afrikaners was not very good. But any reasonable Afrikaner candidate could attain a degree of competence in English adequate to satisfy a selection board made up mostly of Afrikaners.

However, whereas almost all English-speakers had acquired the rudiments of Afrikaans at school, hardly any of them had bothered to acquire a real command of the language, because they had never needed to. True, young English-speaking aspirants to public employment could start brushing up their Afrikaans. But it was not likely that many of them could acquire such a mastery of the finer points of the language as would satisfy a selection board made up mostly of Afrikaners.

With one neat stroke Dr Malan had Afrikanerized the civil service of South Africa. And there was more to it than that. Selection procedures controlled by the Broederbond ensured that all top posts went to Broederbond members and the remaining posts to *regte* Afrikaners of lesser social standing.

The relevance of these transactions to the present situation is that Afrikaners – and especially *regte* Afrikaners – have much more to lose than English-speakers by a transfer of political power. Under 'one man, one vote' the private sector, where most of the English-speakers are, could hope to carry on with business more or less as usual, as in Robert Mugabe's Zimbabwe. Some businessmen – especially in Port Elizabeth – believe that business would be a lot *better* under 'one man, one vote' than it is now. The blacks, if they were well led, would in their own interest be inclined to lay off the private sector. But they would take over the public sector. They would Africanize it just as surely as Dr Malan Afrikanerized it in 1948, and for the same reason: jobs for their own people.

And so, without that power, scores of thousands of Afrikaners would find themselves out in the cold and – unlike the English-speakers – with nowhere outside South Africa to go. Many of them – with few skills that are in demand in the private sector – would be likely to sink back to the condition of poor whites, which was the condition of many of their families in the days before the resurgence of Afrikanerdom.

More generally, the Afrikaners, who came up from their nadir in 1902 to make themselves, forty-six years later, the masters of the great, rich and beautiful land of South Africa, would now fall back to an even more unacceptable position than was theirs in the aftermath of the Anglo-Boer war. Then they accepted defeat at the hands of the mightiest empire in the world. Now they would be lorded over by those over whom they themselves have lorded for so long.

That, no more and no less, is what Afrikaners have to fear – *that*, and not immersion in some generalized doom, such as being 'driven into the sea', in store for all whites (nowhere in Africa have whites been driven into the sea, though some other peoples have). What is at stake is the Afrikaner monopoly of political power. That is why the admonitions of the leaders of the business community fell on deaf ears, as far as the Afrikaner beneficiaries of political monopoly are concerned. Afrikaners see themselves as asked to sacrifice their own, deeply cherished, specific interests for the convenience of *Neef Brit*. Nothing in their history or in the nature of their present situation suggests that they are likely to do this.

Afrikaners are neither the uniquely virtuous *volk* of their own rhetoric – 'the highest work of art of the Architect of the Centuries', as Dr Malan once put it – nor yet the moral monsters depicted by outside rhetoric. They are ordinary human beings, with the normal human quotas of greed, arrogance and so forth, operating within a unique predicament, which they have inherited and are now thrashing around in. I suspect that some of the righteous who denounce them from afar might behave quite like them if they were caught in a similar predicament – if, for example, there had been a black majority in America in the 1950s.

Pride and economic interest are here intertwined. There is probably no people that would willingly accept such a precipitous fall in power, status and income as would be required of Afrikaners in the event of the great transition. So Afrikaners, despite their shaken morale, despite the defection of a certain intellectual elite, and despite their partial Americanization seem likely to go on voting for the parties of the *laager* – the Nationalists and the Afrikaner parties to the right of them – so as to hold the Afrikaner monopoly of political and military power. The mini-election of last October reflected no weakening – rather the contrary – in the determination of Afrikaner voters to hold on to that monopoly.

While holding on to that monopoly to the very last possible moment, the Afrikaner leadership is likely to try various schemes involving the co-optation of blacks or the delegation of subordinate authority to blacks. That is already happening, in a crude but partly effective way, in the Homelands, where black elites and their dependent clansmen have common interests with the Afrikaners rather than with the black revolutionaries (generally the most deadly enemies of the Homelands elites).

But there is available a bolder and more radical form of co-optation than any yet attempted. This is called the Zulu option or the Buthelezi option. This option is already much discussed and is likely to be attempted, in some shape or form, well before the apartheid regime reaches the end of its tether.

So, before we come to consider the possible character of that end game, let us take a look at the Zulu option.

In its roughest outline the Zulu option runs as follows: There are about six million Zulus in South Africa and about five million whites. Under apartheid lines of division, in South Africa's population of 27 million (excluding the four supposedly independent Homelands), blacks (Africans, Asians, coloureds) outnumber whites by more than four to one: whites make up 19 per cent. But if Zulus could somehow be made allies of the whites, then the number of whites and their allies would rise to 41 per cent – more than twice as nice as the way it is now. (It is all more complicated than that, but that is the general idea.)

But how to get Zulus out of the apartheid classification and into an alliance with whites? At this point the Zulu option becomes the Buthelezi option.

Chief Mangosothu Gatsha Buthelezi (he prefers the 'Mangosothu', but the press, for obvious reasons, prefers the 'Gatsha') has been chief minister since 1976 of the Homeland of Kwa Zulu, but he is much more than that. In general the Homeland chief ministers are local bosses, each a ruthless master of his allotted patch of territory, with few ambitions or capacities beyond that. But Buthelezi is a national and international figure, who has followed a line independent of both the South African Government and the ANC-UDF leadership. Because he operates within the Homelands system and because he has campaigned internationally against sanctions and disinvestment, ANC spokesmen depict him as a stooge. But his track record is not that of a stooge. He refused 'independence' status for Kwa Zulu at a time when the South African Government was pushing its fiction of independent statehoods for the Homelands. In 1983 he campaigned against P. W. Botha's disastrous tricameral constitution, at a time when the document was being widely touted (especially in the business community) as 'a step forward'. He is very much his own man.

Buthelezi is often described as 'a Muzorewa' – a comparison to Bishop

Abel Muzorewa, who emerged briefly to nominal leadership in the last stages of Ian Smith's Rhodesia (Zimbabwe) and who was repudiated in the British-organized elections that brought Robert Mugabe to power. There is some point in the comparison, since white South Africans look at Buthelezi as white Rhodesians looked at Muzorewa: as a black option for when things get very bad, a late way of staving off the worst.

But Buthelezi has far more going for him than Muzorewa ever had. Buthelezi has his own power base, in Kwa Zulu, and his own large and dynamic political party, Inkatha, with an embryo militia in Inkatha's Youth League.

The Inkatha youth are a rough lot; they are often referred to as the *Impis*, after the dreaded regiments of the Zulu kings Shaka, Dingaan and Cetshwayo. There is a romantic aura about the whole movement – a Fascist potential, according to its opponents (the ANC and the UDF).

Inkatha today claims a paid-up membership of one million, and even its adversaries do not dispute that the membership is large. The bulk of the membership is drawn from the north-eastern province of Natal (including Kwa Zulu), but there are also many members in urban areas outside Natal. Buthelezi has addressed large meetings in Soweto.

Buthelezi's adversaries accuse him of splitting 'the people' – which consist of all blacks, including Indians and coloureds – along ethnic lines. Buthelezi retorts that Inkatha membership is open to all. Still, almost all the members appear to be Zulus. In a conversation at Jan Smuts Airport with Buthelezi, who had with him John Mavusu, the top Inkatha man in Soweto, I put a question about that. Mavusu replied, 'Inkatha is not a Zulu organization. But the Zulus have always provided the leadership for other Africans.' Chief Buthelezi did not appear to dissent.

The ethnic factor in South African politics is very difficult for an outsider to assess. Perhaps even for an insider – inside *what*, after all? Apartheid, of course, insists on the transcendent importance of ethnicity, and assigns and reassigns ethnicities with ponderous and capricious rigour. The enemies of apartheid sweepingly dismiss ethnic categories as irrelevant. In fact ethnic affiliations – not necessarily as defined by Afrikaners – appear to remain important, though their manifestations can be extremely confusing. I was told by a distinguished and judicious resident of Soweto, Dr Nthato Motlana, of a remarkable incident that occurred during my visit. A mob came down the street chanting, 'Get the Zulus'. What was remarkable was that the words shouted were *in Zulu*. And the shouters were themselves Zulu: Zulu Soweto residents attacking Zulu migrant workers holding Kwa Zulu passes. There are urbanized Zulus, politicized and de-ethnicized by the

ANC, who hate Buthelezi and the very name of Zulu. But it seems that most Zulus are less complicated. Intertribal fighting has been a significant – though relatively little-noted – part of the unrest, and Zulus have often played a leading part in this. About sixty people were reported killed in fighting in Natal between Zulu and Pondo tribesmen on Christmas Day 1985. Such clashes are triggered by local disputes – over matters like access to water – but they can also have some political overtones. The non-Zulu party to any such conflict is much more likely than the Zulu party to use ANC-UDF slogans, and is likely also to accuse the Zulus – and Buthelezi's Inkatha in particular – of tribalism and collaboration with Pretoria. And it is the very fact of this continuing contention among blacks that attracts the attention of some of Pretoria's planners to the Buthelezi option.

Buthelezi himself is a proud African, proud of his people's martial history and of his own dynastic connections: he is a descendant on his mother's side of the last independent Zulu king, Cetshwayo. Buthelezi's manner is aristocratic, in a European rather than an African manner. Some other African chiefs whom I have met are rather obviously indifferent to the opinion of their interlocutor; they have a somnolent, inward-looking hauteur. Buthelezi, though, is charming, affable, considerate. On his visits to Britain he goes down very well, I believe, with members of the House of Lords.

Buthelezi is austere in his personal life. He doesn't drink or smoke, and there is no touch of scandal or corruption about him anywhere. In these respects he is very different from most of the other Homelands chiefs.

The trouble with the 'Buthelezi option' is that Pretoria seems unable to deal with a proud African, or even to register the existence of such a phenomenon. The Buthelezi option, on Buthelezi's terms, would mean power in Natal Province: Natal as a predominantly Zulu state. There can be little doubt that this revival of Zulu glory would rally great numbers of Zulus around Buthelezi and that Pretoria could reap at least some of the benefits of the Zulu option. But that would still mean blacks ruling whites in Natal – even though the whites there are mostly English-speaking, not Afrikaners – and Pretoria still cannot stomach that. The Botha Government at the end of 1985 was still thinking essentially in terms of buying off this (to them) awkward black with some kind of showy job in Pretoria. This is a hopeless version of the Zulu option. But the National Party seems incapable of envisaging any way of dealing with blacks except bludgeoning or bribery.

Racism, like other forms of hubris, tends to blind people to some of their true interests and to the nature of their predicament. And racism wrapped in layers of euphemism – as in contemporary South Africa – remains as blind, and as racist, as before.

157

But even if Pretoria at a later stage brings itself to take the Buthelezi option seriously, it will probably still only be buying a little more time for itself. For the serious trouble, which will not go away, is not in Natal but mainly in the Transvaal and the Cape, and there the pressures are bound to increase. All the demographic odds are heavily against the whites. In 1983, according to official South African statistics, black births outnumbered white by *ten to one*. (And these statistics are geared to *understating* the demographic disparity, by omitting the figures from the four all-black 'independent' Homelands.)

The more black children, the more turbulent the black children. Politicization spreads fast in an expanding population with expanding unemployment, especially as the more energetic and ambitious children realize that politicization brings with it power within the ghettos. The children who count for most are the children with the necklace.

The more children, the more unrest; the more unrest, the more repression; the more repression, the more international pressure and the more economic misery.

Let us suppose that this vicious spiral develops to the point where it overcomes the stiff resistance to change of a large part of the Afrikaner electorate. I doubt whether that will happen, even when things get much worse, but let us suppose it does happen. At some future general election – let us say the next one, in less than three years – large numbers of Afrikaner voters desert the *laager* parties and join forces with the Progressives. You have once again, as before 1948, a British-Afrikaner coalition. And you have a white state president who is pledged to enter into serious negotiations with the ANC about 'one man, one vote'.

Could such a state president count on the loyalty of the South African Defence Force?

I raised that question, in my Proustian way, in conversation with an Afrikaner political analyst who – because his speciality is Marxism – has been in close touch with South African military intelligence.

Could he, I asked, envisage some possible future circumstances in which the South African Defence Force might no longer be amenable to civilian control?

He looked at me, deadpan, and said, 'You are supposing that there is civilian control at the moment.'

Partly he was referring to a matter of structures. Security is the concern of a joint committee – the State Security Council – which includes the head of the Defence Force and the commissioner of police as well as members of the Cabinet. But many well-informed South Africans believe that the security forces are already, at least to some extent, a law unto themselves, prepared to ignore government policies of which they disapprove. Thus in Mozambique an apparently highly successful South African government line of policy seems to have been sabotaged and scorned by the South African military.

On 16 March 1984, the Governments of South Africa and Mozambique concluded a pact – the Nkomati Accord – under which each Government pledged itself to ensure that its territory would not be used for the planning or launching of a military attack on the other. Under that accord – which scandalized former admirers of Mozambique's ruling left-wing party, Frelimo – Mozambique reduced the ANC presence there to a small, purely diplomatic mission. It all seemed quite a coup for South Africa. But in practice the accord was ignored – or rather, systematically violated – on the South African side. The South African military continued to provide logistic backing for the Mozambique Resistance Movement, Renamo. And during October the Mozambique Government published captured documents – the authenticity of which is officially disputed by Pretoria but generally accepted by well-informed South Africans – according to which the military authorities advised Renamo to treat the Nkomati Accord as null and void, and spoke disrespectfully of South Africa's foreign minister, Mr 'Pik' Botha. (As it happens, I have never met a single South African, of any persuasion, condition or colour, who did *not* speak disrespectfully of Pik Botha; but that, of course, is not the point here.)

So it does rather look as if P. W. Botha's Government may not be in full control of its own armed forces. The 'wars' the South African forces have been intermittently waging or supporting beyond South African borders – in Angola and Namibia, Botswana and Lesotho, as well as in Mozambique and possibly Zimbabwe – may well not be P. W. Botha's idea at all; he may have no alternative but to go along, much as the last governments of France's Fourth Republic rubber-stamped the actions of an army over which they had lost control.

And it does seem that the South African Defence Force may already be to a great extent 'Algerianized'. An important recent book, *Pretoria's Praetorians: Civil-Military Relations in South Africa*, by Philip Frankel, suggests as much. It appears that the lectures given at the South African Joint Defence College are entirely based on the work of the French general André Beaufre, a specialist in counter-insurgency, and that they draw on the lessons of France's experiences in Algeria and Indo-China (presumably in order to avoid repeating those experiences). The quotations from this martial guru suggest that the boggling of the Afrikaner mind must be proceeding at an especially accelerated rate in the Joint Defence College. Beaufre, whose doctrine is that of 'the indirect mode', says that the strategist in the indirect mode 'is like a surgeon called upon to operate on a sick person who is growing continuously and with extreme rapidity and of whose detailed anatomy he is not sure: his operating table is in a state of perpetual motion and he must have ordered the instruments he is to use five years beforehand.'

It doesn't sound as if the chances of a successful operation are all that high. All the same, it is clear that the graduates of the Joint Defence College are being conditioned to get their hands on that unfortunate 'sick person' and try out their surgical skills.

It doesn't sound, either, as if the Afrikaner-dominated South African Defence Force would – even in much worsened circumstances – be likely to obey what they would regard as a *hensopper* state president, bent on making a deal with the ANC. Apart from their pride, traditions and anti-Marxist, anti-ANC ideology, they have (like the Afrikaners in the civil service) their professional interests and status to think about, which would be prime casualties of such a deal.

So it seems that even if a majority of the white electorate were prepared to throw in the sponge, the struggle to maintain white, and Afrikaner, supremacy would be carried on by the armed forces, presumably under martial law, with the suspension of the constitution (which is, in any case, not a document that inspires any great veneration, even among white South Africans).

True, there might be questions, under such conditions, about the discipline of some elements of the armed forces. English-speakers – a number of whom already try to evade national service – might desert or be allowed to resign. And there might be even more serious problems concerning the reliability of blacks (including Indians and coloureds) in the Defence Force.

Blacks make up at present about 40 per cent of the South African Defence Force and the South West African Territorial Force (and about 50 per cent of the police). Most of these are 'other ranks', but some have recently been promoted to lieutenant. Most are noncombatants in support roles, but significant numbers have seen active service: it has been reported that at least 20 per cent of the forces serving in Namibia have been blacks. There continue to be more black applicants for places in the Defence Force than there are places. Military analysts report that morale among the black troops is high, and, remarkably, there have apparently been no black desertions to the enemy.

This last phenomenon may be due in part to the extreme ferocity with which the champions of 'the cause of the people' treat not only collaborators but at least some ex-collaborators. In October 1985 an army jeep carrying two black soldiers drove past a 'political' funeral, always a dangerous gathering of mainly militant people. One of the black soldiers jumped out and gave the clenched-fist salute of the Revolution. He was immediately surrounded by a group of mourning children. Perhaps he thought they were coming to congratulate him. They tied a tire around his neck and burned him to death. It was not a news item likely to incite black soldiers to desert.

Of course, the discipline of the black soldiers may weaken under the rising pressures. But even the desertion of many blacks would hardly inflict crippling damage on the Defence Force. Armed blacks are confined to the infantry, with infantry weapons and training only. The armoured units, the artillery and the air force are all-white and mainly Afrikaner; the navy is still predominantly English-speaking but is becoming increasingly Afrikaner.

Even at an advanced phase of the unrest the South African Defence Force would probably still be able to hold, for a prolonged period, those parts of South Africa they would want to hold: primarily the Cape, plus the mineral-rich areas of the Transvaal. The 1977 Security Council embargo on the supply of weapons to South Africa has had the effect of making South Africa largely self-sufficient in conventional arms manufacture. (South Africa is also said to possess a nuclear capability.) The economic difficulties attendant on such unrest would be very serious but probably not crippling. Afrikaners would be prepared to tighten their belts quite a lot rather than abandon their power and status. Sanctions and disinvestment would hurt, but a country with South Africa's resources will always be attractive to the international black market. 'Gold', as the poet Horace remarked, 'has a way of getting through the guards.'

It is true that a general strike, a complete withdrawal of black labour, could defeat this last stand of Afrikanerdom. But it should be noted that the present wave of unrest in the townships is almost exclusively confined to the *unemployed* young. The employed have been mainly quiescent; the black trades union leaders, once the focus of protest against apartheid, have taken a back seat politically since the children took over. A recent strike, in the principal hospital in Soweto, failed in November 1985 despite ferocious intimidation designed to keep it going. One nurse accused of strike-breaking was burned alive. The strike ended a few days later. The children are now threatening to enforce a general strike during this year [1986], but they may find that miners don't burn so easily as nurses. Yet trades union leaders by the end of 1985 were sounding more militant than they had during most of the year. The combination of pressure from the children and resentment at police actions may produce more strikes this year, though probably not the general strike the children call for.

In conditions of high unemployment and no social security, a job (any kind of job) is a most precious possession: hence, among other things, the flow of black recruits into the South African Defence Force. And a black rebel in South Africa is not in the relatively happy position of an IRA rebel in Northern Ireland, able to devote all this time to killing the soldiers of the enemy government, in the secure knowledge that the welfare services of the enemy government will keep the family of the 'unemployed' rebel supplied with all the necessities of life. So a general and protracted withdrawal of black labour seems unlikely.

Up to almost the end of 1985 the unrest consisted mainly of what the children did, together with sporadic and relatively minor attacks, mostly with grenades but more recently with land mines, in border areas. The township unrest, led by the children, precipitated the brutal police repression, which caused most of the deaths in 1985 and attracted almost all the international attention. According to (admittedly approximate) figures published in *The Times* of London on 20 December 1985, there were 685 people killed in the period from 1 January to 31 October 1985, compared with 149 killed in all of 1984. More than half of those killed in 1985 were 'blacks killed by police': 360 people. As against that, only eighteen policemen were killed; significantly, seventeen of these were 'killed by townships residents', as against only one 'killed by guerrillas'. The next largest category of killed after 'blacks killed by police' was 'residents killed by residents': 201 people. These included the victims of the children, and this category may be more subject to underestimation than the others; in any case, in 1985 this category by itself exceeded all of the deaths in 1984. The category 'blacks killed by police' increased nearly five times from 1984 to 1985 (79 to 360), but the category 'residents killed by residents' increased more than ten times (17 to 201) over the same period. The category 'police killed by residents' increased even more sharply: from one in 1984 to seventeen in 1985.

Those *Times* figures showed only one white killed by blacks in 1984 and only one white killed by blacks for 1985 up to 31 October (the latest date covered by the *Times* survey). But in the last days of 1985 the figure for whites killed by blacks suddenly shot up. Six white civilians – including four children – were killed on 15 December by land-mine explosions in a game reserve near the Zimbabwe border. The ANC claimed that these explosions were 'justified'. On 23 December a bomb in a crowded shopping centre at

Amanzimtoti, a white beach resort south of Durban, killed another six white civilians. No organization claimed responsibility for the Amanzimtoti bomb, but Michael Hornsby, the experienced South African correspondent of *The Times*, commented on the incident: 'It is arguably the most indiscriminate act of urban terror to date except in so far as it seems to have been aimed mainly at whites. It has long been predicted that pressure on the ANC leadership from impatient young members of the organization to attack white civilians directly would become irresistible.'

So by the end of 1985 the children seemed to be setting the pace for the guerrillas as well as for the townships. And several correspondents noted a hardening of mood also among whites, especially in the Afrikaner community, following the two major black-on-white incidents of December. Pressure for a tougher military response to black terrorism was rising.

A military – or simply more deeply militarized – government in South Africa might be expected to get a lot tougher than the government of P. W. Botha has yet felt able to be. The model might be General Jacques Massu's successful repression of the Front de Libération Nationale (FLN) in Algiers in the late 1950s. (The Massu repression was itself a response to FLN indiscrimate terror-bombings of Europeans, very much on Amanzimtoti lines.) If an Afrikaner Massu is to persuade people in the townships that he is more frightening than the children with the necklace or the bomb, he is going to have to become very frightening indeed. The least that might be expected – under martial law and a total news blackout – would be house-to-house searches backed by uninhibited use of firepower; torture (on a larger scale than now practised) and execution of suspects; and deportations and concentration camps.

General Charles de Gaulle, by about 1960, was able to bring Massu-style repression in Algeria to an end, and then to abandon French Algeria (in 1962). But there is no Afrikaner De Gaulle and no possibility of one, no general or statesman with anything corresponding to that commanding prestige. For the post of an Afrikaner Massu, though, there would be plenty of competition.

I rejected earlier the current facile tendency to equate present-day Afrikaner nationalism with Nazism. But like all exalted nationalisms, the Afrikaner kind probably has a potential for something like Nazism, which could be evoked by events as they develop. In general, Afrikaner nationalism up to now has been like *pre*-Nazi German nationalism, with a similar tendency to idolize the *volk*. But the idolatry of the *volk* can turn into something very dangerous when the *volk* feels humiliated and deeply threatened. That was how the metamorphosis set in in Germany after 1918, and events in South Africa, in the terminal stages of Afrikaner power, could precipitate a similar metamorphosis.

If South Africa were left to itself, I think Massu-style (or Nazi-style) repression could be a success, in its own ghastly way. I don't see how the ANC or the children could stand up against it.

If South Africa were left to itself. . . . But even already it isn't. I'm not talking about sanctions and disinvestments, which – even combined with the internal unrest – are quite unlikely to end Afrikaner domination over the peoples of South Africa. I'm talking about external *military* intervention.

On South Africa's border external military intervention already exists. About 30,000 Cuban troops are in Angola, where some of them have been (briefly) in combat with South African forces. And the Soviet Union is believed to have warned South Africa in November of 1983 – through its ambassador at the United Nations – that any attempt by South Africa to challenge the Cuban defence positions south of Luanda 'would not be tolerated'.

South African propaganda makes, of course, the most of the red shadow on its borders. And it even appears that some of the more feverish military minds in Pretoria have been hoping to provoke direct Soviet intervention in Angola, in the belief that the United States would then throw its weight behind South Africa.

But to appear as the champion of South Africa is not a coveted international role now. It will be even less coveted if the rulers of South Africa meet rising unrest with far more thoroughgoing repression (as envisaged above). No news blackout could prevent word of Massu-style repression in South Africa from reaching the outside world, probably even in an exaggerated form. The word *genocide* has already been used, wildly, to characterize the actions of P. W. Botha's Government. But future forms of repression may be such as to lead many people not only to throw the word around but also to believe that genocide is actually happening. And then there will be an international call for someone to stop the genocide.

In a book about the United Nations (published in 1968) I put forward as a possible scenario, in some such situation, the following:

The General Assembly passes a resolution calling on its members to supply contingents for military intervention in South Africa. The Soviet Union and its allies announce that they will contribute to such a force and participate in such an intervention. The Soviet Union is then casting itself in the same role – champion of international legality and of aroused world opinion – that the United States did over Korea, with the mandate of the

General Assembly's 'Uniting for Peace' Resolution of 1950.

I don't think that unilateral Soviet intervention will actually happen. But I think that the possibility of something of that order happening is already influencing the course of events. Indeed, the recognition of the existence of the possibility is the principal reason why the possibility is unlikely to come to fruition.

If the Soviet Union seemed to be moving toward assuming the kind of role I have described, the United States would have three options, all of them unattractive.

The first option would be to do nothing. Since the effect of that would be (or be seen as being) to hand over South Africa, its mineral resources and its strategic position, to the Soviets, I take it that this option is in practice impossible.

The second option would be to tell the Soviet Union, 'Hands off South Africa!' Because the Soviet Union seems quite unlikely to want to risk inter-superpower war over a remote region in which it has only contingent interests, it would presumably back away. But as it backed away, it would unleash a propaganda barrage, to which the United States would be extremely vulnerable. The United States would be credibly represented as the protector of a white regime practising genocide against blacks. There are already signs – under the present *relatively* mild conditions – that the United States is increasingly reluctant to appear in the role of protector of South Africa. So the second option seems improbable (though not impossible, like the first one).

The third option is for the United States itself to back a military intervention, which would then become a United Nations operation backed by both superpowers – and probably sanctioned by the Security Council as well as the General Assembly. Under this option the United States could hope to protect its own interests in the region with international approval. So this option – though no doubt repugnant to many U.S. policy-makers – looks like being less repugnant than the other two.

Under certain freak circumstances the normal condition of superpower rivalry can turn into limited superpower consensus. That happened in November of 1956, over Suez, when both superpowers – in different tones of voice – ordered Britain, France and Israel to get out of Egypt, which they did.

And it happened in 1962–3, when United Nations forces, with the support or at least the acquiescence of both superpowers, put an end to the Independent State of Katanga, which with West European support (and also South African support) had seceded from what is now Zaire.

The case of Katanga seems especially instructive in relation to U.S. options regarding South Africa. Katanga was of course a much smaller and less significant territory. But like South Africa, Katanga was exceptionally rich in strategic minerals, and like South Africa, Katanga made much of its anti-Communism. Its motto, everywhere displayed, was, 'Katanga: Central Africa's shield against Communism'. Under the Eisenhower Administration the United States bought the 'shield' idea, and protected Katanga. But under Kennedy the United States slowly and hesitantly reached the conclusion that Katanga, and its anti-Communism and its unpopularity, had become a liability to the United States and an asset to the Soviet Union. The process of thought by which this conclusion was reached is set out in *To Move a Nation*, the memoirs of Roger Hilsman, the director of the Bureau of Intelligence and Research in the Kennedy State Department. Those memoirs make interesting reading today, in the context of South Africa. Because when the United States reached the conclusion that Katanga was a liability, the United Nations put an end to Katanga, by force – a policy that the Soviet Union had long urged and so could not oppose.

A kind of limited superpower consensus on South Africa emerged in 1977, when the Security Council decreed a mandatory embargo against the supply of arms to South Africa. Under such conditions as are contemplated above, that consensus could develop into something much more formidable, on mega-Katangan lines.

The twenty-fourth of October 1985 was the fortieth anniversary of the United Nations. On that day I took part in a debate on South African Television with Dr Brand Fourie, whom I had known when he was South Africa's permanent representative at the United Nations; he was later ambassador in Washington. Before the cameras I talked about the possible line of development examined above: limited superpower consensus, expressed through the United Nations, leading to the extinction of white-controlled South Africa. South African Television is government-controlled, and this kind of thing is not generally discussed on it. Dr Fourie – who happens to be the present chairman of the South African Broadcasting Corporation – was naturally discreet in his reaction. All he said before the cameras about such a possibility was, 'It can't be ruled out.'

As Dr Fourie and I walked out of the studios, after the televised discussion, we went on talking about limited superpower consensus. He told me, 'I said just there it couldn't be ruled out. But there's more than that. That thing is my nightmare and has been for years.'

Of course, it is one thing to snuff out little Katanga and quite another to deal with the South African Defence Force. Presumably there would be a

United Nations naval blockade, with superpower participation, and a blockade along South Africa's land frontiers, combined with a build-up of forces on those frontiers, and followed by an ultimatum requiring South Africa to bring the repression to an end and to assent to the organization, under the United Nations, of free and non-racial elections.

And what would the South African reply be?

I put that question to two Afrikaner political scientists, with whom I discussed this possible scenario. Both of them thought that the South African Government (or junta) might use its 'nuclear capability' against the United Nations.

The Götterdämmerung of the *volk*!

Obviously, there would be *bittereinders* who would favour that course; that is what *bittereinders* are for. But on the whole it seems more likely that the *hensoppers*, in that extremity, would prevail, as they did at the end of the Anglo-Boer war. Militarily, and nationally, there would be no disgrace in capitulation to such overwhelming force. Pride would be saved: it would have taken nothing less than the whole world to overcome the *volk*. And interests could at least be better protected by capitulation than by Götterdämmerung.

In some such way as that, the immensely difficult transition of power might be achieved. In all the above I have of course been guessing. But I have tried, in my guessing, to respect existing patterns of force. Obviously, it would be foolish to attempt any similar analysis of what might happen after the transition. Still, certain shapes can already be dimly made out, looming in the fog.

Even after apartheid and all its elaborate mutations have been thrown to rust on the scrap heap of history, South Africa will still have enormous problems. There will be more and more children, and more and more of the children will be unemployed. It may be nearly as hard for a black government to control Soweto as it is for a white government.

But the new black South Africa, unlike the other African countries, will have a large black middle class. 'We are the fittest for independence, and we shall be the last to get it.' It was Oliver Tambo who said that to me, back in 1960, when I was a delegate to the General Assembly, and he was a 'non-governmental observer' on behalf of the ANC. What he meant was that South Africa, unlike the countries of West, East and Central Africa, then beginning to flock into the United Nations, had a large class of educated blacks: a black bourgeoisie, though he didn't put it that way. (Tambo himself is essentially a liberal; he will get on very well with Dr Slabbert.)

I think that after that transition South Africa's first elected black government is likely to be responsive to, and reliant on, those educated blacks. It will be essentially a middle-class government, though it may be 'middle-class Marxist', like the government of Robert Mugabe.

Such a government would probably be supported by organized labour – the employed – but would be immediately challenged by all the 'outs' of black society, including the politicized unemployed. There likely would be doubts about the loyalty of the lower ranks in the expanded black contingents of the reconstituted armed forces.

In these conditions the new black government would need such allies as it could find. And it would be likely to find allies among the whites. A multi-racial coalition, probably a tacit one, could be expected to emerge: a coalition of all those with something to lose, whatever the colour of their skin.

The multi-racial bourgeois coalition might not be wholly attractive, though it might, with luck, work quite well. But it would be better than apartheid, and better than the Bothaesque mutations of apartheid. It would be a lot better than a possible coming 'Massu apartheid'. And it would be a lot better also than the rule of the children with the necklace, or rather of whichever ominous child emerged as the victor out of the internecine competition for power within a political movement whose sanction, symbol and signature is the burning alive of people in the street.

South Africa and the Academic Boycott*
I: The *Real* Betrayal of Anti-Apartheid

ARDON ME, BUT MY BLOOD IS BOILING. I have just been publicly accused of 'an act of betrayal'. What I am accused of betraying is the anti-apartheid movement. My accuser is the present chairman of the Irish anti-apartheid movement, Mr Kadar Asmal.

My 'betrayal of anti-apartheid' consists of the following:

About two years ago, I was invited to give a course of lectures at the University of Cape Town. In replying, I said that I could only accept, if I could be accompanied by my son, who is black, and be assured that he and I would be treated in all respects on an equal footing at the University. I received the necessary assurances, and accepted the invitation. Later – in November 1985 – I had an opportunity to visit the University of Cape Town and to satisfy myself on the spot that this is a completely integrated campus with classrooms, dining-rooms, dormitories and all other facilities open to members of all races, on an equal footing.

In fact, the University of Cape Town appears more integrated than a number of American universities where a kind of 'voluntary apartheid' is often practised.

So how can lecturing to racially mixed classes, in an institution which rejects apartheid constitute 'an act of betrayal' of anti-apartheid?

I don't know what the answer to that one may be, and after reading Mr Asmal and listening to him, I am still no wiser. But one thing is clear. The Irish anti-apartheid movement, under its current chairman, is seen by him as a branch of a disciplined international revolutionary movement, with no room for deviations of any kind or for the exercise of individual judgement or the individual conscience: you are to toe the line or else.

As Mr Asmal puts it, perhaps a shade unctuously: 'The authentic movement that speaks for the people of South Africa have asked people like him [me, that is] to stay away.'

*Experiences of Conor and Patrick Cruise O'Brien (six articles from *The Irish Independent*, Dublin, and the *New Republic*, Washington).

'Asked' is sweet. If you fail to comply with this polite request, you are immediately convicted of 'an act of betrayal'.

Now, if a person joined a disciplined movement, taking its cue in all things from whatever organizations Mr Asmal is alluding to, then that person could perhaps reasonably be accused of 'an act of betrayal' if he failed to do something which those organizations 'asked' him to do. But I never joined any movement of that kind, or entered into any such commitment.

The anti-apartheid movement which I joined a good many years back, was a movement of open and liberal type. Members were, by definition, against apartheid, but what the opposition might require in practice was left to the individual judgement and consciences of members. The 'do what you are "asked" or we'll brand you a traitor' mentality was not then dominant in the councils of the movement.

I am as firmly opposed to apartheid and all forms of racial discrimination as I ever was. My family is a standing demonstration against the whole value system upon which apartheid is based. My resentment of Mr Asmal's vicious insult is proportionate to that existential commitment.

Mr Asmal now urges me to practise 'humility' before 'the international community', an awesome entity of which Mr Asmal seems to regard himself as the representative in our midst. But Mr Asmal is well aware that, on this question of boycotting South African universities, the relevant section of the international community – that is the international academic community – is deeply divided.

Many scholars emphatically repudiate the whole idea of such a boycott. Indeed it looks as if the boycott is repudiated by a majority of scholars in Western Europe and North America, a not altogether insignificant segment of the 'international community'.

The matter has been put to the test recently, in relation to the world's archaeologists. The World Congress of Archaeologists was – or was to be – held this month [September 1986] in Southampton. South African archaeologists were originally invited, as had always been the practice, to take part in the congress. But the British organizing committee, under pressure from miscellaneous British militants including the British anti-apartheid movement – withdrew the invitation to the South African scholars.

And then the relevant international scholarly body – the International Union of Pre-historians and Proto-historians – withdrew its recognition from the Southampton Congress and announced that the official World Congress of Archaeologists will be held next year at Mainz, West Germany, with participation of South African scholars.

The reason why the IUPPS withdrew its recognition from the South-ampton Congress was that the British organizing committee, in dis-inviting the South Africans, had violated one of the basic rules of the Union, which is that no scholar is to be discriminated against on grounds of race, religion, nationality or philosophical conviction.

That salutary rule was instituted in the 1930s, to mark the rejection by the scholarly community of the principles on which the Nazis were then purging the German universities.

It is sad, but symptomatic, that a rule which is expressive of the essential moral principles of anti-apartheid can now be violated in the name of anti-apartheid.

The decision to dis-invite the South African archaeologists was defended by the British organizers of the Southampton débâcle on the grounds that it was necessary 'to damage the South African regime'. This is transparent nonsense. The regime is in no way vulnerable to actions of this kind. On the contrary, the regime must relish such actions for at least two reasons.

First, on the international plain, the bullyboy mentality manifest in the boycotting of innocent scholars tends to discredit the anti-apartheid cause. Southampton, followed by Mainz, was hardly a triumph for anti-apartheid. Second, the boycotting of scholars solely on grounds of nationality, is helpful to the regime, domestically.

Inevitably, many of the scholars affected are white opponents of the regime. To all such opponents, the regime can now say, wherever the boycott is seen to work: 'Your former friends out there no longer want to know about you. Can't you see now that it is true what we always told you: that all whites in South Africa are in the same boat, whether we like it or not? You wouldn't believe us when we told you that. Maybe you'll believe it now that you're hearing it from the anti-apartheid movement.'

Quite a nice present to the apartheid cause with the compliments of the anti-apartheid movement.

The South African regime has no particular love for the South African universities; the Afrikaner Right distrusts and fears them, and has a particular hatred for certain South African scholars who have challenged some of the myths on which the apartheid ideology is based.

Take the case of the Afrikaner historian Floors van Jahrsfeld, who was tarred and feathered by apartheid extremists in 1979 while attempting to address a theological conference in Pretoria. By the operation of the international academic boycott, Professor van Jahrsfeld himself would be debarred from any international congress of historians, by way of registering international abhorrence of the sort of people who had tarred and feathered him. . . .

Some pretty rum things have been going on in the Irish anti-apartheid movement, as run by Kadar Asmal. Provisional Sinn Fein is now in there, affiliated to the movement, with the right to be represented on its executive. So the Irish anti-apartheid movement is now partly under the control of people who are publicly committed to giving 'unequivocal support to the armed struggle', meaning the murders and other criminal actions perpetrated by the Provisional IRA.

This can hardly do much to help the anti-apartheid cause, in the eyes of the law abiding majority in this country. And, when Mr Asmal attacks me, he knows he can count on the approval of his Provo pals, for reasons which have nothing to do with apartheid.

In general, it seems to me that anti-apartheid is now being used as a flag of convenience under which to attain local objectives in Britain and Ireland. Putting it another way, 'anti-apartheid' can be a useful bludgeon with which radicals and revolutionaries can intimidate and demoralize liberals and moderates on university campuses, in trades unions, in the media and elsewhere. In this way the radicals and revolutionaries increase their personal clout. And the more unreasonable and unjust the demand made in the name of 'anti-apartheid', the more the effectiveness of the clout in question will be demonstrated.

The technique applied is to stampede various bodies into passing restrictive resolutions and then to hound individuals for alleged violations of the restrictions in question. The more resolutions and the more hounding, the more clout. To force liberals to renege on their own principles – as in the case of that miserable academic boycott – is a sweet triumph indeed for people who have always despised liberalism as a bourgeois sham and academic freedom as a bourgeois trick.

Therefore, liberals should not automatically stampede, in a flurry of guilt, at the mere cry of 'anti-apartheid'. They should always look carefully at any particular proposal presented in that name to see whether it is right and just in itself, and whether and in what way it can really help to bring apartheid to an end.

So I'm off to the University of Cape Town with my son Patrick. Newspaper reports have said that I am 'bringing' my son there. I am not bringing him. Patrick is of age and is coming at his own wish and on his own initiative. If our going there together can be construed as 'a betrayal of anti-apartheid', I think that only proves that the term anti-apartheid is being perverted from its true meaning. Therein lies the real 'betrayal of anti-apartheid'.

II: The Racial Chill in Sunshine City

Conor: The University of Cape Town, the oldest in South Africa, has a splendid setting on the lower slopes of Table Mountain, looking out over the city and the bay. It looks idyllic, in the sparkling sunshine of the early South African spring. But humanly there is sometimes a chill in the air.

The University is fully committed against apartheid, and all the practices thereof are firmly banished from the campus. But with the best will in the world you can't keep out some of the racial ill-feeling which prevails in this deeply divided and angry society. Some of the students seem to bring the stuff in on their shoes.

A neatly typed notice outside the lift on our floor reads: 'It appears that a student has been writing racist slogans on the lift in this building. If apprehended, the student will be referred without compunction to the University Court and legal action will be taken against him or her.' (Signed) John De Gruchy, Acting Dean, Faculty of Social Services and Humanities. To which an unknown hand has added in ink, in bright letters, the single word 'HONKIES'.

This is my fourth visit to South Africa. But this time I have Patrick with me, which somehow changes the whole thing. Before, I was looking on, a concerned outsider. Now it's a bit different and distinctly closer to home. Apartheid becomes something that you feel reaching out at you. Now it is in the nature of modern apartheid to camouflage itself from middle class visitors of whatever colour. All the same, apartheid has its ways of making itself known to you, even when it's not supposed to be there.

Patrick: I arrived in South Africa without really knowing what to expect. My initial reaction in the immigration hall of D. F. Malan Airport was one of surprise. Surprise, not because I was treated as a second-class citizen, as I think I had expected to be, but because no notice whatsoever was taken of me, the only 'non-white' in the airport apart from employees.

On our first full day in Cape Town, after sleeping off the effects of the long journey, I left our comfortable hotel to wander the centre of the prosperous suburb of Newlands.

As I walked into Newlands main mall, I thought to myself one of two things will happen. Either I will be physically ejected from 'white' shops or, as in the airport, no notice will be taken.

What actually happened was something in between.

When I walked into my first white area shop I was greeted immediately with cold, unwelcoming suspicious airs. My first impulse was to turn around and leave. Rather than be defeated easily I approached one of these assistants and spoke. At this point his stare softened and he became one of the most helpful men I have ever met.

This pattern repeated itself several times during the past week. It was an American woman who explained it to me. She said: 'When they know you're a foreigner you are no longer a threat.'

Conor: Petty apartheid is supposed to be gone. What are really gone are those aspects of apartheid that are most likely to impinge on middle-class foreigners. In relation to the working-class blacks of South Africa, apartheid grinds on relentlessly: as petty and pedantic and at the same time as gross and overwhelming as ever it was.

A small item on an inside page of the *Cape Times* on Wednesday gives you a whiff of the apartheid that is supposed to be gone: 'Women fined for sleeping with husbands. . . . Six women from Mfulani township near Stellenbosch who pleaded guilty were convicted of contravening the Black Communities Development Act Number 4 of 1984 in the Kuils River Magistrates Court.'

They were found sleeping with their husbands, common-law or otherwise, in a pre-dawn raid on the township's 'Single Quarters'. The women were fined between 30 and 50 rands each.

The title of the act contravened is actually as Orwellian as the date.

A legal system like that is machinery for the manufacture of hatred, and the product is in ample supply in the black townships.

On Thursday, we had lunch in the garden of a white friend, Peter, in a Cape Town suburb. Our fellow guest was a psychologist attached to the University. The psychologist, who has an Afrikaans name, was preoccupied by a report he had to deliver to a law court that afternoon. The report was an effort to demonstrate 'mitigating circumstances' in order to try to save two convicted murderers from the death penalty. The particulars were as follows:

The murdered man was one of the black 'Community Councillors' who are denounced by black radicals – 'the Comrades' – as guilty of collaboration with the apartheid regime. The Councillor's house had been burned down while he was away, and he had come back in the hope of salvaging some of his belongings.

The two comrades had been lying in wait, and when they saw him, they gathered a crowd to attack him. He had a revolver and fired over their heads. While they hung back, he started to get away, but at this point, his luck ran out. Two ordinary thieves, who happened to be in his way, took a fancy to his revolver and grabbed it. Then his political opponents moved in. They smashed his skull in with a rock, then half-decapitated him, then 'necklaced' him with a petrol-filled tyre and set fire to him.

The two comrades were convicted on the evidence of the victim's son, aged twelve – who was with him when he was murdered – supported by the evidence of the two non-political thieves.

The substance of the psychologist's report appeared to be that the whole apartheid system should be taken into account in mitigation of the crime. I didn't think that plea was likely to cut much ice with a South African court and neither did the psychologist think so. Privately, his opinion is that if anyone deserved to hang, those two comrades did; but that nobody should be hanged.

Yet the connection between apartheid and 'the necklace' is there. It's not that apartheid 'drives' people to such crimes – that's a sentimental or pseudo-sentimental way of putting it. It's that apartheid creates conditions in which terrorists can flourish, with some perceived legitimacy.

Our lunch in the sun under the palm trees was suddenly interrupted. . . .

Patrick: A ragged black man with a tattooed chest came walking down the street outside and saw us in the garden. He shouted something incomprehensible over the wall, opened the gate and came in.

Peter, our host, said: 'Oh God, not him again!'

The man walked towards us with an unlit cigarette, demanding a light, while being told to leave. Peter held out his lighter to him. The man stopped, looked at him and said: 'Why you offer me a light – like that? This is not Zimbabwe. This is South Africa.'

The man asked for money, but Peter said no, but offered to give him the address of SHAWCO, the Student Health and Welfare Committee. The man said: 'Anything you can give me I will be appreciative of. I have no money, no food, no blankets.'

Peter explained that SHAWCO would meet his needs. He found the address in the phone book. The man looked over his shoulder. He said: 'Where are you sending me? You are not sending me to P.W.?' (i.e. President Botha). Everyone laughed.

Peter gave him the address. He still refused to go, saying: 'How can I go there with no transport?'

It was only a present of food and a little pressure that finally got him to leave. With Peter gently half-pushing, half-pulling him, he went out the gate, thanking us.

Peter said: 'That's where sanctions get you – more and more beggars. If you give one money, he comes back with his friends.'

Conor: Peter and his wife seemed to feel we might be shocked by their attitude. Actually, Patrick said Peter was far more patient than he, Patrick would have been. In any case, we felt the man would be back. I wouldn't like anyone to infer from any of the above that we are sorry we came, or regret breaking 'The Academic Boycott'. As a matter of fact, 'The Academic Boycott' has been made nonsense of in a quite spectacular way in Southern Africa this week.

An academic delegation from the Cape, including the Vice-Chancellor of Cape Town University, along with staff members and students of both races, has been visiting Lusaka at the invitation of the University of Zambia. The delegation met with the leadership of the African National Congress, which sought the delegation's view on the present educational crisis in South Africa, and asked the University to involve itself more in popular education and social work among the black people. . . .

The only visible on-campus protest at my own presence here has been one graffito in a lift. Unfortunately the graffito – now removed – was neither original nor suitable for reproduction in a family newspaper.

III: Fire in the Eyes of Blacks on Campus

Patrick: I spent Wednesday on the campus of the University of the Western Cape.

Conor: The University of the Western Cape was founded twenty-five years ago, in the confident heyday of apartheid, as a university for coloureds, to indoctrinate them in apartheid ideology. But it does not seem to have worked out as planned.

Patrick: The student body is composed almost entirely of coloured students with very few white students and some black.

I was introduced to a group of about ten students, all of whom were involved with various student bodies on campus. There were members of AZASO, the (left-wing) Azanian Students Organization, both the Catholic and Anglican bodies and Student Representative Council members.

The discussion began on general and wide-ranging subjects: black education, poverty, the economic crisis and the ANC.

During the economic discussions terms such as 'oppressed masses', 'capitalist exploitation', 'class struggle' and 'classless society' were continuously voiced. The inevitable questions, 'Are you Communist and would a black South Africa be?' had to be asked.

The answer to this question was both moving and eye-opening.

Phoebe, one of the more radical students, a short round girl with glasses, said: 'What we want in South Africa is a society where the wealth of the country is not exploited by few at the expense of many. We want a society where all who are sympathetic to our struggle, black and white, can live together. I don't care whether this is called Communism or Capitalism or Socialism.'

Although perhaps idyllic, a nice thought. Nice thought or not it is very unlikely, at least for the near future. What is relevant, however, what I cannot convey fully here, is the emotion with which they spoke of 'all who are sympathetic' and their willingness to look beyond the colour of a person's skin.

Only the most starry-eyed would take anything he hears in this place without several grains of salt. The above is no exception. Although there is all this 'willingness' to cross the race barrier, they do not.

Both the University of the Western Cape and the University of Cape Town are now desegregated universities, in the sense that by university rules there is no segregation: indeed, any manifestation of racism is punishable by legal action.

At the University of the Western Cape, it was explained to me that mixing was not a problem, simply because over 95 per cent of students are coloured.

At the University of Cape Town where there are large groups of every race they don't 'feel comfortable together'. One (black) student told me that blacks either 'try to be white' or don't try at all.

At the University of the Western Cape, the conversation moved on to violence, 'necklacing' and the ANC.

This was a combination of subjects obviously very close to the bone for many of the group. At first no one wanted really to discuss the subject. Then Joey took it up. Joey is a short, semi-bearded, friendly man with sharp eyes and what we would call the gift of the gab.

Joey said that the violence had first to be understood before it was condemned.

'Necklacings' were not premeditated murders, but the spontaneous release of aggression. Only 'collaborators' with the regime, e.g. black councillors, black police, informers were victims, and always had been warned beforehand.

He said, and they all agreed, that he was not at all a supporter of 'the necklace' as it was a horrible way to die, but that the suppressed frustration and anger in the townships is such that he could understand them.

'Suppose you are running from the police, with your brother. Your brother is shot beside you and falls. You can't stop or you too will be shot. Anyone working for the state that killed your brother you immediately hate and want to destroy. People are no longer reasonable.'

With emotions as strong as they are, I can't help wondering if the earlier willingness to forgive and forget is only surface-deep and whether the underlying hatred would prevail.

I wish I was convinced by their arguments to the contrary, but after hearing them talk and seeing the fire in their eyes I would not like to be a white South African under a black government.

Conor: Meanwhile back at the ranch, I was having lunch with the chairman of the South African Rugby Board, Dr Danie Craven, and three of his colleagues. In South Africa, rugby is played by whites and 'coloureds':

blacks play soccer. One of Dr Craven's colleagues, Dougie Dyers, is coloured.

Danie Craven, a legendary scrum half in his day, is now in his eighties, and a folk hero to rugby-worshipping white South Africans. He has a massive round head, attached by a short neck to a short massive frame. He wears an air of quiet authority, restrained and benign.

When I received Dr Craven's invitation, I thought I might be pressed by him and his colleagues, to follow the logic of 'breaking the academic boycott' out towards helping to break the sports boycott as well (which I did not feel inclined to do). But I underestimated the subtlety of the South African Rugby Board. I was not pressed, or even asked, to do anything at all.

Dr Craven began by asking, without overt irony, my views on South African sport, especially rugby. I asked whether he meant the international outlook for South African sport?

'No,' said Dr Craven. 'I mean the domestic scene. That's what matters. If we can get things working properly here, the international part will take care of itself.'

I asked what the score was, to date, on desegregation of South African rugby. At this point, Danie Craven, with a look and a shrug, got the conversational ball away to Dougie Dyers who ran with it.

Dougie Dyers is a tall man in his thirties with an open face and the air of a rather nice Yuppie; but a Yuppie with a tough road up ahead of him. He explained that the SARB, for about ten years, had been fully committed to effective desegregation, but there was still a long way to go.

I said: 'On Saturday, you have the Currie Cup Final here in Cape Town; the biggest event in the South African rugby calendar. Are both teams – Western Province and Transvaal – going to be all white?'

'Yes,' said Dougie Dyers. 'They are. I am a selector myself and I did not recommend the selection of a single coloured player. There isn't at present one who makes that grade, on merit. It is not that the talent isn't there. But the schools are still segregated, and unequal. The facilities in training available to the coloured kids are vastly inferior to what the white kids have. That is what we are trying to change.'

Dr Craven explained that the SARB now has an ambitious programme, with business support, for the provision of rugby equipment and training, and proper playing fields, to coloured schools.

It seems a good effort, but it may have come too late. Apartheid in sport, which whites like Dr Craven are now trying to get rid of is now being applied, on the other side, by left-wing blacks and coloureds under the slogan, 'No normal sport in an abnormal society'.

No doubt by way of enforcing this slogan 'the comrades' burnt down Dougie Dyers' house a few months back, but clearly they didn't succeed in discouraging him. Nor does he seem to be isolated, as far as middle-class coloureds of his age group are concerned.

In industry, as well as in sport, some efforts are being made at forming improvized and unofficial cross-racial coalitions, even under the ponderous disabilities of the apartheid system. In South Africa, class and race lines coincide in some important ways, but not in all.

Employed blacks, and blacks with reasonable hopes of employment have something in common with whites; that is, they all have something to lose. Unemployed blacks – currently estimated at 50 per cent of the potential black workforce – have nothing to lose, except their lives. Those of them who are willing to risk their lives for the revolutionary cause – 'the comrades' – have high prestige in the black (and 'coloured' etc.) community.

Hence, I believe, some of the reactions of Patrick's student contacts at UWC. But older people, like Dougie, are apt to feel different. Workers in Dougie's age and class bracket know that slogans like 'No normal sport in an abnormal society' can easily be extended to 'No normal work in an abnormal society', making every worker – in practice, any unpopular worker – eventually into a perceived collaborator, and so a candidate for the necklace.

On Wednesday last, Winnie Mandela, addressing black miners in the Eastern Transvaal said, 'It is the gold you dig that buys the Casspirs (police armoured personnel carriers), the uniforms and the guns.'

The miners cheered for Winnie but haven't stopped digging.

I think Patrick's students may be caught in a similar contradiction. Their hearts today may be with the radical militants, but if they get the jobs they are training for and no revolution intervenes – most of them are going to have to feel more like Dougie. Even now, they may well feel more torn than they sound – and so indeed may Dougie.

Intelligent whites, like Danie Craven, being well aware of all that, reach out towards people like Dougie. Unfortunately, to judge by voting patterns, stupid whites are still in a majority.

Patrick: I wouldn't give much for Dougie's chances even if whites were smarter.

IV: Archbishop Tutu on 'Being a Leader'

Conor: Monday 29 September was the feast of St Michael and All Angels, so we proceeded to the Church of St Michael and All Angels which is situated, appropriately enough, in what is known as the Observatory district of Cape Town. There we heard Cape Town's new Anglican Archbishop, Desmond Tutu, say the Patronal Mass.

Yes, Mass. Anglicanism in South Africa appears to be quite 'high', generally speaking, and the Church of St Michael and All Angels, Cape Town, is in the liturgical stratosphere: holy water, candles on the altar, Stations of the Cross, genuflections, and above all, incense, till all is no more. As I inhaled the warm, sweet, sickly fumes, I felt that perhaps incense ought to carry a celestial health warning. The Reverend Ian Paisley thinks it already does. Sometimes he has a point.

I had last seen and heard Desmond Tutu officiate when he was still only a common-or-garden bishop, at St Matthew's Church in Soweto. That was a little less than a year ago, but I thought Tutu looked a lot more than a year older; thinner, more stooped, the face a little shrunken, and careworn as it had not been before.

Patrick: He certainly looked much older than I had thought from television. On TV, you could see just those little grey tufts. Now it all looks grey.

Conor: At the beginning of the sermon, the Archbishop referred to his own recent enthronement. 'I got a telegram,' he said, 'congratulating me on my enthornment. Sometimes I think that's really the right word.' He didn't enlarge on that, but I felt it was more than just a joke.

The Church of St Michael and All Angels, Cape Town, and the Church of St Matthew in Soweto belong to the same ecclesiastical communion, but are worlds apart, culturally. St Matthew is totally black African, St Michael is part of English-speaking white South Africa (a few 'coloureds' there too, but very Anglicized).

Desmond Tutu can more than hold his own in both environments, but at St Michael's, it seems to cost him. At St Matthew's, preaching in Xhosa, he had been happy. He cracked jokes and the congregation laughed with him.

His arms spread wide in easy, confident gestures; he even danced, at the end, a kind of 'high life' with members of the congregation.

At St Michael's, the Archbishop, throughout his sermon, gripped the sides of his pulpit firmly with both hands. So no gestures except for a slight rhythmical movement of the head. No jokes, except that single, painful one about 'enthornment'. And no suggestion of dancing; good heavens no!

There was some grumbling at first among white Anglicans when Tutu became their Archbishop. Some of them even left the Church. He seems by now to have won over almost all of those who remained, by his obvious ability and sincerity, by his charm and – indispensably – his dignity. The new Archbishop daily delivers quite a powerful implicit anti-apartheid message, by showing his white flock that it need not be such a terrible thing, after all, to have a black person in authority over you. But the Archbishop is paying a price to get that message over. I feel he has left his heart in St Matthew's.

At a party after the Mass, one of his white hosts offered his Archbishop a drink. 'Are you sure,' he asked, 'that you ought to be offering me that?'

The reference was to the apartheid laws restricting the provision of alcoholic liquor to natives. The hosts laughed rather queasily. I feel that Tutu might be getting a bit of his own back, for having to be so often on his best behaviour, according to standards and conventions laid down by white South Africa.

In a different part of the South African forest this week, at a university, I had my first serious encounter with militant students. I had accepted an invitation from the Social Science Students' Committee, to take part in a debate the subject of 'The Academic Boycott'. I accepted, but what happened was not a debate. When I showed up and asked who would present the case for the other side, I was told: 'Nobody. You are to speak for about five minutes and then it's all questions.'

It began to dawn on me that I had been set up. I couldn't have refused the invitation to a debate. But neither could I walk out, once I found it wasn't going to be a debate. To do so would be seen as chickening out, and would leave the boycotters in possession. So by accepting the invitation, I had let myself in, not for a debate, but for an organized militant grilling. It was a neat trap. Saving what I could, I told them I didn't accept their 'five minute' rule, but would speak as long as was necessary to present my case. Then they could put their questions. This was agreed.

Patrick: The 'debate' was held in a large semi-circular theatre with nearly all of its 250 seats occupied. The audience was composed mainly of white students, with perhaps about fifty non-white students. The proceedings began with the anti-boycott statement.

Conor: I reiterated my support for economic sanctions; as for the academic boycott, I said its impact on the apartheid regime would be nil, but the inroads it was making on academic freedom and freedom of expression were very serious indeed. These values would be vital in the coming non-racial South Africa as to other free societies. What was being conducted in South Africa – and elsewhere – under the banner of academic boycott seemed to be a creeping form of the Cultural Revolution which had wrecked the universities of China, and which the China of today repudiates with abhorrence.

Patrick: Then the 'questions' began. The organizer of the meeting, a thin, wiry, bushy-haired man called Patrick Bulger – a fellow Irishman of course – led off with a string of seven questions, all written out in advance, and so ignoring all of Conor's actual remarks. An article by Bulger, under the title: 'O'Brien Exposed', had been published in a student paper just before the meeting. Bulger's seven questions were really just the same question over and over again: 'What gives you the moral right to break the boycott?' Then the questions from the floor started. Again, these were the same question, over and over, in slightly different language, with the odd variation.

Conor: One question was: 'How can you call yourself a liberal, and be against the academic boycott?' I said it was precisely because I was a liberal that I was against the academic boycott. This answer was met with yells of derision and execration.

Patrick: Later on the questions got worse, like: 'Why have you come here to insult the sufferings of the African masses?' and so on. Tempers were getting hot.

Conor: Mine included.

Patrick: The questioning was conducted mostly by a group of about fifteen students working in relays. They were supported by a larger number – maybe thirty or forty – who hissed or yelled or laughed nastily at each of Conor's answers. Another part of the audience applauded, or laughed when he scored a point. The division was not on racial lines, except that no black (as distinct from 'coloured and Indians') actually spoke. Towards the end, one black fist was raised. But a lot of people just sat there.

Conor: Those who just sat there included most of the faculty members. Only two of these spoke, both of them in favour of boycotting the institution of which they themselves are part. The members who did not utter – or were not present – included several whom I know to be opposed to the academic boycott. The depressing thing about yelling at people is that it so often works.

I remember the Indian student who denounced the University as a capitalist institution, tied to the apartheid regime and so to Fascism. I asked him how he personally could bring himself to be a part of such a detestable institution? I couldn't quite understand his answer. But the general idea seemed to me that for *him* to attend the University of Cape Town was in some way a revolutionary act, but for *me* to visit it was counter-revolutionary. You can't win.

On the whole it was a gruelling but instructive experience. As I came out of it I felt my head was unbowed, but I did notice that it was a bit bloody. And I felt in retrospect the deepest sympathy for those Chinese professors who had their consciousness 'raised' for them by student comrades of that type, not for about forty-five minutes – as in my case – but through all the long years of China's Cultural Revolution.

If students and others of that type came to be in charge in South Africa after the first non-racial elections, it would be a poor look-out, not only for the universities, but for the prospect of any further free election, as well as for freedom of expression in general and for a lot of other things.

But I think it is really quite unlikely that people like that could win power through free elections. They claim – invariably and indefatigably – to speak for 'the people of South Africa', and they do indeed appear to speak for considerable – and probably increasing – numbers of young urban blacks.

But it is clear that there are other large groups of blacks, both urban and rural, who would be most unlikely to vote for the comrades in the townships, or for the middle-class militant students who imitate the comrades' style.

As for the ANC, it is at present a loose coalition, including moderates of the Tutu stamp, as well as comrades and militants.

It is apartheid itself which holds that coalition together. The coming of non-racial elections and the practical choices involved would be likely to dissolve the coalition into competing sections.

(On Monday at St Michael's, Tutu again condemned 'the necklace'; the comrades, whose weapon that is, will never forgive him.)

Nobody can really know what the South African people actually want, until the day when the people, all of them, are for the first time free to say what they want, through non-racial elections, on a common road.

V: Boycott Buster

Patrick: The academic boycott and the breaking of it by Conor Cruise O'Brien has become the hottest issue on the campus of the University of Cape Town. The first I heard of any continuing action on the boycott issue was Tuesday, 7 October. I was handed a flyer printed and distributed by the militant organization AZAPO. The flyer declared: 'O'Brien is a stinking scoundrel and a rogue.' The flyer announced a 'Day of Action' against O'Brien and a lunchtime meeting to discuss tactics. I missed whatever discussion had taken place but did catch the meeting on the move.

The students emerged from the student union headquarters in procession, dancing and chanting in Xhosa. The group, composed of all races, was led by a group of black students, one of whom led the cheer through a megaphone. The students also held aloft a large cardboard placard reading 'Viva UDF' (United Democratic Front). As they descended the steps, they flipped the placard. The other side read 'Viva IRA' (Irish Republican Army). Some thirty people marched to the administration building and demanded – unsuccessfully – the cancellation of O'Brien's lectures.

Conor was due to speak to the Jewish student association that evening. I arrived at the designated hour and place to find the lecture theatre besieged by about 200 students chanting and dancing. All three exits were guarded by campus police, and admission was strictly restricted. I was almost kept out myself.

The lecture began and ended to the background droning of the demonstrators. Just as Conor had finished speaking, the students broke through the police barricade and forced open one of the theatre doors. They decided, after about an hour, that 'O'Brien should never again lecture in the University of Cape Town,' and that they should broaden their action to include all 'boycott-breaking' foreign academics. The following day they began acting on their decisions. Conor's morning class was the next target for disruption.

With Conor safely inside, the campus police barricaded the door of his classroom with two tables and themselves. The students moved slowly down the hall outside the classroom. When they reached the door and were refused entrance, the inevitable scuffles broke out. Before the students succeeded in breaking down the door, the scene turned nasty. Students began kicking and pushing security men, and at least one student took off his belt and swung the buckle end at the police.

Conor: A rough week. Still, there have been some good moments. On Tuesday night, as I finished my lecture to the Jewish students, with a howling mob outside in the corridor busy breaking down the door, members of the audience kept on taking notes of what I was saying about Israel, right up to the moment when the door actually burst open and the mob irrupted. There have always been Jews who have not ceased to study, even with the pogrom, or worse, at the door.

On Wednesday morning, when the same mob, now reinforced from outside, came to break up my regular morning undergraduate class, several of my students went and held the door, keeping the mob out. Afterwards the two elected representatives of my class – I had about a hundred students in all, of all races – wrote a letter to the dean to protest what had happened. They stated that the class is almost unanimous in support of their protest letter, and of me.

On Friday morning the vice chancellor of the University of Cape Town, Dr Stewart Saunders, rang me in Johannesburg, where I was, at the time, a guest of the University of the Witwatersrand (and being subjected to the same kind of militant student attention as in Cape Town). Dr Saunders said he believed that further serious disorders might be imminent on the Cape Town campus. 'If I think it necessary,' he said, 'in order to avert serious violence, will you authorize me to say, on your behalf, that you have cancelled your remaining classes on campus?'

I gave the necessary contingent authorization. What else could I do? What if I refused, and somebody got killed? All the same, I felt pretty sick about it, and so, clearly, did the vice chancellor. After all, he was acknowledging, for the moment, that mob rule has won on his campus, under the flag of 'the academic boycott'.

In the course of the recent campus shenanigans, a faculty member, talking to a student leader, tried to make the case against the academic boycott. 'We are not interested in intellectual argument', replied the 'student'. 'We are only interested in action.' The question is whether people who are not interested in intellectual argument should have any place at a university. If my visit has done some good – and I believe it has – it is in focusing attention on that question, as a matter of urgency, and in eliciting what I believe is a growing determination to answer that question with a clear 'No', and to put that 'No' into effect.

Patrick, along with scores of others, saw that student leader slash at a campus policeman with a belt, in order to gain access to a classroom, for the purpose of breaking up a class. If the University allows the student to get away with that, it will be as good as hoisting a flag with the device 'Mob Rule OK'. Quite a lot of university people are now determined that that flag shall not fly. At Witwatersrand, one professor said to me: 'Your visit and its repercussions have forced us to think about things we didn't want to think about, but need to think about.' Things like taking a stand against mob rule.

Virtually everybody at the Universities of Cape Town and the Witwatersrand is against apartheid. Almost all faculty members, and probably the great majority of students, want free universities and intellectual freedom in general to be an important part of the heritage of a future free and non-racial South Africa. But the students who are now going on the rampage *don't* want that. They want the universities to be under rigid ideological control, by people like themselves, both now and after apartheid has gone.

The signal that brought the academic boycott to the fore – and gave a licence to rampage – was given by the recent Conference of the Non-Aligned States at Harare, Zimbabwe. Now, most of the Non-Aligned don't tolerate dissent in their own countries, and consequently have no time for bourgeois stuff like academic freedom. In the ordering of their own internal affairs the Non-Aligned are very Aligned indeed.

But South Africa is a much more developed country than any of the Non-Aligned, and many South Africans, black as well as white, both hope and believe that free non-racial elections in South Africa will *not* lead to the autocratic rule of one party, or one person. And there are plenty of people in the townships who don't want the rule of the comrades – women, for example, who have seen family planning clinics broken up to the slogan of 'A baby for Azania!' (the name given to revolutionary South Africa).

The attempt to snuff out freedom of speech at the universities can thus be seen as a sort of trial run for what some on the left want to urge upon the society as a whole. In so far as the universities make an effective stand against these pressures, they will be rendering a service also to the future of the wider society. But the primary reason they must resist, and deploy all their resources and sanctions to that end, is that their very *raison d'être* is at stake.

VI: Will Apartheid End in Anarchy?

My son Patrick and I returned from South Africa on Thursday. Our final thoughts on this tour:

Patrick: That there will eventually be a South Africa without apartheid is, as everyone knows, a certainty. What people are not certain about is when it will happen, how it will happen, and what form the new government will take.

The answer to the question *when* it happens will, in fact, probably determine the subsequent answers.

If non-racial elections were to come about in the near future, either by a government decision, or through outside intervention, then South Africa could emerge as the most stable and wealthiest African nation.

Future South African politics are not likely to be divided simply into black and white voting blocks (with whites, of course, outnumbered). As in the US, the nearest outside parallel, there would be multiple factors influencing how a vote would go and dozens of political lobbies.

Again, as in the US, after the initial race problem was solved, the major division in voting patterns would be between the 'haves' and the 'have nots'. This is assuming that the change was fairly soon.

I believe after speaking to several black South African moderates, the claim made by the Government that if they gave the blacks the franchise now, white rule would immediately be replaced by a 'white-hating' black Communist government, to be untrue.

Conor: When the change happens, the new regime will have so many problems that 'revenge on whites' will not be likely to be high on the agenda. In any case, blacks who have worked for the apartheid regime will be more at risk than any whites.

Patrick: The second, more sinister and unfortunately more probable, possibility for South Africa is that the regime will dig its heels in and refuse to budge; rather than ease the apartheid laws, it will tighten them, and deal with the increasing violence more and more ferociously.

As I have already indicated, the only hope for a viable post-apartheid South Africa lies in the emergence of a sense of common interest between moderate South Africans, both black and white. The effect of the Government's continued refusal to budge and the hardening of the ANC line is to make it increasingly difficult for this sense of common interest to prevail.

Already those liberals who can afford it, which in effect means white liberals, are leaving South Africa in considerable numbers. Many of the white liberals do so out of necessity rather than choice. The attitude among many white students is to stay until they have their degrees and then leave with something to offer the outside world.

The picture painted by moderate blacks of their own situation is truly depressing. In the townships the *act* of being a *moderate*, as opposed to a *radical*, is enough for them to be looked on with 'suspicion'. In the townships, if you are looked on with 'suspicion', you can easily become a target for the necklace.

The effect this situation has on black moderates is, naturally enough, to shut them up. It is, in fact, the relatively brave ones who just shut up.

The not so brave publicly toe whatever line 'the ANC or some faction of the ANC', appears to lay down, and prove their radicalism by rioting. The reason some people frighten other people is often that they are frightened themselves.

Conor: As Patrick suggests, there is a 'benign scenario' (as well as various other ones) for a future non-racial South Africa. According to the benign scenario, the first non-racial elections are likely to provide a parliament composed of various regional, ethnic and class interest groups, in which no single group or party has an overall majority.

This situation would result in inter-group bargaining, leading to coalition governments and to conditions favourable to democracy – through renewed elections – to the rule of law, and to freedom of expression and association, including academic freedom.

During our last week in Cape Town, I had dinner with Frederick van Zyl Slabbert, the highly capable former leader of the Parliamentary Opposition in South Africa. I asked van Zyl what he thought of this benign scenario which has been the subject of a much discussed recent book, *South Africa Without Apartheid: Dismantling Racial Domination,* by Herbert Adam and Cogila Moodley (Maskew, Miller, Longman: Cape Town 1986).

Van Zyl said: 'If there were to be non-racial elections soon, they might well work out like that. But they don't seem likely to be soon. It may take as long as a generation. And by that time, things would probably not work out like that.'

That was a bleak enough answer. Roughly, what he had in mind, on such a time-scale, was that the eventual South African non-racial elections would be similar to those through which Rhodesia became Zimbabwe: bandwagon, winner-takes-all elections – just once! – resulting in permanent one-party authoritarian rule.

Even that would be preferable to apartheid. The new government, however authoritarian it might be, would at least be seen as legitimate by most of its subjects: something that can never be the case with the Afrikaner brand of authoritarian rule. And the new government, by rescinding the whole corpus of apartheid law, would relieve most of the people of South Africa from a multitude of oppressive burdens at present experienced in their daily lives.

Also the new government, by reason of its perceived legitimacy and the consequent acceptability of its police, would be able to end the anarchic conditions now prevailing in the townships. The 'comrades' would be brought into line. The 'necklace' would go.

All in all the new government, however regrettable its character might be in terms of Western principles, would have a lot going for it, in the eyes of most of its subjects – in the early years at least. Most South Africans, after all, comprising all South Africa's blacks, have never known democracy, except as a privilege reserved for whites, and have never known the rule of law except through laws devised without their consent and for their oppression.

So they would not be deprived of anything that they have enjoyed, or have learned to value. What would have happened, in the eyes of most people, would be the replacement of an unacceptable form of authoritarian rule by an acceptable form of the same.

Under authoritarian government, all institutions, including universities, are run on authoritarian lines, laid down by the political rulers. So if a non-racial South Africa is authoritarian, its universities will be run by people appointed by the government.

In the social sciences – including history – teachers will be told to teach the prevailing ideology, in order to fit their students for membership of the new ruling class. Teachers who won't do that will be dismissed. Students who object will be sent down. Academic freedom is incompatible with the authoritarian state.

You may well ask whether, if the future is going to be like that, it is worth making a fuss about academic freedom in the here and now, in the South African universities?

This is a good question, but I think it *is* worth making a fuss. First of all, though the 'authoritarian scenario' may at present seem more probable than the more 'benign' pluralist one, we are not obliged to assume that it will happen. South Africa is a far more complicated society than Zimbabwe, or any of the other African countries to the north, and its future forms of government may be widely different.

In the meantime, it seems important to keep South Africa's universities going. The more educated people – black and white, educated together – there are when the great transition comes, the better, surely.

Now what is misleadingly called 'the academic boycott' – in practice, student intimidation of teachers, by the threat and use of violence – is simply incompatible with the continued existence of universities of liberal type, such as are the Universities of Cape Town and the Witwatersrand. Unless student intimidation can be nipped in the bud, teachers are going to start leaving, as many of them are now talking of doing.

In those conditions, the best of South Africa's universities and the ones most opposed to apartheid, would be going into terminal decline.

The fact that at some future date South Africa's universities *may* fall under authoritarian rule is not a reason for destroying them, in the here and now, through making them a prey to mob rule.

Anarchy can be even more destructive than authoritarianism. And the present 'academic boycott' is no more than a licence for the spread of anarchy.

'The Irish Mind'
A Bad Case of Cultural Nationalism*

'THE IRISH MIND'. . . . Oh, dear! Here we go again. There is a split, already, between the title and the subtitle. Richard Kearney is interested in the collective, national-intellectual, concept of 'Irish mind'. Many of the contributors – several of whom are distinguished authorities in their specialist fields – are more interested, most of the time, in exploring particular intellectual traditions. As a result of this, several of the parts are more coherent than the sum. As a collection of essays, *The Irish Mind* contains a variety of material that will be of interest to students of Irish literature or history. But alas! The individual explorers often seem to be looking, rather guiltily, over their shoulders to be sure that they have not lost sight of the governing concept of the collection, and that they are indeed authenticating the existence of the alleged collective intellectual entity in whose name the said explorers are assembled. Even some of the finest scholars seem to pay to this infatuation at least the tribute of appearing in some degree to succumb to it.

I hope the contributors will forgive me if, in this essay, I pay attention to the entity proclaimed in the book's title, and celebrated in the editor's introduction, rather than to the individual essays. After all, if you take part in the setting up of a graven image, you should not complain if people pay more attention to the image than they do to you.

The idea of 'the Irish mind' is a manifestation of cultural nationalism. Cultural nationalism, as explicit ideology, is a German invention under French influence, and now a bit more than 200 years old. It was popularized by Herder, under the general influence of Rousseau, even before the French Revolution. Rousseau's cult of the natural was developed by Herder into the cult of the national. It was *natural* for a German to speak German; *un*natural for him to speak French. 'Spit out that green slime of the Seine!' was

---

* Article on *The Irish Mind: Exploring Intellectual Traditions*, Richard Kearney (ed.), Wolfhound Press, in *Times Literary Supplement*, 1 November 1985.

Herder's advice to his fellow Germans. That was unusually strong language for the meek-seeming Herder. Programmatically and formally, cultural nationalism, in its opening stage, was apolitical, ecumenical and even *gemütlich*. But in its thrust, even then, it was – as it has almost everywhere remained – political. Before the French Revolution the Herderian tendency was towards undermining French intellectual and cultural ascendancy – then towering over Europe – and towards the laying of the intellectual, ideological and cultural foundations of a united Germany. The balance of Europe was already shifting, albeit microscopically.

After the French Revolution, and the emergence of *La Grande Nation*, and especially after the defeat of Prussia by Napoleon at Jena, this cultural nationalism, becoming more overtly political, begins to take on manic forms and it is in this fateful period that the idea of 'the x mind' or 'spirit' (*Geist*) becomes an obsession of certain intellectuals.

Fichte in his *Addresses to the German Nation* (1807–08) – which was to be the Bible of the New Nationalism – argued for a close connection between language, thought and being. Germans, speaking the same language, belonged to the same nation. Speaking in the same way, they thought in the same way, and it was a way in which other people could not think. It was not possible to think in a language which was not one's own. Thus the French (not named, since those people were then in occupation of Berlin, where the lectures were delivered) could not think, in a serious way; they could only give the impression of thinking. The French (or the élite of the French nation) had originally been Germans: Franks. But they had acquired a Latinized language, which had incapacitated their Germanic intellects so that they could no longer understand anything at all. Only a German could understand German. But a Frenchman was not only incapable of understanding German; he was also incapable of understanding French. When a German and a Frenchman converse in either language, the German understands what both parties are saying, but the Frenchman can understand neither.

Cultural nationalism caught on outside Germany, originally in mild Herderian and antiquarian forms, then with something of the Fichtean obsessional intensity, arrogance and political drive. It caught on especially in Italy and Eastern Europe, but in due course its ripples reached the shores of Ireland, around the middle of the nineteenth century.

Cultural nationalism was inherently attractive to many Irish people, but it was also quite baffling (and remains so). The basis of cultural nationalism – whether *à la* Herder or *à la* Fichte – was always language, just as in South Africa the *volk* consists of those who speak the *taal*. But the Irish were already – even by 1848 – a *volk* that was losing its *taal*. Political nationalism had preceded cultural nationalism – instead of the other way around – as among the Germans, the Serbs, the Czechs and the Afrikaners. Indeed in Ireland political nationalism had established itself on the ruins of the cultural (Gaelic) nation (which was never politically unified) as Proinsias MacCana notes in his contribution to the present collection. It was all enough to boggle the Irish mind.

Cultural nationalism emerged in Ireland as a force (or combination of forces) only in the late nineteenth century, after overt political nationalism had reached a kind of *impasse*; following the fall and death of Parnell, cultural nationalism emerged in three main forms. The first was the effort of Douglas Hyde and others to restore the Gaelic language – the basic requirement for a national culture, according to the Herder-Fichte view. 'The Irish mind' would then have meant 'the Gaelic mind', and Irish nationalism would have been placed on the same firm linguistic footing as the other cultural nationalisms of Europe.

It was not to be, as the second school of cultural nationalists saw. What they offered – in the movement known as 'the Irish Literary Renaissance', including the Abbey Theatre – was a vision of a distinctive Irish national culture *in the English language*. 'The Irish mind' was a phrase frequently on Yeats's lips, sometimes in sharp and favourable contrast to 'the English mind'. But it appeared that the medium in which the Irish mind is especially equipped to display its essence is the English language.

Now all this, of course, was the purest heresy in terms of continental cultural nationalism. The Yeatsians, instead of 'spitting out the green slime of the Thames', were taking to the language of their oppressor like ducks to water. Some Irish people, who had not necessarily read Herder, Fichte or Mazzini, were substantially of the same opinion. This was the third school. These were Catholic, populistic and suspicious of Protestants (leaders of the other two schools). Even if it didn't make much use of grand phrases like 'the Irish mind', the third school knew what it meant by 'Irish'. It meant 'Irish Catholic', of Gaelic stock. The culture of this third school was basically that of the Irish Catholic tradition and observance, together with the enthusiastic pursuit of Gaelic games, so organized as to exclude Protestants. As regards language, these people stuck, in practice, to English, but English tempered by the use of the *cúpla focal*: a few tags of Gaelic, in greeting or farewell. The *cúpla focal* were – and are – the disinfectant in the green slime of the Thames.

The intellectual leader of this school was a brilliant journalist, D. P. Moran. Moran ridiculed 'the Irish Literary Renaissance' as a lot of

Protestant flummery and impudence playing to an English gallery. Protestants were not acceptable as leaders, culturally or otherwise. The best they could hope was to be allowed to be absorbed into the real Irish nation, the nation of the Catholics. The *Kulturkampf* went on. You will find it documented in F. S. L. Lyon's *Culture and Anarchy* and now with new examples in Hubert Butler's excellent collection of essays, *Escape from the Anthill* (reviewed in the *TLS* of 6 September 1985). Butler is an Anglo-Irish gentleman who 'stayed on' and got good at coping with School Three. In the 1950s, the poet Patrick Kavanagh adhered for a time to School Three, bringing to it a then much needed (if unappreciated) access of intellectual distinction. Kavanagh was once handed a copy of Arland Ussher's book *Three Great Irishmen* (Yeats, Joyce and Shaw). Kavanagh threw the Three Great Irishmen to one side with a comment, 'A journalist's lie!' What he was understood to mean was that two of the three were Prods, and therefore not really Irish at all. When Kavanagh – in this mood – accused the Protestant poet F. R. Higgins of trying 'to bypass Rome on the way to the heart of Ireland', Hubert Butler had a memorable reply: 'What Mr Kavanagh is trying to do is to by-pass Anglo-Ireland on the way to the heart of London.'

The *Kulturkampf* eventually more or less fizzled out for various reasons, among them a shortage of Protestant fuel in the 97 per cent Catholic Republic. Dublin is today a far more tolerant city than it was in the first half of the century. Eoghan Harris's *Souper Sullivan* has been playing to good houses at the Abbey. This remarkable new play is truly revolutionary, in relation to the traditions of Catholic Ireland. Its heroes are a Protestant pastor and his principal convert, in the Ireland of the Famine. The main villains of the piece are the Catholic clergy and middle class. If that play had been put on in the days of Yeats and Lady Gregory – which it would not have been – the theatre would have been wrecked. But on 26 September 1985, the first night of *Souper Sullivan* went off very well. The reason, I suspect, is that now the audience and the theatre really belong to the same people. There is no longer any feeling that it is a case of 'them' looking out at 'us'; and perhaps 'down' on us. They've gone. We have the place to ourselves. We can relax – while we're at the Abbey, at any rate.

But it would be wrong to conclude that all Ireland has fallen victim to Enlightenment values. In rural Ireland, throughout the last summer, and into this summer, numerous statues of the Blessed Virgin were seen to move, and thousands of people came, by car and minibus, to see them move. At Ballinspittle – the most celebrated scene of such happenings – two local *Protestants* attest to the authenticity of the miracle. D. P. Moran had prophesied that the Protestants would eventually be 'absorbed'. By and large that is what has happened, in the Catholic Republic. And that is what Ulster Protestants don't want to happen to *them*.

The version of cultural nationalism that is represented by *The Irish Mind* has no room for Ulster Protestants, other than those of them – very, very few – who are already, in advance, 'absorbed'. It has not only no room for them; it is fundamentally hostile to them, though in coded language. The language of Kearney's introduction is that of the modern international left, but the spirit is that of old D. P. Moran. Moran was hostile, not only to Protestants ('West Britons', 'sourfaces') but also to those Catholics who were insufficiently anti-British (*shoneens*). Kearney is far too sophisticated to call Seán O'Faoláin a *shoneen*; he just taxes him with 'post-colonial servility', meaning exactly the same thing. I prefer Moran: a bigot, but a plain-spoken one.

An Irish cultural nationalist, expressing his rejection of England in elaborate English, has to find himself in intellectual difficulties, which are perhaps insuperable. Such a person, in Herder's terms, is incapable of thinking genuinely national thoughts. In Fichte's terms, such a person is inherently incapable of thinking any thoughts at all, or even of understanding what he himself is saying. *The Irish Mind* contains a certain amount of evidence in support of the Fichtean theory. Yet oddly enough, what the editor sets out to do, from the first page of his introduction, is to prove that Irishmen *can* think. This seems a curious, even an abject thing to want to prove, but there it is. Certain Victorian English worthies – with whose utterances modern Irish cultural nationalists continue to be much preoccupied – held that Irish people were *not* capable of thought, though they might be capable of imaginative, artistic achievement. So it is urgent, it seems, to refute this offensive and colonialist thesis.

Well, certainly, it can be argued, if you feel the need to do so, that Burke and Berkeley were capable of thought. And the cultural nationalists *need* Burke and Berkeley; in the argument of *The Irish Mind*, these are the clinchers: thinkers, not just artists. But the problem is that Burke and Berkeley were not Irish nationalists, either culturally or politically. They were intimately associated (though not without serious reservations) with the colonialist enterprise which, according to the introduction, generates only 'prejudice' and 'servile discourse', from which we all, even today, need to be saved by the 'intellectually liberating speech' of the modern cultural nationalists. Burke and Berkeley were not intellectually liberated. Richard Kearney, Seamus Deane and Desmond Fennell are. Intellect seems to do better in captivity.

The Irish Mind sets out to show, not only that Irishmen can think, but also that they think in some special way. Having read *The Irish Mind*, I still haven't the faintest idea of what that special way is supposed to be. The first essay in the collection deals with bronze-age cemeteries in purple prose. The last essay deals with the work of some Anglo-Irish scientists in the eighteenth and nineteenth centuries. We are supposed to believe that these two sets of phenomena – together with various other disparate phenomena perceived in between – are linked, by being creations of 'the Irish mind'. In so far as the first and last of the phenomena may be linked it is surely through the *scientific* mind, which is international. To claim the bronze-age Boyne Valley for a national 'mind' imagined by moderns, is – well, perhaps – a shade anachronistic. As for those Anglo-Irish scientists, it seems probable that they would have regarded this idea of a distinctively Irish 'mind' with some suspicion – not only politically and socially, but also scientifically.

The Irish Mind runs some risk of being seen as evidence in support of the offensive Victorian thesis which its editor has set out to refute. I say that, not in condemnation of the individual contributions, but of the doomed intellectual enterprise on which they all imprudently embarked. Most cultural nationalism, at least since Fichte's day, is politically motivated. Irish cultural nationalism, now lacking any linguistic focus of coherence, is more markedly political than most. The politics, now defined as 'anti-colonial', and larded with Third Worldly quotations from the school of Frantz Fanon, is really good old Catholic Irish nationalism, in trendy gear. These cultural nationalists are the latest generation of what used to be called 'the literary side of the movement' – a term formerly employed – with genial derision, by the military leaders of the movement in question: the IRA.

It is all rather a pity. Some of those concerned – Kearney and Seamus Deane in particular – have talents that should not be wasted on this sort of guff, or tied into these sorts of knots. They seem to have few options open to them. They can carry on like this until they are beyond hope of intellectual recovery or they could speak and write Irish rather than English and become serious cultural nationalists. Or they could follow the logic of their political rhetoric and join in the liberation of Northern Ireland. It is true that the majority of the population of Northern Ireland don't want to be liberated, but that is neither here nor there. These people are opposing the general will of the Irish Nation (with 'mind' to match) and must be 'forced to be free', exactly as Rousseau prescribes.

The fourth option for the Irish-Minders would be to come to terms, more humbly, with *their* actual condition, as English-speaking academics, not greatly different from their contemporary colleagues in Britain and the United States (and less different from those than from non-academic Irish people). The differences from the non-Irish are not insignificant but should surely not be hypostatized and then idolized, as in *The Irish Mind*. Such idolaters are – in part – victims of a mysterious spiritual condition once diagnosed by Paul Claudel: '*La quiétude incestueuse de l'âme, assise sur sa différence essentielle.*' 'Incestuous', yes; 'difference', yes. But where, oh where is the *quietude*?

Some of the present cultural nationalists will probably in time embrace that fourth option. But even if they don't, they needn't dominate the field. While I was preparing this essay, I heard over RTE radio the voice of Seán White, the learned head of Dublin's admirable School of Irish Studies. He was asked whether his school was 'teaching Irish culture'. 'No,' he said. 'We tell our students about aspects of Irish experience.' That makes a lot more sense than 'the Irish mind'.

Bobby Sands:
Mutations of Nationalism*

*B*OBBY SANDS AND THE TRAGEDY OF NORTHERN IRELAND is a 151-page piece of propaganda on behalf of the Provisional IRA. It consists in about equal parts of hagiography and bad history. The hagiographical part, of which I shall have more to say, concerns the story of Bobby Sands – the young IRA man and elected MP for Fermanagh, whose death on hunger-strike, in Long Kesh prison, in May 1981, attracted world-wide media attention. The Author, Mr Feehan's, treatment of the story contains little information about Sands, and almost nothing about the activities which led to his arrest and sentence. The 'historical' part of the book applies the usual techniques of propagandist historiography: highlighting of enemy atrocities; failing to mention those of one's own side; converting a far-fetched *interpretation* of a given event into the event itself, and so on.

In itself, *Bobby Sands and the Tragedy of Northern Ireland* would not merit extensive attention here. But the phenomenon – Irish Republicanism – of which this book is a product does, I believe, deserve such attention. I propose, therefore, in this essay, to consider Irish Republicanism, both historically and in relation to the present condition of Northern Ireland and the Anglo-Irish Agreement of 1985. I shall take account of Mr Feehan's book in so far as it sheds light on the Irish Republican mystique.

The father of Irish Republicanism was Theobald Wolfe Tone, in the French Revolutionary period. Wolfe Tone was one of a number of European *patriotes* who during the 1790s – in Belgium, Holland, the Rhineland and various parts of Italy as well as in Ireland – sought to shake off monarchical, aristocratic, clerical and/or alien rule and turn their countries into sister republics, *républiques soeurs,* of *la Grande Nation,* Revolutionary France.

Wolfe Tone died, by his own hand, in 1798, as a prisoner of the British. His life and death remained, and remain, an inspiration to Irish physical-

* Article on *Bobby Sands and the Tragedy of Northern Ireland*, John Feehan, The Permanent Press, Sag Harbor, New York, in the *New York Review of Books*, 24, 21 April 1986.

force separatists. His aim 'to break the connection with England, the never-failing source of all our political evils' was also the political aim of the hero of the 1916 Rising, Patrick Pearse, who called Wolfe Tone's grave at Bodenstown 'the holiest place in Ireland', thus deliberately putting Tone above St Patrick.

Today the Provisional IRA claim, not without some justification, to be following in the footsteps of Tone and Pearse. The considerable element of truth in this claim is a source of constant embarrassment, dull rather than acute, to the principal established democratic political parties in today's Republic of Ireland. These parties – Fianna Fail and Fine Gael, especially Fianna Fail – profess a commitment to the ideals of Tone and Pearse. Yet it is obvious that today's Republic of Ireland is not the Republic for which Tone and Pearse died. *Their* Republic – never attained in fact, but undying or undead, as an ideal – was a Republic of the whole island of Ireland, totally separate from Britain.

The real-life political entity which today bears the same name as that ideal entity – the Republic of Ireland – is territorially deficient, by the exclusion of the six north-eastern counties, still a part of the United Kingdom of Great Britain and Northern Ireland. And today's Republic – the real-life one, as distinct from the ghost one – is spiritually deficient also from an Irish Republican point of view. A real-life Republic, a democracy expressive of the material demands of ordinary citizens, cannot possibly live up to an ideal ever-unrealized Republic, for which heroes and martyrs died. Yet citizens of the real-life Republic feel – at times and dimly, for the most part – a bit guilty about not living up to the ideal Republic, the ghost, and vaguely aspire to catching up with it somehow, some day.

The aspiration is feeble – because commonsense keeps breaking in – and it is also hopeless. It is hopeless because the ghost Republic is not about living up to. It is about dying up to, and killing up to. And these, the sacrificial elements, which are the sole substantial elements of the cult, are looked after by a minority subculture, a sort of hereditary priesthood of blood: the IRA; today, the Provisional IRA.

The ghost Republic and its bloody priesthood have a perennially unsettling effect on the real-life Republic. Most citizens of the real-life Republic don't really want Northern Ireland; that is the real-life Northern Ireland. But they do yearn a bit, when they happen to think of it, for a kind of ghost Northern Ireland, an imaginary entity which will someday be united, by consent, with today's real-life Republic, thus making that Republic identical, territorially at least, with the Republic of Tone and Pearse. This would close a schism (of sorts) in the soul; it would also, it is supposed, make those frightening priests redundant, and end the blood-sacrifices.

So successive democratic governments, in the real-life Republic, are impelled to lay claim to Northern Ireland, and to assert that the separation of Northern Ireland from the Republic constitutes an injustice which must be repaired. It must be repaired, the democratic leaders insist, peacefully and by consent. But as a majority of the population of Northern Ireland passionately and consistently refuses its consent, the injustice in question is most unlikely to be repaired, peacefully and by consent. As this has become rather obvious by now, the attempt to unite Ireland, peacefully and by consent, turns in practice into unintended legitimation of the Provisional IRA, the most committed to the reparation of the injustice which *must*, by common consent of most (around 65 per cent) of the Republic's citizens, be repaired.

Thus there are 'hard' and 'soft' versions of the demand for a united Ireland; the hard version being directly inspired by the vision of the ghost Republic, and the soft version reflecting the same vision, at second hand. And the two versions share the allegiance of the consciously and politically 'Irish' elements in the population of the United States. The hard version in America is what keeps the Provisional IRA going in Ireland itself through money collected in American cities, and through pro-IRA propaganda exercises, using occasions such as the annual St Patrick's Day march along Fifth Avenue. The soft version – of which the principal contemporary exponents are Senators Edward Kennedy and Daniel Patrick Moynihan – condemns the violence of the Provisional IRA. But it agrees with the Provisional IRA to the extent that it insists that the only acceptable 'solution' to the 'problem' is a united Ireland. 'By consent' adds the soft version.

But how exactly do you get unity by consent, when that consent is firmly refused; as it is by the Ulster Protestant population, nearly one million people, a majority of the population of Northern Ireland? I have put that question, on various occasions, to a number of exponents of the soft version, both in Ireland and in the United States. The answers are invariably off-hand and hazy; amounting to little more than a verbal shrug. But what the shrug has to imply in the context of 'we must have unity by consent' is that, if the Ulster Protestants (Unionists) go on refusing their consent, they have no one but themselves to blame, if the Provisionals go on attacking them. Thus the soft version abets the hard version, as the 'nice cop' works together with the 'tough cop'. (New forms of this relationship, under the Anglo-Irish Agreement concluded between Garret FitzGerald and Margaret Thatcher, at Hillsborough, Co. Down, on 15 November 1985, will be considered later.)

At this point, it is necessary to consider the religious dimension of Irish Republicanism, which has undergone a notable mutation since the ideology first took shape under the guidance of Theobald Wolfe Tone, in the 1790s.

Wolfe Tone and his friends, like their contemporary *patriotes* everywhere, were militant secularists, deists and atheists, contemptuous of superstition, and especially of Roman Catholic superstition. Wolfe Tone, like most of his followers in the leadership of the United Irishmen, was a secularist of Protestant background. He and his friends saw themselves as the advance guard of the Enlightenment in still-benighted Ireland, leading their backward Catholic fellow-countrymen towards enfranchisement, both from material despotism and from their Romish superstitions.

But when the flame of Irish Republicanism was re-lit in the early twentieth century by Patrick Pearse, in the name of Tone, it was a different kind of flame. Tone's secular ideology meant less than nothing to Pearse. What interested Pearse about Tone was Tone's *sacrifice*, which Pearse proposed to emulate, and did in 1916. And Pearse was emulating not just Tone, but Jesus Christ: as the dating of the Easter Rising was meant to exemplify. Pearse's ideology, wildly remote from Tone's, was a syncretic mysticism, fusing Irish nationalism and Irish Catholicism into one. And it was Tone's ironic fate to become a major saint in the Pearsean Pantheon. The grave of the man who had set out to emancipate his country from superstition had become 'the holiest place in Ireland'.

Anthropologists tell us that, on the collective farms of contemporary Western Siberia, shamanism has taken on syncratic forms, blending Communist teaching with traditional beliefs. In this way the Parisian communards defeated in 1871 took refuge in Lake Baikal where they were metamorphosed into otters, to whom the Siberian collective farmers of today offer sacrifice in order to ensure fulfilment of their quotas under the Party's fishery plan. (If you doubt me, see Caroline Humphrey, *Karl Marx Collective: Economy, Society and Religion on a Siberian Collective farm*, Cambridge University Press 1983, p. 408.)

The metamorphosis of Theobald Wolfe Tone, in the thaumaturgic hands of Patrick Pearse, is hardly less fishy.

In any case, the mystical Republicanism of Patrick Pearse, unlike the secular Republicanism of (pre-metamorphic) Tone, is an ideology of and for Catholics. Ulster Protestants reject it in all its forms, hard, soft or disguised (as in the Anglo-Irish Agreement). And so, to seek to incorporate Ulster Protestants in any kind of Irish Republic is a recipe for Holy War. Which is what is already going on, on a small scale and intermittently.

The point is made effectively, though quite inadvertently, in John Feehan's book on Bobby Sands. Sands's self-immolation was thoroughly Pearsean, and Mr Feehan's exaltation of Sands is in a Pearsean mode (though lacking any trace of Pearse's power with words). 'The conflict has very little to do with religion,' says Mr Feehan at one point, but his own metaphors and analogies and those of his hero, Sands himself, say something different. Like Pearse, Sands saw himself as one of a line of martyrs for the Republic (beginning with Tone), whose sacrifice repeats the sacrifice of Jesus Christ on the Cross. On receiving a fourteen-year sentence for possession of arms with intent to endanger life, Sands wrote the lines:

> The beady eyes they peered at me
> The time had come to be,
> To walk the lonely road
> Like that of Calvary.
> And take up the cross of Irishmen
> Who've carried liberty.

Mr Feehan takes up this Pearsean hint, which provides the leitmotiv for his book. Near the beginning, commenting on Cardinal Hume's view that men like Sands by deliberately starving themselves to death are committing suicide, Mr Feehan comments: 'Jesus Christ could have saved his life when he came before Pilate, but he refused to do so. Did the founder of Christianity therefore commit suicide?' A few pages later on, the perceived resemblance to the founder of Christianity is more boldly suggested:

> In the quiet evening silence of Milltown graveyard it seemed as if the Republican Movement had reached its Calvary with no Resurrection in sight, that Bobby Sands had lost and the overwhelming power of the British empire had won yet another victory.

The author goes on to suggest that the Resurrection duly followed in the shape of the boost given to the Republican cause by the hunger-strikers. But the clincher is in the last words of Mr Feehan's sixth and last chapter:

> In the early hours of the morning of 5 May the immortal soul of one of the noblest young Irishmen of the twentieth century came face-to-face with his Fellow Sufferer and Maker. Bobby Sands was dead.

There were other fellow-sufferers, lower-case ones: the thousands who were either killed, maimed or bereaved by the devotees of the Irish Republic in Mr Sands's organization, the Provisional IRA. Those other dead, however, being the wrong kind, are implicitly excluded from what's seen as a Celestial Tête-à-Tête.

The effect of elevating anyone prepared to kill and die for the Republic to the status of Jesus Christ, is to annihilate, morally and spiritually, the adversaries of the Republic, whom the Republican Christs feel impelled to bump off. Those adversaries of Christ are necessarily cast in the role, if not of Antichrist himself, then of the agents, or at best the dupes, of Antichrist. They deserve no mercy, and that is exactly what they get. This is the very essence of Holy War. And Mr Feehan shows his hero, on his last birthday, receiving with joy an ikon of Catholic Holy War: 'He was thrilled to get a picture of Our Lady from a priest in Kerry who had encouraged him to take arms for his oppressed people.' To wit, the Catholics of Northern Ireland.

Theobald Wolfe Tone would hardly have been 'thrilled' to get such a present and such a message. But then Wolfe Tone was trying to lead people out of the seventeenth century, while Republicans of our own time have brought the seventeenth century back.

The sole but significant merit of Mr Feehan's book is that it provides such authentic whiffs of the emotional mystique which keeps the IRA going, and for which some (though not all) of its members are not merely willing but anxious to die. (Nine other prisoners followed Sands's example, and fasted to death.) More sophisticated apologists for 'the Republican Movement' (the euphemism for the Provos and their camp-followers) like to stress the 'modern' and 'social' aspects of the movement. Mr Feehan tries to do that too – with his 'very little to do with religion' bit – but he just can't help blurting out – especially at the emotional high points – some of the obstinately archaic and numinous realities.

The Holy War is an incipient reality. But it is not – at least not yet – a war between Catholics-at-large and Protestants-at-large. Most Catholics and most Protestants don't want to fight one another, and have no craving for martyrdom, or for the seventeenth century. But Holy Wars are brought on, not by the mass of people on either side, but by quite small numbers of fanaticized pace-makers. In the Irish case, the pace-makers, for more than fifteen years now, have been a minority on the Catholic side: the Pearsean Catholic-Nationalist fusionist fundamentalists of the Provisional IRA. The Pearseans have long – and well before the emergence of the Provisional strain in 1970 – been a source of considerable embarrassment and confusion to the leaders, and many other members of the Catholic Church in Ireland. On the one hand, a good many churchmen are disconcerted by the tendency of Pearsean Republicans to go around killing people and then – when punished for killing people – to assimilate themselves to Jesus Christ. Some theologians – most notably the late Francis Shaw, S.J. – have discerned a heretical potential in this pattern of behaviour. But most Catholic churchmen are considerably more indulgent than that. As well they might be, for the Church in Ireland, over many years and in many ways, has done much to encourage that assimilation of religion and nationalism which the Pearseans have pushed to extremes (or perhaps merely to its logical conclusion). Generations of Irish Catholic schoolchildren have inscribed on their copy-books the Gaelic words: '*Dochum Glóire Dé agus Onóra na hEireann*', 'For the Glory of God and the Honour of Ireland.'

And what is wrong about that, you may ask. Isn't Ronald Reagan, whenever he links God with America – as in every speech during his last election campaign – doing just the same thing, blending religion and nationalism? He is indeed. But there might just possibly still be something wrong with the practice all the same.

In any case the Catholic Church resolves its ambivalence about the Pearseans – in today's context, the Provos – in ways that have by now become a well-established routine. After each spectacular act of violence admitted, or claimed, by the Provisionals, prominent churchmen express their abhorrence of such acts, and call for an end to them. But whenever people are punished for such acts, by the secular authorities, and when the Provos then launch a spectacular protest – as for example by hunger-strike – prominent churchmen are to be found supporting the protest.

On the Ulster Protestant side, the Catholic Church (like the Dublin Government) is seen as essentially supportive of the IRA, in that the IRA has been able to ignore the Church's reiterated chidings, and to benefit from the Church's backing for its protests. Thus the Ulster Protestant community sees itself as coming under attack from virtually the entire Catholic population of the island: with the Provos forming the actual assault forces, while the democratic parties in the Republic, and the Catholic hierarchy, provide various forms of tacit or oblique – and deniable – support to the Provos, and seek to turn the results of the Provos' activities to their own advantage. This is an over-simplified picture, but it contains more truth than most lay or clerical spokesmen for the Catholic community would admit.

It is the Provos who have been doing the pace-making, and most of the fighting, in the incipient Holy War to date. There are potential holy warriors – and more numerous potential holy warriors – on the Protestant side. And there have been – especially in the mid-1970s – a number of ghastly 'sectarian murders' of Catholics by Protestants. The reader should note that, in Northern Ireland, the murder of a Catholic by a Protestant is generally classified as 'sectarian', whereas the murder of a Protestant by a Catholic is 'political'. This terminology tends to create, or fortify, the misleading impression that only one side – the Protestant – is fighting a Holy War, whereas the other side is engaged in a strictly contemporary sort of struggle. Which is not exactly the case, as you can see from my citations from Mr Feehan's book.

The commitment of many Ulster Protestants to seventeenth-century values is blatant, as in the Orange iconography that commemorates every summer the victory of the Protestant champion King William III over James II and his Irish Catholic followers. There is plenty of fuel for Holy War on the

Protestant side: fuel openly stocked, and not camouflaged as 'anti-sectarian', as in many official pronouncements on the Catholic side.

If the inflammable material on the Protestant side has not been widely ignited as yet, despite the sparks coming from the Catholic side, the reason appears to be that Protestants generally have felt that Holy War might endanger their position in the United Kingdom, seen as their most secure defence against incorporation in a Catholic-majority united Ireland.

The main trouble with the Anglo-Irish Agreement of 1985 is that it weakens that perception of the United Kingdom, and proportionately weakens Protestant inhibition against eventual recourse to Holy War. The Agreement is intended by its sponsors, in London and Dublin, to bring about 'peace and stability' in Northern Ireland, and also 'reconciliation between the two traditions'. With the eye of faith, some signs of increasing 'peace and stability' might indeed be detected (see below); although the Provisional IRA is keeping up its campaign of violence on apparently much the same scale after the Agreement, as it did before the Agreement. But as a measure for 'reconciliation between the two traditions', the Agreement is an obvious and total failure, as could have been (and was) predicted. The Agreement has infuriated one tradition, the Ulster Protestants, who regard it as a betrayal by Britain, at the instigation of their Catholic enemies. If the other tradition, the Catholics of Northern Ireland, accept the Agreement – as most of them do – this acceptance is not based on any perception of a potential for reconciliation in the Agreement, but on a very clear perception, and keen enjoyment, of the Agreement's power to infuriate the Protestant enemy. 'I like hearing Paisley squeal,' as one Catholic put it. So, far from reconciling, this Agreement adds new fuel to a communal animosity now nearly four centuries old.

The main feature of the Agreement is that it creates an institution for consultation between Dublin and London over the affairs of Northern Ireland. The institution is an Anglo-Irish Intergovernmental Conference to deal 'on a regular basis' with the affairs of Northern Ireland; thus for the first time London has accorded to Dublin an officially recognized role in Northern Ireland. This is rejected by the Protestants (Unionists) who see it as giving Dublin 'a toe in the door', which is to be used to break through the resistance of the Protestants to being incorporated in a united Ireland. Privately many, perhaps most, of the supporters of the Agreement (almost all Catholic) view the Agreement in precisely the same light. But officially – and to keep the Agreement with London in existence – the Agreement's Dublin sponsors disclaim any such intention, although in delicate and Delphic language. They point to Articles 1(a) and (b) of the Agreement which affirm that 'any change in the status of Northern Ireland would only come about with the consent of a majority of the people of Northern Ireland'; and recognize 'that the present wish of a majority of the people of Northern Ireland is for no change in the status of Northern Ireland.'

Supporters of the Agreement, on both sides of the Irish Sea, believe that these clauses should reassure the Unionists. Unfortunately for the future of the Agreement, those who should be reassured are in no way reassured. The Unionists believe that a major 'change in the status of Northern Ireland' has already come about, through the Anglo-Irish Agreement, *without* 'the consent of a majority of the people of Northern Ireland', which was not consulted at any stage in the Dublin-London negotiations which produced the Agreement. The Unionists also believe, not without reason, that it is the intention of the Dublin side to use the Agreement to bring about *further* changes in the status of Northern Ireland, to the disadvantage of Unionists and the undermining of the Union itself.

When the Unionist Members of Parliament at Westminster made clear their strong, indeed passionate, opposition to the Agreement, their opponents at first claimed that the Unionist Members were misrepresenting those for whom they purported to speak, and that many ordinary Unionists would find the Agreement perfectly compatible with Unionist principles and traditions.

In order to demonstrate the contrary, and prove that their Unionist constituents were fully with them, the Unionist MPs decided to resign their seats and fight for re-election, standing as declared and determined opponents of the Anglo-Irish Agreement. As Unionists, in 1985, held fifteen out of the seventeen Northern Ireland seats, this meant fifteen simultaneous by-elections. This 'mini General Election' in January 1986 resulted in fourteen of the fifteen Unionists being re-elected. (The loss of the fifteenth seat, Newry-Armagh, did not betoken any Unionist/Protestant tendency to accept the Agreement. Newry-Armagh has a Catholic/Nationalist majority, which had previously split in such a way as to let the Unionist in, and which now came together in such a way as to put the Unionist out.) The Unionists, on their new plank of opposition to the new Anglo-Irish Agreement, held the whole of their previous Unionist/Protestant vote. In this way, the Unionist MPs did demonstrate that their constituents were behind them, against the Agreement.

Naturally, the Catholics were in no way impressed. They merely changed the nature of the indictment against the perennial foe. Before the elections, the Unionist leaders were accused of 'misrepresenting' their community. *Since* the elections the Unionist leaders are accused of 'misleading' the same community.

Those January elections, however, showed a change, of a nature gratifying to the sponsors of the Agreement (as well as to other peace-loving people) in the voting patterns of Northern Ireland Catholics. There was a swing of about 10 per cent away from Provisional Sinn Fein (the political front for the Provisional IRA) and towards Mr John Hume's non-violent Social Democratic and Labour Party. That this benign shift was due to the Agreement is not in doubt. It remains to be seen whether this electoral shift portends – as the sponsors of the Agreement believe – growing isolation for the IRA and a decline in violence. We must hope so, but there is room for doubt. Electoral preference is not a precise guide to actual behaviour. It has not been unknown, in the past, for significant numbers of Northern Catholics to give electoral support to 'constitutional nationalists' – in order to keep out Unionists – while also sympathizing with the IRA, and providing their members with practical help. 'Isolating the IRA', within the community which gave it birth, is not an easy task, nor one which looks like being within the capacity of the Agreement between London and Dublin.

The demeanour of Sinn Fein IRA leaders such as Mr Gerry Adams, on television in 1985–86 did not suggest that they were alarmed by the Agreement as a threat to their movement. They are against the Agreement in principle, but they are also greatly tickled by the Agreement's infuriating effect on the Protestant community, an effect from which the IRA can hope to benefit, by emerging in their favourite role as 'protectors of the Catholic people'. Sinn Fein's loss of votes is not as depressing to the IRA as some democratic observers suppose. Votes are a sideshow; 'the armed struggle' is the real thing.

Protestant opposition to the Agreement is unconditional. But Catholic support for the Agreement, in Northern Ireland, is conditional; dependent on further measures being forthcoming of a nature congenial to the Catholic community, and proportionately distasteful to the Protestant community. The most sensitive areas where change is demanded are those involving security: the Courts, the Royal Ulster Constabulary, the Ulster Defence Regiment. Major changes in these areas would signify to many Protestants that they are being disarmed in the presence, and at the behest, of their hereditary foes. To Protestants seeing the matter in that light, it would look like a case of 'now or never': time to take on the Catholics in earnest, and if necessary throw the connection with Britain to the winds. And at that point the Holy War, now only smouldering, would break into full conflagration.

The danger should not be discounted, but neither should the catastrophe be accepted as meritable. There are signs on the British side of a growing recognition of the danger: of an awareness that they had miscalculated – not for the first time – the depth of the resistance of Ulster Protestants to any changes which look to them like leading to their incorporation in a Catholic-majority united Ireland. The Catholic sponsors of the Agreement had expected some Protestant resistance, though they too underestimated it; as has been the habit of Catholic leaders since John Redmond's time. But the Catholics, in Dublin and Derry, counted, for success, on Mrs Thatcher's celebrated intransigence: a quality which they had all deplored in chorus five years previously, in the days when she was letting all those hunger-strikers die. But in the matter of the Agreement, the Catholic sponsors, and the Catholic media, looked to Mrs Thatcher to give ruthless backing to the Agreement which bears her signature. The Iron Lady was their secret weapon. If the Protestants didn't like the Agreement she would stuff it down their throats, so she would. If they wanted confrontation they would darn well get confrontation, and high time too.

These expectations are excessive. Cabinet responsibility applies, and the Cabinet includes a Secretary of State for Northern Ireland who, virtually *ex officio*, will be likely to oppose implementation of the Catholic agenda, pushed to the point of full confrontation with the Protestant community. Any Cabinet is unlikely altogether to discount very serious misgivings expressed by their colleague with responsibility from the Province. Nor would Mrs Thatcher be likely to want to go the whole way with the Catholic agenda, as long as the Agreement continues to fail to produce significant improvement in the security situation.

If that is the way things go – as looks quite likely at present – then Catholic disappointment will make itself heard, quite loudly. The Irish will have been let down by the Brits, yet again. Now just as the sound of Protestants complaining that they have been let down by the Brits is music in Catholic ears, so the sound of Catholics similarly complaining is music in the ears of Protestants. So – if things develop that way – Catholic disappointment will tend to assuage Protestant resentment, and the Holy War will recede; or, rather more likely, subside into the smouldering condition in which it has continued now for more than fifteen years. Which is about the best that can realistically be expected.

As for the Agreement itself. I doubt whether it can last very long. It is true that it is not as vulnerable, on the Protestant side, as was its predecessor, the Sunningdale arrangement of 1974 (with a power-sharing executive in Belfast, and a Council of Ireland involving both Belfast and Dublin). The Sunningdale executive initially had Protestant participation, and it collapsed when it became plain that the Protestant participants were repudiated by the Protestant community. As the Hillsborough Agreement never had any Ulster Protestant participation, it cannot be overthrown by a withdrawal of

Protestant support, which was never there in the first place. The Agreement's institution, the Anglo-Irish Intergovernmental Conference, lacks any representation from Northern Ireland, and is therefore not *directly* vulnerable to repudiation by either majority or minority in Northern Ireland. But it is indirectly vulnerable; not on the Protestant side this time, but on the Catholic side. If the Catholic 'constitutional' party, Mr Hume's SDLP, should withdraw its support from the Agreement, the position of Dr FitzGerald's Government as a partner in the Anglo-Irish Agreement would speedily become untenable. The opposition in the Republic, led by Mr C. J. Haughey, is already critical of the Agreement (for failing to live up to the ideals of Tone and Pearse). Dr FitzGerald can easily dominate that opposition, in this particular matter, as long as he is fortified by the approval of Mr Hume and his friends, representing the Northern Catholics. Mr Hume is very popular in the Republic, where his views on Northern Ireland are invested with an almost papal authority. So if Mr Hume, after a while, should show disappointment with the progress made under the Agreement, then Dr FitzGerald would be blamed for failure, and the Opposition would dominate the internal debate on the subject in the Republic. The Government of the Republic would be under pressure to withdraw from the Anglo-Irish Intergovernmental Conference, thus bringing the Agreement to an end.

Now Mr Hume and his friends are bound to be disappointed, unless the British Government is willing, for their sake, to plunge the Protestants into desperation and secession. As pointed out earlier, the SDLP's support for the Agreement has been conditional from the beginning. The Agreement was acceptable to them 'as a first step', with a long series of further steps to come, all of them unacceptable to Unionists. If there is not sustained progress in that direction, SDLP support for the Agreement will dry up. Also SDLP support is vulnerable at any moment to any incident involving Catholics and the security forces. Unless each such incident is resolved in a manner acceptable to the Catholic community – and unacceptable to the Protestant community – SDLP members will say the Agreement is not working, and the Irish partner to that Agreement, the Government in Dublin, will be undermined.

So the choice, in relation to the failure of the Agreement, appears to be this:

Either the Agreement will be implemented in accordance with the SDLP's interpretation and demands, in which case the Protestants will be driven in the direction of civil war;

Or the Agreement will not be so interpreted and will collapse, due to the withdrawal of the Irish partner from the Anglo-Irish Intergovernmental Conference.

(However, the fortunes of the Agreement are likely to fluctuate uncertainly, perhaps for a considerable time, between the two alternative outcomes. For example, the Agreement may for a time be sufficiently unpopular with Protestants to keep it popular with Catholics, while not enraging Protestants sufficiently to make them move towards independence. But that is not a balance that seems likely to maintain itself indefinitely, under the strains and shocks of conditions in Northern Ireland. The most likely outcome, in my opinion, is essentially the second alternative: the drying up of Catholic support once it becomes apparent that the limits of British concessions to the minority have been reached.)

Granted the nature of the alternatives, I prefer the second.

Readers may ask what solution to the problem I envisage? None. I think the language of 'problem' and 'solution' is inappropriate to the case. What we have here is a *conflict*, which is likely to continue as long as the island of Ireland contains both a large Ulster Protestant community, and a significant and determined minority of Irish Republicans, with a hold on the Catholic community. That looks like being quite a long time. No tinkering will reconcile those irreconcilables and the effort to reconcile them often serves only to inflame the conflict, by arousing conflicting hopes and fears. On the other hand, if the Governments in London and Dublin learn, from unhappy experience of this Agreement, that it is better to stop tinkering with ambitious 'solutions', and to return to quiet co-operation in security matters, then the level of the violence involved in the conflict of irreconcilable wills could in time be reduced. It would also help if future Dublin Governments and their American backers could desist from their well-meant efforts to bring about progress towards a united Ireland; efforts whose unintended effects help on the Holy War.

Readers are likely to be surprised at the contrast between this bleak survey and the optimistic commentary on the Agreement which has been almost universal in the American (and European) media. The media welcomed the Agreement because *any* agreement between Dublin and London, over Northern Ireland, seemed fit matter for rejoicing. That in itself was understandable. But in the euphoria over that aspect, the media ignored (or glossed over) the obvious fact that the Agreement between London and Dublin was unacceptable in Belfast, and among the great majority of the population for whom the Agreement was intended; or rather on whom the institutions of the Agreement were to be imposed. Anyone who took account of that fact could see that the Agreement was quite unlikely to bring peace and stability to the area which rejected it; or to reconcile two traditions, one of which it outraged. By failing to take anything like adequate account of that fact, the media were able to present their rosy picture, and to convey to the general public the impression that the 'problem' of Northern Ireland, was, if not actually solved, at least well on the way to a solution.

That coverage of the Agreement was one example of the power of wishful thinking in media commentary on international affairs. The distortion was similar in kind to the media-maintained mirage of a comprehensive peace in the Middle East (Israel to acquire lasting peace, through general accept-ability in the Arab world, by handing over the West Bank to Arafat and/or Hussein); the idea that this is attainable ignores the obvious but unpleasant fact that any such 'settlement' would be rejected, and violently sabotaged, by several PLO factions, backed by several Arab States. It is pleasant to contemplate perspectives of peace, even if these can be shown, in the prevailing conditions, to be illusory. The trouble is that if you refuse to recognize how bad certain relationships are, and how durable their badness, you risk making them even worse than they need be.

As an exhibit of Irish Republican ideology and hagiology, *Bobby Sands and the Tragedy of Northern Ireland* has the merit of supplying an antidote to wishful thinking, and to an excessive confidence in the healing power of rationality and compromise.

Note: Except for one paragraph, this essay appears here in the form in which it originally appeared in the *New York Review of Books*. The paragraph beginning 'These expectations' on p. 209 has been rewritten. The original paragraph, written at the time of the Westlands affair exaggerated Mrs Thatcher's political difficulties. For the rest, I believe the analysis stands up in retrospect. Levels of violence have significantly *increased* in Northern Ireland since the Hillsbrough Agreement, and friction between the partners is also increasing at the time for writing.

November 1987

Ireland
The Shirt of Nessus*

MR CRONIN'S BOOK RAISES A FASCINATING SUBJECT: ideology in Irish nationalism. His own treatment of the subject is unsatisfactory, but he deserves some credit for making the attempt. In this article I propose to consider his treatment, briefly, and then the subject in itself, at some length.

Mr Cronin's book is based on a PhD thesis for the New School for Social Research, New York. In his introduction he tells us: 'For the purposes of this study ideology means "the political ideas and outlook of Irish nationalism".' We are plunged immediately into confusion, for, as I shall argue, there is no such continuity of political ideas as might make the idea of Irish nationalism, as a distinct ideology, meaningful or useful. Irish nationalism is a historically formed amalgam of sentiments and traditions. Its 'political ideas' are protean: at the end of the seventeenth century, for example, they took Jacobite form; by the end of the eighteenth century, a Jacobin form. Irish nationalism is not itself an ideology, but it has acquired an ideology: that of Irish Republicanism.

Irish Republicanism affects Irish nationalism – along with other forces, by far the most potent of which is Irish Catholicism – but the Republicanism is neither identical with the nationalism, nor co-extensive with it. By treating Irish nationalism as itself an ideology, Mr Cronin loses touch at the outset with what should be central to his subject matter: the relation between Irish nationalism and a quite distinct entity, the ideology which it has acquired.

The theoretical part of Mr Cronin's book goes down in that confusion, bravely flourishing irrelevant quotations from Mannheim and Morgenthau. But for the most part, the book is not theoretical but 'historical': a rambling survey of recent Irish history from an Irish-Nationalist-Catholic-Republican

*Article on *Irish Nationalism: A History of its Roots and Ideology*, Sean Cronin, Continuum, in the *New York Review of Books*, 29 April 1982.

point of view, proving yet once more how right the Catholic people are, and how wrong the Protestants; politically speaking, of course. The book is not so much an analysis of its subject matter as a specimen of what the subject matter secretes and exudes.

Mr Cronin's title, however, suggests an interesting train of ideas, which I should like to pursue. There is a real continuity of Irish nationalism: not an ideological continuity, but a continuity of the traditions and feelings of a people. That people sees itself as the people of Ireland, and that perception is a large part of the problem. For these are not *all* the people of Ireland. They are the Catholic people of Ireland, formerly Gaelic-speaking. These were the losers in the seventeenth-century wars – wars that were dynastic, social, cultural, national and religious, all at the same time. The forms of oppression which this people suffered – as a result of their decisive defeat – throughout the eighteenth century and into the nineteenth, were economic, social and cultural, but justified by a politico-religious criterion: the presumed disloyalty of Irish Catholics to the British Protestant Crown. This presumption of disloyalty was generally well founded.

The main theme of Irish history, for nearly three centuries now, has been the recovery of the Irish Catholics: the Catholics getting their own back, in more senses than one. Throughout this long period, the Catholic clergy have been at or near the centre of the process of recovery. It was a struggle, after all, not only against alien domination but against domination – until the process of recovery was already well advanced – in the name of an alien and false religion.

The tactics of recovery shifted widely: hence the impossibility of identifying any continuity of their ideology. At the time of the American Revolution, for example, the tactic pursued in the interests of Catholic recovery was demonstration of loyalty to the British Crown. By this tactic, Catholic leaders wrong-footed the Irish Protestant community – whose more radical members supported the American colonists – and at the same time sought to establish that Britain could now safely remove Catholic disabilities. That was the strategy of the leaders. What the mass of the Catholic people – then mainly Gaelic-speaking – thought about this matter, or whether they thought about it at all, we have no means of knowing. Gaelic literature of the period contains hardly any reference to the American Revolution. Contrary to assumptions that later became general among Irish-American Catholics, enthusiasm in Ireland for the American revolutionary cause was exclusively a Protestant affair, at the time.

If the American Revolution left Irish Catholics cold, the French

Revolution was very different. Only at this point does it become meaningful to talk about an Irish nationalist ideology, because up to this point no ideology distinguishable from Irish Catholicism exists among Irish Catholics. From the sixteenth century well into the eighteenth, the Faith and the Nation were one. The people are oppressed for their loyalty to their Faith: the people of Israel enchained by infidels – the parallel is explicit in Gaelic literature. The people had looked for deliverance to the Catholic powers of Europe: to the Pope and the emperor, the kind of Spain, the king of France; or in practice to whichever of these happened to be at loggerheads with England at any particular time.

Long before the French Revolution, however, it had become clear to educated Catholics that no deliverance was at hand, from any Catholic power. The best hope seemed to lie in dropping all that, and pursuing equal rights for Catholics under the British Crown: in effect dropping what had been up to then the political aspect of Irish Catholicism. This was pragmatically sound, but psychologically difficult and divisive. The people's songs were telling them quite different things from what their bishops were telling them. The old unity of Irish Catholicism was under stress.

The French Revolution not only vastly increased that stress; it created new and complex stresses and syntheses of its own. For Irish Catholics, the French Revolution was a wildly confusing and intoxicating phenomenon: anti-English and anti-landlord, and powerful; all that was great, but was it anti-*Catholic* as well?

The confusion was greatly increased by the blazing simplifications of the revolutionary idea itself. There was to be an Irish nation modelled on *la Grande Nation* itself. Irish revolutionaries, Catholic and Protestant together, transcending the outmoded superstitious animosities that monarchy, aristocracy and the English had created, would make the new Ireland, of free, equal, fraternal citizens – 'United Irishmen', as the revolutionaries called themselves.

French revolutionary ideas, more or less in their original form, caught on among radical, educated Irish Protestants – mostly in what is now Northern Ireland – and among a few Catholics of the same class. But where it caught on in rural Catholic Ireland, as in Wexford, it caught on as an opportunity to overthrow Protestant landlords and their Protestant hangers-on, and the English power behind them. The story of the 'United Irish' Risings of 1798 is covered in two splendid modern books which complement each other: Thomas Pakenham's *The Year of Liberty* and Thomas Flanagan's novel *The Year of the French*.

What is relevant to look at here is the condition of Irish nationalism and ideology as these developed in the period following the bloody and comprehensive repression of the 1798 Risings. One should note first the disappearance of Protestants from an Irish nationalism whose 'French revolutionary' manifestations they had done so much to stimulate. Eastern Ulster, the only area where Protestants are in a majority, was henceforward committed, as it is today, to being no part of any united Ireland separate from Britain, or of any political union with Catholics. The course of the Rising (and particularly the massacres of Protestants in Wexford) convinced Protestants generally that 'United Irish' ideas had been a disastrous illusion. Henceforward there would be isolated Protestant adherents to Irish nationalism but they would be adhering, in practice though not in rhetoric, to an Irish Catholic nation.

Some Protestant intellectuals – Thomas Davis, John Mitchel in the early nineteenth century, and later W. B. Yeats – played an important part in keeping 'United Irish' ideas alive among Catholics. Charles Stewart Parnell, at the end of the nineteenth century, was a Protestant leader of Catholic people, on their terms.

Among Catholics, the primary effect of the Rising and its suppression was to reinforce the authority of the Catholic hierarchy, and the more conservative elements generally. The year 1798 was to look romantic in a far later retrospect, but in its immediate aftermath it had to be seen for the bloody disaster it actually was. The bishops, who had warned of the ruin attendant on monkeying around with French revolutionary ideas, were felt to have been proved right: no more of that, was a general feeling. Few Catholics seem to have thought any the worse of Daniel O'Connell for helping to crush the Protestant Robert Emmet's hopeless United-Irish-type rising in 1803. O'Connell, as leader of the Irish Catholic people, pursued, in essentials, the course set by the Irish bishops in the eighteenth century: removal of Catholic disabilities, improvement of conditions for Catholics, under the British Crown. This was the general strategy of Irish nationalism, with mass support, throughout the nineteenth century. As democracy in the United Kingdom developed – Ireland's separate (and Protestant) parliament was abolished in the aftermath of the 1798 Rising – political autonomy for Ireland under the Crown ('Repeal of the Union', 'Home Rule') came to appear an essential goal.

That was the mainstream of Irish nationalism: pragmatic, Church-conditioned. But there was an undercurrent, and this took the form of a distinct ideology: Irish Republicanism. Republicanism, defying the bishops, took its inspiration from 1798 and the United Irishmen and especially from the teaching of Theobald Wolfe Tone, the United Irish leader and martyr. The goal was Tone's: 'To break the connection with England, the never-failing source of all our political evils.' The connection, of course, included the Crown, and this was what made the central formal distinction between the Republicans and the mainstream 'constitutional' nationalists, who were willing to accept autonomous national status under the British Constitution and Crown. The Republican objective could only be attained, if at all, by physical force, and Irish Republicism was and is a physical-force movement.

After yet another hopeless insurrection, in 1848, the Republican movement, like others of its kind in Europe, became embodied in a secret, oath-taking society. This was the Irish Republican Brotherhood, founded in 1858, begetter of the Irish Republican Army. The IRB had strong Irish-American links and its members were known as the Fenians.

The Church, or at least the bishops, condemned the Fenians: as carriers of the alien godless ideology of the French Revolution, as bound by a forbidden oath, and – above all – as inciting people into a hopeless, and therefore by Catholic teaching immoral, insurrection. After the Fenian Rising of 1867, one bishop proclaimed that hell was not hot enough nor eternity long enough to punish the Fenian leaders.

The mass of the people remained loyal to the Church, and supported the constitutional nationalists. But they also admired the Fenians, for their courage, their tenacity and their uncontaminated continuity of Irish Catholic feeling. For what the Fenians were doing, and what the IRA is now doing (in practice, as distinct from rhetoric), was carrying on the *political aspect of the Irish Catholic tradition, as it had existed in the Counter-Reformation times*: root-and-branch hostility to the British Crown and all it stood for. The bishops, with their – relatively – novel doctrine of loyalty to the British Crown (and therefore the Protestant succession!) were on slippery ground, emotionally speaking.

Intellectually, it was the Fenians who were, and are, on slippery ground. Formally the Republican ideology is a modern, secular, post-Enlightenment affair. It preaches, in theory, union between the Irish people of all religious denominations, transcending the tragic sectarian divisions of the past, and so on. It all sounds very nice. At a distance and in a poor light, it is possible to mistake an Irish Republican for some kind of liberal.

But there is a catch, and the catch is that, as well as preaching non-sectarian unity among the Irish people, Republicans have as their prime objective the breaking of the connection with England. So what happens if – as is actually the case – a community of Irish people, the Protestants of Northern Ireland, refuse to break that connection, but on the contrary are determined to defend it?

In that case, with respect to Republican doctrine, the relevant characteristic of these people is not that they are Protestants – in which capacity Republicans, theoretically, welcome them with open arms – but that they are Unionists. Unionists can be regarded either as British, part of the occupying forces, or as Irish traitors. In either case Republicans have warrant from their ideology to shoot these people down, whenever opportunity offers.

So when, in our time, Catholic Republican gunmen systematically pick off Protestant farmers and shopkeepers in the border areas, they are not carrying on a sectarian civil war, as you might imagine, and as Protestants in their ignorance believe. No, they are breaking the connection with England, by killing the people who form that connection.

'We have nothing against Protestants *as such*,' the executioners explain.

You see the importance of ideology.

Sectarian – that is politico-sectarian – civil war in Ireland was always *latent* in Republican ideology. It did not, however, come to the point of actual Catholic-Protestant (Republican Unionist) civil war until as late as 1971, after the emergence of the Provisional IRA, the heirs to the ideology in its purest, perfected and most deadly form.

So let us look back at some of the stages in the maturing of that ideology.

By the late nineteenth century, what looked like a rather stable symbiosis had been achieved in the political culture of the Irish Catholic community (or nation). The people went to Mass, and voted for constitutional nationalists. The Church, through the bishops, condemned the Republicans, and so sometimes did the constitutional nationalists, but not so loudly or so often as the bishops. The constitutional nationalists, unlike the bishops, depended on popular suffrage, and they knew that the people had a 'weakness' for the Republicans. They wouldn't follow them, or swallow their ideology, and they felt uneasy about them, but at the same time they liked to feel that deep down they were on the side of these patriotic men, up to a point and in a way. Under these conditions the Republicans could ignore the Church leaders. A Republican leader knew that, while he would have little visible following in life, there would be a marvellous turnout at his funeral.

So this bloody subcult firmly established itself within an otherwise exceptionally docile body of religious people whose religious leaders fiercely condemned the subcult. Religion is a bit like that: compare non-violent

Hinduism, with its subcult of the Goddess Kali, and her strings of human heads.

A hundred years ago, however, the subcult didn't look serious. The Republicans very seldom actually killed anyone in those days. 'The Church versus the Fenians' was a kind of standing political and cultural Punch-and-Judy show, adding to the fun and colour of life. You knew the Church wasn't *really* all that down on the Fenians. And you also knew that most of the Fenians were really good Catholics, and would probably make their peace with the Church before they died – and there would be a lovely funeral. It was all very cozy. But then around the turn of the century, a number of things happened to dispel the coziness.

The first of these events was the downfall of Charles Stewart Parnell in 1891. Parnell in that year was co-respondent in an undefended divorce suit. In no part of the Victorian United Kingdom, including Ireland, could a political leader expect to retain his leadership under those conditions. Parnell, nonetheless, attempted to hold on. In this way, he created an extraordinary coalition against himself. The coalition consisted of his former allies, the British Liberal Party, headed by Gladstone; the Catholic hierarchy in Ireland; and a majority of the constitutional nationalists, his own party.

This situation presented the Republicans with a truly wonderful opportunity to reshape the whole political culture of Ireland to their own advantage. In their version of history, the English had decreed the fall of the greatest of Irish leaders, and the fawning bishops and fawning constitutional nationalists had hastened to do their bidding. As the writings of W. B. Yeats and James Joyce reflect, this scenario had a powerful appeal to the young, making them at the same time more refractory to Church control and more anti-English: two key points as far as the expansion of Republican influence was concerned.

As far as the young were concerned, the channel of Irish nationalism began to shift its course at this time: away from its tamer shore of Church approval and compromise with Britain and nearer to its wilder shore of Republicanism and human sacrifice. Kali had assumed a higher place in the pantheon.

The post-Parnell period – the last decade of the nineteenth century and the first decade of this one – was a period of apparent political quiet. In fact it was a period of major politico-cultural change. A cultural nationalism grew up – especially among the middle classes and in the cities – highly charged with romantic Republicanism, and resistant to the influence of the Church.

W. B. Yeats of course – a Fenian of sorts himself at the time – played a notable part in all that, especially through his play *Cathleen ni Houlihan* (1902), with its mystical glorification of the blood sacrifice of 1798, and its evocation of further blood sacrifice to come. By this time, a great deal of explosive emotional material had accumulated.

Ironically, it was the triumph of the constitutional nationalists that supplied the detonator. Their triumph, followed by their undoing. For nearly forty years, since Parnell's day, it had been the strategy of the constitutional nationalists to win Home Rule – devolved autonomy – by parliamentary action: in practice by controlling the balance of power in the House of Commons and enacting Home Rule through an alliance with a British party, the Liberals. In 1912, Asquith's Liberals and the Irish nationalists together made up a Home Rule majority in Parliament. The House of Lords, which had vetoed the last Home Rule Bill, no longer had a veto. To Irish nationalists of all descriptions, Home Rule seemed home and dry.

The whole thing then struck a rock, in Ulster. Ulster Protestants first by mass demonstrations, then by arming and drilling, showed their implacable refusal to be incorporated in a Catholic-majority Home Rule State. They were supported by the British Tories. Asquith realized that there was no way by which he could compel Ulster Protestants to accept Home Rule. If Irish Catholics wanted Home Rule, they could have it for themselves, but they would have to do without Protestant-majority eastern Ulster. Rather than get no Home Rule at all, the constitutional nationalists agreed, with bitter reluctance, to a formula of 'temporary exclusion' of eastern Ulster. Everybody knew 'temporary' meant 'permanent'.

The best-known account of these transactions is contained in George Dangerfield's spirited and entertaining *The Strange Death of Liberal England*.[1] The reader should be warned, however, that this account suffers from an underestimation of the autochthonous component in the Ulster crisis. As its title implies, Mr Dangerfield's book is an Anglocentric account, with its emphasis on the amusing and unedifying gyrations of the English parties. The author assumes, without proving his case, that the English Government both could and should have transferred a million Ulster Protestants out of the jurisdiction under which their ancestors had lived for centuries and in which they insisted on remaining, into a new jurisdiction which they passionately refused. This seems a large assumption, and I for one refuse to make it.

It was, however, and is, the almost universal assumption among Irish

Catholic nationalists, and these generally regarded the partitionist outcome of the Home Rule crisis with deep shock and disappointment.

One group, however, that did not share the disappointment was the Republican hard core. For them the Home Rule débâcle – as they saw it – provided an even more favourable conjuncture than the downfall of Parnell had done. That débâcle did two things, both of them satisfactory to the Republican ideologues. First of all, it comprehensively discredited the constitutional nationalists. Second – and even more vital – it reaccredited physical force. Republicans had always said that the only argument England paid any attention to was the gun. The Ulster Volunteers had proved that this was true. In fact it would have been impossible for Britain to force a million refractory Ulster Protestants into Home Rule, even if they had had no guns, but it suited the Republicans to put the emphasis on the guns.

So the Irish Volunteers were founded in response to the Ulster Volunteers. (In reality Irish *Catholic* volunteers, but the religious labels are unnecessary; everybody knows, without saying, what the realities are.)

The Irish Volunteers were nationalists of all descriptions, many still adhering to the constitutional nationalist leaders who, though shaken and demoralized, still at this stage held much of their former respect. But then the First World War broke out and the constitutionally minded among the Irish Volunteers went off to fight the Germans. The Volunteers who remained in Ireland were heavily under Republican influence; the controlling element among the Republicans was the Irish Republican Brotherhood; and the Brotherhood had decided on insurrection. The Easter Rising of 1916 was in preparation.

The IRB, on the outbreak of the First World War, decided, in principle, in accordance with its historic doctrine 'England's difficulty is Ireland's opportunity', to bring about an insurrection at some time during the war. The timing and methods were left to a kind of subcommittee: the Military Council of the IRB. By 1916, the Military Council consisted of seven members, including Patrick Pearse and James Connolly. The members of the Military Council became the signers of the Proclamation of the Republic. When the insurrection had been crushed, within a week, the British executed the members of the Military Council, along with others.

While the insurrection was unpopular in Catholic Ireland when it was actually happening, the executions of the leaders and other events brought about widespread revulsion against the British and the constitutional nationalists, and a corresponding retrospective glorification of the men of 1916. By 1917 this swing to the Republic dominated most of the political life of Catholic Ireland.

It is at this point that the decisive event occurred for nationalism and for ideology. The old antagonists, the Church and the Fenians, now tacitly came to terms. The interlocutors were two exceptionally able and pragmatic men: Eamon de Valera, the senior survivor of 1916, and Archbishop Walsh, of Dublin.

Each had something to gain by coming to terms. De Valera intended to fight the post-war elections through an appeal to the mystique of 1916. Such an appeal was highly vulnerable, from the side of the Church; for according to the traditional teaching of the Irish Church, the enterprise of 1916 was literally damnable: it was a hopeless insurrection irresponsibly precipitated by a secret and oath-bound society, many times condemned by the Church. De Valera did not need the Church's blessing for his political movement (now called Sinn Fein). What he did need was the Church's neutrality: to be able to get on with the political sanctification of 1916 Republicanism, without awkward episcopal interventions reminding the faithful of the traditional theology.

The archbishop and his colleagues, for their part, had some strong reasons for according neutrality, at least. The constitutional nationalists were going downhill rather fast. The Church's interests had to be protected in the event of the disappearance of these politicians. De Valera and his friends showed themselves respectful to the Church, and churchmen. With regard to 1916, there was the traditional teaching of course, and that could not be set aside, but there were other considerations too. The signers of the proclamation may have been secret and oath-bound, but they died exemplary Catholic deaths. Indeed all these people in their ordinary lives seemed to be exemplary Catholics; much better than the constitutional nationalists, many of whom had been contaminated by too much living in London, rubbing shoulders with godless English Liberals.

What exactly happened will probably always remain unknown. Irish historians have generally not looked very hard at this crucial transaction in the history of Republicanism, the Church and Irish ideology. By far the fullest exploration of this is contained in an admirable book by an American historian: David W. Miller's *Church State and Nation in Ireland*.[2] From Miller's account, it looks as if de Valera convinced the Archbishop of the essential point: that in a Sinn Fein Republican Ireland, the Catholic Church would be left with the same tight control over Catholic education as it had achieved under the British. And so indeed it worked out.

In any case, the Church refrained from intruding any awkward theological points into the election campaign of November 1918 – and also generally refrained from warning that a Sinn Fein victory would lead to further violence. (They did not of course know that it would, but as prudent men they ought to have been aware of the danger and warned against it. Archbishop Walsh voted for Sinn Fein himself, and announced the fact.) Sinn Fein, in the name of the Republic proclaimed in 1916, won an overwhelming victory in Catholic Ireland. Republicanism became, and still is, the official political ideology of Catholic Ireland.

Pearse's Republic did not, however, arrive and has not arrived yet. Three years of guerrilla war and reprisals, following Sinn Fein's victory, ended in a treaty with Britain in 1921. That treaty accepted what all Republicans had contemptuously rejected in 1914: autonomy for the homogeneously Catholic part of Ireland, while the Protestant part (with some Catholic areas attached) remained in the United Kingdom. And this of course is still the case today.

The Irish (Catholic) people electorally endorsed the treaty. They had not known what they were letting themselves in for when they voted Sinn Fein, and they were only too happy to let themselves out again. A minority of Republicans, however, opposed the treaty by arms. These were ex-communicated by the Church and crushed militarily by the pro-treaty forces.

Ten years later, however, the most eminent of the excommunicated, Eamon de Valera, came to power through free elections, in the state that the treaty had established. In substance, but not in form, de Valera now accepted the treaty arrangements. But even while doing so he insisted that what he represented was the 1916 tradition. Nineteen-sixteen Republicanism was now tightly fastened as the official ideology of the Irish state, now known as the Republic.

In today's Republic the schools of the Catholic people are controlled by the Catholic Church. And in many such schools there hangs a copy of the Proclamation of the Republic, with the portraits of the seven men who made up the Military Council of a secret and oath-bound society many times anathematized by the Church. The Church acquiesces in the enthronement of the Fenianism that it had so long condemned, as today the official ideology of the state.

The contemporary IRA, however, rejects that state quite consistently, precisely in the name of its own official ideology. They point out that this Republic, not being all Ireland, is not Pearse's Republic; and it is not. They quote, to deadly effect, Pearse's statement, 'Ireland unfree shall never be at peace.' They show from Tone that an Ireland still politically connected with

Britain – through Northern Ireland – is unfree. They claim the right to use violence, as Pearse and Tone did, to achieve the objective of Pearse and Tone. If they are told they have no democratic mandate, they ask what democratic mandate did Pearse and Tone have? To which the only honest answer has to be: none whatever.

The official ideology of the Republic fully legitimizes the IRA's 'war' in Northern Ireland and so helps that 'war' go on and on. The people of the Republic do not endorse that war, very far from it. We are nationalists in the sense of wanting to run our own affairs, not in the sense of wanting to annex territory and crush other people. We dislike the IRA, most of us, and fear it. We are a peaceful and democratic people. But our history, our 'idealistic' pretensions and our fatal ambivalence have stuck us with an ideology that is warlike and anti-democratic, and calls increasingly for further human sacrifice.

Our ideology, in relation to what we actually are and want, is a lie. It is a lie that clings to us and burns, like the shirt of Nessus.

Postcript, November, 1987.

This month, more than two years after the original essay, that 'Shirt of Nessus' has been clinging and burning, even more greviously than it was then.

On 8 November, Remembrance Sunday, the Provisional IRA detonated a bomb in Enniskillen along the route of the town's Remembrance parade. The bomb killed eleven people and wounded many others. Those killed were all civilians. They were also all Protestants. Although Catholics as well as Protestants fought in both world wars with the British forces, in Ireland it is only Protestants – with very few exceptions – who keep Remembrance Day. In Northern Ireland, in particular, when you see a person wearing a poppy, you assume automatically that that person is a Protestant.

'The Poppy Day Massacre', as it came to be called, was the IRA's most spectacular act of war to date against the Protestant population. While murdering and maiming a random sample of that population, the IRA was simultaneously desecrating their sacred day.

The place chosen for the massacre was also significant. Enniskillen is the principal town of Co. Fermanagh. Fermanagh is a border county, and in the districts of the county which are closest to the border, all the Republic Protestants are in a rather small minority. Or rather they were in a minority; now they are gone altogether from those districts. Over more than ten years, the Provisionals have been systematically picking off isolated Protestants – farmers and shopkeepers – along the Fermanagh border. As the pattern became clear, the surviving isolated Protestants left the deadly border districts, often for Enniskillen (which is half and half Catholic and Protestant). And the IRA pursued them there.

The Nazis used to make regions and countries *Jadenrein*: clean from Jews. The IRA is out to make Fermanagh clean from Protestants, and then the rest of Northern Ireland, though that will take longer.

The Poppy Day Massacre was designed to cause the maximum outrage in the Protestant community. But it also brought about a revulsion against the IRA in the *Catholic* community, on a scale never known before. Responding to that mood and participating in it, the Catholic clergy throughout Ireland, on the Sunday following the massacre, denounced the IRA and its accomplices, without the customary ambivalence, and with unaccustomed specifics. People who provided 'safe houses' for IRA fugitives were warned that they were guilty of grave sin as accomplices in murder. Cardinal Tomas O'Fiaich, Archbishop of Armagh and Primate of All Ireland, apologized, on behalf of his community, to the Protestants of Northern Ireland.

In the past, the Cardinal has often seemed ambivalence incarnate in these matters. He has denounced the violence of the IRA but declined to condemn Provisional Sinn Fein, which is nothing more than the political and propaganda arm of the Provisional IRA. But the Cardinal now seems to be troubled by a realization that our ambivalence – not just *his*, but that of the whole Catholic community – has been feeding a monster.

Will Enniskillen prove a turning point? There is some reason to hope that it may. Certainly, I cannot remember a time when the ambivalence count has been as low as it was at the middle of this month. It is as if that single spectacular explosion so lit up the landscape that people suddenly became aware of what the IRA is about, and what helping it means.

Whether that change of mood can be relied on is another matter. It needs to be translated into a determined effort to isolate and defeat the IRA. Personally I do not think that can be done without the introduction of internment without trial *on both sides of the border*. The Anglo-Irish Agreement (see 'Bobby Sands') has not produced any improvement where violence is concerned. Violence has been rising steadily since the Agreement even before Enniskillen, and Protestant rejection of the Agreement remains solid. But if the Agreement were used for the joint implementation of internment, then the Agreement could become acceptable to Protestants. Nothing less will do it. But we are nowhere near that point this November. And as I write, in late November, with the memory of Enniskillen receding, the ambivalence count seems once more to be rising. We have not yet done with that shirt.

Notes

1   Putnam's, 1961.
2   University of Pittsburgh Press, 1973.

Thinking About
Terrorism:I*

ERRORISM IS DISTURBING not just emotionally and morally but intellectually, as well. On terrorism, more than on other subjects, commentary
seems liable to be swayed by wishful thinking, to base itself on
unwarranted or flawed assumptions, and to draw from these assumptions
irrational inferences, muzzily expressed.

Let me offer one example, typical of many more. The following is the
conclusion to a recent *Washington Post* editorial, 'Nervous Mideast
Moment':

> The United States, however, cannot afford to let its struggle against
> terrorism be overwhelmed by its differences with Libya. That gives the
> Qaddafis of the world too much importance and draws attention from the
> requirement to go to the political sources of terrorism. A principal source,
> unquestionably, is the unresolved Palestinian question. The State Depart-
> ment's man for the Middle East, Richard Murphy, has been on the road again,
> cautiously exploring whether it is possible in coming months to bring Israel and
> Jordan closer to a negotiation. This quest would be essential even if terrorism
> were not the concern it is. It marks the leading way that American policy must
> go.

The clear implication is that negotiation between Israel and Jordan can
dry up 'a principal source of terrorism'. Now, nobody who has studied that
political context at all, and is not blinded by wishful thinking, could possibly
believe that. For the Arab terrorists – and most other Arabs – 'the
unresolved Palestinian question' and the existence of the State of Israel are
one and the same thing. The terrorists could not possibly be appeased, or
made to desist, by Jordan's King Hussein's getting back a slice of the West
Bank, which is the very most that could come out of a negotiation between

* From *The Atlantic Monthly*, June 1986.

Jordan and Israel. The terrorists and their backers would denounce such a deal as treachery and seek to step up their attacks, directing these against Jordan as well as Israel.

That *Washington Post* editorial, like many others to the same tune, exemplifies a dovish, or sentimental, variety of wishful thinking on the subject of terrorism. There is also a hawkish, or hysterical, variety. Each has it own misleading stereotype (or stereotypes) of the terrorist. Let us look at the stereotypes:

Sentimental stereotype. According to this stereotype, the terrorist is a misguided idealist, an unsublimated social reformer. He has been driven to violence by political or social injustice or both. What is needed is to identify the measures of reform that will cause him to desist. Once these can be identified and undertaken, the terrorist, having ceased to be driven, stops.

Hysterical stereotype. Less stable than the sentimental variety, this can be divided into subvarieties:

(a) The terrorist is some kind of a nut – a 'disgruntled abnormal' given to 'mindless violence'. ('Mindless violence' may be applicable to the deeds of isolated, maverick assassins. As applied to the planned activities of armed conspiracies, it is itself a mindless expression.)

(b) The terrorist is nothing more than a thug, a goon, a gangster. His 'political' demands are simply a cover for criminal activity.

(c) The terrorist is an agent, or dupe, or cat's-paw of the other superpower. (He might, of course, be a nut or a goon as well as a dupe.)

These stereotypes serve mainly to confuse debate on the subject. There is no point in arbitrarily attributing motives, nice or nasty, to the terrorist. It might be more useful to look at the situations in which terrorists find themselves and at how they act, and may be expected to act, given their situations.

In what follows I shall bear in mind mainly (though not exclusively) the members of the most durable terrorist organizations of the twentieth century: the IRA (including its splinter groups) and the PLO (including its splinter groups).

Terrorists have a grievance, which they share with members of a wider community: the division of Ireland, the division of Palestine, the inroads of secularism into Islam, or whatever. But they also have, from the moment they become terrorists, significant amounts of power, prestige, and access to wealth, and these constitute vested interests in the present irrespective of the attainment or non-attainment of their declared long-term political objectives.

The sentimentalist thinks of the terrorist as driven to violence by grievance or oppression. It would be more realistic to think of the terrorist as hauling himself up, by means of the grievance or oppression and the violence it legitimizes, to relative power, prestige and privilege in the community to which he belongs. For an unemployed young man in a slum in Sidon or Strabane, for example, the most promising channel of upward social mobility is his neighbourhood branch of the national terrorist organization. There are risks to be run, certainly, but for the adventurous, aggressive characters among the unemployed or the otherwise frustrated, the immediate rewards outweigh the risks. In this situation the terrorist option is a rational one: you don't have to be a nut, a dupe or an idealist.

I don't mean that the terrorist is necessarily, or even probably, insincere about the national (or religious or other collective) grievance or in his hatred toward those seen as responsible for the grievance. On the contrary, hatred is one of the things that keeps him going, and the gratification of hatred is among the rewards of the terrorist. The terrorist is not just a goon, out for the loot. His political motivation is genuine. But there are other rewards in his way of life as well as the hazy reward of progress toward the political objective. The possession of a known capacity and willingness to kill confers authority and glamour in the here and now, even on rank-and-file members in the urban ghetto or in the village. On the leaders it confers national and even international authority and glamour, and independence from financial worries.

If we accept that the terrorist's way of life procures him immediate rewards of that nature, and that he is probably not insensible to at least some of the rewards in question, it seems to follow that he will probably be reluctant to relinquish those rewards by voluntarily putting himself out of business.

The situation thus outlined has a bearing of a negative nature on the notion that there are 'negotiated solutions' to the 'problems' that 'cause' terrorism.

First of all, a negotiated solution – being by definition an outcome that offers some satisfaction to both parties – will be inherently distasteful to terrorists and their admirers, accustomed as these are to regarding *one* of the parties (Britain, Israel or another) as evil incarnate.

Second, to exploit that genuine distaste will be in the interests of the terrorists, in relation to the reward system discussed above. So pride and profit converge into a violent rejection of the 'negotiated solution' – which therefore is not a solution to terrorism.

This is most obvious where the solution is to be negotiated between people who are not spokesmen for the terrorists. When Garret FitzGerald and Margaret Thatcher negotiated the Hillsborough Agreement over Northern Ireland, in November 1985, that neither caused the IRA to give up nor deprived it of its hard-core popular support (though there was a drop of about 10 per cent in electoral support for the IRA's political front, Sinn Fein). Similarly, if King Hussein and Shimon Peres were to reach agreement, it would not be likely to cause any of the Arab terrorist groups to go out of business or forfeit their hard-core support.

Suppose a terrorist (or putatively *ex*-terrorist) organization joined in the deal. That would presumably earn a cessation, or at least a suspension, of terrorist activity by the negotiating group and its immediate following. But the deal would be repudiated by other organizations, who would see no reason to go out of business; and since these intransigents would be demonstrably in line with the absolutist policies previously proclaimed by the whole movement, they would have high credibility and widespread support.

So the prospects for ending terrorism through a negotiated settlement are not bright, whether or not the terrorists are involved in the negotiations. But the insistence that a negotiated solution *can* end terrorism actually helps the terrorists. It does so because it places the responsiblility for continuing terrorism equally on the terrorists and those they seek to terrorize. The enhanced respectability with which the terrorist is thereby invested gives him a foretaste of success and an encouragement to persevere. This is the opposite of what the dovish advisers desire, but it is the main result of their ill-advised endeavours.

Not only do doves sometimes help terrorists but some hawkish advisers also give inadvertent aid and comfort to the forces they abhor. The combating of terrorism is not helped by bombastic speeches at high levels, stressing what a monstrous evil terrorism is and that its elimination is to be given the highest priority. I'm afraid that the most likely terrorist reaction to such a speech, whether it comes from a president, a secretary of state or other important official, is: 'You see, they *have* to pay attention to us now. We are hurting them. Let's give them more of the same.' And it all helps with recruitment. A movement that is denounced by a president is in the big time. And some kind of big time is what is most wanted by the aggressive and frustrated, who constitute the pool on which terrorist movements can draw.

What applies to speeches applies *a fortiori* to unilateral military action against countries harbouring terrorists. Whatever short-term advantages may be derived from such attacks, a price will be paid – in increased international sympathy for the 'cause' of the terrorists in question, and so in enhanced glamour and elbow room for them, all tending to legitimize and so facilitate future 'counterattacks'.

Nor does it help to suggest that terrorism is about to be extirpated – because it almost certainly isn't. Today's world – especially the free, or capitalist, world – provides highly favourable conditions for terrorist recruitment and activity. The numbers of the frustrated are constantly on the increase, and so is their awareness of the lifestyle of the better-off and the vulnerability of the better-off. Among the better-off themselves are bored young people looking for the kicks that violence can provide, and thus for causes that legitimize violence, of which there are no shortage. A wide variety of people feel starved for attention, and one surefire way of attracting instantaneous worldwide attention through television is to slaughter a considerable number of human beings, in a spectacular fashion, in the name of a cause.

Although the causes themselves hardly constitute the sole motivation of the terrorists – as terrorists claim they do – they are not irrelevant, either. The cause legitimizes the act of terror in the terrorist's own eyes and in those of others belonging to his nation faith or culture. Certain cultures and subcultures, homes of frustrated causes, are destined breeding grounds for terrorism. The Islamic culture is the most notable example. That culture's view of its own rightful position in the world is profoundly at variance with the actual order of the contemporary world. It is God's will that the House of Islam should triumph over the House of War (the non-Moslem world), and not just by spiritual means. 'Islam Means Victory' is a slogan of the Iranian fundamentalists in the Gulf War. To strike a blow against the House of War is meritorious; consequently, there is widespread support for activities condemned in the West as terrorist. Israel is one main target for these activities, but the activities would not be likely to cease even if Israel came to an end. The Great Satan in the eyes of Ayatollah Khomeini – and of the millions for whom he speaks – is not Israel but the United States. The defeat of Israel would, in those eyes, be no more than a portent of the impending defeat of the Great Satan. What the West calls terrorism should then be multiplied rather than abandoned.

The wellsprings of terrorism are widespread and deep. The interaction between modern communications systems and archaic fanaticism (and other sources of resentment and ambition) is likely to continue to stimulate terrorist activity. In these conditions, talk about extirpating terrorism – and unilateral exploits backing such talk – are likely to be counterproductive. They present terrorists with a 'victory', merely by the fact of being able to continue their activity. Similarly, solemn promises never to negotiate with terrorists can play into the hands of terrorists. Terrorists holding hostages can force a democratic government to negotiate, as happened in the case of the hijacked TWA airliner in June 1985. If the democratic government then pretends that no negotiation took place, this helps the credibility of the terrorists, not that of the democratic government.

It is not possible to extirpate terrorism from the face of the globe, but it should be possible to reduce the incidence and effectiveness of terrorism, through co-ordinated international action. The Reagan Administration's efforts to get better co-operation in this matter from the European allies are justified in principle but flawed in practice. They are justified because the performance of several European countries in relation to international terrorism has often amounted to turning a blind eye, for commercial reasons. The British Government, for example, tolerated the conversion of the Libyan Embassy in London into a 'Revolutionary People's Bureau', and ignored all reports that the bureau was a centre of terrorist activity, until the point was reached at which the revolutionary diplomats actually opened fire from the embassy windows into St James's Square, killing a British policewoman. Even after that the policy of playing ball with Qaddafi, as long as there was money to be made out of it, did not altogether disappear, either in Britain or elsewhere in Europe. (Mrs Thatcher's support for the recent US air strikes against Libyan targets seems to stem from a wish to be seen as the most dependable ally of the United States, rather than from any spontaneous change of heart about the proper way in which to deal with Libya.)

So President Reagan had good reasons for urging the European allies to adopt less complaisant attitudes toward international terrorism. But, unfortunately, the President's remonstrances lack the moral leverage they need to have. They lack such leverage because a very wide international public sees the Reagan Administration itself as engaged in supporting terrorism in Central America, in its backing for the contras in Nicaragua. Public cynicism about American anti-terrorist rhetoric is increased by the strong component of Cold War ideology that the Reagan Administration has been putting into its anti-terrorism, implying that almost all terrorism has its ultimate roots in the Soviet Union. Most of the interested public outside the superpowers tends to see each superpower as calling the terrorists whom it favours 'freedom fighters', while reserving the term 'terrorists' for the 'freedom fighters' favoured by the other side. That view of the matter is debatable, but the point, in the present context, is that it is shared by so many people that it inhibits effective international co-operation against international terrorism.

Such co-operation is unlikely to have a strong impact unless both superpowers are prepared to participate in it. Bringing about such co-operation will be difficult but is not inconceivable. Limited superpower consensus has emerged, in the second half of the twentieth century, on at least three occasions: in 1956, against the Anglo-French-Israeli invasion of Egypt; in 1963, against the continued existence of the secessionist 'state' of Katanga; and in 1977, against the supply of arms to South Africa.

Can limited superpower consensus be attained for co-ordinated action against terrorism? I think it can, especially if international terrorist activity grows to the degree that it begins to pose a clear threat to international peace and stability – not just as these are perceived by one superpower, but as perceived by both. There is a historical precedent, flawed – like all such precedents – but suggestive. This is the case of the Barbary pirates, who used to operate in the Mediterranean, out of North African ports. In the seventeenth and eighteenth centuries, rivalries between the European powers provided the Barbary pirates with conditions propitious to their activities, much as global rivalries tend to protect state terrorism today. The Barbary pirates were a general nuisance, but they were a worse nuisance to some powers than to others, and so the enemies of the powers for whom the pirates were making the most trouble were apt to give the pirates a helping hand from time to time. In the first half of the nineteenth century, however, the powers decided, in effect, that the pirates should be treated as a common enemy: the enemy of the human race, *hostes humani generis*. With that change in international approach piracy was brought under control in the Mediterranean.

International terrorism has yet to reach the stage that Mediterranean piracy reached in the nineteenth century. Terrorism is a worse nuisance to one superpower – the United States – than it is to the other. Democratic societies, committed to freedom of information and having governments necessarily sensitive to changing public moods, are far more vulnerable to terrorist blackmail, and offer a far more stimulating environment for terrorist activity, than closed societies like the Soviet Union. (We are often told that there is no terrorist activity in the Soviet Union; in reality we don't know whether there is terrorism or not. But the fact that we don't know and that the Soviet public doesn't know would certainly be advantageous to the Soviet authorities in coping with any terrorists that they may have.)

So the Soviets have no clear and present incentive to join in international activity against terrorism. On the contrary, they have given cautious aid and encouragement to some forms of terrorism (less than right-wing propagandists suggest, but more than the left admits). But it would be wrong to conclude, as most right-wing analysts do, that the Soviets are operating under a doctrinal imperative to destabilize the West. The Soviet authorities – despite their ideological bravado – know well that a destabilized West could be extremely dangerous, and specifically dangerous to the Soviet Union. The superpowers do have an elemental common interest – in survival. That is why limited superpower consensus has been possible in the past, and that is why it remains a possibility for the future with regard to terrorism. Such consensus could take the form of a joint warning that any country harbouring terrorists would no longer be allowed to invoke its sovereignty as a protection against international intervention. Once super-power agreement had been reached, that warning could be embodied in a mandatory resolution of the Security Council.

We are very far indeed from that point, though here as elsewhere thought should not treat present actuality as if it were eternal. In the meantime, it appears that the United States has two main alternatives for anti-terrorist policy.

The first alternative, which seems likely to be followed for the remainder of the Reagan Administration, is to go on backing the contras and simultaneously calling for an end to terrorism, with occasional armed spectaculars to lend conviction to such calls. As already indicated, I think this policy is internationally incredible and hopeless, and unnecessarily dangerous, whatever its merits may be in terms of domestic electoral politics.

The second alternative is to provide clear and consistent political and moral leadership in this matter to US allies and the rest of what is called the free world. That would require the United States both to abandon completely its support for the contras in Nicaragua and to accept, without the present reservations, the authority of the World Court. I believe that a President of the United States who had taken these steps would be in a far stronger position than is now the case to give the world a lead in combined action against terrorism and to prepare the way for eventual superpower consensus on this matter. And I think that a President who took such a stand would be bringing new hope on other matters, also, to many people in the world.

Thinking About Terrorism: II

TERRORISM: HOW THE WEST CAN WIN* is a collection of essays by more than thirty contributors. The editor, Benjamin Netanyahu, is Israel's Permanent Representative to the United Nations. He is a brother of the Israeli hero Jonathan Netanyahu – who was killed in action leading the brilliantly successful Entebbe raid – and he himself served for five years in the special forces of the Israeli Defence Forces.

Contributors include senior American officials and public representatives – Secretary of State George P. Shultz, Attorney General Edwin Meese III, FBI Director William H. Webster and Senators Daniel Patrick Moynihan and Paul Laxalt; members of the Government of Israel – Moshe Arens and Yitzhak Rabin; as well as a number of eminent academics and journalists, mainly American, but with some French and British contributors.

Terrorism: How The West Can Win contains some important and illuminating analytical pieces: notably the essays by Professors Bernard Lewis, Elie Kedourie and P. J. Vatikiotis in the section 'Terrorism and the Islamic World'; and also some acute comments on the difficult subject of 'Terrorism and the Media' by journalists John O'Sullivan and Charles Krauthammer.

But in the main *Terrorism: How The West Can Win* is designed – as its title implies – not so much to shed light on the problem as to mobilize public opinion in favour of more drastic action, against those forms of terrorism which threaten the West, especially the United States and Israel. Certain specific proposals are made. In a powerfully argued and well written concluding essay – which bears the same title as the book itself – Ambassador Netanyahu argues in favour of graduated and co-ordinated action by Western countries against States known to be giving active support to terrorists – he names Syria, Iraq, Iran, Libya and South Yemen. He

---

* *Terrorism: How The West Can Win*, Benjamin Netanyahu (ed), Weidenfeld and Nicolson.

envisages, first, political pressure, including the closing of embassies: 'Offending States will be denied their fortresses of terror in our midst.' Second, economic pressure including 'the denial of landing rights to the commercial planes of terrorist States'. Finally, 'military action cannot be ruled out, nor should we be bashful about discussing it.' For these purposes Ambassador Netanyahu proposes 'an anti-terrorist alliance' headed by the United States.

This programme is likely to be taken rather more seriously in the wake of the horrors of Karachi and Istanbul than might have been the case earlier. Personally, I think the suggested political and economic pressures would be justified, in relation to the States named, and could help to inhibit support for terrorism. I also agree that military action 'cannot be ruled out' nor should it be given a blank cheque. It is possible to hold that Entebbe was right, but Tripoli wrong.

As editor, Ambassador Netanyahu appears to have sought contributions from two categories of people: those who had something of value to say on the subject, and those whose support could be of value to the programme advocated. The latter category includes Reaganites and other right-wingers who believe that all terrorism originates ultimately in the Soviet Union, and that no violence backed by the United States can ever be classified as terrorism even where – as in the case of *contra* activities in Nicaragua – the forms of violence practised are covered by any definition of terrorism offered in this book. Contributions of this kind may help win political support in America, but they seriously weaken the intellectual and moral force of the book as a whole. The editor is certainly aware of that and opted for political effectiveness, as he saw it. If I had been Ambassador of Israel, I should no doubt have done the same. If your country is permanently top of the international terrorist hit-list, you don't turn away any supporters, just because they happen to say that the earth is flat.

James Adams in *The Financing of Terror*,* sees *both* superpowers – and other countries also – as paying terrorists wherever they wish to encourage 'a degree of instability in areas under the control of their enemy'. But he doesn't attach decisive importance to governmental support for terrorism, or discern any 'master plan' behind such support. For him, the really successful modern terrorist movements are not creatures of any government. They are business enterprises, integrated into the international capitalist economy. The PLO, the most prosperous of the terrorist enterprises, 'has control of some $2 billion' in the Palestine National Fund,

* *The Financing of Terror*, James Adams, New English Library.

and may have as much as $5 billion, when the total assets of the component groups are added up. The computerized financial empire of the PNF survived the Israeli onslaught in Lebanon, and looks like enabling the PLO to carry on indefinitely.

The IRA, though less prosperous than the PLO, is also now largely self-sufficient financially. Mr Adams cites a secret Northern Ireland office study of 1983 listing the estimated sources of finance for the Provisional IRA:

Covert
1 Bank robberies in the North and South
2 Extortion
3 Tax exemption frauds
4 Gaming machines
Overt
1 Clubs, social functions, shops, direct collections and subscriptions
2 Overseas sympathetic contributions

I would guess that, in 1986, 'extortion' has moved to the top of that list. The new IRA policy designating as a 'legitimate target' anyone who supplies the security forces with anything has almost limitless capacity for terrorist blackmail.

Terrorism and organized crime have often mutually profitable relationships. In Colombia the terrorist organization flourishes on a basis of 'protecting' the drug traffic. In Italy, the Red Brigades and the Camorra have worked together happily. And legitimate business enterprises have also contributed heavily to keeping terrorism going. An outstanding example of this is the growth in Lloyd's kidnap-and-ransom insurance business, which yields very satisfactory profits both to Lloyds's and to the terrorist.

I find Mr Adam's survey of 'terrorism as business' chillingly impressive. He demonstrates that winning the battle against terrorism is not just a question of 'the West against the rest', as the first book reviewed here often implies.

Terrorism is now very much *part of the West*: integrated into the world of free enterprise. If terrorism is to be fought effectively, the financial institutions of the West will have to become committed to the struggle against it, instead of being neutral or worse, as at present.

Effective international action against terrorism would also require co-operation between the superpowers. They would have to drop the silly and dangerous game of, '*I* back freedom fighters! *You* back terrorists.' Unfortunately, we still seem a long way from finding any such basis for co-operation. At the moment, the terrorists are sitting pretty, with the connivance of a number of governments and financial institutions. There is no sign that the horrors of Karachi and Istanbul have changed that basic situation. The funding for further Istanbuls and further Karachis can still go ahead. It looks very much as if international terrorism has become a permanent feature of modern society. Mr Adams, it is true, finds a silver lining:

> Even if nothing is done, there are still some grounds for optimism. Terrorists set out to overthrow the society in which they are operating. However, the more they succeed, the richer they become and the more dependent they are on the survival of that society for a regular source of income to fund the revolution. Capitalism can evidently corrupt the most idealistic of terrorists.

I find the silver lining even more depressing than the cloud. Corrupt terrorists are even more deadly than 'idealistic' ones, because they are more likely to get away with murder.

Press Freedom and the Need to Please*

THERE IS ONE THING the free press and the Soviet press have in common. Both must please.

Any organ of the Soviet press must please, and go on pleasing, a limited number of relevant party officials and through them the party hierarchy generally, the effective owners of the press in question. The Soviet press may also please its general readership, if it can, but only in ways that first please its owners.

Left-wing critics of the free press – which they call, accurately enough, the capitalist press – would mostly be slow to acknowledge the pattern of priorities of pleasing which exists in the Soviet press. But these same critics – who abound, or used to abound, in panels of 'experts' advising Unesco – depict, as existing in the capitalist press, a pattern of pleasing which is closely symmetrical to the Soviet pattern. According to this view of the matter, any organ of the capitalist press must please, and go on pleasing, its capitalist owners and capitalist advertisers, and through them the capitalist class in general. The capitalist press may also please its general readership, if it can, but only in ways that first please the capitalists.

There is some truth in that picture; and significantly more than is acknowledged on those occasions in Western societies when the virtues of a free press are ritually extolled. Few if any editors of newspapers in Western societies could afford to ignore altogether the views of their proprietors, on political and other matters. And these views are likely to be those prevalent in the social class to which proprietors belong. The press as a whole reflects those views to a greater extent, and with greater stability, than they are generally reflected in the electoral choices of the public which reads it.

Yet the extent of the symmetry of 'communist-subordination' and 'capitalist-subordination' in relation to the press stops just about there. Nobody could examine the end-products in question – Soviet newspapers on

---

* From *Times Literary Supplement*, 21 February 1986.

the one hand and, say, British or American newspapers on the other – without being immediately aware of the enormous contrast in the characters of the two kinds of effort to please. The Soviet press concentrates its effort into pleasing the party hierarchy, the ultimate sole controllers of the *entire* Soviet press. The capitalist press diversifies its efforts in competition to please a very wide variety of readers.

The Soviet press can afford to bore most of its readers, and indeed cannot afford *not* to bore most of its readers. Endless reiteration is boring down below, but it is reassuring at the top: the line is the line is the line, and evermore will be so. The capitalist press, on the other hand, cannot afford to bore any significant number of its readers. Each capitalist paper is in the grip of what has been called 'the Scheherezade Syndrome'. Its readers form a kind of collective Sultan who conveys the unspoken message: 'If you bore me, you die.'

The reader, under conditions of capitalist competition, is a more formidable figure than any proprietor or advertiser. If a proprietor's newspaper cannot attract or hold readers, then obviously that proprietor will soon be out of business. As for advertisers, they must follow the readers, without question. The idea of advertisers dictating policy is wide of the mark (with occasional minor exceptions). If someone were to produce a Marxist or anarchist newspaper which attracted lots of readers, then people would buy space in that newspaper to sell their goods to all those lovely Marxists and anarchists. Similarly with a Fascist newspaper. Any policy is commercially acceptable, provided it attracts readers. (Again with some exceptions. For example it would be unwise to be associated, through choice of an advertising medium, with a newspaper which gave serious offence to a body of people more numerous and with more purchasing power than the readers of the newspaper in question.)

The power of the proprietor in the free (or market) press should not, however, be underestimated. What is called 'editorial freedom' or 'editorial independence' can, in certain circumstances, restrain or fend off a given proprietorial intervention. But not for long; not if the proprietor is determined, and certainly not if the paper is losing money. If a journalist, for any reason whatever, incurs the serious and sustained displeasure of the proprietor of the newspaper for which he works, that journalist will not be able to go on writing for that newspaper for long, even if he still pleases the readers. The power of the capitalist proprietor, in relation to the newspaper or newspapers he owns, is almost as full, and may therefore be exercised almost as arbitrarily, as is the power of the Communist bosses in relation to the press of a Communist country. (Only 'almost', because the need to please the general readership is a restraining factor on the power of the capitalist proprietor, which has no equivalent in the press of Communist countries.)

But there is an enormous difference in the overall situations, because of the concentration of power within Communist-ruled societies as contrasted with the diffusion of power in capitalist competitive societies. If, for example, you are fired from the *Irkutsk Inquirer*, for political deviation, your chances of getting a job on the *Vladivostok Vindicator* are practically nil. On the other hand, if you are fired from a given capitalist newspaper – for failure to please its proprietors – you still have a variety of opportunities within the capitalist market generally.

Clearly there is a great deal to be said, with validity, in favour of the free, or capitalist, or market, press. But there is rather less to be said in its favour, with validity, than it is in the habit of saying for itself. So let us consider, first, what may be said, with validity, in favour of this kind of press; and then the limits of that. I shall use the description 'the market press' from here on because I think it is more precise than the other terms and lacks the pejorative overtones of 'capitalist', as well as the laudatory overtones of 'free'.

The market press is, by definition, more *satisfactory* than its ideological rivals. It is more satisfactory because providing satisfaction – the satisfaction of demand – is what it is all about. The ideological press is not about providing satisfaction to the generality of its readers. It is about dispensing guidance, direction, warning, and a certain kind of instruction: instruction to the reader-citizen on what he or she is expected to say or do in order to give satisfaction to his or her rulers, the masters of the press in question.

Because it is required to give satisfaction to its reader-consumers (who are also, by and large, the citizens of the society in question) the market press is necessarily far more *democratic* than the ideological press, which demands satisfaction for its hierarchical controllers, rather than satisfying the demands of its reader-citizens. Indeed the market press is more democratic than the democratic political system itself. Democratic governments are generally accountable to the citizen-voters not much more often than every few years. But a market newspaper is accountable to its reader-consumers every day of its life, and if it is found consistently less satisfactory than its competitors, its life will soon be at an end.

That the market press is more *entertaining* than the ideological press is something that even the most ardent advocate of the latter would not contest. The market press is also more *informative* than the ideological press, because market demands elicit a far wider variety of information than centralized control, combined with political censorship, permits. For similar reasons, the market press is more *truthful* than the ideological press. Competitive conditions make it far less likely that any truth which would interest readers will be suppressed than is the case with a hierarchically controlled and centralized ideological press.

More satisfactory, more democratic, more entertaining, more informative, more truthful. . . . So the market press is preferable to the ideological press in virtually every relevant way. Unless, of course, we allow for the possibility that the ideology dispensed by the ideological press is indeed the only correct one. In that case, the ideological press is vastly more instructive than the market one, and the readers of the market press are being systematically deprived of the only valid means of understanding human history and the world they live in. But unless you can actually believe that (which I don't), then the market press wins hands down, any day, against the ideological press, as exemplified in the Soviet Union and other 'socialist countries'.

But if you look at the market press in its own right, without the aid of that striking and flattering comparison, things don't look quite so rosy.

The functions of the press are usually defined as threefold: 'to inform, to instruct and to entertain'. But there is a wider imperative, affecting the exercise of all three functions: the need to please. This need, inseparable from a market press, enters into the supply, not only of entertainment, but also of information and of instruction.

In the case of information – news – the workings of the pleasure-principle are quite subtle. Bad news seems to be more pleasing than good news: or at least more productive of the kind of pleasure that sells newspapers, or boosts broadcasting ratings. Perhaps readers, viewers etc, feel more alive for hearing of terrible things that have just happened to other people. Perhaps also there is a biological need to pay some attention to perceived danger-signals, and newspapers meet this need: a case of pleasing by alarming. Somewhere in there are the roots of that 'sensationalism' in the presentation of news which is so marked a feature of the mass-circulation market press. But along with sensationalism, there can also be sedation. However, the reality-principle enters into it, as well as the pleasure-principle. There is such a thing as a genuine thirst for information and the market press tries to satisfy that simple thirst, as well as gratifying other and more obscure needs, in the guise of information.

Then there is the question of instruction. The exercise of this function is not confined to the up-market ('quality') press, but it is taken more seriously there, or at least with greater apparent seriousness, than is the case down-market. And the relation of instruction to pleasure is more complex and more fraught up-market than down. It is generally taken to be one of the characteristics of the up-market press that it is genuinely instructive, and not merely informative-cum-entertaining. I believe that that impression is partly true, and partly delusive. The up-market press, it seems to me, dispenses both genuine instruction and pseudo-instruction. And perhaps there is more pseudo-instruction around than is generally admitted. The basic problem is, of course, how to instruct people, without boring or annoying them. The areas in which this is least a threat are those in which instruction and entertainment are intrinsically connected: reviews of books, films, concerts, art exhibitions; also articles on sport. These tend to be the departments where the best writing is found, and the most seriousness, together with the most entertainment. Here many of the readers are *really* interested, and that makes life more rewarding all round.

On the other hand, those departments which are the most remote from entertainment, and from the direct experience of the reader, are also the most likely to be in the grip of *solemn frivolity*, an intellectual and moral ailment for which there is no known cure. Writers on international affairs, and especially on international terrorism, seem the most liable to succumb to this scourge.

Before going on to speculate about why that should be, and what it may have to tell us about the market press, let me exhibit an example of the kind of thing I have in mind. My example, as it happens, comes from the *Observer*. The *Observer* is, of course, an excellent newspaper, especially in those departments where entertainment and instruction can be happily related. And the most interesting thing about the passage from which I am going to quote is that it could appear, in an otherwise excellent newspaper, in discharge of that newspaper's responsibility to provide its readers with instruction concerning international affairs. The passage occurred in an end-of-year editorial, on 29 December 1985, entitled 'When the world began to come together'. As that quasi-millennial title implies, the writer set out to interpret the events of the year with systematic optimism, even though some of the events on the face of them, may seem hard to interpret in such a way. On the Middle East, the editorial writer had this to say.

> In the Middle East, a slow but inexorable progress towards direct talks between Israel and representatives of the Palestinian people seems to be under way. The peace initiative launched by King Hussein has been so often written off that one needs reminding from time to time that it is in fact still alive. Its pace is slow, and setbacks frequent; but there is movement, and that mostly in the right direction.

The two terrorist outrages at Rome and Vienna airports which soured the end of the Christmas break are almost certainly evidence of this. They bear the marks of having been an attempt by dissident Palestinian groups outside the PLO to disrupt the peace process and discredit Yasser Arafat, the PLO leader, in two capitals where he has enjoyed some diplomatic support. In the aftermath of such a horror, Israel should be wary of hasty and ill-directed reprisals, which could play into the hands of those who carried out the attacks.

So the two terrorist attacks on Israeli targets at Rome and Vienna were 'almost certainly evidence' that the peace process in the Middle East is making satisfactory progress.

The conclusion is remarkable; the method of reasoning through which the conclusion is reached, no less remarkable. In particular, the concept of 'evidence' is introduced here with no warrant whatever. The writer attributes a motive to the terrorists without citing evidence for that motive, and then decides that their acts of terror *in themselves* were 'almost certainly evidence' of the motivation attributed to them by him. And as it happens, the editorial interpretation of the background to all this is utterly at variance with the interpretation of the *Observer*'s own Middle East specialist, Patrick Seale, in the same issue of the paper. The editorial writer thought that extremists were so distressed by the progress which moderates in the PLO, led by Arafat, were making towards peace that they, the extremists, lashed out in despair in order to wreck the peace process, thus inadvertently showing that the peace process was working. For Mr Seale, however, it was the moderates, not the extremists, who were 'in despair' – Seale's words – at their *failure* to make progress through negotiation. So the PLO were turning back to terrorism, according to Seale. Thus it appeared that a tendency towards increased terrorism was due to the success of the peace process, or to the failure of the peace process, depending on which bit of the *Observer* you read. Those readers who were looking to the *Observer* for instruction on Middle Eastern affairs must have had their minds well and truly boggled by that issue of 29 December.

It is not clear, however, what proportion of readers are looking for instruction on such subjects as that, and what proportion are looking for other things: the pleasures of wishful thinking, for example, or a capacity for appearing well informed. If there is a market for genuine instruction, there is also a market for congenial or pleasing pseudo-instruction: *le confort intellectuel*. It is not always easy to see where one kind ends and the other begins (although sometimes the pseudo-instruction stands out rather clearly, as in the sample above).

Reading news and commentary in various up-market British newspapers,

I have the feeling that the commentary is often a sort of antidote to the news. The news is often shocking: the commentary more often sedative. The commentary would claim to put the news 'in perspective', and so in a way it does. But the sense of perspective conveyed is often that associated with sedation: the calming sense of having recovered a sense of proportion, which accompanies the operation of a drug. The physical results of war and terrorism often require recourse to anaesthetics. But it seems that even the intellectual contemplation of the threats of war and terrorism cannot be borne for long without some recourse to verbal anaesthetics, and this need also is met by the market press, in the form of what it likes to think of as 'instruction'.

The reign of wishful thinking, in the press, in relation to international affairs especially, is nothing new. Fifty years ago, at a time when the expansionism of the dictators could probably have been stopped without major war, people in the democracies preferred to believe that that expansionism would somehow stop of itself, without the democracies having to run any kind of risk at all of any kind of war. The free press of the democracies did not throw its collective weight against that preference. The free press, being the market press, agreed with the readers. The right-wing press argued that Hitler, being basically a reasonable man, was bound to get even more reasonable, provided his reasonable demands were met. The left-wing press wrote 'against Fascism and War'; a determined show of pacifism would soon bring Hitler to his knees. Intellectually, the right-wing argument was barely tenable: the left-wing argument not tenable at all. But emotionally both were very tenable indeed. Newspaper editorials rational-ized the relevant emotions, in language appropriate to their particular readership.

We are all accustomed to hearing it said, and some of us are accustomed to saying, that freedom of expression is the great safeguard of a democracy. But it didn't turn out to be much of a safeguard in the circumstances of fifty years ago. And the same tendencies to wishful thinking – or rather to wishing dressed up as thinking – that were present then are still present in the press today. They are present because there is a demand for them and it is in the nature of the market press to try to satisfy demand, whatever form it takes.

By this I do *not* mean that freedom of expression is not in any way a safeguard of democracy. I think it is a very important safeguard against *internal* threats to democracy, such as abuses of power by elected persons. The classical modern demonstration of that was Watergate. And there have been recent and healthy signs of a 'Watergate investigating potential' in British public life – although 'freedom of expression' in Britain is a much more restricted concept than it is in America. But I don't think that either in Britain or America – or elsewhere – the market press is anything like as serviceable to democracy, in relation to international affairs, as it is in relation to domestic affairs. The reasons for that seem fairly clear. On domestic affairs, the reader – especially the 'A' and 'B' reader – is likely to be quite well informed, and genuinely anxious to be better informed. Also, capable of distinguishing, and anxious to distinguish, between sense and nonsense with a definite preference for the former. These are conditions and dispositions making for a reasonably healthy press, so far as domestic affairs are concerned.

In relation to the vast – and partly veiled – range of international affairs, however, the reader cannot hope to be anything like as well informed as he often is in relation to his own country. He is not likely to be prepared to make more than a rather perfunctory effort to become better informed about world politics. So he will find it quite hard to distinguish sense from nonsense in this domain. He may even have a tendency to prefer the latter, since nice nonsense is more readily acceptable than bleak sense. In these conditions there is a certain demand for bogus punditry, and the bogus pundit duly makes his appearance, conjured up by the mysterious power of the market, as was of old the Genie, by Aladdin's Lamp.

The farther away the place is, as a general rule, the more nonsense you can get away with about it. This happens to be exemplified in that veritable treasure-house of editorial bogus punditry, 'When the world began to come together'. The Genie in charge of that one lit up the Middle East for his readers through the discovery that multiple murder is a harbinger of peace: then he went on to discuss Northern Ireland, where he found things had been also coming together, this time as a result of the Anglo-Irish Agreement of 15 November 1985. But the interesting thing was that, although exactly the same category of 'evidence' was available in relation to Northern Ireland as that which the editorial writer found convincing in relation to the Middle East, the evidence in question is *not* introduced in the context of Northern Ireland. In Northern Ireland as in the Middle East, terrorists had a busy year, in 1985. In reality the IRA kept on killing people, after the Hillsborough Agreement, as before that Agreement; just as in the Middle East various terrorist organizations kept on killing people, without any ascertainable relevance to the status or alleged status of the peace process. In the Middle East, the commentator interpreted continuing terrorism as evidence of the success of the peace process. So why not see continuing terrorism in Northern Ireland as evidence of the success of the Hillsborough peace process? The evidence is fully as convincing in the second case as in the first, for the sufficient reason that the evidence doesn't exist at all, in either case. The reason for the difference in the nonsense content in the two cases is probably that nonsense is more readily distinguishable, and therefore offered with less abandon, the nearer the topic under discussion is to home.

The *level* of the acceptability of nonsense in relation to commentary on international affairs seems to be constant, or nearly so. The *character* of the nonsense which the market finds acceptable varies widely, according to place, time and circumstances. In Britain of the mid-1980s as in Britain of the mid-1930s (though in widely different circumstances) it is the sedative variety which seems to be in most demand. In other contexts, it has been the alarmist variety: in Britain for example in the mid-1950s ('Nasser equals Hitler'); or in America, at fairly frequent intervals throughout the century. But in both kinds of case, the reader is demanding, and consuming, disquietingly large quantities of some kind of intoxicant, whether sedative or stimulating. The sedative kind can make people fail to notice the reality of Hitler. The stimulating kind can get people into a war in Vietnam.

The inadequacy of the market press, in relation to international affairs, is worth bearing in mind, as a significant weakness in our democratic societies. Individual journalists, here and there, do what they can to remedy that inadequacy. (They could perhaps do more if there were less of the 'dog doesn't eat dog' principle within the profession. That principle protects the more nonsensical breeds of dog.) But the reasons for the inadequacy are rooted in the market itself and the inadequacy is therefore inherent in the nature of a market press. And the market press, with all its manifold inadequacies and blemishes, is vastly better than any known alternative. Nothing I have said here is intended to give any aid or comfort to Unesco, and its 'free and balanced flow of information'.

One thing that might help a bit, in spreading an awareness of the dangers inseparable from the advantages of the kind of press we actually have, would be a more widespread use of the expression 'market press' instead of 'free press'. 'Market' gives due warning that along with the goods and services go dangers of deception. And 'market' replacing 'free' already gets rid of one deception: the suggested absence of constraints and servitudes where in fact these abound, in the empire of demand, and of the need to satisfy demand. You are not really free, if you are under unrelenting pressure to please.

I don't remember by now what the Five Freedoms are supposed to be, but I would propose a Sixth Freedom: the Freedom to Displease.

A Neo-Conservative Ideologue

Norman Podhoretz*

THE TITLE AND SUBTITLE of Podhoretz's book together make up a quotation from Lionel Trilling. The book is made up of nine essays: On the writers of *The God That Failed* group: on Camus and his critics; on Orwell; on F. R. Leavis; on Henry Adams; on 'the Adversary Culture and the New Class'; on Kissinger, on Milan Kundera and on Solzhenitsyn. All of the essays contain – though in varying proportions – both literary criticism and political comment. In his introduction, Mr Podhoretz reasserts his belief 'that it is possible for a critic to speak openly from a particular political perspective and to make political judgements without permitting such judgements to replace or obscure literary values as such.'

I agree with Mr Podhoretz that this is indeed possible. I also believe that Mr Podhoretz genuinely set out to separate 'political judgements' from 'literary values'; and that he also genuinely believes that he has been successful in this undertaking. I think he has been partly successful, and partly not. He tries to be good, but when his 'political' blood is up – and it is, most of the time – he can't help forcing a 'literary' point (or any other point if it comes to that).

I should, however, at this point, declare interest. I happen to be among Mr Podhoretz's targets, in his essay 'Camus and his Critics'. A short book of mine on Camus, published in the 1970s, is found by Mr Podhoretz to be a 'travesty' offered 'in the name of art', but actually in the service of my 'anti-anti-Communist political passions'. So I am accused of having succumbed to the very temptation – that of politicizing literature – which Mr Podhoretz believes himself to have consistently resisted. And when – as here – I doubt the extent of his success, I fear such criticism may be imputed again to the power of those political passions which he assumes to hold me in their fell grip.

* Article on *The Bloody Crossroads: Where Literature and Politics Meet*, Norman Podhoretz, Simon and Schuster, in the *New York Review of Books*, 9 October 1986.

As the reader will already appreciate, argument along those lines could become tiresome. I mention the matter as a kind of 'health warning', in justice to Mr Podhoretz and to the reader, and leave it there.

Politically speaking, the most ambitious of these essays is 'If Orwell Were Alive Today'. This essay ends with the words, 'I am convinced that if Orwell were alive today he would be taking his stand with the neo-conservatives and against the Left'. The claim here is, of course, made on behalf of a group of which the essayist is himself a leading member: Mr Podhoretz is described on the jacket of this book as 'America's most outspoken neo-conservative intellectual'. How important it is for the essayist to be able to claim Orwell for his neo-conservatives may be inferred from a passage near the beginning of the essay 'If Orwell Were Alive Today'.

> This enormous reputation by itself would make Orwell one of those writers that are well worth stealing [a phrase of Orwell's own, about Dickens]. It is, after all, no small thing to have the greatest political writer of the age on one's side: it gives confidence, authority, and weight to one's political views.

This passage is not, of course, programmatic. That is, Mr Podhoretz is not here signalling his own intention to 'steal' George Orwell; although he may possibly be inadvertently revealing the power of a temptation to do just that. Rather, he is rebuking other people for their efforts to steal a writer who properly belongs to the neo-conservatives – Mr Podhoretz's own group. As a matter of fact, Mr Podhoretz's point about left-wing efforts to 'steal Orwell' has acquired more force since he first made it. In Britain, the year 1984 brought on an influential and misguided effort to depict the book *Nineteen Eighty-Four* as a satire impartially – from a democratic socialist point of view – directed at *both* East and West, the Soviet Union and the United States. This effort, backed (or rather, led) by the considerable authority of Professor Bernard Crick – Orwell's biographer, and editor of the annotated *Nineteen Eighty-Four* – may indeed rightly be described as 'stealing Orwell'. *Nineteen Eighty-Four* is highly specific in its satire of Soviet society – and in its warning to Britain against the danger presented by Soviet sympathizers – and contains hardly anything that can be construed, without twisting and wrenching, as satire on the West.

Mr Podhoretz's resistance to the Orwell-stealers of the Left is fully justified. His claim to Orwell, on behalf of the neo-conservatives is another matter. Certainly, Orwell's last two books – *Animal Farm* and *Nineteen Eighty-Four* are (*pace* Professor Crick) as anti-Communist as the stoutest neo-conservative could desire. But this doesn't mean that Orwell would necessarily be attracted to neo-conservatism. He was essentially a loner, with a marked and consistent distaste for cliques and coteries, and for politico-literary intellectuals hunting in packs, on the scent – usually a distant scent – of power. In Orwell's own day – and especially in his last years – the most conspicuous groups of that kind were active on the Left. But I see no reason to suppose that he would have liked these phenomena any better when they turned up on the Right, as they have in the last quarter of the twentieth century. For example, one of the intellectual manifestations which Orwell most despised was what he called 'back-scratching': the politico-literary coterie practice of puffing the works of fellow-members. And as it happens, the back-jacket of *The Bloody Crossroads* – in which a number of Mr Podhoretz's political friends praise him for his literary prowess – is a classic case of politico-literary back-scratching. I really can't see George Orwell *dans cette galère*.

Mr Podhoretz quotes Orwell on 'smelly little orthodoxies'. Without entering into the game of 'if Orwell were alive today', one may point out that while Orwell actually *was* alive, some of the things he most disliked about the 'smelly little orthodoxies' were characteristics which are today salient or sniffable in neo-conservatism.

In his essay on F. R. Leavis – the best in the collection, and the most free from polemics – Mr Podhoretz finds that Leavis (whom he generally admires) in his writing on D. H. Lawrence 'sins against the disinterestedness in whose absence literary criticism becomes a species of covert ideologizing'.

Coming from Norman Podhoretz, that is a breathtaking judgement. What is admirable about it is its transparent innocence. Mr Podhoretz really does believe himself to possess the kind of disinterestedness against which even a Leavis could sin. And this disinterestedness which he confidently attributes to himself seems to be felt as a kind of talisman which automatically preserves his criticism from turning into ideologizing. Few readers of *The Bloody Crossroads* – outside the neo-conservative camp – are likely to be convinced that Mr Podhoretz's talisman is really in working order. Not all the time, but much of the time, he appears to be forcing a critical judgement to make a political point.

This is perhaps most apparent in the essay on Camus. Mr Podhoretz doesn't annex Camus outright, as he does with Orwell. He is content with having 'the best of Camus' on his side. Mr Podhoretz, the literary critic, discovers, in his disinterested way, that the best of Camus is to be found in the work by Camus which happens to be most to the political taste of Mr Podhoretz, the neo-conservative ideologue. This is Camus' anti-Communist essay of 1951, *L'Homme Révolté* (translated as *The Rebel*). This is an eccentric opinion – since Camus' reputation is based mainly on his three novels – but it might be none the worse for that, if Mr Podhoretz were to establish it, by bringing out the neglected excellences of the essay he values so highly, and which other critics (including myself) have considered tedious and pretentious. But Mr Podhoretz devotes only a few lines, with several laudatory adjectives, to *The Rebel* itself. His strategy for validating this particular piece of literary reassessment consists of:

(a) Flat assertion that *The Rebel* is 'the best of Camus';

(b) Attacks on the supposed political motivations – failure of dis-interestedness – of critics who fail to rate the work so highly as Mr Podhoretz says is its due;

(c) Depreciation, on what appear to be random grounds, of Camus' other works, including the best known and most admired.

Camus' sin, in Mr Podhoretz's eyes, was that he failed to keep going on about anti-Communism as he had done in *The Rebel*. For Mr Podhoretz to think thus is quite understandable. But Mr Podhoretz goes much further than this. He has convinced himself that *Camus himself* felt this way. The sense of guilt which pervades *The Fall* has nothing to do with Christianity or anything of that kind, according to this critic. No, what Camus' guilt was all about was his own failure to stand up for the United States, as Sartre had stood up for the Soviet Union. 'Sartre . . . chose the Soviet Union and was not afraid to say so'; Camus, in effect, chose the United States and was afraid to say so. *That* is what made Camus a penitent. All that religious stuff in *The Fall* is just there to disguise and deaden Camus' actual political guilt, for his desertion of Uncle Sam. Religion 'provides Camus with a pretentious way to avoid the full and rigorous accounting with himself he so desperately needed and wanted to undertake.'

What a pity the novelist did not have a neo-conservative father-confessor at his side, to get his penance right for him, and see his books got rewritten.

Mr Podhoretz does not produce any evidence in support of this interpretation of *The Fall*, but then he can't be expected to, can he? Camus himself – Mr Podhoretz's Camus – didn't know what he was doing or, in so far as he did know what he was doing, was anxious to cover up the evidence, even from himself. So it is for Mr Podhoretz, the literary critic, to divine intuitively what Camus was up to in *The Fall*. And it happens, as so often in these pages, that which Mr Podhoretz, the critic, is able to divine is very much to the taste of Mr Podhoretz, the neo-conservative ideologue.

Mr Podhoretz's idiosyncratically Americanocentric interpretation of *The Fall* is I think symptomatic of the main intellectual weakness of neo-conservatism, its obsessive reductivism. Everything has to be about *us* and *them*, the United States and the Soviet Union, God and Satan. That, for example, a French-Algerian writer, Albert Camus, might have been more interested, in the late 1950s, in the Franco-Algerian war, then raging, and in his own painfully conflicting feelings about that, than in either the United States or the Soviet Union, does not occur to Mr Podhoretz even as a possibility. *Of course* the author of *The Fall* had to be thinking about the United States. What else, after all, when you get down to it, is there to think about? Except the Soviet Union.

The Orwell and Camus essays are, I think, fairly representative of Mr Podhoretz's politico-critical *modus operandi*. I don't propose to consider the other essays in the collection in the same way, but shall instead consider a theme that greatly preoccupies the author and runs, in one way or another, through almost all the essays. That theme is the relation of intellectuals to power.

Mr Podhoretz believes that intellectuals are powerful, whether for good or ill, and whether they know it or not. In 'Henry Adams: the "Powerless" Intellectual in America, Mr Podhoretz argues that Adams, who felt himself to be powerless, is actually powerful, for evil. 'Thus one can say', says Mr Podhoretz, 'that Adams has been kept alive as an incitement to and justification of the hunger of the American intellectual class for the power, and especially the political power, that he himself for all that he denigrated it, could never stop wanting and envying.' Yet Adams, in Mr Podhoretz's view, actually attained power posthumously at least: 'The great irony is that the case of Adams – who remains a force when the names of Rutherford B. Hayes or Chester Arthur are scarcely even remembered – demonstrates how much more powerful intellectuals can be in the long run than even the most successful of politicians.' Yet this is a bad thing, in the case of Adams, who exercises a 'malignant influence' in encouraging 'a bigoted contempt for this country and in subtly denigrating and devaluing the life of the mind.'

The bracketing of 'this country' and 'the life of the mind' in this passage is significant. According to Mr Podhoretz's view of things in all these essays, uncritical nationalism and intellectual integrity always tend to converge, in the case of America (though not presumably in certain other countries). On this view 'the treason of the clerks' and treason to the United States are in essence the same thing. I prefer Julien Benda's original version, according to which uncritical nationalism was among the causes which could induce the intellectual to abdicate his proper function and deviate systematically from the truth. But Mr Podhoretz does not mention the author of *La Trahison des Clercs*.

In his essay on Adams, Mr Podhoretz, by the context in which he uses the expression 'the American intellectual class', leaves the class in question firmly in the grip of the leftist baddies with their twisted minds. But things brighten up considerably, in Podhoretzian terms, in the very next essay, 'The Adversary Culture and the New Class'. The baddies are still at work – inside the Adversary Culture and the New Class – but now some intellectuals in white hats have shown up, in the form of 'a group of dissident intellectuals, mostly, but not exclusively associated with magazines like *Commentary* and *The Public Interest*' and 'often called neo-conservatives'. Although this group still remains 'a minority within the intellectual community', its influence is not to be underrated, in Mr Podhoretz's book: 'Certainly these intellectual adversaries of the adversary culture were exerting a marked influence by the mid-1970s. Their writings were being read and discussed in many circles, and the election of Ronald Reagan in 1980 could be, and was, seen as a mark of their spreading influence.'

Could it be? And was it? And by whom? Clearly it could be and was by Mr Podhoretz and some of his pals; afflicted by galloping swelled heads. But did anyone else see it that way? Possibly some besotted left-wing intellectual, disposed to magnify the importance of his intellectual opponents, may have suggested something of the kind; though I don't happen to know of any such case. But could anyone, outside the charmed circle of a few intellectual coteries and counter-coteries, ever have dreamed of such a thing? How could a couple of magazines, and a couple of dozen individuals of whom most Americans, and most other people, have never heard possibly have exercised a determining influence over an American national election? Of course you can imagine – if you are a neo-conservative – the esoteric influence of *Commentary* etc., as spreading out at second hand, through the media, and so filtering down to the plebs who, when they pressed those levers, were indirectly under the spell of Mr Podhoretz and his friends, without ever having heard of them. But it all seems a mite fanciful to me. Far from thinking of that election result as 'a mark of the spreading influence of neo-conservative intellectuals', I think that the only intellectual who clearly exercised a significant influence in bringing about the defeat of Jimmy Carter and the election of Ronald Reagan was that eminent palaeoconservative scholar, Imam Khomeini.

In general, the essays in this collection seem to be the work of a writer who knows quite a lot about literature, without any longer being much interested in the subject – and who is passionately interested in politics, without knowing much about them. As I read Mr Podhoretz, that phrase of Edmund Burke came to mind: 'those who have nothing of politics save the passions they excite'. Such people exist, obviously, both on the left and on the right. But some of those on the right, these days, who fall into that category, like to attribute to themselves, with some insistence, the possession of an exceptional and disinterested intellectual rigour: a quality not readily discernible in their writings to those outside the fold.

Politically, I don't suppose the neo-conservatives matter all that much. They are not so much turning America round – as Mr Podhoretz, perhaps in one of his wilder moments, supposed – as sending a message to mainstream America: that not all eggheads are baddies. I don't know whether mainstream America is much interested in that message, but the Reagan administration seems less interested in it than the leading neo-conservatives may perhaps have hoped. There has been no neo-conservative equivalent to the political career of Henry Kissinger. Incidentally, Mr Podhoretz's essay on Kissinger seems astonishingly reverential coming from a writer usually free from that defect. When Mr Podhoretz meets his old master, F. R. Leavis, in heaven he will have to answer for attributing literary 'greatness' to the author of *White House Years*. But perhaps what sounds unpleasantly obsequious is just harmless wistfulness. Mr Podhoretz wrote *Making It*, but Kissinger really and truly made it. Had Kissinger, the politician, *not* made it I doubt whether Podhoretz, the critic, would have discerned greatness in anything Kissinger wrote. The literary greatness went with the political job.

In case there are still any neo-conservative intellectuals who would like to be Presidential advisers, but have not yet received the Call, let me offer a helpful hint or two.

First of all, let Talleyrand be your guide. Both Burke and Machiavelli are more interesting as political thinkers, certainly, but in terms of making it, and keeping it, Talleyrand is the man. Burke spent most of his life in opposition, and had only one brief period of junior office. The author of *The Prince* ended a generally dismal political career by leading a delegation to the Friars Minor at Carpi, and glad to get that tiny job. Talleyrand, on the other hand, achieved the really astonishing feat of remaining close to the centres of political power in France – with only brief and absolutely indispensable intervals – for the best part of forty-five years (1789–1834) and under five regimes. So Talleyrand's worth listening to, if making it is what you want. And it happens that Talleyrand's best-known piece of political advice is also the most relevant: '*Surtout, pas de zèle*'.

(English writers often render this advice, with insular fogginess, as 'not too much zeal' and some of them then put their own amendment back into French: '*Pas trop de zèle*'. But the actual advice, accurately Englished, remains: 'Above all, no zeal.' (*No* zeal; none at all.)

Now this means that a prudent Prince or President will not be inclined to include among his close advisers an intellectual who is publicly known as a zealous champion even of the very ideas to which the Prince or President is publicly committed. For the ideas which that intellectual is out there championing only *sound* identical to those to which the Prince or President (henceforward P.P.) is committed. The P.P. is committed to those ideas *as he personally interprets them*, and with the knowledge that it may become politically expedient for him, in certain circumstances, to interpret them in ways that may seem peculiar, on the face of it, to some of those who have most admired the P.P's commitment to the ideas in question.

For example, a given P.P. may be widely admired for his determination to resist some Evil Empire or other. But then political necessity may require the P.P. to flog a lot of grain or something to the E.E. in question, thereby presumably feeding its capacity to do evil. In such circumstances, the kind of intellectual the P.P. needs to have around the place is the kind that will help draft the kind of speeches that are needed in the circumstances: *not* the kind of intellectual that will ask, 'What the hell's going on around here?', or talk about bolting, or even perhaps actually bolt. And the more vehemently an intellectual has *published* the ideas to which the P.P. is thought of as committed, the less reliable that intellectual is likely to be found to be, when the going gets rough.

A politic intellectual who wants to get close enough to a P.P. to wield some P.P.-derived power must be prepared to serve the P.P., *on the P.P.'s terms*, especially when the going gets rough; rough that is, on principles, ideas, consistency and so on. It is true that, in certain circumstances, the politic intellectual may ditch his P.P.; Talleyrand ditched no fewer than four sets of his (sometimes by getting himself ditched by them, while they were slipping). But in the nature of things, an American intellectual adviser is unlikely to have many opportunities to ditch his P.P., Talleyrand-style. Loyalty to the P.P. has necessarily a higher place in the equipment of the politically-ambitious American intellectual than any such quality had in the case of Talleyrand. Otherwise, Talleyrand remains the examplar: the *service* intellectual, without ideology, enthusiasm, or worries about principles.

Henry Kissinger is in the Talleyrand line, although he has had more to say about Metternich, the man of principles. Talleyrand would have approved of that, too.

Now I greatly fear that Norman Podhoretz yearns to be the Kissinger of the Right. Perhaps he does not – I am not in his council – but it seemed to me as I read the Podhoretz essay 'Kissinger Reconsidered' that that yearning was rising at me from the page, like a feverish miasma. Mr Podhoretz should stifle any such yearning. He is most unlikely ever to make it that way. He is burdened with ideology, attachment to principles, zeal. He has published far too much, and too pugnaciously, about contemporary politics, and so given too many hostages to fortune. He lacks too many relevantly desirable qualities: patience, good humour, smoothness, masked cynicism. Any P.P. could see from a mile off that Mr Podhoretz would be an awkward crew-member to have on board. So – for reasons the foremost of which are creditable to his personal honesty and integrity – Mr Podhoretz seems unlikely to get the Call.

Once actual political power is denied, there remains, theoretically, another kind of power. This is the kind that Mr Podhoretz attributes to Henry Adams: the power of the writer, through his writing, over others, through generations. But I doubt whether Mr Podhoretz is really much interested in that stuff. Paul Valéry's 'horribly-laurelled consolatrix' is hardly everyone's cup of tea. Mr Podhoretz's writing seems mainly concerned with the other kind of power. He writes competently, but in an off-the-cuff sort of way, like a man who has a bus to catch. I think his bus is a mirage, and I don't think the things he writes, in that rush to the mirage, are likely to be memorable. In short, Mr Podhoretz is neither Henry Kissinger nor Henry Adams. And he is no more an authority on 'the Bloody Crossroads' than any other of the romantic and power-infatuated victims with whom that crossroads is bestrewn.

Mr Podhoretz will no doubt have the satisfaction of ascribing this largely negative review to the 'anti-anti-Communist passions' which he believes are seething in the bosom of this reviewer. It would be unkind to deny Mr Podhoretz that satisfaction.

About anti-Communism and anti-anti-Communism, and the general phenomenon of neo-conservatism, I hope to have something to say on another occasion.

Three Zionists
Weizmann, Ben-Gurion, Katznelson*

THE PUBLICATION OF THESE THREE BOOKS considerably enriches the literature on Zionism available in English. Regrettably, the enrichment is rather less than it might have been. The books about Ben-Gurion and Katznelson are translations from Hebrew originals, and both are quite drastic abridgments. In his introduction, Mr Teveth says: 'This work is a rendition in English of a rather weightier tome in Hebrew. The English version is distinguished from the Hebrew by an economy of expression and documentation, which I believe will be appreciated by the English reader.' It seems a pity. Only those seriously interested in Zionism will read any of these books, and they are not likely to appreciate the economy. Surely a university press, when it finds a text worth translating, should translate it in full, and let the reader do such skipping as he chooses to.

Chaim Weizmann is the first volume of a long-awaited scholarly biography. Jehuda Reinharz, professor of modern Jewish history at Brandeis University, was selected in 1977 to write the biography along with Walter Laqueur, who later had to drop out of the project. The present volume takes the story only as far as the outbreak of the First World War; the period of Weizmann's major achievement is left for the projected second and final volume. But this volume whets the appetite for it. Its scholarship, obviously, is beyond question, but Reinharz has other qualities not always to be taken for granted in academic writing about politicians. He has a sure sense of his subject's political position (or political predicament) at any given time, and explains his political motivations convincingly. (Reinharz handsomely acknowledges his indebtedness to 'insights and formulations' of the late R. H. S. Crossman, who was originally designated as Weizmann's

* Article on *Chaim Weizmann: The Making of a Zionist Leader*, Jehuda Reinharz, Oxford University Press; *Ben-Gurion and the Palestinian Arabs: From Peace to War*, Shabtai Teveth, Oxford University Press; *Berl: The Biography of a Socialist Zionist*, Anita Shapira, Cambridge University Press; in *The New Republic*, 17 June 1985.

biographer, and it may be in this area that Crossman's political experience has been helpful.) Reinharz's approach to his subject is respectful without being reverential, and never verges on the hagiographic. (The same is true of the Ben-Gurion book and also, though perhaps to a slightly lesser extent, of the Katznelson biography.) Indeed, Weizmann's admirers, who include this reviewer, are likely to be a little shocked by the prominence, in the portrait, of a few warts.

This study sheds a great deal of light, for example, on the fascinating subject of the political relationship between the young Weizmann and Theodor Herzl, the founder of the Zionist movement. Weizmann was not a very important figure in Zionism during Herzl's lifetime, but he was beginning to make his mark by means of a youth movement he founded, on which he based his so-called Democratic Faction within the Zionist movement. During Herzl's lifetime, Weizmann was no more than, as Reinharz puts it, 'the leader of the Russian Zionist student colonies in the West'. But Herzl took note of him, and he watched Herzl avidly. Herzl, for his part, could use him politically, and Weizmann could use Herzl's use of him.

Weizmann's Youth Conference in 1901 represented a challenge to Herzl's leadership, and some of Herzl's colleagues called on the leader to denounce the Youth Conference. This Herzl refrained from doing. Reinharz analyzes Herzl's reasons convincingly:

> Herzl had his own reasons for co-opting rather than further alienating the young Zionist intelligentsia. He considered the source of his troubles within the World Zionist Organization to be the vested interests and veteran leadership of the local organizations. Thus, any new leadership that arose might be preferable, and perhaps also more responsive to his own influence.

Weizmann met Herzl, and a compromise was worked out. Reinharz comments:

> As much as the results of the meeting attest to Weizmann's powers of persuasion, they also indicate Herzl's ability to defuse a potentially dangerous opposition before it got out of hand. Both showed themselves to be seasoned politicians who understood the advantages of eliminating unnecessary direct confrontation. . . .
> The negotiations with Herzl reveal important characteristics in Weizmann. The young *Privat-Dozent* whose experience in the movement hitherto was mainly as a propagandist now showed that he was a first-rate tactician. Weizmann was essentially a pragmatic empiricist, not an opportunist, who believed in attaining the possible. He revealed an ability to maintain a flexible

posture toward both the content of the ideas he represented as well as their method of implementation. He did not seek a final, decisive, and irrevocable break with the established leadership since he knew his own position and power base to be quite weak. Though he stood by his principles, at the same time he retained a sceptical attitude toward rigid ideological positions.

At the Fifth Zionist Congress, in December 1901, Weizmann's Democratic Faction staged an attack on the religious Zionists; when Herzl deflected the attack procedurally, the Democratic Faction, including Weizmann, walked out. Again Herzl was asked to intervene and again he refused. 'Don't get upset,' said Herzl. 'Those are not the worst people amongst us.' And at the final session of the Congress – which was still being boycotted – Herzl expressed his pleasure at the existence of 'a youthful group, which is faithful, sometimes in a rather lively way'. On the following day, Weizmann presented the members of his Democratic Faction to Herzl with the words: 'Before you stands His Majesty's most loyal opposition.'

In the great controversy that broke out at the Sixth Zionist Congress, at Basel in 1903, over the British Government's offer of Uganda for Jewish settlement, Weizmann originally wished to support Herzl and accept the offer. He changed his mind, however, when he realized the strength of the resistance of the Russian Zionists. 'Despite his sympathy with Herzl's position, Weizmann preferred being in the camp of the Russian Zionist leadership since it was his only chance to survive politically.'

A little less than a year later, Herzl was dead, and on 6 July 1904, Weizmann wrote to his fiancée, Vera Khatzman: 'I have had to experience a heavy blow . . . the death of *Herzl* . . . At this moment all the differences between us have disappeared, and I only have the image of a great creative worker in front of my eyes. . . . He has left us a frightening legacy. . . . I feel that a heavy burden has fallen on my shoulders. . . .' But about a week later Weizmann wrote on the same subject, with a significantly different emphasis, to Menachem Ussishkin, the leader of the Russian Zionists and Herzl's most implacable opponent. 'One feels that a terrible burden has fallen on our shoulders. Herzl left a terrible legacy, but now less than ever is there time for tears. *Einigkeit macht stark*. I repeat once again: I am entirely at your disposal.'

And he was. It was as the trusted agent, among Western Zionists, of Ussishkin's Russian Zionists that Weizmann built up his own position as a force in world Zionism in the years after Herzl's death. It was with the support of Herzl's greatest opponent that Weizmann began to establish his claim to the mantle of Herzl. Both as a politician and as an artist, Herzl would have appreciated the irony.

The Balfour Declaration, Weizmann's greatest achievement, does not come within Reinharz's purview in this volume. But the first meeting between Balfour and Weizmann – on 9 January 1906 – does. Reinharz is sceptical about the colourful account that Weizmann gives of this meeting in his autobiography, *Trial and Error*. Such scepticism is understandable. One of Weizmann's weaknesses was a tendency to fantasize. (For example, he gave Dorothy Rothschild a detailed account of how he personally helped to defend the Jewish quarter of Kishinev in April 1903 – at a time when, as Reinharz points out, Weizmann was actually in Geneva.) But I am not convinced that the account of the meeting with Balfour in *Trial and Error* is seriously misleading. Reinharz casts doubt on it by pointing out that Weizmann's 'record of the meeting the very same day of the interview is a great deal less dramatic and no doubt more accurate'. In his autobiographical account, Weizmann sets out the arguments he used with Balfour. In the contemporary account he simply says, 'I explained to him why this – 'territorialism', the substitution of Uganda for Palestine – was not possible.' But Weizmann was writing to his fiancée, who knew what he would have had to say on that subject. She didn't have to be told. I see no reason to doubt that Weizmann was impressive – he always was, when he wanted to be – or that Balfour was impressed.

Reinharz makes the point that Balfour did not show any interest in Zionism, or meet Weizmann again, until December 1914. But a Zionism with no legitimate outlet other than Palestine was not a practical object for a British statesman at any time before Britain found itself at war with the Ottoman Empire. What was remarkable, rather, is how quickly Balfour met Weizmann afterwards. It will be very interesting to see how Reinharz handles the preliminaries to the Balfour Declaration in his next volume.

Spokesmen for Ben-Gurion's party – Mapai, or what is now called the Labour Alignment – have tended, naturally enough, to idealize their founder in retrospect. This communicated itself to outside critics of Israel, after Likud came to power in 1977, and especially during the Lebanon war in 1982. Thus a writer in *The Times* of London during that war wrote of the moral decline he saw in Israel by comparing it with the days of Ben-Gurion. (This view of the matter happens to fit into the ancient grid through which the Christians have perceived the Jews: the Jews were once very holy, and are now very much not.)

The retrospectively idealized version of Ben-Gurion represents him as conciliatory in his approach to the Arab question – in sharp contrast to the approach of Begin's mentor, Vladimir Jabotinsky, Begin himself and the

Likud. Shabtai Teveth's valuable volume makes the contrast considerably less sharp than the idealized version does. In fact, the main difference between Ben-Gurion and Jabotinsky, in relation to the Palestinian Arabs, seems to have been that Jabotinsky was a lot more candid on the subject than Ben-Gurion (or Weizmann) judged it expedient to be. Jabotinsky himself was well aware of this. When, in 1936, a member of the Peel Commission suggested that Jabotinsky thought himself brainier than Ben-Gurion and Weizmann, Jabotinsky replied: 'It is a great question whether it requires more "brains" to be straightforward than not to be straightforward. It is a moot point, as I think you call it in English.'

In his earliest public statements on the Arab question, as in his later ones, Ben-Gurion stressed the prosperity and 'renewal' that the Zionist enterprise would bring to the Palestinian Arabs. His private thoughts – first recorded in the 'Omaha papers', notes made in 1916 during his American tour – were more complex. Shabtai Teveth writes:

> For although in his published articles Ben-Gurion denied any conflict between Arab and Jewish interests, he admitted secretly that 'yes, there is this certain measure of Arab opposition.' 'But this can't stop us. First, *we did not come here to expel the Arabs*,' but to build. This the Arabs 'must understand', for 'the Arabs themselves are incapable of such building.' Second, 'they don't have the power to expel us.' Here Ben-Gurion analyzed the reasons for Arab incompetence: 'The Arabs are not organized as a nation and they haven't one national party but many; some want to separate from Turkey while others are satisfied with things as they are, and believe that only tied to Turkey can they develop. But they have no national movement in our sense.' Once the Arabs understood that they were powerless to be rid of the Jews, 'then we can work together.'
>
> And if they refused? With this possibility in mind, Ben-Gurion advocated the reinforcement of the Yishuv with the volunteers of Hehalutz. In short, Ben-Gurion foresaw armed struggle between Jews and Arabs. 'It is possible to come to terms with the Arabs. This is a matter of strategy,' he wrote in his Omaha notes. And so it was just as possible, for tactical reasons, not to come to terms. In any event, this was a secondary question, since he believed that the attitude of the power ruling Palestine would determine all.

In the first years of the Mandate, Ben-Gurion believed – or at least toyed with the fancy – that the Palestine *fellahin* would become assimilated into the Jewish community, known as the Yishuv. (He believed the Palestinians to be at least partly of Jewish descent.) After the first outbreaks of Arab mob violence against Jews, in 1920 and again in 1921, the assimilation theory must have worn thin. Still, in public Ben-Gurion played down Arab hostility, and put all the blame for the outbreaks on the British authorities. As Teveth says:

> Ben-Gurion would have made a political calculation before settling on a public interpretation, with the welfare of the Yishuv in mind. Would he have chosen Jabotinsky's blunt approach, and declared that 'a voluntary settlement between us and the Arabs in Palestine is unthinkable, now and in the foreseeable future'? To posit an irreconcilable conflict in this manner would have harmed the prospects of the Yishuv, for it would have deepened Arab hatred and could have cost the Jews the sympathy of world public opinion. No one was prepared to impose the Jews on the Arabs by brute force with Wilsonian talk of self-determination in the air. Ben-Gurion rejected Jabotinsky's demand for an 'Iron Wall', that is, that only under the shield of an armed force could Zionism achieve its aim. In the event, and in the absence of a Jewish armed force, the British army would have to defend the Yishuv against implacable foes. But Ben-Gurion maintained that the land could not be won by reliance on others.
>
> 'The homeland cannot be given as a gift,' wrote Ben-Gurion. 'It cannot be purchased like a concession through political contracts, bought with gold, or seized by force. The land can be earned only by building, by the sweat of one's brow.' Ben-Gurion was not blind to what Jabotinsky saw; he already had written of the depth of Arab hatred for Zionism. But to reiterate this point and inscribe it as a principle of Zionist doctrine would have been pointless. He preferred a positive and beneficial tactic, one that burned no bridges and left open a chance for peace, however remote. It is difficult to establish Ben-Gurion's considerations with assurance, since his tactical denial of the real conflict had to be total to be convincing. In 1939, Ben-Gurion confessed that he often took positions on the Arab question for tactical reasons, and not out of conviction. This might well have been such an instance.

By 1922 Ben-Gurion is acknowledging, in his diary, the existence of 'an Arab national movement' waging 'a national war' against the Zionists. In November 1929, after the widespread acts of Arab violence in that year, Ben-Gurion made the same acknowledgment, in the form of a warning, to a gathering of members of his party: 'In a political sense, [the Arab movement] is a national movement.'

In the early 1930s Ben-Gurion thought that it might be possible to come to some kind of terms with this Arab national movement, perhaps on a 'cantonal' or 'federal' basis, by which he meant, substantially, partition. Negotiations in fact occurred between Ben-Gurion and Arab representatives in Geneva in September 1934, but they culminated in a stinging public rebuff by the Arabs to Ben-Gurion – whom they said they had met only in order 'to know the enemy'.

After that Ben-Gurion gave up on negotiations with the Arabs, as long as the Jews in Palestine remained in a minority:

> And so on April 16, 1936, Ben-Gurion informed Mapai that he had reached the conclusion that '. . . there is no chance for an understanding with the Arabs unless we first reach an understanding with the English, by which we will become a preponderant force in Palestine. What can drive the Arabs to a mutual understanding with us? . . . *Facts*. . . . Only after we manage to establish a *great Jewish fact* in this country . . . only then will the pre-condition for discussion with the Arabs be met.'

What Ben-Gurion had come to realize, after the total breakdown of the 1934 negotiations, was that there was no hope of Arab consent to unrestricted Jewish immigration. And once Hitler came to power in Germany, there was no way the leader of the Yishuv could accept restrictions on Jewish immigration to Palestine. As Ben-Gurion explained to Judah Magnes, the most ardent advocate of Arab-Jewish reconciliation:

> The difference between me and you is that you are ready to sacrifice immigration for peace, while I am not though peace is dear to me. And even if I was prepared to make a concession, the Jews of Poland and Germany would not be, because they have no other option. For them immigration comes before peace.

On this, Teveth comments:

> Zionism was no longer a movement of absolute justice; it was, Ben-Gurion now believed, a movement of relative justice. The tragedy of the Jews outweighed the minor dispossession of the Arabs, and to that extent, Zionism remained for Ben-Gurion a moral force. Thus, although Zionism was peace-loving, immigration still came before peace. This was a slogan of struggle, and henceforth, Zionism was to rely much more on the desperate situation of the Jews in Europe as a moral prop. Concern for justice for the Arabs diminished. Rights became functions of tragedies; the greater the tragedy, the greater the rights it conferred on its victims. Few but the Arabs doubted that the Jewish tragedy was the greater.

Ben-Gurion no longer hoped for any concrete results from talks with Arabs. All the same, he had three long talks with George Antonius, a prominent Arab intellectual and author of *The Arab Awakening*, in April 1936. 'Readiness for talks was a weapon Ben-Gurion could brandish in his campaign for the support of British public opinion,' Teveth writes. 'But from now on, there would be no more pursuit of compromise. The actual talking had come to an end.'

In a letter in November 1937 to Moshe Sharrett, Ben-Gurion showed his complete understanding of Arab resistance to Jewish immigration: 'Were I an Arab,' he wrote,

> . . . an Arab with nationalist political consciousness . . . I would rise up against an immigration liable sometime in the future to hand the country and all of its Arab inhabitants over to Jewish rule. What Arab cannot do his math and understand that immigration at the rate of 60,000 a year means a Jewish state in all of Palestine?

Finally in February 1938, with a greatly enlarged Yishuv behind him, Ben-Gurion, in a conversation with the British high commissioner, Harold MacMichael, could be as candid as Jabotinsky. 'Almost every Arab,' he said, opposed Zionism 'because he is an Arab, because he is a Muslim, because he dislikes foreigners, and because we are hateful to him in every way.'

In his epilogue, Teveth concludes:

> A careful comparison of Ben-Gurion's public and private positions leads inexorably to the conclusion that this twenty-year denial of the conflict was a calculated tactic, born of pragmatism rather than profundity of conviction. The idea that Jews and Arabs could reconcile their differences through class solidarity, a notion he championed between 1919 and 1929, was a delaying tactic. Once the Yishuv had gained strength, Ben-Gurion abandoned it. The belief in a compromise solution, which Ben-Gurion professed for the seven years between 1929 and 1936, was also a tactic, designed to win continued British support for Zionism. The only genuine convictions that underlay Ben-Gurion's approach to the Arab question were two: that the support of the power that ruled Palestine was more important to Zionism than any agreement with the Arabs, and that the Arabs would reconcile themselves to the Jewish presence only after they conceded their inability to destroy it.

Berl Katznelson became one of the leading members of the Second Aliyah, the critical wave of Jewish immigration to Palestine between 1904 and 1915, and his influence was strongly felt also by the members of the Third Aliyah (1919–1923). These were the immigrations that did most to shape the character of Israel. Katznelson, by inclination and personality, was one of the great character-moulders, though he later came to have some doubts about the nature of his achievement. He did much, along with Ben-Gurion, to shape the principal institutions of Labour Zionism – the political party Ahdut ha-Avoda, later Mapai, and the trade union the Histadrut. Through the Hebrew newspaper *Davar*, which he did most to found and which he personally controlled, and the Hebrew publishing house Am Oved, which he also founded and ran, he exercised a unique cultural influence over the Yishuv. Katznelson admired and generally followed Ben-Gurion, but he had little use either for Ben-Gurion's gestures in the direction of the Arabs or for his desire, at certain times, to impress the British. In fact Katznelson disliked Gentiles of all descriptions. 'No non-Jews', says Anita Shapira, 'ever entered his home.' He was inclined to sarcasm, which he used with effective restraint, and he applied this gift against Zionists in the Diaspora who argued for *rapprochement* with the Arabs. He described one proposal as 'the outcome of the uncomfortable situation of our comrades who often come into contact with the outside world and must explain our case there'.

Yet Katznelson liked and admired Chaim Weizmann, the greatest of the explainers to the outside world, whom he considered the foremost Zionist of his day. Still, he could have his little dig at Weizmann, too. At one meeting in 1936, comparing his own Zionist role with Weizmann's, he said:

> When a patient is gravely ill, they bring him a great professor and he does what he can. But by the professor's side stands a Jew, a poor relation, and he too does what he can – he recites Psalms. I have come to recite Psalms by the professor's side.

Katznelson and his *Davar* were, of course, in the thick of Labour's fight in the 1930s against Jabotinsky and his Revisionists. Katznelson compared Jabotinsky's loud candour and open demand for a Jewish state to 'a man walking through a forest full of bears, shouting at the top of his lungs, thereby attracting the attention of the predators'. (It was a remark that made Jabotinsky tear up his delegate's card and walk out of the meeting.) Yet Katznelson was to be the first Labour leader to follow Jabotinsky's example and call openly for a Jewish state. This was in December 1940 at a Zionist conference at Ayanot. Ben-Gurion did not formulate that demand publicly until nearly eighteen months later, at the famous Biltmore Conference of May 1942.

Both Jabotinsky and Katznelson had an exceptionally early and keen sense of the dimensions of the catastrophe impending in Europe. Indeed, Katznelson may well have acquired his sense of it from Jabotinsky, with whom he had several long and painful meetings in London in late August 1939, just after the conclusion of the German-Soviet Pact. Katznelson reported on these conversations to Mapai's Central Committee on 21 September 1939. In their last conversation, as Katznelson recalled it, Jabotinsky had said, sadly and bitterly: 'You have won. You have America, the rich Jews. I had only poor Polish Jewry, and now it is gone. I have lost the game.'

A little more than a year later – at the same conference at which he called, like Jabotinsky, for a Jewish state – Katznelson spoke of European Jewry, as Jabotinsky (now dead) had, as already condemned to death:

'The essence of Zionist awareness must be that what existed in Vienna – will never return, what existed in Berlin will never return, nor in Prague, and what we had in Warsaw and Lodz – is finished, and we must realize this! . . .

'And I declare,' he reiterated with great emphasis, 'that the fate of European Jewry is sealed, not because I wish it to be so, but because cruel destiny has so determined.'

In the last years Katznelson suffered intensely, not only because of what was happening to the Jews in Europe, but because of the failure of young Jews in Palestine to identify with European Jews. Am Oved had published a series of 'Letters from the Ghetto', but the book was not in demand. 'I do not think', wrote Katznelson in June 1944, 'that these terrible events, which we are all consciously aware of, are being experienced on the personal level, as part of our own destiny.' Anita Shapira adds:

Berl did not absolve himself of responsibility for this alienation. As the mentor of the movement, who had left his indelible stamp on its consciousness through lectures, seminars and talks, he had shared in creating it. The denial of the Diaspora, which implied, on the one hand, rejection of the Jewish way of life in the Diaspora, and, on the other, denial of the possibility of the continued existence of the Jewish people there, was one of the underlying tenets of Zionism. It had, however, been interpreted by both teachers and students as a rejection of the *Jewish people* in the Diaspora, thus inevitably enhancing the specific value of the new tribe growing up in Palestine. This had not been the intention of the Second Aliyah teachers. In their revolt against their own past, their home towns and villages had appeared to them as the epitome of ugliness and degradation. They were well aware, however, that this was not the whole truth, and even while attacking their own background, they had remained inextricably bound to it, and through it to the fabric of Jewish life. The young generation in Palestine did not regard their origins in the same fashion. Their associations lacked the existential dimension, absorbed with mother's milk, with Sabbath and festival rituals, with the dread of pogroms, with the grief which followed in their wake. For them, identification was an intellectual process, in the course of which the Jewish people was weighed and found wanting. For the young the Diaspora was everything against which their parents had rebelled. The denial of the Diaspora in Berl's generation implied the duty to rescue the Jewish people; for young people bred in Palestine it meant the severing of the link binding them to the Jewish people and to Jewish history. In his twilight years Berl witnessed the utter failure of the education of 'the children of Zionism'. The estrangement between the new Jewish people in

Palestine and the suffering Jewish people elsewhere was a constant reminder to him of his own failure.

It may well be that here, too, in Katznelson's sense of failure concerning 'the children of Zionism', there is a reflection of those last conversations with Jabotinsky. Jabotinsky had accused Mapai of indifference to the plight of the Jewish masses in Europe. 'For me,' he had told Katznelson, 'Zionism is the concern of those Jews who are not in Palestine.'

These books are works of lucid, honest scholarship. Their combined effect is bleak. We are very far here from the sugar versions of the Zionist pioneers as some kind of all-purpose 'idealists'. Weizmann, Ben-Gurion, and Katznelson were indeed all idealists, but they were not all-purpose idealists. Their ideal was a Zionist ideal (somewhat differently conceived by each one) to which they dedicated their whole lives. To that ideal, however, they were prepared to subordinate other ideals, if they found them to be in conflict. All three were Russian Jews who grew up under an anti-Semitic regime. They all lived to see an unimaginably intensified anti-Semitism explode throughout Europe and engulf the European Jews. And they were all conscious of the fact that the environment in which most of the survivors among the Jews of the Old World lived – in the Middle East and especially in Palestine – had become no less hostile to the Jews and their state than the Russia in which they were born had been to the Jews in the ghetto. They lived all their mature lives with the consciousness of being among the leaders of besieged people. And they developed qualities appropriate to the leaders of besieged people: extreme alertness, intellectual lucidity, pragmatism, resourcefulness (including reliance, where necessary, on ruse), and a concentrated will toward collective survival.

They were well aware, of course, that those who besieged the Jews in the Middle East had done nothing to create the predicament, and finally the horror, which had brought the Jews to the Middle East in the nineteenth and twentieth centuries. Europeans, not Arabs, had done all that. But what to do with the awareness that that was so? Take it back to Europe, where it belongs, was essentially the Arab answer. But neither these men, nor those whom they led, were prepared to do that. Nor were they prepared to dismantle the Jewish state, the need for which they felt had been proved for all time by the Nazis.

The demand that the Jewish state be dismantled is still at the top of the agenda of most Palestinian Arabs, and of most other Arabs. Thus the work of Weizmann, of Ben-Gurion, of Katznelson, of all the others who gathered at the call of the author of *Der Judenstaat*, is subject to a challenge over which compromise is not possible. The Jewish state will either be or not be. These books leave me with an enhanced sense of the harshness of the Zionist predicament, and of the extra measure of hardness in certain characters moulded by that predicament. They also leave me with even less faith than before in the possibility of the kind of comprehensive Arab-Israeli settlement for which so many Western politicians and publicists call, which, when stripped down to its essentials, requires a negotiated agreement between people who are committed to the preservation of the Jewish state and people who are committed to its destruction.

The Fall of Africa*

THE TITLE OF MARTIN MEREDITH'S BOOK is taken from one of Lord Byron's *Detached Thoughts* of 1821–22. 'I sometimes wish I was the Owner of Africa; to do at once what Wilberforce will do in time, viz – sweep Slavery from her desarts, and look on upon the first dance of their Freedom.' When Byron wrote, of course, most of black Africa was, in a sense, 'free': that is, it was not – with the exception of fairly small coastal enclaves – ruled by powers from outside the continent. Most of Africa between the Sahara and the Cape was under the control of indigenous despotisms. Very much as now, in fact, except that the boundaries of the new despotisms are those established in the colonial period, less than a hundred years ago and more than sixty years after Byron wrote those words.

Byron was not thinking of freedom in the modern sense of national independence – what 'nations' in Africa, then? He was talking about going in there, to free slaves: 'I sometimes wish I was the Owner of Africa. . . .' The poet, in fact, was already in the grip of one of the urges that went into the making of colonialism: the urge to go in there and clean the place up, for the benefit of its unfortunate people.

Mr Meredith, as is his privilege, is using the poet's words in a sense that the poet could not have intended. Mr Meredith's point is that the 'dance of freedom' – in the sovereign independence of African states – has turned out to be, on the whole, a macabre fiasco. The last paragraph in his book runs:

> The predictions made in the 1980s about Africa's future were increasingly gloomy. No solution to its myriad problems seemed available. Experts like the French agronomist René Dumont spoke only in pessimistic terms: 'Most of the countries of tropical Africa, with one or two exceptions, are up to their ears in debt, without any hope of ever being able to repay what they owe,' he said. 'Twenty years after independence these countries are in reality bankrupt,

* Article on *The First Dance of Freedom: Black Africa in the Post-War Era*, Martin Meredith, Harper and Row, in *The New Republic*, 18 March 1985.

reduced to a state of permanent beggary.' The World Bank noted in a 1983 report that despite billions of dollars of international aid poured into Africa, the region faced 'a deepening crisis'. A study published by the Economic Commission for Africa in 1983, attempting to look twenty-five years ahead, made particularly chilling reading. It predicted that on existing trends poverty in rural areas would reach 'unimaginable dimensions', while the towns would suffer increasingly from crime and destitution. 'The picture that emerges', it said, 'is almost a nightmare.'

Mr Meredith is a reporter with long experience of post-independence Africa. He writes without polemical intent, and I think that, like several others who write about Africa, he would wish that things were different from what he has to report that they are. Where there is a bright side, he gladly acknowledges it.

The advances that Africa made in those circumstances were remarkable. In the two decades between 1960 and 1980, school enrolment grew faster in Africa than in any other developing region. At primary level, enrolment increased from thirty-six per cent to sixty-three per cent of the age group; at secondary level, it increased from three to thirteen per cent; universities produced thousands of graduates each year. A World Bank study published in 1981 observed: 'The African record is unique; nowhere else has a formal education system been created on so broad a scale in so short a time.' In the field of medical care, similar improvements were recorded. Child death rates fell from thirty-eight to twenty-five per thousand; life expectancy increased from thirty-nine to forty-seven years; the numbers of medical and nursing personnel per capita doubled, despite a large increase in the population. New infrastructures were built at record-breaking pace: ports, railways, roads and buildings. The number of miles covered by all-weather roads tripled, opening up vast areas of the interior for the first time.

But the darkness surrounding these bright patches is awesome:

Despite these achievements, the magnitude of the problems facing Africa proved overwhelming. Economic growth in much of the continent was slow. In the first two decades, per capita income in nineteen countries increased by less than one per cent a year; in the 1970s it actually fell in fifteen countries. Output per person rose more slowly than in any other part of the world. In many countries agricultural production declined sharply, making them dependent on foreign food supplies. The population meanwhile expanded at one of the fastest rates in the world. As African governments embarked on one development project after another, they accumulated huge and unmanage-able debts. During the 1970s many were beset by severe economic crises, threatening to undermine what progress had been made. Hospitals and clinics ran short of medicines; schools lacked textbooks; factories closed through lack of raw materials or spare parts for machinery. Even when the accomplishments were taken into account, Africa remained perilously far behind other areas of the world. Life expectancy was by far the lowest of any region in the world, still twenty-seven years shorter than in industrialized countries and less than in any other developing region. The African child death rate in 1980 was sixty-seven per cent greater than in South Asia, three times higher than in Latin America, and twenty-five times higher than in the developed world. The African population was more exposed to endemic diseases like malaria and to other diseases stemming from poor sanitation, malnutrition and poverty. In the field of education, the advances made were still limited: in about one third of African countries, less than half of the child population received primary education; in only six countries were more than twenty per cent of the age group in secondary school.

On the whole (there are exceptions) the failure of the polities has matched the failure of the economies; and the twin failures merge. Ghana, the most advanced of all the territories of colonial Africa, and the first to gain its independence, is today in economic ruin, apprehensively and incompetently guarded by a puritanical military dictatorship. And Ghana has been lucky, compared with some. Everyone knows about the horrors of Idi Amin's Uganda. What is less well known is that the people of Uganda are just as terrorized now as they were in his day. The only difference is that whereas terror in Amin's day was a centralized institution, terror today is dispersed, meted out by various bands of armed brigands, in or out of government uniform.

The continent is crawling with dictators, sane and insane. Hastings Banda in Malawi: 'Anything I say is law. Literally law. It is a fact in this country.' Jean-Bedel Bokassa, in 1977, declared an empire in the Central African Republic,

and himself Emperor of its two million subjects. The following year, using as a model the ceremony in which Napoleon had crowned himself Emperor of France in 1804, he arranged for his own coronation. No expense was spared. From France, Bokassa ordered all the trappings of monarchy: a crown of diamonds, rubies and emeralds; an imperial throne, fifteen feet high, shaped like a golden eagle; thoroughbred horses; carriages; coronation robes; brass helmets and breastplates for the imperial Guard; and tons of food, wine, fireworks and flowers for the festivities. To the strains of Mozart and Beethoven, mixed with the throb of tribal drums, Bokassa duly crowned himself Emperor in Bangui's sports stadium on the mosquito-infested banks of the Oubangui river. The cost, amounting to $22 million, was nearly equivalent to one quarter of the entire national revenue for the previous year.

Malawi and the Central African Republic (or Empire) are small and poor states, but big, rich ones have not always been more fortunate in their rulers. Joseph-Désiré Mobutu in Zaire (the former Belgian Congo):

> In time, Mobutu accumulated vast personal power, appropriating at will government revenues, deciding on all appointments and promotions and ruling by decree. The personality cult which surrounded him became all-pervasive. He assumed grand titles like 'Guide' and 'Messiah'. His deeds were endlessly praised in songs and dances; officials took to wearing lapel badges with his miniature portrait. The television news was preceded by the image of the president descending, as it were, through the clouds from heaven.

The failure of the polities and the failure of the economies are linked, partly because of the crippling cost of megalomania and arbitrary power, but also because, even in relatively benign cases, the political class helps itself to a wildly disproportionate share of the national income. René Dumont – who was the first to diagnose, back in the early 1960s, that 'black Africa is off to a bad start' – has written about the political superstructure of the small Francophone of the West African state of Gabon (once the abode of Albert Schweitzer):

> As for the cost of the Gabonese presidency, parliament and ministers, with all their supposedly useful trips, it probably represents, in relation to the national income of the country, more than the cost to France of the court of Louis XVI in 1788.

Unfortunately in Africa such conditions have generated not social revolutions but military coups, which generally (though not always) make no difference, except that there are more uniforms around on those expensive state occsions.

Mr Meredith thinks that it also makes no difference whether the state chooses a capitalist road or a socialist road or any other ideological road. He writes:

> What was so striking about Africa's plight was its universality. Whatever economic and political system was devised, whatever ideology was chosen, the same pattern of economic crisis developed.

I dissent from this view, and I can find a good deal of support for my dissent in the pages of Mr Meredith's book. Not all the capitalist African states have been successful, but all the (relatively) successful states have been capitalist. 'African socialism' has no success stories to tell. I say this not because I wish to make a fashionable Reaganite point, but simply because it is true, and important.

Mr Meredith tells of a meeting at Abidjan in April 1957 between Ghana's Kwame Nkrumah, then in the pristine glory of the presidency of the first of the newly independent African states, and Félix Houphouet-Boigny, the leading politician of the neighbouring Ivory Coast. Nkrumah was a proud African socialist, already dreaming of a united socialist Africa under his leadership. Houphouet-Boigny was a cautious politician committed to co-operation with France; his Ivory Coast became independent, in association with France, three years later. As Mr Meredith tells the story of that meeting between the two West African leaders in the dawning period of African independence:

> Houphouet feigned indifference to Ghana's independence, predicting that in ten years the Ivory Coast, with the assistance of France, would have surpassed its neighbour Ghana in economic and social progress. Between them a wager was made to see who turned out to be right. 'You are witnessing the start of two experiments,' Houphouet told his compatriots.

Although Mr Meredith refrains (oddly) from acknowledging the fact, Houphouet won that wager hands down. The Ivory Coast and its neighbour Ghana started out more or less level, around 1960, but the Ivory Coast is now the most flourishing economy in tropical Africa. As Mr Meredith records:

> In the 1950s, the Ivory Coast produced a single crop, coffee. The government encouraged diversification, guaranteed profitable prices for major cash crops, provided extension services and a marketing organization. Private enterprise was given free rein. New crops were developed under the direction of parastatal companies. Between 1960 and 1980 agricultural production tripled. The Ivory Coast overtook Ghana as the world's largest producer of cocoa; it became Africa's largest exporter of coffee and a major exporter of pineapple, bananas, palm oil and hardwood; and at the same time it managed to increase food production at a higher rate than population growth.

Mr Meredith's index entry under 'Ghana' provides a succinct guide to the progress of the rival 'experiment'.

Ghana
    collapse of cocoa production, 1965–79, 356;
    history: name chosen for old Gold Coast colony, 91; independence achieved, 1957, 93; economic and political strength on day of independence, 94; comes under Nkrumah's dictatorship, 188; ruinous industrialization of, 189–90; financial confusion, 190–1; decline of agriculture, 191; corruption under Nkrumah, 191–2; fall in living standards by 1963, 192; political confusion, 192–3; made one-party state, 1964, 194; university purge, 1964,

Guinea, the Francophone West African state whose leader, Sekou Touré, chose Nkrumah's way, rather than Houphouet's, also ended up in economic ruin, amid socialist and anti-colonialist rhetoric.

In general, the socialism of African states turns out, in any particular case, to be either a racket or a façade. Let me consider, a little more closely, one case of the 'racket' variety – Nkrumah's Ghana – and one of the 'façade' variety – Nyerere's Tanzania.

I lived for three years (1962–65) in Nkrumah's Ghana, where I was vice chancellor of the University at Legon, near Accra. Nkrumah invited me to take the job, and I accepted, once I found that the faculty of the university – both Ghanaian and foreign – also wanted me to take the job. I found Nkrumah's anti-colonialist record not unsympathetic at the time I went to Ghana, partly because I had just recently been politically clobbered by certain colonialists while I was on a UN mission in Katanga, Congo (which was mainly why Nkrumah had invited me). I was not particularly starry-eyed about Nkrumah; I expected him to be a despot, but thought he would be a fairly enlightened one. I was sceptical about Ghanaian socialism, but I did expect Nkrumah to be serious about trying to make it work, for the benefit of his people. What I found was different.

The first state occasion I attended in Ghana was the annual opening of parliament by Nkrumah. It was an imposing spectacle: the full panoply of Westminster, plus certain ceremonies associated with the formal appearances of the great chiefs of the Twi-speaking peoples. The parliamentary benches were lined with the members of Nkrumah's Convention People's Party, fat men all wearing the *kente*, the multicoloured toga traditionally worn by Ashanti and Fanti of status.

Nkrumah read a prepared speech. Most of it was about Africa at large, but at one point he did get down to Ghanaian specifics. Ghanaians, he said, were not allowed to hold funds deposited in banks abroad. He said he knew that even certain members of parliament had infringed this rule. Still, he offered an amnesty to all who would repatriate their foreign currency holdings by a certain date. Those who continued to hold moneys on deposit abroad after that date would be severely penalized.

Throughout this entire passage of their president's speech, his entire parliament rocked with laughter. They found the bit about the amnesty and the bit about the penalties equally hilarious. And as the parliament laughed, the president was smiling.

As we left the parliament building, I asked Alex Kwapong, my Ghanaian colleague and deputy at the university (later my successor, always my friend), what all that meant. He smiled and said: 'If you stick around with us here for a while, you'll find out exactly what it means.' And so I did. I found out, for example, what Ghana's gigantic Development Programme meant. A senior Ghanaian civil servant told me why he was leaving.

> The Farmers Co-operative wanted currency and clearance to import 24 more tractors. I wanted to know just what use they had made of the last 24 tractors they imported. They wouldn't tell me, so on a hunch I went down to the harbour at Tema and found all 24 of them, rusting in the rain with their tyres flat.
>
> So I went to Nkrumah and told him about it. Nkrumah appeared to be shocked. He sent for the chairman of the Farmers Co-operative. I told my story in the presence of the two of them, and Nkrumah said to the chairman: 'How do you explain this, Joe?'
>
> At that, Joe went on his knees in front of Nkrumah, and clutched Nkrumah's knees. He said: 'Osagyefo' – Nkrumah's title – 'if I ever let you down, you may hang me in the public square. Hang me in the public square!' Nkrumah lifted him up and embraced him, and that was that.

Of course there is corruption in every state, and in every form of society. But Nkrumah's state was one huge rip-off. Note also that graft disguised as development is many times more expensive than just plain graft. Joe the socialist farm-boss was interested in his 10 per cent cut on every tractor imported. But the people of Ghana had to pay for ten times that cut, in the shape of tractors paid for but not used. Meanwhile favourable commentators from foreign parts cited the tractor-import statistics, one index of Ghana's dynamic expanding socialist economy.

I attended two more of Nkrumah's annual openings of parliament. Each of them contained the same homily about moneys deposited abroad, and each time it was greeted with the same laughter, followed by the same smile on the part of the homilist. The third such occasion for me – in 1965 – was also the last for Nkrumah. He was ousted by military coup in February 1966. But Ghana has never made good the damage his regime inflicted on it. The main damage was not the direct cost of the waste, the reckless running down of the currency reserves. The main damage was the destruction of the most valuable part of Ghana's inheritance from the colonial days: its honest and competent civil service, the best in tropical Africa. But the honest and competent administrators had to be shoved aside, because they stood between Nkrumah's socialist cronies and the loot.

African-socialism-as-racket I came to know quite intimately, in my three years in Nkrumah's Ghana. African-socialism-as-façade I knew only from the outside (appropriately, in a way). I met Julius Nyerere during my Ghana days – I was representing the University of Ghana in Nairobi, at one of those mirage-like occasions so frequent in the history of post-colonial Africa. This was the opening ceremony of the supposed University of East Africa, a concept that was related to the alleged Federation of East Africa, consisting of Kenya, Tanzania and Uganda. The EAF was a phantom milestone on the road to the ultimate and most dazzling of all the mirages: African Unity.

At the UEA dinner I found myself seated beside Nyerere. I think he had asked me to be put there because he wanted to pump me about the Congo, which he did. I found him very pleasant company. His charm of manner is well known. Kwame Nkrumah could be charming too, when he wanted to; but there was always a touch of godlike condescension in Nkrumah's charm. Nyerere, on the other hand, was down-to-earth and unassuming, talking like one human being to another. I found this a refreshing change, and wished I had had Julius to work with, instead of Kwame.

In later years, when I visited Tanzania, I was impressed by the modesty of Nyerere's lifestyle, by the absence of palaces and other evidence of conspicuous consumption. I also heard much talk of Tanzanian socialism and the principle of *ujemaa*, 'self-reliance'. The cornerstone of the whole system, it seemed, was the *ujemaa* village: putatively a vaguely kibbutz-like affair, a matter of building and being built. On my last visit to Tanzania, at the end of the 1970s, I made an effort to see some *ujemaa* villages. I had come to Dar-es-Salaam to interview Nyerere about Rhodesia (then in one of the crises of its mutation into Zimbabwe). Nyerere was travelling at the time, so I had a few days with time on my hands. I told Nyerere's secretary – a European woman – that I would like to see some *ujemaa* villages. I had assumed this would be a welcome request, but it wasn't. 'What do you want to see *ujemaa* villages for?' she asked, with something like loathing in her voice. I said I understood these were the cornerstone of Tanzania's self-reliance development programme. She made an appointment for me to see the minister for information.

Even though one of the main tasks of the minister for information was telling the world about *ujemaa* villages, he didn't seem too happy at finding himself face to face with someone anxious to look at some of these inspiring collectivities. He asked me how long I would be in Tanzania. I told him four or five days. 'Then it is quite impossible. You know, you can't just go and *see* an *ujemaa* village. You have to give us time to, well time to organize some kind of manifestation.' Even the famous Potemkin, Catherine the Great's equivalent of a minister for information, needed a little time before he could provide those idyllic 'Potemkin Villages' that so edified the more trusting of the visitors to the czarina's dominions.

Ujemaa may be a bit of a joke, but at least – unlike Nkrumah's socialism – it is a harmless joke. The illusions it generates are even helpful, to some extent. Paradoxically, 'self-reliance' is a great begetter of foreign aid. Mr Meredith is very good on this.

> Much was achieved during Tanzania's independence, notably in the field of education, health and social services. Between 1960 and 1980, primary school enrolment increased from one quarter of the school-age population to ninety-five per cent; adult literacy grew from ten percent to seventy-five per cent; four in ten villages were provided with clean tap water, three in ten had clinics; life expectancy increased from 41 years to 51 years; only half as many children – 18 in 100 – died before the age of four. Yet what progress was made was financed largely by foreign aid. During the 1970s, Tanzania received no less than $3 billion, mostly from the West. The level of aid increased from $10 million in 1967 to $600 million in 1982, when as much as two thirds of the development budget was derived from foreign funds and grants. Nyerere's achievement, therefore, was related not to the success of his strategy for improving the economic and social welfare of his countrymen, but to his ability to persuade foreign sponsors that his objectives were sincere.

Socialism, real or imaginary, is something exotic in Africa; a fad of Westernized élites. The market, on the other hand, is indigenous, and readily comprehensible. Those regimes that interfere least with the market are those that are least alien to those over whom they rule. Houphouet was supposed to be the stooge of a foreign power; Nkrumah the proud, free African. Yet Houphouet made more sense to the people of the Ivory Coast than Nkrumah did to the people of Ghana. That is how Houphouet won his bet.

States of the Union*

MRS THATCHER DESCRIBES HERSELF AS A UNIONIST, and there is no reason to doubt her sincerity. Yet she has probably done more than any previous Prime Minister to undermine the Union. Both Northern Ireland and Scotland are now less securely attached to the Union than they were when Mrs Thatcher first took office. And in both cases, the weakening of the attachment has been due mainly to Mrs Thatcher's policies and – no less important – Mrs Thatcher's personality and style.

In Northern Ireland, there is probably not a single person who feels happy with the province's relation to the rest of the United Kingdom. Catholics never *did* feel happy with it, though they seem mostly to have felt less *un*happy than some of their propaganda suggested. The Hillsborough Agreement was sold, very successfully, in Dublin, London, Washington and elsewhere as something which would end the 'alienation' of the Catholics. In what exactly this 'alienation' consisted was never precisely spelled out. There were good political reasons for that. In Britain, the impression given was that what would be ended would be Catholic alienation *from the United Kingdom*. But that way of looking at things could not be sold in Dublin or in Derry. Catholics are *nationalists* – interchangeable terms in ordinary speech. Being alienated from inclusion in the United Kingdom is an essential part of the nationalist heritage (even in its moderate forms). So the alienation – as understood in Derry and Dublin – will remain as long as the United Kingdom of Great Britain and Northern Ireland exists. The Anglo-Irish Agreement tends to 'end alienation' only in the sense that it tends towards the political conclusion that can alone end the alienation of nationalists: the dissolution of the United Kingdom of Great Britain and Northern Ireland.

Looked at from London, the Hillsborough Agreement is supposed to be a Unionist document. Looked at from Dublin and Derry it represents a

* From *The Times*, 28 July 1986.

subtle, gradualist and effective way of moving in an anti-Unionist direction.

As often happens, Catholics and Protestants (Nationalists, Unionists) in Ireland understand what is going on in precisely the same way, while entertaining radically conflicting feelings about the events. As the most candid of Zionists, Vladimir Jabotinsky, used to say about relations between Jews and Arabs: '*There is no misunderstanding.*' In Northern Ireland, both sides understand that the Nationalists have stolen a march on the Unionists. So the Hillsborough Agreement, without ending the alienation of Catholics, has trebled the general level of alienation by poisoning the Union for the Protestants, the only people in the Province who have ever been attached to the Union. (The idea, now quite prevalent, that Protestants are becoming reconciled to the Agreement, is mistaken. They are simply trying new tactics for getting rid of it.)

Visiting Scotland this month, I found that the word 'alienation' is hanging in the air there also. The *Glasgow Herald* – an excellent and hardly an extremist organ of opinion – has been warning of the danger of 'permanent alienation'. As the paper said editorially: 'The Government is perceived as Southern English rather than British.'

This sense that many Scots now have almost of observing a foreign power at work is quite new. It arises from the hostility expressed at the highest levels of the Government to the very idea of the Scottish interest as a legitimate concept.

Privately, Scottish people put all this more bluntly, and more personally. It is *Mrs Thatcher* who is getting Scotland's goat. Mrs Thatcher comes across, especially on television, as intensely bossy and at the same time intensely English: a combination guaranteed to set Scottish teeth on edge.

In the nineteenth century heyday of the United Kingdom of Great Britain and Ireland, the phrase, 'the predominant partner' was much in use, and went down quite well in the Home Counties. I don't recall seeing or hearing that particular phrase recently, but Margaret Thatcher, on television, appears as the predominant partner, in the flesh.

There are *some* significant differences here betewen Northern Irish and Scottish forms of alienation. In Ireland, the distinction between 'British' and 'English' has never seemed particularly important, so that Margaret Thatcher's quintessential Englishness does not markedly affect reactions to her. Nor does her bossiness, in itself. What has mattered is the distribution of her bossiness; Lenin's 'who, Whom'? When she was letting hunger-strikers die, Protestants praised her 'firmness', while Catholics deplored her 'intransigence'. When she holds to the Anglo-Irish Agreement, the ethnic epithets are reversed. In neither case did it matter much that Mrs Thatcher is distinctively English.

But in Scotland, that does matter, because Britishness matters, and the idea of partnership, in making up the United Kingdom. Of course, Britishness matters to Ulster Protestants, too, but as a way of not being Irish, not as a way of not being English. Indeed, I think Ulster Protestants *used* to like Margaret Thatcher all the better for being so very English, since being so very English is such a thoroughgoing way of not being Irish. All the greater the pain, therefore, and the incomprehension, when the English-woman pulled the rug from under their version of 'Ulster is British'.

Whatever else Ulster is, it is not English, as the English can plainly see, especially in the month of July. And what Scotland has most in common with Protestant Ulster is a feeling that something has gone badly wrong with common Britishness, and with the Union. The United Kingdom has turned into England plus its subject provinces.

Of course, it was always like that, to a great extent, in reality. But the harsh, utilitarian light of Thatcherism makes the contrast between England – especially Southern England – and the dependencies stand out more starkly than ever. This is of special importance in relation to the union of England and Scotland. The workings of that Union have been lubricated by romanticism, for more than a hundred and fifty years now. The key note was set, very deliberately and successfully, by the Wizard of the North himself, in that brilliant pageant of tartanry, the Scottish version of Pastoral, which he designed for George IV's visit to Edinburgh in 1822. Scottish nationalists have never forgiven Walter Scott for that one, and rightly so from their point of view. Scott, and the many who followed him along that line, over the generations, helped fellow-Scots to feel that the Union did really and truly belong to them, and that their share in it was respected by their partner.

Now, Margaret Thatcher has no more use for that sort of stuff than a Marxist has for a feudal vestige. Indeed I suspect that she regards Scotland and all its peculiar institutions as one big complex of feudal vestiges.

Of all the great Victorians, Karl Marx is the one who would have liked Margaret Thatcher best. Marx was always looking for bourgeois who would really *be* bourgeois, and get on with *their* revolution, so preparing the way for *his*. But the bourgeois of his day were wets, all dripping with respect for tradition and other characteristics inappropriate to their class. Margaret Thatcher, though, is different.

What Marx would have liked most about England's Thatcherite revolution of the 1980s is the sharpening of social contradictions that accompanies it, and the appetizing smell of political disintegration now proceeding from the northern parts of the United Kingdom. And enemies of the United Kingdom, in those northern parts, tend to agree with that Marxist analysis, believing that Thatcherism is doing their work for them.

Perhaps – as the intrepid little band of Scottish Thatcherites believes – Mrs Thatcher can convince Scotland that Thatcherism is good, not only for the Home Counties, but for Scotland as well. She has announced that she will now be devoting special attention to the inner cities, as well as to Scotland. Some Scots seem to think that she referred to 'the inner cities, especially Scotland', but this is unfounded.

It doesn't follow, however, that the more attention Mrs Thatcher pays to Scotland, the better Scotland will like Mrs Thatcher and the Union. It is at least equally possible that the more attention Mrs Thatcher pays to Scotland, the more the Scots will feel that the Union means being pushed around everlastingly by a bossy Englishwoman.

Just before the election, I got a whiff of how unpopular Mrs Thatcher is in Scotland. I was following Mr David Steel around the more Liberal parts of Scotland in his 'Battlebus'. The day before, Mr Steel had first said that he would not serve under Mrs Thatcher; then, under pressure from Dr David Owen, he had indicated that he might, after all, serve under Mrs Thatcher. Mr Steel was now questioned about this. Everywhere that battlebus stopped little knots of people gathered round Mr Steel, to make plain that they liked his first answer a lot better than his second. They weren't aggressive about this, but – something more frightening to a politician – they showed in a cold, flinty way that their votes depended on the right answer. After about an hour of this treatment, Mr Steel dropped his second answer, and Dr Owen along with it. 'No', said Mr Steel. 'I will *not* serve under Mrs Thatcher.' After that, the going got much easier.

I think many Scots voted for Labour because they thought that Labour – or some combination of Labour and Alliance – had the best chance of putting Mrs Thatcher out. If it becomes apparent that Labour has no chance of putting Mrs Thatcher out, then Scottish support for Labour is likely to wilt, and Scottish nationalism likely to declare itself in more overt and uncompromising forms.

The Government's official view is, of course, that Scottish nationalism is of no significance, since Scotland voted overwhelmingly for 'a British party'. This is a good lawyer's debating point, but liable to lack political staying-power. If you vote for a British party, and find that it never wins, you may perhaps go on voting for it regardless, or you may switch sides, within British politics. Or you may decide that, since you are on a permanent loser, within the Union, you might do better to set up on your own. There is at present a trend in that direction. And that trend is likely to accelerate sharply, if the British Government really tries to collect poll tax (community charge) in Scotland.

It remains true that people in Northern Ireland – among both sets – are far more bitterly alienated from Thatcherite England than Scotland is. All the same, Scotland may be nearer to going it alone (via, initially, a devolved Assembly) than Northern Ireland is. For the hard fact, known to every adult in Northern Ireland, is that Northern Ireland cannot go it alone and stay in one piece. Northern Ireland is in a state of latent civil war; 'independent Northern Ireland' would be in a state of *real* civil war. There may come a time when Ulster Protestants, goaded by the combined attentions of Dublin, London and the IRA, will decide to run even that risk. But for the present it seems to be a case of sticking to nurse, for fear of finding something worse. Even if nurse's name is Margaret Thatcher.

The Scots talk much of the divisions within their society but those divisions, real though they are, are nothing like the Northern Irish kind. A Scottish Assembly, which most of Scotland's elected representatives say they want – might indeed move in the direction of independence – which over thirty per cent of Scots tell pollsters they want. But an independent Scotland, within the EEC might, in certain circumstances appear less scary to middle-class Scots, than a Scotland in the throes of anti-Thatcherite resentment. And the choice may boil down to that, if present trends continue.

Index

Index

Index

Mandela, Nelson 127, 136, 150
Mandela, Winnie 129, 180
Mannheim 213
Mannin, Ethel 43, 46, 52, 60n, 61n
Mapai *see* Labour Alignment party, Israel
March on Rome 33, 41
Marie Antoinette, Queen of France 62
Mark (South African) 127–9
Markiewicz, Countess Constance 8, 34–5, 52, 55n
Marriage of Figaro, The (Beaumarchais) 66
Marx, Karl 65, 66, 67, 136, 279
Marxism: Orwell on 18–19; and Nicaragua 90–1, 92–3, 111, 113–4; and Poland 90–1; and Pope John Paul II 77, 78; and press 239; and South Africa 126, 158, 168; and Thatcher 279–80; and Yeats 18–19, 54
Mary, Virgin 78–9
Maryknoll Order 95, 101
Massu, General Jacques 163, 164, 168
Matanzima, Kaiser 148
Mauriac, François 19
Mavusu, John 156
Mayorga, Silvio 112
Mazzini, Giuseppe 194
Medellin 88–9
Meese, Edwin 234
Melville, Herman 136
Mercier, Dr Vivan 42
Meredith, Martin 268–72, 268n
Merwe, Dr Piet van der 130
Metternich, Prince Clemens 254
Mexico 86
Meyer, Dr P. J. 145, 146
Meynier, Albert 72n
Miami 86
Michelet, Jules 72
Middle East 242–3, 245, 266
Miller, David W. 222
Mobutu, Joseph-Désiré 271
Modern Philosophy 54n, 60n
Moloise, Benjamin 129
Montesquieu, Baron Charles de 71
Moodley, Cogila 189
Moran, D. P. 196
Morgenthau 213
Morris, William 19
Motlana, Dr Nthato 156
'Mourn and then Onward' (Yeats) 15, 16
Moynihan, Senator Daniel Patrick 201, 234
Mozambique 159

Mugabe, Robert 153, 156, 158, 168
Munster Bank, Cork 57n
Murphy, Richard 226
Murphy, William Martin 21–7, 35, 56n, 57n
Mussolini, Benito 33, 42, 51, 58n, 59n
Muzorewa, Bishop Abel 155–6

Nairobi 275
Namibia 159, 160
Napoleon I, Emperor of France 193, 270
Nasser, Gamal Abdel 246
Natal 156, 157
Nation, The 58n, 59n
National Guard, Ireland (*see* Blueshirts, Nicaragua) 110
National League, Ireland 26
National Literary Society, Ireland 16
National Party, South Africa 5, 122–4, 136, 137, 138, 143, 148, 150–1, 153, 154, 157
National Press Club, Washington 122
Nationalists, Irish 278
Naudé, Dr Beyers 138
Nazism, 2, 43, 53, 124, 143, 145, 163–4, 171, 225
'Nervous Mideast Moment' 226
Netanyahu, Benjamin 234, 235
Netanyahu, Jonathan 234
New Republic 169
New Republic Party (formerly United Party), South Africa 137
New School for Social Research, New York 213
New York 130
New York Review, The 213
Newlands 173–4
Newry-Armagh 207
Newsweek 81
Nicaragua 3, 80–121, 231, 233, 235; Catholic Hierarchy 80, 82, 85, 92, 103, 105, 106, 107; Episcopal Conference 82, Episcopate 84, 86; National Guard 110
Nineteen Eighty-four (Orwell) 77, 248
'Nineteen Hundred and Nineteen' (Yeats) 52–3
1916 Rebellion 10, 55n, 200, 221
1913: Jim Larkin and the Dublin Lock-out (Workers' Union of Ireland) 56n
Nkomati Accord 159
Nkrumah, Kwame 272–6
Nobel Committee 60n
North, Colonel Oliver 3

Index